D1286044

BK ENGLISH

COMMUNICATION SKILLS IN THE NEW MILLENNIUM

LEVEL IV

LANGUAGE HANDBOOK

J.A. Senn
Carol Ann Skinner

BK

Educating tomorrow today

BARRETT KENDALL PUBLISHING
AUSTIN, TEXAS

PROJECT MANAGER
Sandra Stucker Blevins

EDITORIAL DIRECTOR
Sandra Mangurian

EDITORIAL STAFF
Marianne Murphy
Marlene Greil
Donna Laughlin
Susan Sandoval
Vicki Tyler
Catherine Foy
Michelle Quijano
Elizabeth Wenning
Cheryl Duksta
Margaret Rickard

PRODUCTION DIRECTORS
Gene Allen
Pun Nio

PHOTO RESEARCH AND
PERMISSIONS
Laurie O'Meara

ART AND DESIGN
Pun Nio
Leslie Kell
Rhonda Warwick

PRODUCTION
Bethany Powell
Isabel Garza
Rhonda Warwick

COVER
Leslie Kell Designs
Pun Nio
Images © Photodiscs, Inc.

EDITORIAL AND PRODUCTION
SERVICES
Book Builders, Inc.
Gryphon Graphics
Inkwell Publishing
Solutions, Inc.
NETS

Barrett Kendall Publishing has made every effort to locate the copyright holders for the images and text used in this book and to make full acknowledgment for their use. Omissions brought to our attention will be corrected in a subsequent edition.

Copyright © 2002 by Barrett Kendall Publishing
All rights reserved. No part of this publication may be reproduced or transmitted in any form or by any means, electronic or mechanical, including photocopying, recording, or any information storage and retrieval system, without permission in writing from the publisher. Requests for permission to make copies of any part of the work should be mailed to: Rights and Permissions, Barrett Kendall Publishing, P.O. Box 685168, Austin, Texas 78768.

Printed in the United States of America.

ISBN 1-58079-402-5   1 2 3 4 5 6 7 RRD 06 05 04 03 02 01

Senior Consultants

Tommy Boley, Ph.D.
Director of English Education
The University of Texas at El Paso
El Paso, TX

Deborah Cooper, M.Ed.
Coordinating Director of PK-12
    Curriculum
Charlotte-Mecklenburg Public Schools
Charlotte, NC

Susan Marie Harrington, Ph.D.
Associate Professor of English,
    Director of Writing, Director of
    Placement and Assessment, and
    Adjunct Assistant Professor
    of Women's Studies
Indiana University-Purdue University,
    Indianapolis
Indianapolis, IN

Carol Pope, Ed.D.
Associate Professor of Curriculum
    and Instruction
North Carolina State University
Raleigh, NC

Rebecca Rickly, Ph.D.
Department of English
Texas Tech University
Lubbock, TX

John Simmons, Ph.D.
Professor of English Education and
    Reading
Florida State University
Tallahassee, FL

John Trimble, Ph.D.
University Distinguished Teaching
    Professor of English
The University of Texas
Austin, TX

Contributing Writers

Jeannie Ball

Grace Bultman

Richard Cohen

Elizabeth Egan-Rivera

Laurie Hopkins Etzel

Bobbi Fagone

Lesli Favor

Nancy-Jo Hereford

Susan Maxey

Linda Mazumdar

Elizabeth McGuire

Shannon Murphy

Carole Osterink

Michael Raymond

Duncan Searl

Jocelyn Sigue

Lorraine Sintetos

James Strickler

Diane Zahler

Kathy Zahler

CRITICAL READERS

Alan Altimont
St. Edwards University,
Austin, TX

Larry Arnhold
Deer Park High School,
Houston, TX

Kerry Benson
Santa Fe Public School,
Santa Fe, NM

Elaine Blanco
Gaither High School,
Lutz, FL

Peter Bond
Randolph School,
Huntsville, AL

**Christina M.
Brandenburg**
Rancho Cotate High
School, Rohnert Park, CA

Paulette Cwidak
John Adams High
School, South Bend, IN

Jean Ann Davis
Miami Trace High
School, Washington
Courthouse, OH

Terri Dobbins
Churchill High School,
San Antonio, TX

Susan Drury
Springwood High
School, Houston, TX

David Dunbar
Masters School
Dobbs Ferry, NY

Chuck Fanara
Brebeuf Preparatory,
Indianapolis, IN

Jason Farr
Anderson High School,
Austin, TX

Marilyn Gail
Judson High School, San
Antonio, TX

Gary Gorsuch
Berea High School,
Berea, OH

Monica Gorsuch
MidPark Sr. High School,
Cleveland, OH

Donna Harrington
Churchill High School,
San Antonio, TX

Janis Hoffman
John Adams High
School, South Bend, IN

Norma Hoffman
John Adams High
School, South Bend, IN

David Kidd
Norfolk Academy,
Norfolk, VA

Kate Knopp
Masters School, Dobbs
Ferry, NY

Suzanne Kuehl
Lewis-Palmer High
School, Monument, CO

Michelle Lindner
Milken Community High
School, Los Angeles, CA

Stephanie Lipkowitzs
Albuquerque Academy,
Albuquerque, NM

Sarah Mannon
Hubbard High School,
Chicago, IL

Linda Martin
Valley Torah, North
Hollywood, CA

Lisa Meyer
Lincoln High School,
Tallahassee, FL

Karla Miller
Durango High School,
Durango, CO

Stacy Miller
Santa Fe High School,
Santa Fe, NM

Eddie Norton
Oviedo High School,
Oviedo, FL

Diana Perrin
Johnson High School,
Huntsville, AL

William Petroff
R. Nelson Snider High
School, Ft. Wayne, IN

Linda Polk
Deer Park High School,
Houston, TX

Lila Rissman
Suwanne Middle School,
Live Oak, FL

Carmen Stallard
Twin Springs High
School, Nickelsville, VA

Jeanette Taylor
Rye Cove High School,
Duffield, VA

Eric Temple
Crystal Springs Uplands
School, Hillsborough, CA

Sherry Weatherly
Denton High School,
Denton, TX

Grammar

CHAPTER 1   The Parts of Speech

CHAPTER 2 The Sentence Base

> **CHAPTER 3** Phrases

CHAPTER 4 Clauses

Usage

CHAPTER 5 Using Verbs

CHAPTER 7 **Subject and Verb Agreement**

CHAPTER 8 Using Adjectives and Adverbs

Mechanics

CHAPTER 9 · Capital Letters

CHAPTER 10 · End Marks and Commas

CHAPTER 11 **Other Punctuation**

Spelling

CheckPoint

Another Look

Posttest

Study and Test-Taking Skills Resource

Glossary

Index

Acknowledgments

LANGUAGE

firs
almo
oped for so
hless. The ho
miraculo
fe

The Parts of Speech

 **Pretest**

Directions

Write the letter of the term that correctly identifies the underlined word in each sentence.

EXAMPLE **1.** What is realism in a literary <u>work</u>?

    1 **A** noun

        B pronoun

        C verb

        D adverb

ANSWER   **1** **A**

1. Realistic writing emphasizes accuracy <u>of</u> detail.

2. Realism generally concerns <u>itself</u> with common people.

3. A realistic novel <u>is</u> neither moralistic nor preachy.

4. Realism became <u>trendy</u> in the nineteenth century.

5. It may have started <u>earlier</u> with the writings of Defoe and Fielding.

6. In <u>America</u>, Howells and James were important realists.

7. French realists include Flaubert <u>and</u> Balzac.

8. An outgrowth of realism was the <u>naturalism</u> of Zola and Dreiser.

9. Naturalists <u>believed</u> in social and economic determinism.

10. Their subjects primarily come from the <u>lowest</u> depths of society.

1 **A** adjective
   B adverb
   C preposition
   D noun

2 **A** noun
   B pronoun
   C verb
   D adverb

3 **A** preposition
   B pronoun
   C verb
   D adverb

4 **A** adjective
   B adverb
   C preposition
   D noun

5 **A** adjective
   B adverb
   C preposition
   D noun

6 **A** adjective
   B adverb
   C preposition
   D proper noun

7 **A** conjunction
   B interjection
   C preposition
   D adjective

8 **A** adjective
   B adverb
   C preposition
   D noun

9 **A** noun
   B pronoun
   C verb
   D adverb

10 **A** conjunction
    B interjection
    C preposition
    D adjective

Andy Warhol.
Moonwalk, 1987.
Screenprint, 38 by 38 inches.
Courtesy of Ronald Feldman
Fine Arts, New York.

Describe What historic event is portrayed in this famous print by Andy Warhol? What colors does the artist use?

Analyze How has the artist used a few key figures to symbolize an event?

Interpret Suppose a poet were to write about this particular historic event, man's first landing on the moon. How might he or she use a few key words—such as colors and/or symbols—to signify the entire episode?

Judge Do you think art or writing works better to capture the significance of historic events? Explain your answer.

At the end of this chapter, you will use the artwork to stimulate ideas for writing.

Nouns and Pronouns

Nouns and pronouns are two of the eight parts of speech. The grammatical elements covered in this chapter include all eight parts of speech. Remember, though, that the part of speech of a word can vary depending upon its use in a sentence.

Understanding the function of grammatical elements can help you as a writer. If you know, for example, when a word is a noun and when a word is a verb, then you can diagnose a problem such as incorrect agreement between a subject and a verb as you edit your work.

THE EIGHT PARTS OF SPEECH	
noun (names)	**adverb** (describes, limits)
pronoun (replaces)	**preposition** (relates)
verb (states action or being)	**conjunction** (connects)
adjective (describes, limits)	**interjection** (expresses strong feeling)

 Nouns

A **noun** is the name of a person, place, thing, or idea.

There are more nouns in our language than any other part of speech. Nouns can be classified in several ways.

Concrete and Abstract Nouns

A **concrete noun** names a person or an object that can actually be seen, touched, tasted, heard, or smelled. An **abstract noun** names qualities, conditions, and ideas that cannot be perceived through the senses.

CONCRETE AND ABSTRACT NOUNS	
CONCRETE NOUNS	table, feather, lemon, salt, bells, roses
ABSTRACT NOUNS	courage, joy, friendship, loyalty, freedom

Common and Proper Nouns

A **common noun** names any person, place, or thing. Always beginning with a capital letter, a **proper noun** names a particular person, place, or thing.

COMMON AND PROPER NOUNS	
COMMON NOUNS	quarterback, state, city
PROPER NOUNS	Sam Levin, New Jersey, Houston

Some proper nouns, such as *Sam Levin* and *New Jersey*, include more than one word; but they are still considered one noun. *Sam Levin* is one person, and *New Jersey* is one state.

You can learn about capitalizing proper nouns on pages L399–L409.

Compound Nouns

A **compound noun** is made up of more than one word. Since a compound noun can be written as one word, written as a hyphenated word, or written as two or more separate words, it is always best to check a dictionary for the correct, up-to-date form.

COMPOUND NOUNS	
ONE WORD	peacemaker, falsehood
HYPHENATED WORDS	sister-in-law, hobby-horse
TWO WORDS	life jacket, city hall

You can learn about spelling the plural forms of compound nouns on page L557.

Collective Nouns

A **collective noun** names a group of people or things. Following are some collective nouns.

COMMON COLLECTIVE NOUNS			
band	congregation	flock	nation
class	crew	gang	orchestra
committee	crowd	herd	swarm
colony	family	league	team

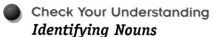

CONNECT TO WRITER'S CRAFT

Some nouns are more colorful and convey meaning more vividly than other nouns. For instance, a noun such as *building* is a general term, but *skyscraper*, *Sears Tower*, *factory*, and *hut* are more specific and lively. In your writing, whether formal or informal, use the most precise nouns possible.

You can learn about spelling plural nouns on pages L552–L560. You can learn about possessive nouns on pages L471–L473.

PRACTICE YOUR SKILLS

Check Your Understanding

Identifying Nouns

General Interest **Write the nouns in the following paragraphs.** A date should be considered a noun.

The Eiffel Tower is perhaps the most familiar human-made landmark on Earth. It was designed for the Paris Exposition in 1889. The tower can now accommodate 10,000 visitors annually. Some people, however, go there for publicity, not for enjoyment. A man once climbed 363 steps on stilts, and a stuntman came down on a unicycle.

The tower is repainted every seven years, requiring thousands of gallons of paint. As a part of one cleanup, nearly 1,000 tons of rust and dirt were shaved off. This kind of effort signifies the tremendous pride the city takes in its famous structure—even if only a very small percentage of its visitors are Parisians.

● **Connect to the Writing Process:** Drafting
Using Specific Nouns

For each general noun below, write at least two specific, lively alternatives. Then write sentences using 10 of your new and improved word choices.

1. visitor	**4.** driver	**7.** building	**10.** happiness
2. car	**5.** hat	**8.** picture	**11.** fruit
3. store	**6.** bag	**9.** money	**12.** furniture

● **Connect to the Writing Process:** Editing
Capitalizing Proper Nouns

Write each proper noun in the paragraph. Capitalize any proper nouns that are not capitalized.

Distinctive geographical features serve as landmarks across the united states. Each year Carlsbad Caverns attracts crowds of sightseers to new mexico. In Arizona, tourists flock to view the grand canyon. Popular for its beaches, florida lures tourists to its swamps and bayous as well. A famous geyser named old faithful draws nature enthusiasts to yellowstone national park. Avid downhill skiers throng the snowy slopes of colorado. Vacationers to Hawaii enjoy waterfalls and volcanoes. Carved into mount rushmore are the faces of four presidents: george washington, thomas jefferson, abraham lincoln, and theodore roosevelt. Landmarks in America celebrate our nation's natural and historical heritage.

Communicate Your Ideas

APPLY TO WRITING

Descriptive Paragraphs: *Nouns*

Just as the Eiffel Tower is a Paris landmark, structures such as the Gateway Arch in St. Louis, Missouri, and the Golden Gate Bridge in San Francisco, California, are landmarks in those cities. You are a travel writer, and you have received an assignment to write about a landmark of your own choosing. Write two paragraphs describing a landmark you have seen, whether it is in your hometown or across the world. Make your descriptions as specific and interesting as possible by using a variety of nouns: concrete nouns, abstract nouns, common nouns, proper nouns, compound nouns, and collective nouns. Be prepared to identify the nouns you used.

▶ Pronouns

A **pronoun** is a word that takes the place of one or more nouns.

The word the pronoun replaces or refers to is called its **antecedent**. The antecedent of a pronoun can be in the same sentence or in another sentence. In the following examples, an arrow has been drawn from each pronoun to its antecedent.

Stephen wore **his** new jacket to study hall.

Rob and Beth are at the library. **They** have **their** exams tomorrow.

Occasionally the antecedent will follow the pronoun.

"That homework is **mine**," Heather said.

You can learn more about pronouns and their antecedents on pages L267–L273.

Personal Pronouns

Personal pronouns, the most commonly used type of pronoun, are divided into the following groups.

PERSONAL PRONOUNS	
FIRST PERSON	(the person speaking)
SINGULAR	I, me, my, mine
PLURAL	we, us, our, ours
SECOND PERSON	(the person spoken to)
SINGULAR	you, your, yours
PLURAL	you, your, yours
THIRD PERSON	(the person or thing spoken about)
SINGULAR	he, him, his, she, her, hers, it, its
PLURAL	they, them, their, theirs

FIRST PERSON	**We** want to publish a study guide.
SECOND PERSON	Did **you** ever find **your** article?
THIRD PERSON	**He** told **them** to call **him** if **they** needed more study advice.

Reflexive and Intensive Pronouns

Reflexive and intensive pronouns are formed by adding *–self* or *–selves* to personal pronouns.

REFLEXIVE AND INTENSIVE PRONOUNS	
SINGULAR	myself, yourself, himself, herself, itself
PLURAL	ourselves, yourselves, themselves

A **reflexive pronoun** refers to the noun or pronoun that is the subject of the sentence. It is an essential part of the sentence. An **intensive pronoun** is included in a sentence to add emphasis— or intensity—to a noun or another pronoun. Because an intensive pronoun is not a necessary part of a sentence, it can be removed without affecting the meaning of the sentence.

REFLEXIVE PRONOUN   Rob taught **himself** to speak French.

(*Himself* cannot be removed from the sentence without changing the meaning.)

INTENSIVE PRONOUN   Rob **himself** volunteered to help.

(*Himself* can be removed from the sentence. *Rob volunteered to help.*)

PRACTICE YOUR SKILLS

● Check Your Understanding
Identifying Personal Pronouns and Their Antecedents

Contemporary Life   **Write the personal, reflexive, or intensive pronoun(s) in each sentence. Then beside each one, write its antecedent.**

1. Roberto lost his essay test in the subway when he was going home.

2. "Is this essay yours?" Megan asked Roberto the next day.

3. Roberto was relieved that Megan had found his test, and he thanked her for returning it.

4. Megan told herself that she could do better on the next essay test.

5. Roberto told Megan, "I myself have developed a study technique that I could share with you."

6. "An essay test is not as difficult if I write a practice answer ahead of time," Roberto said.

7. "We should study together for the next test," Megan told Roberto.

8. "I will set up a study group with you and Roger," Roberto said to Megan.

9. "When I helped Roger study for the last test, he made excellent progress for himself," Roberto continued modestly.

10. Megan was glad that she could study with Roberto and Roger, and she was certain that her grades would improve with her hard work.

● **Connect to the Writing Process:** Revising
Replacing Nouns with Pronouns

Rewrite the following paragraph, replacing repetitious nouns with pronouns.

Bill always waits as long as Bill can before Bill studies for a test. On the night before a test, Bill calls several friends and asks the friends if the friends will lend Bill the friends' notes. Bill sometimes does not attend the classes, so Bill is missing notes from several lectures. Usually Bill can find some sympathetic friends. Are the friends doing Bill a favor by lending Bill the friends' notes? Would you lend Bill your notes?

Indefinite Pronouns

Indefinite pronouns often refer to unnamed persons or things and usually do not have specific antecedents.

COMMON INDEFINITE PRONOUNS	
SINGULAR	another, anybody, anyone, anything, each, either, everybody, everyone, everything, much, neither, nobody, no one, one, somebody, someone, something
PLURAL	both, few, many, others, several
SINGULAR/PLURAL	all, any, most, none, some

Few attended the meeting.
Most of the teachers did **something** to help **everybody** who failed the midterm.

You can learn about indefinite pronouns functioning as antecedents on pages L270–L273.

Demonstrative Pronouns

A **demonstrative pronoun** is used to point out a specific person, place, or object in the same sentence or in another sentence.

DEMONSTRATIVE PRONOUNS	
SINGULAR	this (points out an object close by)
	that (points out an object in the distance)
PLURAL	these (points out objects close by)
	those (points out objects in the distance)

This is the perfect place for a rest.
Of all the books, **these** were the best.

Interrogative Pronouns

An **interrogative pronoun** is used to ask a question.

INTERROGATIVE PRONOUNS				
what	whom	which	whose	who

Which is the best class on filmmaking?
Who wrote that screenplay?
Whose is better?

CONNECT TO SPEAKING AND WRITING

In casual conversation, you often can use a single pronoun to express your thoughts without causing confusion.

Your friend says, "You'll never guess what I just did!"
You respond, **"What?"**

Your brother asks, "Which boots are yours?"
You answer, **"Those."**

A classmate asks, "Who can join that study group?"
You tell her, **"Anyone."**

Relative pronouns are another kind of pronoun. They are used to introduce adjective clauses. You can learn about relative pronouns on pages L148–L152.

PRACTICE YOUR SKILLS

Check Your Understanding
Identifying Pronouns

Contemporary Life

Write each pronoun in the following sentences. Beside each pronoun, write what type it is.

1. Who is going to lead our study group this week?

2. Few attended last week's session.

3. We have to do something to increase involvement.

4. These should generate a definite interest.

5. I will post some of the fliers near the lockers.

6. Which of the boxes do you want Krista to take?

7. Tell her to take those.

8. Whose is this?

9. That is Tyrell's drawing, and this is Lee's photograph.

10. Either could win an award.

Communicate Your Ideas

APPLY TO WRITING
Speech: *Nouns and Pronouns*

Attributed to Tamura Suio. *Ladies' Pastimes in Spring and Autumn*, 18th century. On handscroll, ink and color on paper, 12⅜ by 96⅛ inches. The New York Public Library.

You have volunteered to talk to a fifth grade class about a painting, and you have chosen *Ladies' Pastimes in Spring and Autumn*. Write an informal speech that you could give, discussing any aspect of the painting that appeals to you. One idea is to explain what each group of women is doing and then relate these activities to modern careers. After you have written your speech, underline each noun and circle each pronoun.

Verbs

A **verb** is a word that expresses action or a state of being.

A verb is an essential part of a sentence because it tells what the subject does, is, or has.

▶ Action Verbs

An **action verb** tells what action a subject is performing.

Action verbs can show several types of action.

ACTION VERBS	
PHYSICAL ACTION	drive, march, soar, sing, talk, paint
MENTAL ACTION	believe, think, dream, imagine, wish
OWNERSHIP	have, own, possess, keep, control

CONNECT TO SPEAKING AND WRITING

Many action verbs can be used alone to create a one-word action command. These commands can be particularly effective in grabbing a listener's attention.

A drill sergeant tells a soldier: **"March!"**
Your older brother tells you: **"Move!"**
A teacher tells her student: **"Think."**

Transitive and Intransitive Verbs

An action verb is **transitive** if it has an object. You can find an object by asking the question *What?* or *Whom?* after the verb. An action verb is **intransitive** if it has no object.

| TRANSITIVE | I **found** a new restaurant. (*Found* what?) |
| INTRANSITIVE | We **met** there Friday. (*Met* what or whom?) |

Some action verbs may be either transitive or intransitive.

| TRANSITIVE | She **writes** restaurant reviews in her spare time. |
| INTRANSITIVE | She often **writes** to me. |

You can learn more about the objects of transitive verbs on pages L72-L75.

PRACTICE YOUR SKILLS

● Check Your Understanding
Identifying Transitive and Intransitive Verbs

Science Topic **Write each action verb. Then label each one *transitive* or *intransitive*.**

 1. Rings on the scales of some fish show the age of the fish.

 2. The electric eel throws a charge of 600 volts.

 3. Rays live on the ocean bottom.

 4. The Nile catfish swims upside down.

 5. Minnows have teeth in their throat.

 6. The female marine catfish hatches her eggs in her mouth.

 7. The trout belongs to the salmon family.

 8. The flounder changes its color.

 9. Some fish thrive in underground streams and caves.

 10. Sharks, despite their reputation, rarely attack humans.

● Connect to the Writing Process: Drafting
Writing Sentences

Use each word to write sentences about a science class. If the verb is a transitive verb, draw an arrow to its object.

11. speak	**16.** carry
12. write	**17.** find
13. copy	**18.** have
14. walk	**19.** lock
15. study	**20.** paint

Verb Phrases

A **verb phrase** is a main verb plus one or more helping verbs.

Another name for **helping verb** is **auxiliary verb.**

COMMON HELPING VERBS	
be	am, is, are, was, were, be, being, been
have	has, have, had
do	do, does, did
OTHERS	may, might, must, can, could, shall, should, will, would

In the following examples, the helping verbs are in **bold** type, and the verb phrase is underlined.

> Jeff **has been** bringing our food promptly.
> You **should have been** notified of the reservations.

A verb phrase is often interrupted by contractions or other words.

> Marvin **will** soon **apply** for that job.
> **Have** you always **taken** the server's suggestions?
> I **don**'t **want** any dessert.

CONNECT TO SPEAKING AND WRITING

You probably use many contractions in your everyday conversations. When you are writing, though, you need to consider whether contractions are appropriate. The use of contractions depends on your purpose and audience. If you are writing a letter to a friend, contractions are appropriate. If you are writing a research report, you probably should avoid using contractions.

You can learn more about contractions on pages L479–L480.
Throughout the rest of this book, the term verb *will refer to the whole verb phrase.*

PRACTICE YOUR SKILLS

● Check Your Understanding
Identifying Verbs

> Social Science **Write the verb in each sentence. Include all helping verbs.**

1. Sushi comes from Japan.
2. Some sushi is carefully rolled in a wrapper of very thin, edible seaweed.
3. Sushi consists of raw fish, raw shellfish, and cooked rice.
4. The Japanese have been making sushi for more than a thousand years.
5. Sushi was originally made with salt as a preservative.
6. The fish and salt were aged over several weeks or months.
7. Nowadays, chefs often prepare sushi without the preservative.
8. The sushi is immediately served to the customer.
9. The preparation and display of sushi can be considered an elegant art form.
10. The sushi chef does consider all details of color, texture, and taste.

● Connect to the Writing Process: Revising
Writing Sentences with Verb Phrases

Each of the sentences below contains a verb phrase. Rewrite the sentence, adding an interrupter so that the meaning of the sentence changes. Underline the verb.

11. I have liked that Mexican restaurant.
12. We can give our order to the server.
13. Our order was sent to the kitchen.
14. The server has returned with our water.
15. The dish for the chips and salsa has been empty.

APPLY TO WRITING

Instructions: *Verbs*

A nearby restaurant has announced a search for a new dish for the "Local Favorites" section of its menu. You have decided to enter one of your favorite dishes. You must write clear, simple, step-by-step instructions for preparing the food. Use precise, colorful verbs. For example, instead of *mix*, you might write *whisk* or *whip*. After you write your instructions, underline each verb.

▶ Linking Verbs

A **linking verb** links the subject with another word in the sentence. The other word either renames or describes the subject.

A linking verb serves as a bridge between the subject and another word in the sentence.

> History **is** my favorite subject. (*Subject* renames *history*.)
>
> This election **has been** exceptionally competitive. (*Competitive* describes the subject *election*.)

The most common linking verbs are the various forms of *be*.

COMMON FORMS OF *BE*		
be	can be	has been
is	could be	had been
am	should be	could have been
are	would be	should have been
was	may be	would have been
were	might be	might have been
shall be	must be	must have been
will be	have been	

Diane **may be** our new class president.

These votes **should have been** anonymous.

The forms of *be* are not always linking verbs. Only a verb that links the subject with another word in the sentence that renames or describes the subject can be a linking verb. In the following examples, the verbs simply make a statement or describe a state of being.

Her running mate **is** here.
She **was** in Memphis on Tuesday.
The campaign buttons **could be** in the box.
They **must have been** there all the time.

Forms of *be* are not the only linking verbs. The verbs in the following box may also be used as linking verbs.

ADDITIONAL LINKING VERBS		
appear	look	sound
become	remain	stay
feel	seem	taste
grow	smell	turn

Jonathan **became** my campaign manager.
(*Manager* renames the subject *Jonathan*.)

The campaign posters **look** very professional.
(*Professional* describes the subject *posters*.)

Most of the additional linking verbs listed in the box can be linking verbs in some sentences and action verbs in other sentences.

| LINKING VERB | The governor **appeared** weary.
(*Weary* describes the subject *governor*.) |
| ACTION VERB | The bodyguard **appeared** beside him.
(No word describes the subject *bodyguard*.) |

Subject complements complete the meaning of linking verbs. You can learn more about subject complements on pages L77–L81.

PRACTICE YOUR SKILLS

● Check Your Understanding
Identifying Linking Verbs

History Topic **Write each linking verb. If a sentence does not have a linking verb, write *none*.**

1. During the Civil War, Abraham Lincoln was the president of the United States.

2. Lincoln was assassinated while in a theater.

3. Other leaders have been targets for assassins also.

4. Dr. Martin Luther King, Jr., was shot on April 4, 1968.

5. James Earl Ray grew old in prison for that crime.

6. President John F. Kennedy appeared in Texas in November 1963.

7. His assassination seemed a conspiracy to some people.

8. President Ronald Reagan nearly became the victim of John Hinckley.

9. Reagan was whisked away to a hospital and survived.

10. Hinckley had been insane at the time of the crime.

Write two sentences for each verb. In the first sentence, use the word as an action verb. In the second sentence, use the word as a linking verb.

11. become   **13.** seem   **15.** appeared

12. look   **14.** felt   **16.** remains

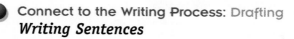

Communicate Your Ideas

APPLY TO WRITING

Writer's Craft: *Analyzing the Use of Verbs*

Writers usually choose vivid action verbs so that readers can experience what is happening. In "Araby," James Joyce tells the story of a young man hopelessly in love who goes to a fair to find a gift for a young woman. This passage describes what the young man sees when he arrives. Read the passage and then follow the instructions.

> Nearly all the stalls were closed and the greater part of the hall was in darkness. I recognized a silence like that which pervades a church after a service. I walked into the center of the bazaar timidly. A few people were gathered about the stalls which were still open. Before a curtain, over which the words *Café Chantant* were written in colored lamps, two men were counting money on a salver. I listened to the fall of the coins.
>
> —*James Joyce,* "Araby"

- List all the verbs in the passage.
- How many of the verbs are forms of *be* or verb phrases with *be*?
- Does the use of *be* make the passage more vivid or less vivid? Why do you think Joyce chose to use these verbs? Explain your answer.

Adjectives and Adverbs

An adjective and an adverb have similar functions in a sentence. They both modify or describe other parts of speech. Adjectives and adverbs improve the style of sentences by adding vividness and exactness.

 Adjectives

An adjective is a word that modifies a noun or a pronoun.

An adjective answers one of the following questions about a noun or a pronoun.

ADJECTIVES		
WHAT KIND?	**fresh** ideas	**plaid** shirt
WHICH ONE(S)?	**red** curtain	**those** few
HOW MANY?	**six** actors	**many** pages
HOW MUCH?	**extensive** role	**much** publicity

An adjective may come in one of three places.

BEFORE A NOUN OR A PRONOUN	The **young, eager** playwright wrote a script about Homer.
AFTER A NOUN OR A PRONOUN	The playwright, **young** and **eager**, wrote a script about Homer.
AFTER A LINKING VERB	The playwright of the script about Homer was **young** and **eager**.

You can learn about adjectives that follow linking verbs on pages L78–L81.

PUNCTUATION WITH TWO ADJECTIVES

Sometimes you will write two adjectives before or after the noun or pronoun they describe. If those adjectives are not connected by a conjunction—such as *and* or *or*—you might need to put a comma between them.

To decide if a comma belongs, read the adjectives and add the word *and* between them.

- If the adjectives make sense, put a comma in to replace *and*.
- If the adjectives do not make sense with the word *and* between them, do not add a comma.

COMMA NEEDED	I read a realistic, scary book. (*Realistic* and *scary book* reads well.)
NO COMMA NEEDED	It was an unusual mystery story. (*Unusual* and *mystery story* does not read well.)

You can learn more about using commas to separate adjectives before a noun on pages L438–L441.

CONNECT TO WRITER'S CRAFT

A talented writer chooses adjectives that are fresh, vivid, and specific. For example, a ***good*** steak expresses a general idea, but a ***succulent*** steak expresses a more specific, vivid idea. A football player's ***strong*** muscles are one thing, but ***Herculean*** muscles are another.

Proper Adjectives

Because a **proper adjective** is formed from a proper noun, it begins with a capital letter.

PROPER ADJECTIVES	
Roman emperor	**Greek** cuisine
Hawaiian island	**Shakespearean** play

You can learn more about capitalizing proper adjectives on pages L409–L411.

Compound Adjectives

A **compound adjective** is made up of more than one word. Since a compound adjective may be one word, a hyphenated word, or two or more separate words, you may need to check a dictionary for the correct form.

COMPOUND ADJECTIVES	
seaworthy vessel	**spellbound** audience
long-term project	**high school** play

Articles

The words *a*, *an*, and *the* form a special group of adjectives called **articles**. The article *a* comes before words starting with a consonant sound, and *an* comes before words starting with a vowel sound.

ARTICLES		
a comedy	**an** understanding	**the** apple
a harp	**an** hour	**the** ball

You will not be asked to list articles in the exercises in this book.

PRACTICE YOUR SKILLS

● Check Your Understanding
Identifying Adjectives

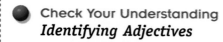 Write each adjective. Then write the word the adjective modifies.

1. Homer was a famous Greek poet.
2. He told the great story of the Trojan War.
3. Homer also recounted the fantastic adventures of Odysseus in *The Odyssey*.
4. The larger-than-life man lived in a seaside city.
5. An important philosopher of ancient times was Plato.

6. Even today, ambitious scholars choose the study of Platonic philosophy.

7. One of Plato's well-known works is *The Republic*.

8. A Roman writer, Ovid, composed the long poem, *Metamorphoses*.

9. *Metamorphoses* includes the romantic story of the handsome Pyramus and the beautiful Thisbe.

10. Nick Bottom and Francis Flute are characters in a Shakespearean play.

11. Bottom and Flute play Pyramus and Thisbe in a hilarious production of Ovid's story.

12. Sappho, a Greek poet, wrote beautiful poems about love, marriage, and friendship.

● **Connect to the Writing Process:** Revising
Using Specific Adjectives

Work with another student. Ask your partner to look around the room and describe ten things that he or she sees. Write down each description. Then, working together, revise each so that it contains vivid and specific adjectives.

Other Parts of Speech Used as Adjectives

Sometimes a word will be used as a noun in one sentence and as an adjective in another sentence.

NOUNS USED AS ADJECTIVES	
NOUNS	flower, glass, refrigerator
ADJECTIVES	**flower** garden, **glass** vase, **refrigerator** door

Also, the same word may be a pronoun in one sentence and an adjective in another sentence. The words in the box on the following page are adjectives when they come before a noun and modify that noun. They are pronouns when they stand alone.

WORDS USED AS ADJECTIVES OR PRONOUNS		
Demonstrative	**Interrogative**	**Indefinite**
this	what	all many
these	which	another more
that		any most
those		both neither
		each other
		either several
		few some

ADJECTIVE   **These** scripts must be yours.
PRONOUN   **These** must be yours.

ADJECTIVE   **Each** actor was given a new costume.
PRONOUN   **Each** of the actors was given a new costume.

The possessive pronouns *my, your, his, her, its, our,* and *their* are sometimes called **pronominal adjectives** because they answer the adjective question *Which one(s)?*

Throughout this book, these words will be considered pronouns.

Practice Your Skills

 Check Your Understanding
Identifying Adjectives

 History Topic **Write the adjectives in the following paragraph.**

According to the ancient Greeks, eyes could reveal a personality. The Greeks compared the eyes of people to the eyes of various animals. Then they attributed the personality traits of those animals to people. Lion eyes, for example, are almond-like. In a person they signified a sense of fairness, a sense of justice, and leadership skills. Monkey eyes are small in relation to the face, but they have large irises. The Greeks thought that people with these eyes were unpredictable and shy. Elephant eyes are long and narrow with several folds of skin on the upper and lower eyelids. People with elephant eyes, it was believed, could handle difficult problems and solve them in a thoughtful, methodical manner. This unusual list of eye types also included the eyes of sheep, horses, wolves, hogs, snakes, and fish.

● Connect to the Writing Process: Drafting
Writing Sentences

Write two sentences for each word. In the first sentence, use the word as an adjective. In the second sentence, use the word as a noun or a pronoun. Above the word, label it *adjective*, *noun*, or *pronoun*.

  1. these
  2. other
  3. baseball
  4. porch
  5. book
  6. science
  7. both
  8. all
  9. stone
  10. wool

APPLY TO WRITING

Analysis: *Adjectives*

Georges
Rouault. *The
Old King*,
1871–1958.
Oil on canvas,
30¼ by 21¼
inches. The
Carnegie Museum
of Art, Pittsburgh,
Patrons Art Fund,
40.1.

Study Georges Rouault's painting *The Old King*. Look at the
expression on the king's face. Are those flowers in his
hands? Observe the colors the painter chose to use. Now
imagine that this king is Oedipus, and he has blinded
himself after discovering the horrible truth that he has
killed his father. Write an essay describing the emotions
and thoughts you think this king must be experiencing.
Express your ideas vividly and precisely by using specific
adjectives. Share your essay with your classmates.

 **Adverbs**

An **adverb** is a word that modifies a verb, an adjective, or another adverb.

Although many adverbs end in –*ly*, some do not. Common adverbs that do not end in –*ly* are listed in the box.

COMMON ADVERBS			
afterward	fast	now	soon
again	hard	nowhere	still
almost	here	often	straight
alone	just	outside	then
already	late	perhaps	there
also	long	quite	today
always	low	rather	tomorrow
away	more	seldom	too
down	near	so	very
even	never	sometimes	well
ever	next	somewhat	yesterday
far	not (n't)	somewhere	yet

Adverbs That Modify Verbs

Adverbs answer the questions *Where? When? How?* and *To what extent?* Notice in the following examples that adverbs that modify verbs modify the whole verb phrase.

WHERE?   Enrique went **outside**.

WHEN?   Donna will be swimming **tomorrow**.

HOW?   The divers have been competing **fiercely**.

Be careful not to confuse an adverb that ends in *–ly* with an adjective that ends in *–ly.*

ADVERB	Enrique meets **weekly** with his team. (When?)
ADJECTIVE	The **weekly** meeting is a time to plan strategy. (What kind?)

CONNECT TO SPEAKING AND WRITING

Sometimes when you are performing an action, another person will use a single adverb to tell you how to do it.

You are carelessly stacking china dishes, and your mother says, *"Carefully."*

You are driving rapidly through a school zone, and your passenger reminds you, *"Slowly."*

You are slowly picking up your clothes, and your dad says, *"Quickly!"*

Adverbs That Modify Adjectives and Other Adverbs

When adverbs modify adjectives or other adverbs, they usually answer the question *To what extent?* Notice in the following examples that the adverbs that modify the adjectives and the other adverbs come before that word.

MODIFYING AN ADJECTIVE	This swimsuit is **too** loose.
	The **extremely** hot sand burned the soles of his feet.
MODIFYING AN ADVERB	Sammy moves through the water **very** quickly.
	She **almost** always spends the day collecting shells.

You can learn about using adjectives and adverbs to show degrees of comparison on pages L327–L345.

PRACTICE YOUR SKILLS

● Check Your Understanding
Identifying Adverbs

Contemporary Life **Write the adverbs from the sentences below. Then beside each adverb, write the word the adverb modifies.**

1. Enrique always keeps the members of the swim team in stitches.

2. Yesterday he solemnly asked someone for directions in a fake language.

3. The person listened courteously to him and then walked rapidly in the opposite direction.

4. Another time, he impulsively popped popcorn without the lid on the pan.

5. Popcorn flew crazily around the kitchen, and the dog ran around in circles.

6. When Enrique drove too fast, he irritably paid the fine in pennies.

7. Last week Enrique secretly started an odd rumor about himself.

8. The rumor evolved radically before it eventually came back to him.

9. He was bored in math class today and carefully wrote his work in Roman numerals.

10. Occasionally he dresses his little brother and cheerfully sends him to preschool with his clothes on backward.

● Connect to the Writing Process: Drafting
Using Adverbs to Modify Adjectives and Other Adverbs

Write a sentence for each adjective and adverb below. Then add an adverb to modify each adjective and adverb.

11. clearly	**15.** well	**19.** warmly
12. fast	**16.** slowly	**20.** neat
13. loud	**17.** badly	
14. loudly	**18.** thin	

Nouns Used as Adverbs

The same word may be used as a noun in one sentence and as an adverb in another sentence.

NOUN   The **outdoors** is the best location for the reptile habitat.

ADVERB   We will move the reptile habitat **outdoors**. (Where?)

NOUN   **Tomorrow** is the day for the lizards' release.

ADVERB   I will release the lizards **tomorrow**. (When?)

PRACTICE YOUR SKILLS

● **Check Your Understanding**
Identifying Adverbs

Science Topic **Write the adverbs from the sentences below. Then beside each one, write the word or words each adverb modifies.**

1. Southwest deserts appear totally empty of life.

2. Many animals, birds, and insects survive very well in this barren land.

3. An unusually hardy inhabitant of these bleak areas is one type of lizard.

4. This lizard can swiftly skim along the sandy surface and can easily burrow into the sand.

5. You have probably watched swimmers at the ocean or a lake on a hot summer day.

6. These bathers often run quickly to the water, dive in, and then disappear beneath the surface.

7. In the same way, this lizard runs very fast, dives into the sand, and disappears without a trace.

8. During the course of this swift run, the lizard may actually fly for a few seconds.

9. The body of the lizard is perfectly suited for this incredible stunt.

10. During the dive a group of scales cleverly protects the eyes of the lizard.

⬤ Connect to the Writing Process: Drafting
Using Adverbs and Nouns to Write Sentences

Write two sentences for each word. In the first sentence, use the word as a noun. In the second sentence, use the word as an adverb.

11. yesterday

12. downstairs

13. there

14. downtown

15. afternoon

16. more

17. later

18. tomorrow

19. well

20. outside

Communicate Your Ideas

APPLY TO WRITING

News Story: *Adverbs*

Imagine that you are a reporter for your local newspaper. You have been asked to cover a high school competition for the readers of the newspaper. You may choose any competition you wish—for example, cheerleading, soccer, football, dance team, tennis, quiz team, or any other. Be sure you use adverbs as you explain the action of the contest.

Contemporary
Life

Divide your paper into two columns. In the first column, write the adverbs and the word each adverb modifies. In the second column, write the adjectives and the word each adjective modifies.

1. Yesterday I went to an unusual water park.

2. In a huge tank, baby dolphins swam peacefully.

3. The older dolphins and their trainers performed daily water shows indoors.

4. I most enjoyed the activities available outside.

5. A few visitors can swim with the dolphins.

6. I was incredibly pleased about this unusual opportunity.

7. The trainers carefully gave me several instructions.

8. There was a trainer beside me constantly.

9. I quickly became friends with a large, happy dolphin. I swam playfully beside him for an hour.

Other Parts of Speech

Prepositions, conjunctions, and interjections are the three remaining parts of speech.

 Prepositions

A **preposition** shows the relationship between a noun or a pronoun and another word in the sentence.

In the following examples, the words in **bold** type are prepositions. Notice how the different prepositions change the relationship between the plant and the table.

> The plant **on** the table is a geranium.
> The plant **beside** the table is a geranium.
> The plant **near** the table is a geranium.

Following is a list of common prepositions. Prepositions of two or more words are called **compound prepositions**.

COMMON PREPOSITIONS				
aboard	before	down	off	till
about	behind	during	on	to
above	below	except	onto	toward
across	beneath	for	opposite	under
after	beside	from	out	underneath
against	besides	in	outside	until
along	between	inside	over	up
among	beyond	into	past	upon
around	but ("except")	like	since	with
as	by	near	through	within
at	concerning	of	throughout	without

COMPOUND PREPOSITIONS		
according to	by means of	instead of
ahead of	in addition to	in view of
apart from	in back of	next to
aside from	in front of	on account of
as of	in place of	out of
because of	in spite of	prior to

A preposition is always part of a group of words called a **prepositional phrase**. A prepositional phrase begins with a preposition and ends with a noun or a pronoun called the **object of a preposition.** One or more modifiers may come between the preposition and its object. The prepositional phrases in the following examples are in **bold** type.

> **During history class** we watched a film **about carrier pigeons**.
>
> **On account of the war**, pigeons carried mail **throughout the country**.

Preposition or Adverb?

The same word may be a preposition in one sentence and an adverb in another sentence. A word is a preposition if it is part of a prepositional phrase. An adverb stands alone.

PREPOSITION	I saw the pigeon *outside the window.*
ADVERB	I saw the pigeon **outside**.
PREPOSITION	Professor Reilly speaks well *before an audience.*
ADVERB	Have you heard this lecture **before**?

You can learn more about prepositional phrases on pages L97–L103.

PRACTICE YOUR SKILLS

● Check Your Understanding
Identifying Prepositional Phrases

History Topic **Write the prepositional phrases in the following paragraph.** (There are 20 prepositional phrases.)

In a sense the French were the originators of airmail service. During the siege of Paris in the Franco-Prussian War of the 1870s, mail was sent from the capital by balloon, along with hundreds of homing pigeons. Return letters were photo-reduced on thin film, which held an average of 2,500 letters. Then pigeons delivered the letters to the capital. Approximately 300 pigeons carrying the mail were dispatched. Some of these got past the Prussian pigeon snipers. In Paris the messages were enlarged on a projection screen, copied by clerks, and delivered to addresses within the city.

● Connect to the Writing Process: Drafting
Writing Sentences with Prepositions and Adverbs

Write two sentences about mail for each word. In the first sentence, use the word as a preposition. In the second sentence, use the word as an adverb.

1. around
2. below
3. near
4. by
5. down
6. up

APPLY TO WRITING

Web Site Sample Page: *Prepositional Phrases*

You are a Website developer, and you are writing a proposal to the marketing director of a company that specializes in historical memorabilia. You decide to end your proposal by writing a sample page about the era of history that interests you most. For your sample page, write a short summary about your chosen time period. Use prepositional phrases to make your sample page as specific and vivid as possible.

 Conjunctions

A **conjunction** connects words or groups of words.

Coordinating conjunctions are single connecting words, and **correlative conjunctions** are pairs of connecting words.

CONJUNCTIONS				
Coordinating			**Correlative**	
and	nor	yet	both/and	not only/but also
but	or		either/or	whether/or
for	so		neither/nor	

Following are some uses of a conjunction.

Neither *Marty* **nor** *Lana* has a credit card. (connects nouns)
Either *write* her a check **or** *pay* cash. (connects verbs)
That dollar bill is *old* **and** *dirty*. (connects adjectives)
I can't pay the balance, **for** *I don't have the money.*
(connects sentences)

Subordinating conjunctions are used to introduce adverb clauses. You can learn about subordinating conjunctions on pages L142–L143.

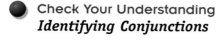

CONNECT TO SPEAKING AND WRITING

In casual conversation, your listener may prompt you to finish a thought by stating an appropriate conjunction for you to use.

You say, "I went to the airport yesterday."
Your friend does not understand why you're telling him this, so he says, **"And ..."**
You are prompted to finish the thought. "I went to the airport yesterday **and** applied for a job."

PRACTICE YOUR SKILLS

● Check Your Understanding
Identifying Conjunctions

General Interest **Write and label the coordinating and correlative conjunctions in the following paragraphs.**

Visitors to the Bureau of Engraving and Printing in Washington can buy 150 dollars' worth of United States currency for 75 cents, but there is a catch. The money is real, but it has been shredded. Every day the bureau shreds not only new, misprinted currency but also stamps and other items that are not fit for circulation. Anyone can take home some souvenir money, for in the bureau's visitor center, machines automatically dispense 75-cent packets of shredded currency.

Each of the twelve Federal Reserve district banks is also authorized to dispose of unusable currency whether it be old, soiled, or worn. Residents of Los Angeles can either drop by the district bank or request a delivery. For the sum of 83 dollars, the branch will deliver an entire day's output—up to 5,550 pounds—to your door if you live closer than the nearest dump. Some of this currency later appears in novelty stores in one form or another.

● **Connect to the Writing Process:** Revising
Using Conjunctions

Revise the following paragraphs to make them less repetitive and choppy. Use coordinating and correlative conjunctions to join words, phrases, and sentences.

Every year criminals think they have discovered a fool-proof way to counterfeit money. They use color copiers. They use scanners. They use high-quality printers. They scrutinize watermarks. They scrutinize paper quality. They scrutinize tiny markings. In 1997, more than 135 million dollars in counterfeit U.S. currency appeared worldwide. Three-fourths of it was discovered. Three-fourths of it was confiscated before it was circulated.

The United States government is well versed in detecting counterfeit money. It issued the first paper currency in 1861. Fewer than five years later, one-third of all notes in circulation were counterfeit. It created the Secret Service in 1865. Its sole mission was to quell the usage of fake currency. It is part of the U.S. Department of Treasury. It has developed new security features such as inks that change color when viewed from different angles. It has developed new security features such as fine-line printing patterns that are hard for printers and scanners to duplicate.

Communicate Your Ideas

APPLY TO WRITING

Journal Entry: *Conjunctions*

If you received a million dollars as an unexpected legacy, what would you do with the money? Brainstorm a list of possibilities. Then arrange the items in that list from most important to least important. Finally, write a journal entry explaining what you would do with the money and why you would use it this way. Underline each conjunction you use.

Interjections

An **interjection** is a word that expresses strong feeling or emotion.

Fear, anger, surprise, and happiness are just some of the emotions expressed by interjections. A comma or an exclamation point always separates an interjection from the rest of the sentence, depending on whether strong or mild feeling is being expressed.

> **Wow!** This price is unreasonable.
> **Yes,** I will lend you money.

PRACTICE YOUR SKILLS

● Check Your Understanding
Identifying Interjections

Contemporary Life
Write the interjections in the sentences below. If there is no interjection, write *none*.

1. Help! I've been robbed.
2. Whew! It could have been worse.
3. The thief wanted my cash but not my credit cards!
4. No, I did not see his face well enough to identify him if I saw him again.

5. Stop! Don't touch my arm there.

6. The thief hit my arm to make me let go of the cash I was holding.

7. Yes, I was standing in line to pay for my candy and gasoline.

8. Oh! I remember a distinctive ring he wore.

9. Come back!

10. Well, I can sketch the ring as I remember it, and I think you'll be able to use the information to catch the thief.

Connect to the Writing Process: Revising
Adding Interjections

You can change the intensity of each sentence below by adding an interjection to it. Write each sentence, adding a correctly punctuated interjection.

11. That was my favorite ring.

12. I have to get it back.

13. Wait a minute.

14. I see something shiny on the floor.

15. The thief must have dropped it as he ran away.

Communicate Your Ideas

APPLY TO WRITING

Letter: *Prepositions, Conjunctions, and Interjections*

Your guidance counselor has invited each student in your class to write her an informal letter describing the ideal job fair. She is interested in your ideas and reactions to different careers, pay rates, work environments, and so on. Take this opportunity to influence what type of job fair you and the other students are provided, and write an expressive letter describing your ideas, opinions, and feelings. Be prepared to identify each preposition, conjunction, and interjection.

Parts of Speech Review

A chameleon can change its color to blend with its surroundings. Many words in English are like chameleons. They can become different parts of speech, depending on how they are used in different sentences.

NOUN	The **last** of the books has arrived.
VERB	The rare book sale will **last** two more days.
ADJECTIVE	The **last** book to sell was by George Eliot.
ADVERB	Her signed edition of *Silas Marner* sold **last**.

To determine what part of speech a word is, read the sentence carefully. Then ask yourself, *What is each word doing in this sentence?* The following summary of the eight parts of speech will help you determine how a word is used in a sentence.

NOUN	Is the word naming a person, place, thing, or idea? The **friendship** between **Silas Marner** and his **neighbor** lasted for many **years**.
PRONOUN	Is the word taking the place of a noun? **Everything they** said about **him** was true.
VERB	Is the word either showing action or linking the subject with another word in the sentence? I **read** the book. It **was** fascinating.
ADJECTIVE	Is the word modifying a noun or a pronoun? Does it answer the question *What kind? Which one(s)? How many?* or *How much?* **That large stone** fireplace was very **cozy**.
ADVERB	Is the word modifying a verb, an adjective, or an adverb? Does it answer the question *How? When? Where?* or *To what extent?* Baby Eppie was **rather** curious and found Marner's fireplace **very quickly**.

PREPOSITION	Is the word showing a relationship between a noun or a pronoun and another word in the sentence? Is it part of a phrase? ***By means of*** her determination, Molly carried Eppie ***through*** the snowstorm.
CONJUNCTION	Is the word connecting words or groups of words? Molly was **either** unconscious **or** dead, **for** she lay motionless in the snow.
INTERJECTION	Is the word expressing strong feeling? **Wow!** Godfrey Cass is really selfish.

PRACTICE YOUR SKILLS

● Check Your Understanding
Identifying Parts of Speech

Write each underlined word in the following paragraph. Beside each one write its part of speech, using these abbreviations.

noun = *n.*
pronoun = *pron.*
verb = *v.*
adjective = *adj.*

adverb = *adv.*
preposition = *prep.*
conjunction = *conj.*
interjection = *interj.*

Adam Bede, considered a masterpiece by some, was written by George Eliot and published in 1859. Today this book is still one of the most widely read Victorian novels. Eliot's purpose in telling this story was to show her readers what ordinary life was like. What does that mean? Well, the setting is not any more colorful or the characters any more heroic than readers of her day were likely to find in their own experience.

Determining Parts of Speech

Write the underlined word in each sentence. Then, beside each word, write its part of speech using the following abbreviations.

noun = *n.*   pronoun = *pron.*   verb = *v.*
adjective = *adj.*   adverb = *adv.*   preposition = *prep.*
conjunction = *conj.*   interjection = *interj.*

1. He walked <u>out</u>.
2. <u>These</u> are delicious.
3. He writes very <u>well</u>.
4. Jane has a new <u>cat</u>.
5. He <u>leaves</u> at ten.
6. Did you see <u>my</u> hat?
7. We <u>can</u> tomatoes.
8. Finish your banana <u>split</u>.
9. Fill the car with <u>gas</u>.
10. <u>Both</u> children slept well.
11. The <u>gas</u> heater warmed us.
12. <u>Cat</u> fur makes me itch.
13. I like <u>these</u> songs.
14. The <u>leaves</u> are turning red.
15. <u>My</u>! You are quite funny.
16. The dog went <u>out</u> the door.
17. May I have <u>both</u>?
18. <u>Well</u>! That was rude.
19. Recycle that <u>can</u>.
20. <u>Split</u> some logs for the fire.

Understanding Parts of Speech

Write five sentences that use the following words as the different parts of speech. Then underline each word and label its use in the sentence.

1. some—pronoun, adjective
2. alarm—verb, noun
3. either—pronoun, adjective, conjunction
4. down—adverb, preposition, adjective
5. chilled—verb, adjective

Using Parts of Speech

Write a paragraph in which you use each of the eight parts of speech at least once. Write about one of the following topics or one of your choice: someone whose actions you admire or an author whose work you enjoy. Then underline and label one use of each part of speech.

Language and *Self-Expression*

Andy Warhol was a founder of the Pop Art movement of the 1960s, a movement that made art out of the icons of popular culture. In this print Warhol took a famous photograph of a moonwalk and made it his own, silkscreening it onto canvas and transforming the colors and rhythms of the photograph.

In this work two key figures, an astronaut and an American flag, are shown on the surface of the moon. These figures are all you need to conjure up this historic event. Think of a recent significant event in local or world history. Boil down the event to two or three key images. Then use those images to write an unrhymed poem that captures the event in words. As you write, think about precise nouns, verbs, and adjectives you might use to make your images come alive for a reader.

Prewriting Choose an event in recent history. Quickwrite two or three adjective-noun pairs that seem to be key images related to the event. Some examples from the moonwalk might be *white uniform, horizontal flag, rough surface.*

Drafting Include your adjective-noun pairs as you describe the key images in your unrhymed poem.

Revising Reread your poem or have a classmate critique it. Replace dull, ordinary nouns, verbs, and adjectives with vivid, precise ones.

Editing Review your poem, looking for errors in grammar, capitalization, punctuation, and spelling. Make any corrections that are necessary.

Publishing Prepare a final copy of your poem. Then publish it in a notebook of poems by your classmates. Take the time to read your classmates' poems. As a class, discuss the power of a few words to portray the essence of an event.

Another Look

The Parts of Speech

A **noun** is the name of a person, place, thing, or idea.

A **common noun** names any person, place, or thing. *(page L6)*
A **proper noun** names a particular person, place, or thing. *(page L6)*

A **pronoun** is a word that takes the place of one or more nouns.

A **reflexive pronoun** is formed by adding *–self* or *–selves* to personal pronouns. *(page L11)*
An **intensive pronoun** is included to add emphasis or intensity. *(page L11)*
An **indefinite pronoun** often refers to unnamed persons or things. *(page L13)*
A **demonstrative pronoun** points out a specific person, place, or thing. *(page L13)*
An **interrogative pronoun** is used to ask a question. *(page L14)*

A **verb** is a word that expresses action or a state of being.

An action verb is **transitive** if it has an object. *(page L16)*
An action verb is **intransitive** if it has no object. *(page L16)*

An **adjective** is a word that modifies a noun or pronoun.

The words *a, an,* and *the* form a special group of adjectives called **articles**. *(page L26)*

An **adverb** is a word that modifies a verb, an adjective, or another adverb.

A **preposition** is always part of a group of words called a **prepositional phrase**.

A **conjunction** connects words or groups of words.

An **interjection** is a word that expresses strong feeling or emotion.

Directions
Write the letter of the term that correctly identifies the underlined word in each sentence.

EXAMPLE
1. My mother <u>introduced</u> me to the work of the Brontë sisters.

1 **A** noun
   B pronoun
   C verb
   D adverb

ANSWER   1 **C**

1. The Brontë <u>family</u> produced three novelists: Emily, Charlotte, and Anne.

2. Charlotte worked as a teacher and governess, <u>but</u> she wrote verse on the side.

3. In 1845, she discovered that <u>her</u> sisters Emily and Anne also wrote poetry.

4. The sisters collected their <u>poems</u> in a volume, using the pseudonyms Currer, Ellis, and Acton Bell.

5. Neither the poems nor Charlotte's first novel <u>was</u> successful.

6. However, in 1847, Charlotte's book *Jane Eyre* became very <u>popular</u>.

7. *Wuthering Heights,* Emily's one novel, is considered the Brontës' <u>best</u> work.

8. <u>My</u>, it is a passionate and inspired work of fiction!

9. Anne, the youngest Brontë, is the <u>least</u> famous of the sisters.

10. She published two novels <u>before</u> her death in 1849.

1 **A** adjective
   B adverb
   C preposition
   D noun

6 **A** conjunction
   B interjection
   C preposition
   D adjective

2 **A** adjective
   B adverb
   C preposition
   D conjunction

7 **A** adjective
   B adverb
   C preposition
   D noun

3 **A** adjective
   B adverb
   C pronoun
   D noun

8 **A** conjunction
   B interjection
   C preposition
   D adjective

4 **A** noun
   B pronoun
   C verb
   D adverb

9 **A** noun
   B pronoun
   C verb
   D adverb

5 **A** noun
   B pronoun
   C verb
   D adverb

10 **A** conjunction
    B interjection
    C preposition
    D adjective

CHAPTER 2

The Sentence Base

 **Pretest**

Directions
**Write the letter of the term that correctly identifies the
underlined word or words in each sentence.**

EXAMPLE

1. *The New Yorker* <u>was founded</u> by
   Harold Ross.

   1 **A** simple subject
   B simple predicate
   C complete subject
   D complete predicate

ANSWER

1 **B**

1. Among the early contributors to the magazine were
   <u>Dorothy Parker and E. B. White</u>.
2. *The New Yorker* <u>specializes</u> in short fiction, essays,
   and cartoons.
3. After Harold Ross's death, <u>William Shawn</u> became
   the editor.
4. The magazine sometimes <u>carries</u> entire books in
   installments.
5. You <u>should look at a copy someday</u>.
6. <u>Ogden Nash</u> and <u>S. J. Perelman</u> contributed to the
   magazine's reputation for humor.
7. Nash <u>wrote</u> light satirical verse and <u>served</u> as an editor
   for many years.
8. His collections of verse include *<u>Everyone But Thee and
   Me</u>* and *<u>Bed Riddance</u>*.
9. East Coast intellectuals were <u>targets</u> of Nash's wit.
10. Perelman often used dreadful <u>puns</u> in his satires.

1	**A**	simple subject	**6**	**A**	compound subject
	B	simple predicate		**B**	compound verb
	C	complete subject		**C**	compound direct object
	D	complete predicate		**D**	compound predicate nominative

2	**A**	simple subject	**7**	**A**	compound subject
	B	simple predicate		**B**	compound verb
	C	complete subject		**C**	compound direct object
	D	complete predicate		**D**	compound predicate nominative

3	**A**	simple subject	**8**	**A**	compound subject
	B	simple predicate		**B**	compound verb
	C	compound subject		**C**	compound direct object
	D	complete predicate		**D**	compound predicate nominative

4	**A**	simple subject	**9**	**A**	direct object
	B	simple predicate		**B**	indirect object
	C	complete subject		**C**	predicate nominative
	D	complete predicate		**D**	predicate adjective

5	**A**	simple subject	**10**	**A**	direct object
	B	simple predicate		**B**	indirect object
	C	complete subject		**C**	predicate nominative
	D	complete predicate		**D**	predicate adjective

Chuck Jones. *Love Is in the Hare,* 1998.
Limited edition giclée, 20 by 15 inches. © Warner Bros.

Describe Who is the focus of this caricature? How does the title suggest that this artwork is meant to be humorous?

Analyze How does the cartoonist use exaggeration in the caricature?

Interpret Exaggeration is a technique also used by writers in tall tales and satires. If you were to describe Bugs Bunny in words, how would you express the ridiculous aspects of his appearance and character?

Judge If you wanted to satirize someone, do you think it would be more effective to do so in the form of a cartoon or in writing? Why do you think so?

At the end of this chapter, you will use the artwork to stimulate ideas for writing.

Subjects and Predicates

A well-constructed house has a foundation, which basically holds all the other parts of the house together. Like a house a sentence must also have a foundation. The foundation, or base, of a sentence is composed of a subject, a predicate (verb), and sometimes a complement. All other words in the sentence are added to this foundation.

A **sentence** is a group of words that expresses a complete thought.

A group of words that does not express a complete thought is called a **fragment**. In many cases a group of words is a fragment because it does not have a subject or a predicate.

FRAGMENT	SENTENCE
Under the briefcase.	The script is under the briefcase.
The characters.	The characters seem real.
Designing the set.	Mike is designing the set.
Auditioned for the part.	She auditioned for the part.

To express a complete thought, a group of words must have both a subject and a predicate.

A **subject** names the person, place, thing, or idea the sentence is about.

The **predicate** tells something about the subject.

COMPLETE SUBJECT	COMPLETE PREDICATE
My aunt from Alabama	is performing in *Hamlet*.
The box on the counter	contains costumes for the actors.
The audience	clapped for ten minutes today.
The final cast member	took a bow.

You can learn more about sentence fragments later in this chapter on pages L68–L71.

● Simple Subjects and Predicates

A **simple subject** is the main word in the complete subject.

A **simple predicate**, or **verb**, is the main word or phrase in the complete predicate.

Each complete subject and predicate can be narrowed down to a single word or phrase. In the following examples, the simple subjects and the verbs are in **bold** type.

> ⌐——— complete subject ———⌐ complete predicate ¬
> The narrow wooden **stage curved** to the right.
>
> complete
> ⌐— subject —¬ ⌐——— complete predicate ———¬
> Two **reviews** recently **appeared** in the *Chronicle*.
>
> ⌐——— complete subject ———¬⌐——— complete predicate ———¬
> The **New Globe** in Acton **is raising** money for new seats.

In the last example, *New Globe* is a single proper noun; therefore, both words make up the simple subject. Notice also that the verb phrase *is raising* is considered the verb of the sentence.

Throughout the rest of this book, the term *subject* will refer to a simple subject, and the term *verb* will refer to a simple predicate, which may be a single verb or a verb phrase.

You can learn more about using verbs on pages L16–L23 and about subject-verb agreement on pages L289–L317.

CONNECT TO SPEAKING AND WRITING

Anyone—even a three-year-old—can express ideas using a few random words. However, you will express yourself much more precisely and persuasively if you have mastered the basic sentence. You will argue more effectively, describe more vividly, and entertain more creatively. People will pay more attention to what you say because you say it with skillfully formed sentences. By understanding the two main parts of a sentence, the subject and the verb, you will be able to create these powerful sentences. ●

Finding Subjects and Verbs

To find the subject of an action verb, ask yourself *Who?* or *What?* before the verb. The answer to either question will be the subject of the sentence. In the following examples, each subject is underlined once, and each verb is underlined twice.

Mandy has taken drama classes for two years. (The action verb is *has taken*. Who has taken? The subject is *Mandy*.)

His performance is improving rapidly. (The action verb is *is improving*. What is improving? The subject is *performance*.)

To find the subject of a linking verb, ask yourself, *About whom or what is the statement being made?* When you have answered that question, you will have identified the subject.

My brother is a stagehand at a dinner theater. (The linking verb is *is*. About whom is the statement being made? The subject is *brother*.)

The stage curtains feel exceptionally heavy. (The linking verb is *feel*. About what is the statement being made? The subject is *curtains*.)

You can learn more about linking verbs on pages L20–L23.

When you look for a subject and a verb, it is often helpful to eliminate all modifiers and all prepositional phrases from the sentence. Remember: *A subject is never part of a prepositional phrase.*

Numerous masterpieces by Shakespeare are performed throughout England. (*Masterpieces* is the subject; *are performed* is the verb.)

His plays can still be seen at the reconstructed Globe Theatre in London. (*Plays* is the subject; *can be seen* is the verb.)

You can learn more about modifiers on pages L107–L111 and L120–L122 and prepositional phrases on pages L97–L103.

PRACTICE YOUR SKILLS

● Check Your Understanding
Identifying Subjects and Verbs

Literature
Topic **Write the subject and the verb in each sentence.**

1. William Shakespeare lived from 1564 to 1616.

2. At his death this famous playwright left a most unusual will.

3. Considerable real-estate holdings in and near Stratford went to his two daughters, Susanna and Judith.

4. Shakespeare did, however, make some curious bequests.

5. The following line from his will is still confusing many historians.

6. "I give unto my Wiffe my 2nd-best bed with the furniture."

7. He apparently had just scribbled these words into the will as an additional note.

8. His will never mentions his plays.

9. This omission has raised serious doubts in some historians' minds.

10. The writer of this will may not have been the author of the Elizabethan dramas.

● Connect to the Writing Process: Drafting
Writing Simple Subjects and Verbs

Add subjects or verbs to the following words to create complete sentences. If you are given a verb, add a simple subject. If you are given a subject, add a verb.

11. auditioned for the role of Duncan, King of Scotland.

12. For the next three weekends, tryouts.

13. painted the wooden props.

14. will practice each night.

15. The flamboyant drama teacher.

16. Everyone's favorite actor.

17. wants her own room with a star on the door.

18. had never read *The Tragedy of Macbeth*.

19. Seth Ramsey.

20. said she will write a letter of recommendation for him.

Communicate Your Ideas

APPLY TO WRITING
Play Scene: *Subjects and Verbs*

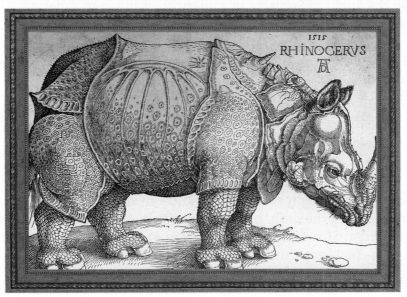

Albrecht Dürer. *Rhinoceros,* 1515.
Woodcut, 9¼ by 11¾ inches. Prints Collection, New York Public Library.

A writer's choice of verbs determines how clearly the reader pictures the action. In *Macbeth*, Macbeth says that he would rather face an "arm'd rhinoceros" than the ghost that is in front of him. In Shakespeare's time, *armed* meant that one not only carried weapons but also was covered with armor—much like the thick-skinned rhinoceros armed with a sharp horn.

Which do you think would be scarier for Macbeth to confront, a rhinoceros or a ghost? Study Dürer's drawing

Rhinoceros, and assume that this rhinoceros, rather than the ghost, appears to Macbeth. Write an action scene in which Macbeth is faced with this rhinoceros. Be prepared to identify the subjects and verbs in your scene.

Different Positions of Subjects

When a sentence is in its **natural order**, the subject comes before the verb. For various reasons a sentence may also be written in **inverted order**, with the verb or part of the verb phrase coming before the subject. Subjects in sentences in inverted order are sometimes difficult to find.

Questions are often phrased in inverted order. To find the subject and the verb in a question, turn the question around to make a statement.

QUESTION	Have you seen my model of the inner ear?
STATEMENT	You have seen my model of the inner ear.

There **and** *here* begin sentences that are in inverted order. To find the subject and the verb, place the words in the sentence in their natural order. Sometimes the word *there* or *here* must be dropped before the sentence can be put in its natural order.

INVERTED ORDER	Here is your inner-ear model.
NATURAL ORDER	Your inner-ear model is here.
INVERTED ORDER	There will be a test given on the ear.
NATURAL ORDER	A test will be given on the ear. (Drop *there*.)

Emphasis and variety are other reasons for inverted sentences. To create emphasis or variety, you may sometimes deliberately write a sentence in inverted order. To determine the subject and the verb, put the sentence in its natural order.

INVERTED ORDER	Throughout the body are innumerable muscle fibers.
NATURAL ORDER	Innumerable muscle fibers are throughout the body.
INVERTED ORDER	Across the gym lay the muscle-building equipment.
NATURAL ORDER	The muscle-building equipment lay across the gym.

Understood *You* is the subject of most commands and requests. Although *you* seldom appears in such sentences, it is still understood to be there. In the following examples, *you* is the understood subject of each sentence.

Smell this fragrant lotion!
(*You* is the understood subject.)

Cathy, breathe deeply.
(*You* is the understood subject even though the person receiving the command is named.)

You can learn more about subject-verb agreement and inverted order on pages L303–L305.

PRACTICE YOUR SKILLS

 Check Your Understanding
Identifying Subjects and Verbs in Inverted Order

 Write the subject and the verb in each sentence. If the subject is an understood *you*, write *you* in parentheses.

Science Topic

1. Listen to this fascinating information!
2. Within the skull is the average three-pound human brain.
3. Here is the detailed diagram of the respiratory system.
4. Have you studied the respiratory system yet?

5. There are millions of tiny air sacs in the lungs.

6. Think of this fact at your next mealtime.

7. On the table in the food is your supply of vitamins and minerals.

8. There are 9,000 taste buds on a person's tongue.

9. With increased age comes an inability to hear fewer high-pitched sounds.

10. How does the circulatory system transport 680,000 gallons of blood a year?

● Connect to the Writing Process: Drafting
Writing Sentences in Inverted Order

11.–18. Write two sentences for each type of inverted order sentence: *Questions, There and Here, Emphasis or Variety,* and *Understood You.* Then underline the subjects and circle the verbs.

Communicate Your Ideas

APPLY TO WRITING

Expository Essay: *Inverted Sentences*

Choose one system of the body, such as the respiratory system, the circulatory system, or the central nervous system, and write a short expository essay about some aspect of it for your science teacher. (You may first want to do some research.) The main point of your essay should be the remarkable functions that a system has. Incorporate some inverted sentences to give your essay variety and interest.

▶ Compound Subjects and Verbs

A **compound subject** is two or more subjects in one sentence that have the same verb and are joined by a conjunction.

A sentence can have more than one subject and more than one verb. You can ask yourself the same questions to find compound subjects and verbs as you did to find simple subjects and verbs.

> The rings and bracelets disappeared suddenly.
> Maria, Barry, and Martin searched for the jewels.

A **compound verb** is two or more verbs that have the same subject and are joined by a conjunction.

> You can join the treasure hunt or stay in the cabin.
> This map will assist our search and will guarantee success.

A sentence can have both a compound subject and a compound verb.

> Paul and his sister had the jewelry and buried it deeply.
>
> Maria and Barry received a treasure map and immediately organized a search party.

You can find out more about conjunctions on pages L40–L43. You can learn about subject-verb agreement with compound subjects on pages L298–L301.

PRACTICE YOUR SKILLS

 Check Your Understanding
Identifying Compound Subjects and Verbs

General Interest **Write the subjects and the verbs in the following sentences.**

1. Gold and silver in the *Atocha's* hold lay on the bottom of the sea and tempted treasure hunters for centuries.
2. In 1622, the ship was bound for Spain but sank in the waters off the Florida coast during a hurricane.
3. Because of a second hurricane, other vessels could not rescue the *Atocha's* treasure.
4. The position of the ship either was not recorded or was forgotten.
5. Eventually ocean currents covered the ship with sand and hid it from searchers.

6. The legend of the *Atocha* and the promise of great wealth brought many treasure hunters to Florida.

7. Mel Fisher and his family joined the others and became full-time treasure hunters.

8. Mel had once run a chicken farm and then had operated a diving shop.

9. He not only had some original ideas about the possible location of the ship but also used clever techniques in the search.

10. Both Mel and his family continued their search in the face of many hardships and much scorn.

● Connect to the Writing Process: Prewriting
Brainstorming for Ideas

Read the following paragraph to find out what eventually happened to the *Atocha*'s treasure. Write each subject and each verb. Using these subjects and verbs for ideas, brainstorm and list additional subjects and verbs that relate to treasure-hunting. Be sure to include plenty of compound subjects and verbs.

Critics constantly laughed at the efforts of the Fishers. Finally, in June 1975, Fisher's crew found a cannon from the *Atocha* and silenced the critics. The joy of the Fisher party was intense yet brief. On the night of July 18, 1975, Fisher's son, his daughter-in-law, and another diver drowned. Neither Mel nor his wife stopped their work. The tragedies would then have been meaningless. They continued and salvaged more and more objects. They could not keep all of the treasure. The state of Florida claimed a portion of the treasure and held much of it for a long period of time.

APPLY TO WRITING

Newspaper Story: *Subjects and Verbs*

Using the lists of subjects and verbs you wrote for the preceding exercise, write a newspaper story of a treasure found years after being lost and forgotten. Be sure to use compound subjects and compound verbs in some of your sentences.

QuickCheck Mixed Practice

Contemporary Life

Make two columns. Label one column *Subjects* and the other *Verbs*. Then write the subjects and verbs in each sentence under the appropriate heading.

1. Jamaica is a lush, green island in the Caribbean Sea.
2. There is sparkling clear water surrounding this popular vacation destination.
3. Deep-sea divers and eager swimmers rent boats and buy snorkeling equipment for water recreation.
4. Have you seen the beautiful coral reefs off the coast of Jamaica?
5. Just below the calm surface of the sea grows living coral.
6. Wear a scuba mask for the best view of the coral.
7. Trisha, Jerry, and Ling saw a baby octopus and accidentally frightened it away.
8. Tomorrow I will windsurf, shop, and sunbathe until nightfall.
9. Here are the picture postcards and small souvenirs from our shopping trip.
10. In the early morning hours, enjoy your breakfast and then meet me at the beach for a swim.

Sentence Fragments

A sentence fragment is not a sentence at all. It is an incomplete thought that usually leaves the reader confused with unanswered questions.

A **sentence fragment** is a group of words that does not express a complete thought.

To communicate clearly and completely when you write, be sure to check your work for sentence fragments like the following.

Fragments due to incomplete thoughts are a common kind of fragment. A fragment that expresses an incomplete thought is often missing a subject or a verb.

FRAGMENT	Applied to five different colleges.
CORRECTED	Jackie applied to five different colleges.
	(*Jackie* is the subject.)
FRAGMENT	All of my friends in homeroom.
CORRECTED	All of my friends in homeroom graduated.
	(*Graduated* is the verb.)

Fragments due to incorrect punctuation are another kind of fragment. If you place a period between the parts of a compound verb, you create a fragment. Likewise, if you place a period before a list of items, you create a fragment.

FRAGMENT	Martin rewrote his application essay five times. And made it stronger each time.
CORRECTED	Martin rewrote his application essay five times and made it stronger each time.
	(*Rewrote* and *made* are a compound verb.)
FRAGMENT	Sarah consulted many sources for advice. Books, teachers, relatives, and friends.
CORRECTED	Sarah consulted many sources for advice: books, teachers, relatives, and friends.
	(A colon precedes the list of sources.)

You can find out about other kinds of sentence fragments on pages L123–L125 and L164–L166.

Ways to Correct Sentence Fragments

You can correct a fragment in one of two ways. You can add words to it to make a complete sentence, or you can attach it to the sentence next to it. Sometimes when you attach a fragment to a sentence next to it, you may have to add or drop words.

FRAGMENT	Asked her guidance counselor for direction.
ADD WORDS	Katia asked her guidance counselor for direction.
	(Who asked for advice? Words are added to complete the sentence.)
FRAGMENT FOLLOWING A SENTENCE	Leon wanted an academic scholarship. Studied diligently all year.
ATTACH TO PREVIOUS SENTENCE	Leon wanted an academic scholarship and studied diligently all year.
	(The conjunction *and* is added to connect the fragment to the sentence before it.)
FRAGMENT PRECEDING A SENTENCE	Good grades, social skills, and academic potential. These are all important to the application committee.
ATTACH TO FOLLOWING SENTENCE	Good grades, social skills, and academic potential are all important to the application committee.
	(*Grades, skills*, and *potential* form a compound subject for the verb *are*.)

CONNECT TO **W**RITER'S CRAFT

Writers of fiction use sentence fragments to make written dialogue sound more realistic. They know that in daily life, few people speak in complete sentences all the time. Poets often use fragments to focus readers' attention on the thought or idea expressed by the fragment rather than on a complete thought. All formal writing, however, requires complete sentences. An essay, business report, or formal letter free of sentence fragments is the sign of an educated writer.

PRACTICE YOUR SKILLS

● Check Your Understanding
Identifying Sentence Fragments

Contemporary Life **Write *F* if the item is a sentence fragment and *S* if it is a sentence. Then correct each sentence fragment.**

1. The most important preparation for college admission. Begins long before you fill out the application.

2. Do homework and take thorough notes. In every class.

3. Most college freshmen. They wish they had taken high school more seriously.

4. Don't forget the value of exercise and sleep.

5. Community involvement.

6. Verbal, math, and analytical skills. Tested by standardized tests.

7. Many smart people. Afflicted by test anxiety.

8. Become familiar with the SAT and ACT formats. And take a few practice tests beforehand.

9. Many tips and facts about tests and applications. Freely available from guidance counselors and college admissions offices.

10. Your best plan is simple. Study, practice, and plan.

Read the following advice on writing college admission essays. Then rewrite the paragraph, correcting each sentence fragment you find.

Two important things. They will help you write a strong college admission essay. First, one or several admissions officers. Dedicated, overworked, experienced. Will read your essay. Sentence fragments, poor grammar, and spelling errors. These will destine an essay for the rejection stack. Second, each reader will look for a connection with you through the essay. You can make this connection. By keeping the focus of the essay on the most important topic—you. For example, if you are writing about "An Event That Changed My Life," which do you think is a better statement: "My parents divorced when I was ten. And they spent the next seven years fighting over the house, the furniture, and me" or "I was ten when my parents divorced. And I quickly learned. Responsibility, self-discipline, and dedication"? Is the better sentence. Focuses on the positive qualities in you. Will help make you a successful college student.

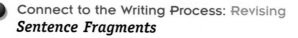

Communicate Your Ideas

APPLY TO WRITING

College Admission Essay: *Complete Sentences*

The Director of Admissions of your choice of colleges has requested that you send a writing sample. Write a short college admission essay about an event that changed your life. Then team up with a writing partner to check for sentence fragments in your and your partner's writing. Help each other correct any fragments you find because you want to impress the Director!

Complements

Sometimes a sentence needs more than a subject and a verb to sound complete. Such a sentence also needs a completer, or complement. None of the following sentences, for example, would be complete without the complements in **bold** type.

> Todd wrapped the **gift.**
> Dan gave **me flowers.**
> Kate has become an **expert** on customs.
> The stores are **open.**

There are five kinds of complements. Direct objects, indirect objects, and objective complements complete the meaning of action verbs. Predicate nominatives and predicate adjectives, which are called subject complements, complete the meaning of linking verbs.

● Direct Objects and Indirect Objects

A **direct object** is a noun or a pronoun that receives the action of the verb.

To find a direct object, ask yourself *What?* or *Whom?* after an action verb. Notice in the third example below that a direct object can be compound.

> d.o.
> Leo removed the **packages** from his briefcase. (Leo removed what? *Packages* is the direct object.)
>
> d.o.
> I drove **Heather** to the airport. (I drove whom? *Heather* is the direct object.)
>
> d.o. d.o.
> Heather will visit **associates** and **clients** in Japan. (Heather will visit whom? *Associates* and *clients* make up the compound direct object.)

Each part of a compound action verb can have its own direct object.

>   d.o.   d.o.
> Heather focused her **camera** and snapped the **picture**.
>
> (*Camera* is the direct object of *focused*, and *picture* is the direct object of *snapped*.)

You can learn more about action verbs and transitive verbs on pages L16–L17.

An **indirect object** is a noun or a pronoun that answers the question *To or for whom?* or *To or for what?* after an action verb.

If a sentence has a direct object, the same sentence may also have an indirect object. To find an indirect object, first find the direct object by asking *What?* or *Whom?* after the action verb. Then ask *To or for whom?* or *To or for what?* after the direct object. An indirect object always comes before a direct object in a sentence.

>   i.o.   d.o.
> I bought **Paul** a new catcher's mitt.
>
> (*Mitt* is the direct object of the verb *bought*. I bought a mitt for whom? *Paul* is the indirect object. Notice that the indirect object comes before the direct object.)
>
>   i.o.   d.o.
> The students gave **Mr. Beacon** tokens of appreciation.
>
> (*Tokens* is the direct object of the verb *gave*. The students gave tokens to whom? *Mr. Beacon* is the indirect object.)

An indirect object may be compound.

>   i.o.   i.o.   d.o.
> Sashina Chi is teaching **Lee** and **Kelly** Japanese.
>
> (*Japanese* is the direct object of the verb *is teaching*. Sashina Chi is teaching Japanese to whom? *Lee* and *Kelly* make up the compound indirect object.)

Remember that neither a direct object nor an indirect object is ever part of a prepositional phrase.

>   i.o.   d.o.
> We gave **Roger** an album for his birthday.
>
> (*Roger* is the indirect object. It comes before the direct object *album* and is not part of a prepositional phrase.)
>
>   d.o.
> We gave an album to Roger for his birthday.
>
> (In this sentence *Roger* is not the indirect object because it follows the direct object *album* and is the object of the preposition *to*.)

You can learn more about prepositional phrases on pages L97–L103.

PRACTICE YOUR SKILLS

 Check Your Understanding
Identifying Direct and Indirect Objects

Contemporary Life   **Write the direct and indirect objects in the following sentences. Then beside each one state whether it is a *direct object* (d.o.) or an *indirect object* (i.o.).**

1. My Japanese friend Keiko shipped me a collection of herbal teas.
2. Last month I gave her a tea service for her birthday.
3. Later Keiko recommended a book about gifts to me.
4. I read the book with great interest.
5. I learned several facts about gift customs in Japanese culture.
6. During the year-end gift-giving season, called *O-seibo*, employers treat employees and clients lavishly.
7. Department stores stock special sections of appropriate gift items and wrappings.
8. Friends, relatives, students, and teachers surprise others with gourmet candy, cookies, and other treats.

9. They sometimes send overseas friends souvenir stamps, small pins, or fancy soaps.

10. Visitors to Japan should learn the customs about gifts.

 ## Objective Complements

An **objective complement** is a noun or an adjective that renames or describes the direct object.

To find an objective complement, first find the direct object. Then ask the question *What?* after the direct object. An objective complement will always follow the direct object. Notice the compound objective complement in the third example.

Chin-yau declared the gift **perfect**. (*Gift* is the direct object. Chin-yau declared the gift what? *Perfect* is the objective complement. It follows the direct object and describes it.)

The Chinese consider red a joyful **color** for gift wrap. (*Red* is the direct object. The Chinese consider red what? *Color* is the objective complement. It follows the direct object and renames it.)

The award made Ming **happy** and **proud**. (*Ming* is the direct object. The award made Ming what? The words *happy* and *proud* make up the compound objective complement. These words follow the direct object and describe it.)

PRACTICE YOUR SKILLS

● Check Your Understanding
Identifying Complements

General Interest **Write the complements in the following sentences. Beside each one, write whether it is a *direct object* (d.o.), *indirect object* (i.o.), or *objective complement* (o.c.).**

1. The right bouquet will make the recipient happy and appreciative.

2. The Spanish consider chrysanthemums a flower of sadness.

3. This flower forms floral arrangements for funerals.

4. Don't give your girlfriend a chrysanthemum arrangement in Spain.

5. In France yellow flowers symbolize infidelity.

6. Mexicans use yellow flowers in their "Day of the Dead" events.

7. In either country, give loved ones bouquets of flowers in a different color.

8. The Japanese comfort the ill with flowers and use flowers at times of death.

9. The Japanese also give a future spouse flowers during courtship.

10. Like the Spanish, the Japanese use yellow chrysanthemums for funerals.

Connect to the Writing Process: Prewriting
Freewriting for Ideas

You are a member of the committee that organizes activities for International Student Celebration Week. You will not only advise the committee on international gift etiquette, but you will write a feature article on the topic for a small booklet the committee will distribute. To develop ideas for your article, freewrite for ten minutes on anything that comes to mind regarding gifts and etiquette. Then underline and label the complements: *direct object* (d.o.), *indirect object* (i.o.), and *objective complement* (o.c.).

Communicate Your Ideas

APPLY TO WRITING

Informative Article: *Complements*

Using the ideas you developed in your freewriting activity, write an informative article on gifts and etiquette. Your audience will be students at your school who participate in festivities during International Student Celebration

Week. You may want to plan a trip to the library or a search session on the Internet to gather interesting facts for your article. Use direct and indirect objects and objective complements to make your writing accurate and engaging. Be prepared to identify them.

Subject Complements

Two kinds of complements, called **subject complements**, complete the meaning of linking verbs.

> A **predicate nominative** is a noun or a pronoun that follows a linking verb and identifies, renames, or explains the subject.

To find a predicate nominative, first find the subject and the linking verb. Then find the noun or the pronoun that follows the verb and identifies, renames, or explains the subject. Notice in the second example that a predicate nominative can be compound.

p.n.
Bart will become an art **teacher**. (*teacher = Bart*)

p.n.   p.n.
The winners of the art scholarships are **Bryan** and **Julie**.
(*Bryan* and *Julie = winners*)

p.n.
David was a visiting art **scholar**. (*scholar = David*)

Like other complements, a predicate nominative is never part of a prepositional phrase.

p.n.
Pamela is **one** of the artists at the Colorado Artists' Colony.
(*One* is the predicate nominative. *Artists* is the object of the preposition *of*.)

p.n.
Jeff and Luis were a **couple** of the sculptors there.
(*Couple* is the predicate nominative. *Sculptors* is the object of the preposition *of*.)

Often when someone asks you a question beginning with *Who is,* he or she wants a predicate nominative for an answer.

> "Who is that man?"
> "He is the **photographer**."
> "Who is your favorite cartoonist?"
> "Scott Adams is my favorite **cartoonist**."

The other subject complement is a predicate adjective.

> A **predicate adjective** is an adjective that follows a linking verb and modifies the subject.

To find a predicate adjective, first find the subject and the linking verb. Then find an adjective that follows the verb and modifies, or describes, the subject. Notice in the third example that a predicate adjective can be compound.

> p.a.
> That painting was **impressionistic**. (*Impressionistic* describes the subject: *the impressionistic painting.*)
>
> p.a.
> The colors were **vivid**. (*Vivid* describes the subject: *the vivid colors.*)
>
> p.a.   p.a.
> The paints looked **dry** and **lumpy**. (*Dry* and *lumpy* describe the subject: *dry, lumpy paints.*)

Remember that a predicate adjective follows a linking verb and modifies, or describes, the subject. Do not confuse a predicate adjective with a regular adjective.

> PREDICATE ADJECTIVE   Carlos is **brilliant**. (*Brilliant* describes the subject *Carlos.*)
>
> REGULAR ADJECTIVE   Carlos is a **brilliant** sculptor. (*Brilliant* describes the word *sculptor.*)

You can review lists of linking verbs on page L21.

Now that you've studied subjects, verbs, and complements, you may notice something about newspaper headlines. Usually the headline is not a complete sentence. Instead, it contains the simple subject, the main verb, and perhaps the complement. Consider these examples:

Murderer Declared Insane (subject-verb-complement)
Philanthropist Donates Millions (subject-verb-complement)
Election Results Disappointing (subject-verb)
Hurricane Approaching! (subject-verb)

PRACTICE YOUR SKILLS

● Check Your Understanding
Identifying Subject Complements

Art
Topic
Write the subject complement in each sentence. Beside it, label it *p.n.* for predicate nominative or *p.a.* for predicate adjective.

1. Shelby has become a cartoonist.
2. My favorite colors have always been blue and purple.
3. *Hue* is another word for *color* or *shade*.
4. The silver sequins felt too brittle and fragile.
5. My brother is a senior at the Savannah College of Art and Design in Georgia.
6. The art museum in my hometown has grown old and drafty.
7. After graduation my sister became a graphic artist for a local publisher.
8. Woodcarving is a forgotten art form.
9. This color scheme seems progressive.
10. The foreground appears bright, and the background seems shadowy.

Using Subject Complements

Complete each sentence by adding a predicate nominative or adjective. Then write five sentences of your own to continue discussing the ideas. Use at least one compound predicate nominative and one compound predicate adjective. Label the predicate nominatives and adjectives in all 10 sentences.

11. The colors in the mural seemed ■.

12. Across the room, the mural artist was ■.

13. Her favorite subject is obviously ■.

14. The exhibition room felt ■.

15. The award-winners are ■.

Communicate Your Ideas

APPLY TO WRITING
Oral Report: *Complements*

William Wegman. *Cinderella,* 1992.
Unique Polacolor ER photograph, 20 by 24 inches. © William Wegman. From the book *Cinderella.* Hyperion Books for Children, New York, New York, 1993.

Write a short oral presentation about William Wegman's photograph *Cinderella*. Describe the artwork for your classmates and express your opinions about it. Also, use the five types of complements to add detail and clarity to your opinions.

QuickCheck Mixed Practice

Literature Topic **Write each complement. Then label each one using the following abbreviations:**

direct object = *d.o.*   predicate nominative = *p.n.*
indirect object = *i.o.*   predicate adjective = *p.a.*
objective complement = *o.c.*

1. Mr. Williams gave the class a list of fiction genres.
2. I consider the western a boring category of fiction.
3. I read approximately three mystery novels every month.
4. Two best-selling mystery novelists are Patricia Cornwell and Sue Grafton.
5. The category of science fiction is amazing and exciting.
6. My friend declared Toni Morrison her favorite author of all time.
7. Many bookstores devote special shelves, large posters, and special sales to popular books.
8. Several of my classmates are eager readers and devoted fans of Larry McMurtry's intricate novels about the Southwest.
9. Well-informed bookstore employees show patrons the current favorites in each section of the store.
10. Regular customers often buy themselves a new book and a cup of coffee on the weekend.

Sentence Patterns

Using Sentence Patterns

Each sentence you write seems unique—like the patterns and shapes of snowflakes. Looking more closely at the sentences you write, however, you will see that each falls into one of six basic sentence patterns. You can vary your writing style by expanding these basic sentence patterns. They can be expanded by adding modifiers, appositives, prepositional phrases, and verbal phrases. Any of these patterns can also be expanded by making the subject, the verb, or any of the complements compound. In this way you create many variations within a particular pattern itself.

Pattern 1: S-V (subject-verb)

```
  S     V
Cattle graze.
```
```
————————S———————    ————————V————————
Cattle belonging to Matt always graze in the far pasture.
```

Pattern 2: S-V-O (subject-verb-direct object)

```
  S     V    O
Girls swam laps.
```
```
————————S————————   ————V————   —O—
The girls on the swim team effortlessly swam many laps.
```

Pattern 3: S-V-I-O (subject-verb-indirect object-direct object)

```
  S    V    I    O
Todd sent me tickets.
```
```
—S—  ——————V——————  —I—  ——————O——————
Todd unexpectedly sent me tickets to the Ice Capades.
```

Pattern 4: S-V-N (subject-verb-predicate nominative)

```
   S     V    N
Campers are hikers.
```
```
————————S————————  —V—  ———————N———————
Many campers in this group are enthusiastic hikers.
```

Pattern 5: **S-V-A** (subject-verb-predicate adjective)

$$\begin{array}{ccc} \text{S} & \text{V} & \text{A} \end{array}$$

Spectators grew restless.

┌─────── S───────┐ ┌─── V───┐ ┌── A ────┐
The eager spectators suddenly grew very restless.

Pattern 6: **S-V-O-C** (subject-verb-direct object-objective complement)

$$\begin{array}{cccc} \text{S} & \text{V} & \text{O} & \text{C} \end{array}$$

Everyone considers Roy trustworthy.

┌────── S──────┐ ┌─V─┐ ┌O┐ ┌──── C ────┐
Everyone in my school considers Roy absolutely trustworthy.

PRACTICE YOUR SKILLS

Check Your Understanding

Write the sentence pattern for each of the five following sentences.

1. Freshly cut hay always smells clean and sweet.
2. Many historians consider Harriet Tubman a major personality in United States history.
3. The coach of the field hockey team gave each member a certificate of achievement.
4. Fallen meteors have been discovered by scientists in various parts of the world.
5. The correct answer to the question is the last one.

Writing an Expository Paragraph

Have you ever wondered how food is canned or how the ancient Egyptians built the pyramids? Brainstorm for a list of *How?* questions you would like answered and then choose one question. Research the answer on the Internet or in reference books at school or in the media center. Take notes on the information you find that will answer your question and then organize your details in a logical order. Write a topic sentence for your paragraph. Then write the first draft of an expository paragraph that answers the *How?* question you chose. As you revise and edit your paragraph, make certain it includes a variety of sentence patterns. Then write a final copy.

Diagraming the Sentence Base

A **diagram** is a picture of words. By placing the words of a sentence in a diagram, you can often see the relationship between the parts of a sentence more clearly.

Subjects and Verbs   All diagrams begin with a baseline. The subject and the verb go on the baseline but are separated by a vertical line. Capital letters are included in a diagram, but punctuation is not. Notice in the second diagram that compound subjects and verbs are placed on parallel lines. The conjunction joining the subjects or the verbs is placed on a broken line between them.

He is working.

He | is working

Lupe and Carl both sang and danced.

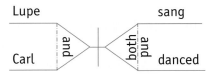

Inverted Order and Understood Subjects   An inverted sentence is diagramed like a sentence in natural order. The understood subject *you* is diagramed in the subject position with parentheses around it.

Have you eaten?

you | Have eaten

Listen!

(you) | Listen

Adjectives and Adverbs   Adjectives and adverbs are connected by a slanted line to the words they modify. Notice that a conjunction joining two modifiers is placed on a broken line between them. Notice, too, how an adverb that describes another adverb is written parallel to the word it modifies.

Her small but valuable diamond sparkles quite brilliantly.

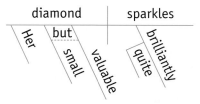

Note: Possessive pronouns, such as *Her* in the example above, are diagramed like adjectives.

Complements

All complements except the indirect object are diagramed on the baseline with the subject and the verb.

Direct Objects   A short vertical line separates a direct object from the verb. Notice in the second example that the parts of a compound direct object are placed on parallel lines. The conjunction is placed on a broken line.

I have already seen that movie.

Buy four oranges and six bananas.

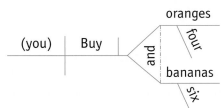

Indirect Objects   An indirect object is diagramed on a horizontal line that is connected to the verb by a slanted line. Notice in the second example that the parts of a compound indirect object are diagramed on horizontal parallel lines. The conjunction is placed on a broken line between them.

Send them an invitation.

Aunt May bought David and me identical sweaters.

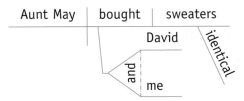

Objective Complements   Since an objective complement renames or describes the direct object, it is placed to the right of the direct object on the baseline. A slanted line that points toward the direct object separates the two complements. Notice in the second example that a compound objective complement is placed on horizontal parallel lines. The conjunction is placed on a broken line between them.

We named our dog King.

Mom will paint the kitchen yellow or green.

Subject Complements   A predicate nominative and a predicate adjective are diagramed in exactly the same way. They are placed on the baseline after the verb. A slanted line that points back toward the subject separates a subject complement from the verb. Notice in the second example that a compound subject complement is placed on horizontal parallel lines. The conjunction is placed on a broken line between them.

This camera was a birthday present.

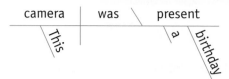

This lecture was not only interesting but also informative.

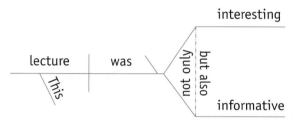

PRACTICE YOUR SKILLS

Diagraming Sentences

Diagram the following sentences or copy them. If you copy them, draw one line under each subject and two lines under each verb. Then label each complement using the following abbreviations.

direct object = *d.o.*   predicate nominative = *p.n.*
indirect object = *i.o.*   predicate adjective = *p.a.*
objective complement = *o.c.*

1. Would you be an astronaut?

2. The first American astronauts were Abe and Miss Baker.

3. These very brave astronauts were monkeys!

4. They gave scientists important information.

5. Space travel could be safe and reliable.

6. The space shuttle has been a really huge success.

7. NASA named the first shuttle *Columbia*.

8. Shuttles quite often carry many astronauts and large cargo.

9. Astronauts now successfully repair satellites.

10. Tell us more.

Finding Subjects and Verbs

Write the subjects and verbs in the following sentences. If the subject is an understood *you*, write *you* in parentheses.

1. The giant tortoise of the Galápagos Islands may weigh as much as 500 pounds and may live up to 150 years.
2. Here are the balloons and streamers for Leah's birthday party.
3. Did you contact the Better Business Bureau about the problem with your new television set?
4. Most people remember Paul Revere's patriotism but forget his work as a silversmith and engraver.
5. Over the horizon that August day sailed the ships of Columbus's small fleet.
6. Revise your report carefully.
7. There are many inlets and bays along the coast of Nova Scotia.
8. There are more than 200 CDs of classical and popular music in the cabinet.
9. Have you seen the exciting new computers on sale?
10. Brad, take these shirts back to the store for a refund.
11. There is no living descendant of William Shakespeare.
12. Hasn't he answered your letter yet?
13. American Indians do not pay taxes on their land.
14. John Adams, John Quincy Adams, John F. Kennedy, and George Bush were all born in Norfolk County, Massachusetts.
15. Slowly over the mountaintops rose the brilliant morning sun.

Finding Complements

Write each complement. Then label each one, using the following abbreviations:

direct object = *d.o.*   predicate nominative = *p.n.*
indirect object = *i.o.*   predicate adjective = *p.a.*
objective complement = *o.c.*

1. The Puritans considered buttons a sign of vanity.
2. At first the old trunk in the basement appeared empty.
3. Michelle showed Mom a copy of the yearbook.
4. Many early American settlers found the Indians friendly and helpful.
5. In Williamsburg, Virginia, we visited several old shops.
6. Their grandfather clock is quite old and very valuable.
7. James Monroe was the fourth president from Virginia.
8. Tell Alma and James that funny story about your uncle.
9. From the top of Mount Irazu in Costa Rica, a person can see the Atlantic Ocean and the Pacific Ocean.
10. Centuries ago a collection of books was a sign of wealth.

Using the Sentence Base

Write five sentences that follow the directions below. (The sentences may come in any order.) Write about this topic or a topic of your choice: a trip back in time to a historic event.

Write a sentence that . . .

1. includes a direct object.
2. includes an indirect object.
3. includes a predicate nominative.
4. includes a predicate adjective.
5. includes an object complement.

Underline each subject once, each verb twice, and label each complement.

Language and *Self-Expression*

Chuck Jones brought characters such as Bugs Bunny, Elmer Fudd, Roadrunner, and Porky Pig to life. He has won three Academy Awards for his animated films, and his artwork has been shown at museums worldwide.

Jones uses exaggeration and word play to add humor to his cartoons. The disproportionate cheeks, feet, and teeth on Bugs Bunny and his friend add to the amusing quality of their appearance. The title of the artwork includes a pun that involves the substitution of *hare* for *air.*

Let this cartoon inspire you to write your own humorous sketch. Choose a person who is in the news or a character from history. Write a character sketch that exaggerates that person's features and actions for humorous effect. If possible, title your character sketch with a phrase that includes a play on words.

Prewriting Choose a famous person whom you would like to lampoon in a character sketch. Quickwrite a list of phrases and images that come to mind when you think about that person's appearance and actions.

Drafting Use your list to draft a character sketch. Begin by introducing the character. Add details that exaggerate the person's appearance and actions. Try to give your character sketch a title that includes a play on words.

Revising Reread your character sketch critically, analyzing its flow and clarity. Cut and add details as needed. Vary your sentence patterns to add interest to your writing.

Editing Review your paragraph, looking for errors in grammar, capitalization, punctuation, and spelling. Make any corrections that are necessary.

Publishing Prepare a final copy of your character sketch. You might try to publish your paragraph in your school newspaper or magazine.

Another Look

The Sentence

A **sentence** is a group of words that expresses a complete thought.

A **sentence fragment** is a group of words that does not express a complete thought.

Subjects and Predicates

A **subject** names the person, place, thing, or idea the sentence is about. *(page L57)*

A **simple subject** is the main word in the complete subject. *(page L58)*

A **predicate** tells something about the subject. *(page L57)*

A **simple predicate**, or **verb**, is the main word or phrase in the complete predicate. *(page L58)*

A **compound subject** is two or more subjects in one sentence that have the same verb and are joined by a conjunction. *(page L64)*

A **compound verb** is two or more verbs that have the same subject and are joined by a conjunction. *(page L65)*

Other Information About Subjects and Predicates

Recognizing inverted order *(page L62)*

Recognizing understood *you* *(page L63)*

Complements

A **direct object** is a noun or a pronoun that receives the action of the verb. *(page L72)*

An **indirect object** answers the questions *To or for whom?* or *To or for what?* after an action verb. *(page L73)*

An **objective complement** is a noun or an adjective that renames or describes the direct object. *(page L75)*

A **predicate nominative** is a noun or a pronoun that follows a linking verb and identifies, renames, or explains the subject. *(page L77)*

A **predicate adjective** is an adjective that follows a linking verb and modifies the subject. *(page L78)*

 **Posttest**

Directions
Write the letter of the term that correctly identifies the underlined word or words in each sentence.

EXAMPLE

1. Before 1914, Carl Sandburg <u>was</u> an unknown poet.

1 **A** simple subject

B simple predicate

C complete subject

D complete predicate

ANSWER

1 **B**

1. The now famous <u>Carl Sandburg</u> was born in 1878 in Galesburg, Illinois.

2. Sandburg <u>served as a soldier during the Spanish-American War</u>.

3. His political beliefs <u>would influence</u> his poetry.

4. <u>Have</u> you <u>read</u> any of his early work?

5. <u>Many of his poems</u> reveal a vision of democracy.

6. Industrial <u>America</u> and American <u>workers</u> are a recurrent theme.

7. Besides free verse, Sandburg also wrote <u>biographies</u> and <u>books</u> for children.

8. Sandburg's biography of Lincoln is a remarkable <u>study</u> and a powerful <u>memorial</u> to that great president.

9. *The American Songbag* is a <u>collection</u> of almost 300 folk songs.

10. Sandburg recorded <u>several</u> of the songs himself.

1 **A** simple subject
   B simple predicate
   C complete subject
   D complete predicate

6 **A** compound subject
   B compound verb
   C compound direct object
   D compound predicate nominative

2 **A** simple subject
   B simple predicate
   C complete subject
   D complete predicate

7 **A** compound subject
   B compound verb
   C compound direct object
   D compound predicate nominative

3 **A** simple subject
   B simple predicate
   C complete subject
   D complete predicate

8 **A** compound subject
   B compound verb
   C compound direct object
   D compound predicate nominative

4 **A** simple subject
   B simple predicate
   C complete subject
   D complete predicate

9 **A** direct object
   B indirect object
   C predicate nominative
   D predicate adjective

5 **A** simple subject
   B simple predicate
   C complete subject
   D complete predicate

10 **A** direct object
    B indirect object
    C predicate nominative
    D predicate adjective

CHAPTER 3

Phrases

Directions

Write the letter of the term that correctly identifies the underlined phrase in each sentence.

EXAMPLE
1. <u>In the 1970s</u>, Maya Angelou and Toni Morrison had their first fame as writers.

   1 A prepositional
      B participial
      C gerund
      D infinitive

ANSWER
   1 A

1. <u>Growing up in Arkansas</u>, Maya Angelou knew sorrow and hardship from a young age.
2. Maya Angelou's autobiographical work, *I Know Why the Caged Bird Sings*, appeared in 1970.
3. <u>Triumphing over adversity</u> is a recurring theme in her work.
4. It is evident in her collection <u>of poetry</u>, *And Still I Rise*.
5. <u>Distilling the female and black experience</u>, Angelou writes sensitive, hopeful poetry and prose.
6. She prefers <u>raising up</u> to casting down.
7. Her optimism has appealed <u>to critics and presidents alike</u>.
8. Toni Morrison, <u>an editor and novelist</u>, published three important novels in quick succession.
9. *The Bluest Eye, Sula,* and *Song of Solomon* owe some of their color <u>to folklore and myth</u>.
10. The experience <u>of black women</u> is Morrison's focus.

1 A prepositional
   B participial
   C gerund
   D infinitive

2 A prepositional
   B participial
   C appositive
   D gerund

3 A prepositional
   B participial
   C gerund
   D infinitive

4 A prepositional
   B participial
   C appositive
   D gerund

5 A prepositional
   B participial
   C gerund
   D infinitive

6 A prepositional
   B participial
   C appositive
   D gerund

7 A prepositional
   B participial
   C gerund
   D infinitive

8 A prepositional
   B participial
   C appositive
   D gerund

9 A prepositional
   B participial
   C gerund
   D infinitive

10 A prepositional
    B participial
    C appositive
    D gerund

Andy Goldsworthy.
Sand Brought to an Edge to Catch the Light, August, 1991.
Shore of Lake Michigan.
©Andy Goldsworthy.
Photograph courtesy of the artist.

Describe   What are three adjectives you might use to describe this artwork?

Analyze   This artist creates art by manipulating landscapes and natural objects. How does he connect the natural and human-made worlds in his art?

Interpret   How do writers you know get across the message that commonplace objects in nature have a peculiar beauty? Can you think of any examples?

Judge   Unlike a painted landscape or a written poem, this artwork's life was fleeting. If you wished to convey this artist's message in a more permanent way, how might you do it?

At the end of this chapter, you will use the artwork as a visual aid for writing.

Prepositional Phrases

The subject, the verb, and sometimes a complement are the foundation of a sentence. Once you are familiar with the basic structure of a sentence, you can build on it. In a way, you become an architect. Instead of adding rooms, however, you are adding grammatical elements, such as phrases. The rooms in a house have specific purposes, and their different shapes and sizes make the house interesting and unique.

Similarly, different phrases have different purposes. Some phrases are used to expand or to qualify an idea, while others are used to show relationships between ideas. Using different kinds of phrases will make your writing more varied and more interesting.

A **phrase** is a group of related words that functions as a single part of speech. A phrase does not have a subject or a verb.

In this chapter you will first review prepositional phrases and appositive phrases. Then you will review the three kinds of verbal phrases: participial, gerund, and infinitive. Finally, you will review misplaced and dangling modifiers and phrase fragments.

A **prepositional phrase** is a group of words that begins with a preposition and ends with a noun or pronoun called the **object of the preposition**. The prepositional phrases in the following sentences are in **bold** type.

Before midnight the athlete **from Canton** withdrew **from the competition.**

In spite of the weather forecast, all teams are proceeding **with their plans for the outdoor events**.

Prepositional phrases are used like single adjectives and adverbs to modify other words in a sentence.

You can find a list of prepositions on page L37.

Adjective Phrases

An **adjective phrase** is a prepositional phrase used to modify a noun or a pronoun.

The following examples show how an adjective phrase works exactly like a single adjective.

SINGLE ADJECTIVE
Did you see **that** score?
(*That* tells which score.)

ADJECTIVE PHRASE
Did you see the score **on the scoreboard**?
(*On the scoreboard* also tells which score.)

A single adjective and an adjective phrase answer the same questions: *Which one(s)?* and *What kind?*

WHICH ONE(S)?
The runner **in the first lane** is Morgan.

WHAT KIND?
I like athletic events **with music**.

An adjective phrase usually follows the word it modifies. That word may be the object of a preposition of another prepositional phrase.

Thousands *of* **athletes** *of* **the highest skill** become Olympic competitors.

All *of* **the winners** *of* **the medals** *for* **first place** have arrived.

Two adjective phrases occasionally will modify the same noun or pronoun.

Pick up those programs *of* **events** *on* **the counter.**

Adverb Phrases

An **adverb phrase** is a prepositional phrase used to modify a verb, an adjective, or an adverb.

An adverb phrase works exactly like a single adverb. Notice in the following examples that an adverb phrase, like a single adverb, modifies the whole verb phrase.

SINGLE ADVERB   The discus throwers will compete **soon.**
                 (*Soon* tells when the discus throwers will compete.)

ADVERB PHRASE   The discus throwers will compete **on Friday.**
                 (*On Friday* also tells when the discus throwers will compete.)

A single adverb and an adverb phrase answer the same question: *Where? When? How? To what extent?* or *To what degree?* An adverb phrase also answers the question *Why?*

WHERE?   I left my sneakers **in my locker**.

WHEN?   The practice lasted **until ten o'clock.**

HOW?   I performed the move **according to his instructions**.

WHY?   **Because of the heavy traffic**, we missed the opening ceremony.

CONNECT TO WRITER'S CRAFT

Writers use prepositional phrases to add clarity to their writing and to enhance the images in their audience's minds. Sports writers, for example, could not write effective articles without using prepositional phrases to identify the types and locations of games and players. Many questions in a reader's mind will be answered by the prepositional phrases the writer uses.

Which baseball player? The player **in left field** caught the fly ball.

To what extent did the team practice? The team practiced **until eleven o'clock**.

Where did the team play? The team played **at Fenway Park in Boston**.

Two or more adverb phrases may modify one verb.

For the game days, all the flags were flying **above the stadium.**

Over the weekend I put my medals **into the cabinet.**

Although most adverb phrases modify a verb, some modify adjectives and adverbs.

MODIFYING AN ADJECTIVE   Coach Margo is kind **to everyone.**

MODIFYING AN ADVERB   My team arrived late **in the afternoon.**

PUNCTUATION WITH ADVERB PHRASES

- Do not place a comma after a short introductory adverb phrase unless it is a date or is needed for clarity.
- Place a comma after an adverb phrase of four or more words or after several introductory phrases.

NO COMMA	**From my seat** I can see the finish line.
COMMA	**From my seat at the edge of the track**, I can see the finish line.

CONNECT TO SPEAKING AND WRITING

When you are speaking, you pause for various lengths of time so your listeners can better understand you. When you are writing, you use punctuation to indicate these pauses. Since the reader does not have the benefit of listening to you, he or she must rely on your placement of commas to understand your meaning. Sometimes, using a comma is advisable though not required. Compare the following sentences.

Behind Peggy Sue sat and watched the competition.
Behind Peggy, Sue sat and watched the competition.

Without the comma, it is easy to misread the sentence.

PRACTICE YOUR SKILLS

● Check Your Understanding
Recognizing Prepositional Phrases as Modifiers

Sports Topic **Write the prepositional phrases in the following sentences. Then beside each phrase, write the word it modifies.**

1. The first champion of the modern Olympic Games was James Brendan Connolly.

2. In 1896, when he was a 27-year-old undergraduate at Harvard, he read about the revival of the ancient Greek games.

3. At that time Connolly was the triple-jump champion of the United States.

4. Connolly left school and went to Athens in March.

5. Ten American athletes and one trainer spent 16½ days on a ship to Naples and another day on a train to Athens.

6. On the following day, the Olympics began with the triple jump.

7. Before his turn Connolly surveyed the mark of the leader on the ground and threw his cap beyond it.

8. He then jumped beyond his cap and became the first champion of the modern Olympics.

9. He later became a journalist and the author of 25 novels.

10. Connolly died in 1957 at age 88.

● Check Your Understanding
Identifying Uses of Prepositional Phrases

General Interest **Write the prepositional phrases in the following sentences. Then beside each phrase, label it *adjective* or *adverb*.**

11. In 1936, Jesse Owens, a famous track star, beat a horse in the hundred-yard race.

12. During the following year, an Olympic hurdler named Forest Towns beat a horse in the hundred-yard hurdles.

13. Micki King, a gold-medal winner in the 1972 Olympics, became a diving coach at the U.S. Air Force Academy.

14. Award-winning gymnast Cathy Rigby had a lung ailment during her youth.

15. For six years Hugh Daily played baseball for several major-league teams.

16. As a pitcher he held a long-standing record of 19 strikeouts in a single game.

17. Hugh Daily was a man with only one arm.

18. Fourteen-year-old Nadia Comaneci had seven perfect scores in gymnastics at the Montreal Olympics.

19. She scored the first perfect 10 in the history of Olympic gymnastics.

● Connect to the Writing Process: Revising
Using Prepositional Phrases

Make the following sentences more exact by adding an adverb phrase to each one. Use a comma where needed.

20. Stan could see every gymnastic event.

21. Sarah could see only the backs of people's heads.

22. The competitors stretched and practiced.

23. The events would begin in ten minutes.

24. The gymnasts exited the floor and waited in an outer hall.

25. Mary Lou Retton stood ready to narrate the events for television cameras.

26. The judges entered.

27. The gymnasts entered.

28. They marched slowly and prepared to perform.

29. The music began to play.

30. The first gymnast stepped forward.

APPLY TO WRITING

Writer's Craft: *Analyzing the Use of Prepositional Phrases*

Read several sports articles from a newspaper and choose one to use in this exercise. Read the article carefully and then follow these instructions:

- Write each prepositional phrase and then beside it, write the word it modifies.

- Read the article *without* the prepositional phrases. What do you think of this version? What images or ideas are lost when the prepositional phrases are not included?

- Write a paragraph describing in detail the images and ideas that came to your mind as you read the article. Then review your writing and underline each prepositional phrase you have used. Label each one *adjective* or *adverb*.

QuickCheck Mixed Practice

General Interest **Write the prepositional phrase or phrases in each sentence and label them *adjective* or *adverb*.**

1. Some youngsters under the age of four are learning gymnastics skills.

2. Parents take these children to the gym each week.

3. They jump on the trampoline.

4. On the low balance beam, they walk carefully.

5. Their instructors encourage them with words of praise.

6. Somersaults are a common sight on the gym floor.

7. The older siblings of these young children are often found on the high bars.

8. They gather momentum and swing from one bar to the next.

Appositives and Appositive Phrases

An **appositive** is a noun or a pronoun that identifies or explains another noun or pronoun in the sentence.

An appositive usually follows the word or words it identifies or explains.

My friend **Bart** is working at an art gallery.

The museum houses an exhibit of sculptures by the French artist **Auguste Rodin.**

I enjoyed my favorite hobby, **sketching.**

Most often an appositive is used with modifiers to form an **appositive phrase.** Notice in the second example that one or more prepositional phrases may be part of an appositive phrase.

Chicago, **the Windy City of the Midwest**, is home to the Art Institute of Chicago.

I just bought *Twentieth-Century Painting and Sculpture,* **a pictorial of art at The Art Institute of Chicago**.

PUNCTUATION WITH APPOSITIVES AND APPOSITIVE PHRASES

If an appositive contains information essential to the meaning of a sentence, no punctuation is needed.

- Information is essential if it identifies a person, place, or thing.

If an appositive or an appositive phrase contains nonessential information, a comma or commas should be used to separate it from the rest of the sentence.

- Information is nonessential if it can be removed without changing the basic meaning of the sentence.
  An appositive that follows a proper noun is usually nonessential.

ESSENTIAL	The famous artist **Manet** was born in 1832. (No commas are used because *Manet* is needed to identify which artist.)
NONESSENTIAL	Manet, **a famous French artist**, was born in 1832. (Commas are used because the appositive could be removed from the sentence: Manet was born in 1832.)

PRACTICE YOUR SKILLS

● Check Your Understanding
Identifying Appositives and Appositive Phrases

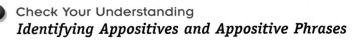 Art Topic **Write each appositive or appositive phrase.**

1. Georgia O'Keeffe, an American abstract painter, was famous for her paintings of the desert region of the Southwest.

2. The painting *Sunflowers* is one of van Gogh's most recognized masterpieces.

3. Claude Monet, one of the most well-known impressionist painters, had undergone operations for cataracts when he painted *The Japanese Bridge* from around 1923 to 1925.

4. John William Waterhouse painted a picture of the ill-fated woman in Tennyson's poem *The Lady of Shallott*.

5. The Victorian artist William Holman Hunt also painted a scene from *The Lady of Shallott*.

6. Alexandra Nechita, a painter in the abstract cubist style, published a book of her work at age ten.

7. This book, *Outside the Lines*, includes her popular painting *Variation on the Lion King*.

8. The 1995 Caldecott Award–winning artist, Trina Schart Hyman, received the award for illustrating *Saint George and the Dragon*.

9. The French artist Eugène Delacroix painted a battle scene, *Combat Between the Giaour and Hassan*, after becoming inspired by Lord Byron's poem "The Giaour."

10. Byron's poem is about a Venetian man who sets out to avenge his mistress's murder by Hassan, a Turk.

Using Commas with Appositive Phrases

Write each sentence, punctuating the appositives or appositive phrases correctly. If a sentence is correct, write C.

11. Theodor Seuss Geisel Dr. Seuss was born in 1904 in Springfield, Massachusetts.

12. Dr. Seuss a writer and cartoonist is famous for his rhyming children's books.

13. *And to Think That I Saw It on Mulberry Street* the first of his children's books was published in 1937.

14. *The Cat in the Hat* one of his most famous books was published in 1957.

15. *The Cat in the Hat* a story with only 237 different words was based on a word list for first-grade readers.

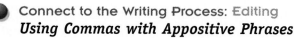

APPLY TO WRITING

Biographical Oral Report: *Appositive Phrases*

Prepare to give a five-minute oral report to your classmates. Choose an artist whose life interests you and look up biographical information on this person. Read the material and take notes. Then write the first draft of a report that summarizes the artist's life. Remember to put the information into your own words. Also, devote special effort to creating smooth and effective sentences by using appositives and appositive phrases. Be sure you punctuate appositive phrases correctly.

Verbals and Verbal Phrases

Verbals are part of your everyday speech. If you have ever apologized for your *unmade* bed or told someone that you would be ready *to leave* at six o'clock, you have used verbals. A **verbal** is a verb form that is used not as a verb, but as a noun, an adjective, or an adverb. Because verbals are verb forms, they are usually lively words that add action and vitality to your writing. The three kinds of verbals are participles, gerunds, and infinitives.

Participles and Participial Phrases

A **participle** is a verb form that is used as an adjective.

Used like an adjective, a participle modifies a noun or a pronoun and answers the adjective question *Which one(s)?* or *What kind?* The participles in the examples are in **bold** type. An arrow points to the word each participle modifies.

> The **rising** sun was reflected on the **frosted** glass of the mayor's limousine.
>
> **Broken** campaign promises are sometimes the downfall of an **elected** official.

There are two kinds of participles: a present participle and a past participle. A **present participle** ends in *–ing*, while a **past participle** has a regular ending of *–ed* or an irregular ending of *–n*, *–t*, or *–en*.

PARTICIPLES	
PRESENT PARTICIPLES	spinning, shrinking, ringing, winning
PAST PARTICIPLES	buried, defeated, worn, bent, stolen

Be careful not to confuse a participle, which is used as an adjective, with the main verb of a sentence. A participle will have one or more helping verbs if it is used as a verb.

PARTICIPLE	The governor's **reserved** seats are in the sixth row of the mezzanine.
VERB	We **have reserved** four seats for the senator's speech.
PARTICIPLE	The **broken** clock on the mantel in the living room belonged to President Johnson.
VERB	During the voter registration, a small table **was broken**.

Participial Phrases

Because a participle is a verb form, it may have modifiers and complements. Together these words form a participial phrase.

A **participial phrase** is a participle with its modifiers and complements—all working together as an adjective.

The following examples show three variations of a participial phrase. As you can see, a participle may be followed by an adverb, a prepositional phrase, or a complement.

PARTICIPLE WITH AN ADVERB	**Ordered early**, the campaign posters were ready for the rally.
PARTICIPLE WITH A PREPOSITIONAL PHRASE	Our mayor, **speaking to the senior class**, described her path to success.
PARTICIPLE WITH A COMPLEMENT	Who is that political aide **raising his right hand**?

The present participle *having* is sometimes followed by a past participle.

Having met **the senator in person**, I was surprised at how tall she was.

Sometimes an adverb that modifies a participle may come before the participle. The adverb in this position is still part of the participial phrase.

The post-election ball is a grand event *usually* **involving bands and caterers**.

Never **having entertained at such a function,** the members of the chorus were nervous.

PUNCTUATION WITH PARTICIPIAL PHRASES

Always place a comma after an introductory participial phrase.

Arriving at the White House, I registered for the tour.

Participial phrases that come in the middle or at the end of a sentence may or may not need commas.

- If the information in a phrase is essential to identify the noun or the pronoun it describes, no comma is needed.

- If the information is nonessential, a comma is needed to separate it from the rest of the sentence. A phrase is nonessential if it contains information that can be removed from the sentence without changing the basic meaning. A phrase that follows a proper noun is usually nonessential.

ESSENTIAL	The FBI agent **guarding the limousine** is Jason Jackson.
	(No commas are used because the phrase is needed to identify which agent.)
NONESSENTIAL	Jason Jackson, **guarding the limousine**, has twelve years of experience with the FBI.
	(Commas are used because the phrase can be removed, and the meaning is still clear: Jason Jackson has twelve years of experience with the FBI.)

● Check Your Understanding

Recognizing Participial Phrases as Modifiers

Government Topic **Write each participial phrase. Then beside each one, write the word or words it modifies.**

1. Winning the confidence of many voters, women have become the mayors of several large cities in the United States.

2. One report identifies some of the women elected in recent years.

3. Jane Byrne of Chicago captured the office held by Mayor Richard J. Daley for 21 years until his death.

4. Isabelle Cannon, having won the support of young people, became the mayor of Raleigh in a major upset.

5. Having complained unsuccessfully about a dangerous intersection, Janet Gray Hayes ran for mayor of San Jose.

6. Gaining prominence in a nonpartisan campaign, she went on to win the election.

7. Demonstrating her leadership abilities, Mayor Margaret Hance of Phoenix won a second term.

8. Mayor Carole McClellan of Austin, gathering 79 percent of the vote, also won a second term.

9. Effectively governing San Francisco, Dianne Feinstein became nationally prominent.

10. All of these remarkable women led the way for other women entering politics.

● Connect to the Writing Process: Editing

Using Commas with Participial Phrases

Write each sentence, adding or deleting commas if necessary. If a sentence is already correct, then write C.

11. The candidates, running for Town Council, will hold a debate in the town hall.

12. Arriving early I took a seat up front.

13. That is my sister, passing out campaign buttons.

14. Spoken with sincerity, the candidate's words stirred the voters.

15. Kathleen Sullivan elected to the School Committee by a wide margin instituted many changes.

16. Having lived in the district her entire life, she had some practical ideas.

17. Ms. Sullivan convinced of the value of school uniforms rallied the other board members to her point of view.

18. Less convinced some parents and many students objected to the notion of a mandatory dress code.

● Connect to the Writing Process: Drafting
Distinguishing Between Verbs and Participles

Work with a writing partner. Together, form a list of five verbs that you associate with the activities of government or politics. Then each of you write two sentences for each word. The first sentence should use the word as a verb. The second sentence should use the word as a participle in a participial phrase. Use punctuation where needed. Compare your sentences.

Communicate Your Ideas

APPLY TO WRITING

Opinion Essay: *Participles and Participial Phrases*

Prepare for a class summit on politics. You will have an opportunity to speak your mind on any political issue you choose. You can review the sentences you wrote above to get ideas and to "break the blank page barrier." Write the first draft of your opinion essay to get as many ideas on paper as possible. Then review your writing, looking for opportunities to use participial phrases to help clarify your ideas and to create sentence variety. Finally, prepare the final copy.

Gerunds and Gerund Phrases

A **gerund** is a verb form used as a noun.

Because a gerund ends in *–ing*, it looks like a present participle. A gerund, however, is used as a noun. The gerunds in the following examples are in **bold** type.

> **Dating** brings out the creativity in some people. (subject)
>
> Kyle and Sasha enjoy **rollerblading**. (direct object)

Gerund Phrases

Like other verbals, a gerund may be combined with modifiers and complements to form a phrase.

A **gerund phrase** is a gerund with its modifiers and complements—all working together as a noun.

A gerund or a gerund phrase may be used in all the ways in which a noun may be used. A gerund may be followed by an adverb, a prepositional phrase, or a complement.

SUBJECT	**Playing tennis** is an enjoyable date.
DIRECT OBJECT	I like **riding on roller coasters**.
INDIRECT OBJECT	My brother gave **writing a love poem** his full attention last Saturday.
OBJECT OF A PREPOSITION	We drove to the pizza parlor across town without **making a single stop**.
PREDICATE NOMINATIVE	Her most enjoyable date was **riding a two-person bicycle**.
APPOSITIVE	Heather's weekend plan, **applying for jobs for date money**, is admirable.

The possessive form of a noun or a pronoun comes before a gerund and is considered part of the gerund phrase.

> What do you think of **Eric's asking Cindy for a date**?
>
> **Her asking Todd out** was surprising.

You can learn more about possessive nouns and pronouns on pages L471–L475.

PRACTICE YOUR SKILLS

● Check Your Understanding
Identifying Gerund Phrases

Contemporary Life

Write each gerund phrase. Then underline each gerund.

1. We can get good seats for the movie by buying our tickets early.

2. Buying snacks at the concession stand takes time and a great deal of money.

3. I couldn't understand her refusing the buttery popcorn and soda.

4. My creative cousin is capable of planning some very unusual dates.

5. His idea last Saturday was renting a large moving van for the day.

6. Decorating the van's interior like a four-star restaurant was his morning activity.

7. After shopping carefully for ingredients, he cooked a gourmet meal.

8. His date was thrilled with his creating this enjoyable dinner experience.

9. Going to a local bookstore was my most recent memorable date.

10. Our afternoon activity, listening to the children's story hour, was different and fun.

Determining the Uses of Gerund Phrases

Contemporary Life **Write each gerund phrase. Then label the use of each one, using the following abbreviations.**

subject = *subj.*   object of a preposition = *o.p.*
direct object = *d.o.*   predicate nominative = *p.n.*
indirect object = *i.o.*   appositive = *appos.*

11. Dancing by the lake is Julie's idea of the perfect evening.

12. Jackie's spontaneous nature welcomes jumping puddles in the rain.

13. Last month Mike surprised his girlfriend by taking her to a fruit orchard.

14. His idea, picking fruit together, was a success.

15. One date I'll never forget was test-driving a new car together.

16. For a sweet evening, give baking cinnamon rolls a try.

17. Two of my friends succeeded in running a marathon together.

18. My bright idea, pretending to be an artist at the beach, was hilarious.

● Connect to the Writing Process: Prewriting
Distinguishing Between Gerunds and Participles

Work with a writing partner to brainstorm at least ten gerunds and participles. Use word association to generate words, beginning with the word *dating*. Write down the first –*ing* gerund or participle you think of, and then your writing partner will write down the first –*ing* word that comes to mind. Continue until your combined list totals ten words. Then each of you choose five words and write two sentences for each word. The first sentence should use the word as a gerund. The second sentence should use the word as a participle. Use punctuation where needed. Compare your sentences.

APPLY TO WRITING

Guidebook: *Gerunds and Gerund Phrases*

Your class will write a handbook of dating tips and ideas that will be useful to anyone who is interested in dating. Each student will write one entry for this handbook. Use your prewriting from the preceding exercise to start your first draft. Write a first draft, devoting extra care to using gerunds and gerund phrases. Edit your writing for errors in spelling, punctuation, and grammar. Then prepare the final copy.

 Infinitives and Infinitive Phrases

An **infinitive** is a verb form that usually begins with *to*. It is used as a noun, an adjective, or an adverb.

Infinitives do not look like the other verbals because they usually begin with the word *to*. An infinitive has several forms. The infinitives of *change*, for example, are *to change*, *to be changing*, *to have changed*, *to be changed*, and *to have been changed*. The infinitives in the following examples are in **bold** type.

Pat wanted **to win**. (noun, direct object)

She couldn't think of a story **to write**. (adjective)

The unexpected ideas from Jill were nice **to receive**. (adverb)

Do not confuse a prepositional phrase that begins with *to* with an infinitive. A prepositional phrase ends with a noun or a pronoun; an infinitive ends with a verb form.

Prepositional Phrase	Give the book **to me**.
Infinitive	When is it time **to read**?

Infinitive Phrases

An infinitive may be combined with modifiers and complements to form an infinitive phrase.

> An **infinitive phrase** is an infinitive with its modifiers and complements—all working together as a noun, an adjective, or an adverb.

The following examples show how an infinitive phrase may be used as a noun, an adjective, or an adverb. Notice that like other verbals, an infinitive phrase may also take several forms. An infinitive, for example, may be followed by an adverb, a complement, or a prepositional phrase.

NOUN	**To write well** requires patience. (subject)
	I tried **to buy two rare books**. (direct object)
ADJECTIVE	These are the fables **to read for tomorrow**.
ADVERB	We printed the story **to create public awareness**.

Occasionally the word *to* is dropped when an infinitive phrase follows such verbs as *help, dare, feel, make, let, need, see,* or *watch.* It is, nevertheless, understood to be in the sentence.

> We helped **collect** (to collect) **picture books for the preschool.**

Unlike other verbal phrases, an infinitive phrase can have a subject. An infinitive phrase with a subject is called an **infinitive clause.**

>   d.o.
> Everyone expected **Pat to win the storytelling contest.**
>
> (*Pat* is the subject of *to win*. The whole infinitive clause is the direct object of *everyone expected. Everyone expected* what?)

$$\overbrace{\text{We asked } \underline{\underline{\textbf{her to distribute the awards}}}}^{\text{d.o.}}.$$

(*Her* is the subject of *to distribute*. The subject of an infinitive clause is in the objective case. The whole infinitive clause is the direct object of *we asked*.)

PRACTICE YOUR SKILLS

● Check Your Understanding
Identifying Infinitive Phrases

Literature Topic
Write each infinitive or infinitive phrase.

1. To be brave from a distance is easy. —*Aesop*
2. Aesop created fables to teach people lessons.
3. The ant wanted to store food.
4. The grasshopper was the one to play all summer.
5. The shepherd boy promised to tend sheep.
6. He cried "Wolf!" to get a little excitement.
7. However, there really was a wolf to fear.
8. Later the wolf came to eat the sheep.
9. The shepherd boy tried to get help, but no one believed him.
10. A runaway slave named Androcles helped pull a thorn from a lion's paw.

● Check Your Understanding
Determining the Uses of Infinitive Phrases

Literature Topic
Write the infinitive or infinitive phrases in the following sentences. Then label how each one is used: *noun, adjective,* or *adverb.*

11. The fables to read are by Aesop and other Greek storytellers.
12. To credit Aesop with writing all Greek fables has been the tendency.

13. Legend says that Aesop was freed from slavery to become a diplomat for King Croesus.

14. To starve a free man is better than being a fat slave. —*Aesop*

15. A young wife wants her husband to look more like herself.

16. She plucks out his gray hairs each night to create a younger appearance.

17. The second wife to pluck hairs from the man's head is older.

18. This wife decides to remove all the brown strands.

19. As a result, each wife helped make the husband bald.

20. To bend with the wind is the Reed's wise choice in "The Tree and the Reed."

● Connect to the Writing Process: Drafting
Writing Sentences with Infinitive Phrases

Write sentences that follow the directions below.

21. Use an infinitive phrase as a subject.

22. Use an infinitive phrase as a direct object.

23. Use an infinitive phrase as an adjective.

24. Use an infinitive phrase as an adverb.

25. Use two infinitive phrases.

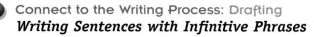

Communicate Your Ideas

APPLY TO WRITING

Fable: *Infinitives and Infinitive Phrases*

If possible, read several fables by Aesop to get ideas for writing a fable of your own for middle-schoolers. You'll notice that in fables the animals talk and think as people, and the story always teaches a lesson or moral. Also, fables are usually only 150 to 200 words long. When you write your fable, use infinitive phrases to add variety and interest. Be prepared to identify how you used infinitive phrases—as *subject, direct object, adjective,* or *adverb.*

QuickCheck Mixed Practice

General Interest **Write the verbal phrases in the following sentences. Then label each one *participial, gerund,* or *infinitive.***

1. Born in New York in 1856, Louise Blanchard Bethune is considered the first woman architect.

2. After designing many buildings, she became the first woman to gain membership in the American Institute of Architects.

3. The first American woman to receive the Nobel Peace Prize was Jane Addams.

4. In 1931, she was recognized for establishing a center for social reform in Chicago.

5. The first woman to be pictured on a United States coin in circulation was suffragist Susan B. Anthony.

6. Treasury officials had first considered picturing only a representative female figure such as Miss Liberty.

7. Anthony, appearing later on a one-dollar coin, was selected over Jane Addams and Eleanor Roosevelt.

8. Long before Sarah Walker became the first African American woman millionaire, she supported herself by taking in laundry.

9. In 1905, after eighteen years as a launderer, she decided to create a line of hair products especially for African American women.

10. Working at home, she formulated shampoos and oils.

11. Concerned for other African American women, Walker created many college scholarships.

Misplaced and Dangling Modifiers

The meaning of a sentence sometimes gets confused because a modifier is placed too far away from the word it describes. When that happens, the modifier appears to describe some other word. Such modifiers are called **misplaced modifiers**. Remember to place phrases used as modifiers as close as possible to the word or words they describe.

MISPLACED   Rob will answer this ad for a gardener **in the Globe**.

CORRECT   Rob will answer this ad **in the Globe** for a gardener.

MISPLACED   I found the seedlings **looking through a catalog**.

CORRECT   **Looking through a catalog**, I found the seedlings.

Another problem sometimes arises when a phrase that is being used as a modifier does not have a word to describe in the sentence. This kind of phrase is called a **dangling modifier**.

DANGLING   **To be a good park ranger**, knowledge of animals is needed.
(*Knowledge* cannot be a good park ranger.)

CORRECT   **To be a good park ranger**, you need knowledge of animals.

DANGLING   **Filling the bird feeder**, birds will be attracted to your yard.
(*Birds* cannot fill the bird feeder.)

CORRECT   **Filling the bird feeder**, you will attract birds to your yard.

PRACTICE YOUR SKILLS

● Check Your Understanding

Recognizing Misplaced and Dangling Modifiers

Contemporary Life
Write the misplaced or dangling modifier in each sentence. If a sentence is correct, write C.

1. Walking through the nature preserve, we saw many interesting sights.
2. Rummaging through the trash can, we saw the raccoon.
3. I found the raccoon family picking up litter.
4. I followed Lisa as she ran around the pond on my bike.
5. Booming in the distance, I was startled by the thunder.
6. Enjoying the sound of the rain, he fell asleep.
7. Trotting through the forest, Kate's ears detected a babbling brook.
8. My little brother wanted to play with the baby frogs wearing shorts in the pond.
9. Roaring loudly, Juan took a picture of the lion.
10. Rowing steadily, the canoe was brought to the dock.
11. Jenny stood on a rock trying to get a good view of the baby birds.
12. Having eaten the food, the dish was empty.
13. Following the posted rules, we did not attempt to feed any of the animals.
14. Bending over, we could see the tall giraffe.
15. Walking around the preserve, the many kinds of plants were amazing.

● Connect to the Writing Process: Revising

Correcting Misplaced and Dangling Modifiers

16.–27. Correct each of the misplaced and dangling modifiers in the previous exercise. Either place the phrase closer to the word it modifies, or add words and change the sentence so the phrase has a noun or a pronoun to modify. Use punctuation where needed.

APPLY TO WRITING

Description: *Modifiers*

Alma Gunter, *Dinner on Grounds,* 1979–1980.
Acrylic on canvas, 24 by 18 inches. African American Museum, Dallas, Texas.

You are spending the afternoon with a friend who is blind, and she asks you to describe a painting to her. Study the painting *Dinner on Grounds*, and then write a description that would make your friend feel as though she were taking part in this scene. Along with describing what you see, describe the other senses—touch, taste, hearing, and smell. Use plenty of modifiers to help make these sensory experiences come alive. Finally, edit for dangling and misplaced modifiers before preparing your final copy.

Phrase Fragments

Since a phrase is a group of words that does not have a subject and a verb, it can never express a complete thought. As a result, when a phrase is written as if it were a sentence, it becomes a **phrase fragment**.

To correct a phrase fragment, add a group of words that contains a subject, a verb, or both; or like the following examples in **bold** type, attach a phrase fragment to a related sentence.

PREPOSITIONAL PHRASE FRAGMENT	After 1945, many new words and expressions came into our language. **Such as *baby-sit, cutback, rat race,* and *soap opera*.**
CORRECTED	After 1945, many new words and expressions, such as *baby-sit, cutback, rat race,* and *soap opera,* came into our language.
APPOSITIVE PHRASE FRAGMENT	Alice Walker wrote *The Color Purple*. **The 1983 Pulitzer Prize–winning novel.**
CORRECTED	Alice Walker wrote *The Color Purple*, the 1983 Pulitzer Prize–winning novel.
PARTICIPIAL PHRASE FRAGMENT	O. Henry produced a story a week for the *World*. **Living in New York City.**
CORRECTED	Living in New York City, O. Henry produced a story a week for the *World*.
GERUND PHRASE FRAGMENT	**Winning the Nobel Prize in literature.** This is the dream of many authors.
CORRECTED	Winning the Nobel Prize in literature is the dream of many authors.

INFINITIVE PHRASE FRAGMENT	**To provide facts about authors, works of literature, and literary terms.** This is the primary purpose of a literary encyclopedia.
CORRECTED	To provide facts about authors, works of literature, and literary terms is the primary purpose of a literary encyclopedia.

You can find information about other types of fragments on pages L68–L71 and L164–L166.

CONNECT TO WRITER'S CRAFT

If you are like most writers, your first drafts probably contain fragments. That is because writers are primarily thinking about subject matter, not accuracy or style. After you have written your first draft, however, you should always edit your work to make sure all your sentences are complete.

PRACTICE YOUR SKILLS

● Check Your Understanding
Recognizing Phrase Fragments

Literature Topic

Write the phrase fragments in the following paragraph. Then label the use of each one *prepositional, appositive, participial, gerund,* or *infinitive.*

Admired as a great writer. Mark Twain was also an inventor. To make millions on his ideas. This was Twain's hope. Twain predicted innovations such as microfilm, data storage and retrieval, and television. He had great ideas, but he was not a good businessman. He lost $300,000, for example. On an automatic typesetting machine. It had moving parts, but it seldom worked. Numbering 18,000. Twain did make a small profit on one of his ventures. Mark Twain's Self-Pasting Scrapbook. Finally, having lost a fortune. Twain had to earn a living by writing.

● **Connect to the Writing Process:** Revising
Correcting Phrase Fragments

Revise the above paragraph on Mark Twain by correcting the phrase fragments. Either add a group of words that contains a subject or a verb or attach the phrase fragment to a related sentence.

Communicate Your Ideas

APPLY TO WRITING
Summary: *Complete Sentences*

You have adopted a pen pal in a retirement home, and you want to include some entertaining information in your next letter to this person. Skim the table of contents of a current almanac or other book of interesting information. (You might also search the Internet.) Find a topic particularly interesting to you, read it, and take notes. Then write the first draft of a paragraph that summarizes the topic you chose. Remember to put the information into your own words. After you have revised your summary, edit it, correcting any phrase fragments, and prepare the final copy.

Diagraming Phrases

The way a phrase is used in a sentence determines how and where the phrase is diagramed.

Prepositional Phrases   An adjective or an adverb phrase is connected to the word it modifies. The preposition is placed on a connecting slanted line. The object of a preposition is placed on a horizontal line that is attached to the slanted line. The following example includes two adjective phrases and one adverb phrase. Notice that an adjective phrase can modify the object of the preposition of another phrase.

The assignment for Mr. Marshard's class in English literature must be completed by tomorrow.

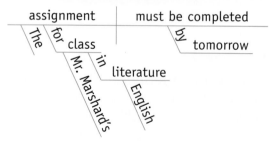

An adverb phrase that modifies an adjective or an adverb needs an additional horizontal line that is connected to the word modified.

The two trophies stood close to each other on the mantel.

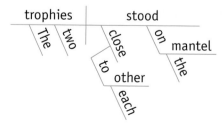

Appositives and Appositive Phrases An appositive is diagramed in parentheses next to the word it identifies or explains. Its modifiers are placed directly underneath it.

The appetizer, egg rolls with hot mustard, arrived before a huge meal of several Chinese dishes.

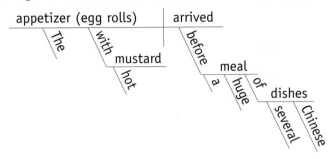

Participial Phrases Like an adjective, a participle is always diagramed under the word it modifies. The participle, however, is written in a curve. In the first example below, the participial phrase modifies *Marcy*, the subject of the sentence. In the second example, the participial phrase modifies the direct object *tree*.

Seeing the time on the kitchen clock, Marcy rushed out the door.

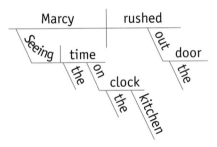

I transplanted the maple tree growing in our backyard.

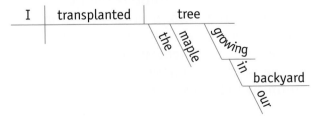

Gerund Phrases   A gerund phrase is diagramed in any position in which a noun is diagramed. In the next diagram, the gerund phrase is used as a direct object. In the diagram after that, a gerund phrase is used as a subject, and another gerund phrase is used as the object of a preposition. Notice that an adverb, a prepositional phrase, and a complement may be part of a gerund phrase.

During my summer vacation, I enjoy sitting quietly by the lake.

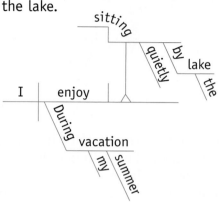

Studying hard is a sure way of guaranteeing a good grade.

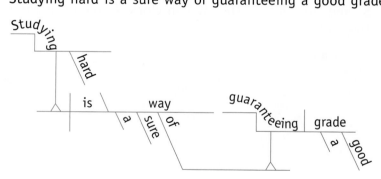

Infinitive Phrases   Because an infinitive phrase may be used as a noun, an adjective, or an adverb, it is diagramed in several ways. In the following example, one infinitive phrase is used as an adjective and one is used as a predicate nominative. In the example after that, the infinitive phrase is used as a direct object. Notice that these infinitive phrases all have complements.

The only way to have a friend is to be one.   —Emerson

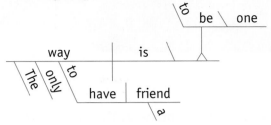

If the *to* of an infinitive is omitted from the sentence, it is diagramed in parentheses.

Do you dare interview the mayor?

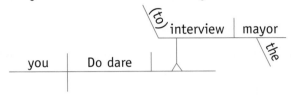

PRACTICE YOUR SKILLS

Diagraming Phrases

Diagram the following sentences or copy them. If you copy them, draw one line under each subject and two lines under each verb. Then put parentheses around each phrase and label each one *prepositional, appositive, participial, gerund,* **or** *infinitive.*

1. I like to visit my relatives in Tennessee.
2. We always go to Opryland in Nashville.
3. Buddy, the first dog for the blind, was trained in Nashville.
4. Born in Tennessee, Davy Crockett became a national legend.
5. You can visit his home by taking a tour through the mountains.
6. I liked learning about the real Davy Crockett.
7. Arriving in Memphis, we went to Graceland, the home of Elvis Presley.
8. To visit his home was my idea.
9. We saw his gold records hanging on the walls.
10. The best way to travel through Tennessee is by car.

Identifying Phrases

Write the phrases in the following sentences. Then label each one
prepositional, appositive, participial, gerund, **or** *infinitive.*

1. Seaweed sometimes grows to 200 feet in length.
2. At the end of February, Jonathan decided to send in his application.
3. Transporting pollen is the worker bees' job.
4. Meteors, known as shooting stars, may be seen on almost any clear night.
5. Both Cervantes and Shakespeare, two enormously important writers, died on April 23, 1616.
6. Scoring five runs immediately, the Red Sox took command of the game.
7. I enjoy swimming laps every morning.
8. An old game, played since ancient times, is marbles.
9. Do you want to frame your diploma?
10. Running the bases clockwise was the custom during baseball's early years.
11. Joan, my oldest aunt, was an Olympic swimmer and a distance runner.
12. The club's secretary handed me the minutes, typed neatly on bond paper.
13. Dan's father enjoys restoring antique cars.
14. The President, planning an important Cabinet appointment, studied the list of possible candidates.
15. In some places in the world, people actually train geese to tend sheep.

Identifying Phrases

Write each phrase in the following paragraph. Then label each phrase *prepositional, appositive, participial, gerund,* **or** *infinitive.*

Early Will

Little is known about the early life of William Shakespeare, the playwright. There are, however, many legends like these. Abandoning his family to pursue a more carefree life, Shakespeare became a soldier, lawyer, or teacher. Joining an acting troupe, Shakespeare left his home in Stratford-upon-Avon and went to London. Shakespeare, having stolen Sir Thomas Lucy's deer, left his birthplace to avoid prosecution. Little or no proof exists, though, to support these legends.

Using Phrases

Write five sentences that follow the directions below. (The sentences may come in any order.) Write about one of the following topics or a topic of your choice: why you enjoy speaking up in class or why you fear public speaking.

Write a sentence that . . .

1. includes at least two prepositional phrases.
2. includes an appositive phrase.
3. includes an introductory participial phrase.
4. includes a gerund phrase.
5. includes an infinitive phrase.

Underline and label each phrase. Then check for correct punctuation in each sentence.

Language and *Self-Expression*

British sculptor Andy Goldsworthy has created sculptures out of ice, grass, twigs, and sand—among other natural objects. He has worked in places as varied as the shores of Lake Michigan, where this artwork was created, and the North Pole.

Imagine the public reaction to this artwork. Suppose you were a journalist reporting on the artwork's creation and unveiling. Write a newspaper article explaining how the work was made, what the public thought about it, and how you yourself reacted when you saw it for the first time. Your article might include "interviews" with the artist, invited guests, and passersby. Vary your sentences as you write by including phrases of all sorts in different positions within the sentence.

Prewriting Jot down ideas that answer these questions about the artwork: *Who? What? When? Where? How? Why?* As you reread your notes, use the information you included to come up with a lead for your story.

Drafting Begin with a lead that introduces the artwork. Add details that answer the questions you responded to in Prewriting. If you wish, include "quotes" from people you "interviewed" for the article.

Revising Reread your article, focusing on the flow of ideas and sentence variety. Find places where you might add phrases to clarify details or move phrases to vary sentence construction.

Editing Check your article for errors in grammar, capitalization, punctuation, and spelling. Make any needed corrections.

Publishing Prepare a final copy of your article by typing it up on a computer and printing it. Exchange articles with students in your class and discuss how different writers recorded the same event.

Another Look

A **phrase** is a group of related words that functions as a single part of speech. A phrase does not have a subject and a verb.

Prepositional Phrases

An **adjective phrase** is a prepositional phrase that is used to modify a noun or pronoun. *(page L98)*

An **adverb phrase** is a prepositional phrase that is used to modify a verb, an adjective, or an adverb. *(page L98)*

Appositives and Appositive Phrases

An **appositive** is a noun or pronoun that identifies or explains another noun or pronoun in the sentence. *(page L104)*

An **appositive phrase** is a group of words that contains an appositive and its modifiers. *(page L104)*

Verbals and Verbal Phrases

A **participle** is a verb form that is used as an adjective. *(page L107)*

A **participial phrase** is a participle with its modifiers and complements—all working together as an adjective. *(page L108)*

A **gerund** is a verb form that is used as a noun. *(page L112)*

A **gerund phrase** is a gerund with its modifiers and complements—all working together as a noun. *(page L112)*

An **infinitive** is a verb form that usually begins with *to*. It is used as a noun, an adjective, or an adverb. *(page L115)*

An **infinitive phrase** is an infinitive with its modifiers and complements—all working together as a noun, an adjective, or an adverb. *(page L116)*

Other Information About Phrases

Punctuating adverb phrases *(page L100)*
Punctuating appositives and appositive phrases *(page L104)*
Punctuating participial phrases *(page L109)*
Recognizing misplaced modifiers *(page L120)*
Recognizing dangling modifiers *(page L120)*
Avoiding phrase fragments *(page L123)*

Posttest

Directions

Write the letter of the term that correctly identifies the underlined phrase in each sentence.

EXAMPLE

1. Eugene O'Neill is surely one <u>of our most brilliant playwrights</u>.

   1 **A** prepositional
   B participial
   C gerund
   D infinitive

ANSWER

1 **A**

1. Eugene O'Neill grew up <u>in a theatrical family</u>.

2. Both of his parents, <u>James and Ella</u>, were actors.

3. O'Neill worked as a merchant seaman before tuberculosis forced him <u>to rest and educate himself</u>.

4. <u>Writing</u> <u>twelve one-act plays and two longer works</u> kept him busy for two years.

5. <u>Falling into three main phases</u>, O'Neill's work grew stronger during his life.

6. His early plays feature sailors and their dreams <u>of a better life</u>.

7. *Beyond the Horizon* and *Anna Christie* are his most important plays <u>written before 1921</u>.

8. Both plays won the Pulitzer Prize, <u>an award from the trustees of Columbia University</u>.

9. *The Emperor Jones,* <u>considered America's first expressionist play</u>, owes a lot to Swedish playwright August Strindberg.

10. It marks the beginning <u>of a more experimental phase</u>.

1	A	prepositional	6	A	prepositional
	B	participial		B	participial
	C	gerund		C	appositive
	D	infinitive		D	gerund
2	A	prepositional	7	A	prepositional
	B	participial		B	participial
	C	appositive		C	gerund
	D	gerund		D	infinitive
3	A	prepositional	8	A	prepositional
	B	participial		B	participial
	C	gerund		C	appositive
	D	infinitive		D	gerund
4	A	prepositional	9	A	prepositional
	B	participial		B	participial
	C	appositive		C	gerund
	D	gerund		D	infinitive
5	A	prepositional	10	A	prepositional
	B	participial		B	participial
	C	gerund		C	appositive
	D	infinitive		D	gerund

CHAPTER 4

Clauses

Directions
Write the letter of the term that correctly identifies each sentence or underlined part of a sentence.

EXAMPLE
1. Aesop may have been a Phrygian slave.

1 **A** simple sentence
B compound sentence
C complex sentence
D compound-complex sentence

ANSWER
1 **A**

1. Aesop, who lived from 620 to 560 B.C., was a writer of fables.
2. We can infer from Aristotle's descriptions that Aesop was a freed slave, but little else is known about him.
3. Some scholars doubt that he ever lived.
4. His fables exist, however, and fortunately they have been passed down to us.
5. Some fables attributed to Aesop appear on Egyptian papyri dated 1000 years before his birth.
6. <u>What we know as *Aesop's Fables*</u> certainly includes tales from older sources.
7. The translators <u>who collected the fables</u> added other stories they knew.
8. <u>Some stories may have originated in Asia</u>, and others may come from Africa.
9. Do you know <u>what a fable is</u>?
10. A fable is a story <u>that illustrates a moral</u>.

1	**A**	simple sentence	**6**	**A**	independent clause
	B	compound sentence		**B**	adverb clause
	C	complex sentence		**C**	adjective clause
	D	compound-complex sentence		**D**	noun clause
2	**A**	simple sentence	**7**	**A**	independent clause
	B	compound sentence		**B**	adverb clause
	C	complex sentence		**C**	adjective clause
	D	compound-complex sentence		**D**	noun clause
3	**A**	simple sentence	**8**	**A**	independent clause
	B	compound sentence		**B**	adverb clause
	C	complex sentence		**C**	adjective clause
	D	compound-complex sentence		**D**	noun clause
4	**A**	simple sentence	**9**	**A**	independent clause
	B	compound sentence		**B**	adverb clause
	C	complex sentence		**C**	adjective clause
	D	compound-complex sentence		**D**	noun clause
5	**A**	simple sentence	**10**	**A**	independent clause
	B	compound sentence		**B**	adverb clause
	C	complex sentence		**C**	adjective clause
	D	compound-complex sentence		**D**	noun clause

Leo and Diane Dillon. Illustration from *Why Mosquitoes Buzz in People's Ears*, by Verna Aardema. Watercolor, pastel, and ink.

Describe What animals are visible in this watercolor? Describe the patterns and shapes you see.

Analyze In what way do you think this illustration is suitable as an accompaniment to an African folk tale?

Interpret How do you think the painting shows the character of each animal? How might a folk tale use description to do the same thing?

Judge When this folktale was told originally, only the teller's words conveyed the imagery and characterization. How can illustrations help a reader better understand a story?

At the end of this chapter, you will use the artwork to stimulate ideas for writing.

Independent and Subordinate Clauses

You could paint a landscape with just one color, but it would be a dull, unrealistic picture when you finished. You could also write only simple sentences in essays, reports, and letters. People would certainly understand what you wrote. Like the picture painted all in one color, however, your written work would be a dull, unrealistic representation of ordinary speech.

You can add color and interest to your writing by varying the structure of your sentences. One way to do this is to include various combinations of clauses within your sentences.

A **clause** is a group of words that has a subject and a verb.

This chapter will cover independent clauses and subordinate clauses and show you how a subordinate clause can be used as an adverb, an adjective, or a noun. This chapter will also show you how clauses form different kinds of sentences.

An **independent** (or **main**) **clause** can usually stand alone as a sentence because it expresses a complete thought.

When an independent clause stands alone, it is called a sentence. When it appears in a sentence with another clause, it is called a clause. In the following examples, each subject is underlined once, and each verb is underlined twice. Notice that each independent clause can stand alone as a separate sentence.

> ┌─independent clause─┐   ┌────independent clause────┐
> Greg waited a long time, but his new saddle never arrived.

> ┌──independent clause──┐ ┌──independent clause──┐
> Greg waited a long time. His new saddle never arrived.

A **subordinate** (or **dependent**) **clause** cannot stand alone as a sentence because it does not express a complete thought.

A subordinate clause has a subject and a verb; nevertheless, it does not express a complete thought. It can never stand alone as a sentence. A subordinate clause is dependent upon an independent clause to complete its meaning.

> ┌──── subordinate clause ────┐ ┌── independent clause ──┐
> When we attended the rodeo, we sat in the bleachers.
>
> ┌── independent clause ──┐ ┌── subordinate clause ──┐
> We found some red paint that matches the barn.
>
> ┌────── independent clause ──────┐ ┌── subordinate ──
> Nobody at the livestock show knew that you were a
> ── clause ──┐
> newcomer.

PRACTICE YOUR SKILLS

● Check Your Understanding
Distinguishing Between Independent and Subordinate Clauses

Contemporary Life **Label each underlined clause *I* for independent or *S* for subordinate.**

1. We had an enjoyable weekend when we spent two days on Lloyd's farm.

2. Before the sun came up, we had eaten a huge breakfast.

3. Jeremy helped milk several cows, and Tamara spread grain for the chickens.

4. I slowly drove the tractor to the barn, but Steven attached the tractor's trailer.

5. After we loaded the trailer with bales of hay, we hauled the load into the pasture.

6. I wasn't afraid of the cows until one of them lumbered toward me.

Uses of Subordinate Clauses

Like a phrase, a subordinate clause can be used in a sentence as an adverb, an adjective, or a noun. Keep in mind, however, the basic difference between a clause and a phrase. A clause has a subject and a verb; a phrase does not.

 Adverb Clauses

An **adverb clause** is a subordinate clause that is used as an adverb to modify a verb, an adjective, or an adverb.

An adverb clause is used just like a single adverb or an adverb phrase. In the following examples, the single adverb, the adverb phrase, and the adverb clause all modify the verb *arrived*.

SINGLE ADVERB	The hockey team arrived **early**.
ADVERB PHRASE	The hockey team arrived **at five o'clock**.
ADVERB CLAUSE	The hockey team arrived **before the rink opened**.

In addition to the questions *How? When? Where? How much?* and *To what extent?,* adverb clauses also answer *Under what condition?* and *Why?* Although most adverb clauses modify verbs, some modify adjectives and adverbs.

MODIFYING A VERB	**After the snow stopped**, we organized a snowball war.
	(The clause answers *When?*)
MODIFYING AN ADJECTIVE	Some ice sports are faster **than others are**.
	(The clause answers *How much?*)

The snow was piled higher **than I had ever seen before**.

(The clause answers *To what extent?*)

Subordinating Conjunctions

An adverb clause usually begins with a **subordinating conjunction.** Notice in the following list such words as *after, before, since,* and *until*; these words can also be used as prepositions. Notice also that subordinating conjunctions can be more than one word, such as *even though*.

COMMON SUBORDINATING CONJUNCTIONS		
after	because	though
although	before	unless
as	even though	until
as far as	if	when
as if	in order that	whenever
as long as	since	where
as soon as	so that	wherever
as though	than	while

An adverb clause that describes a verb modifies the whole verb phrase.

You may watch the team's photo session **as long as you are quiet**.

When you get your hockey equipment, you must call me.

The goalie, **after he blocked the puck**, was lying on the ice.

PUNCTUATION WITH ADVERB CLAUSES

Always place a comma after an adverb clause that comes at the beginning of a sentence.

Since the country roads were icy, I drove at a slow and safe speed.

When an adverb clause interrupts an independent clause, place a comma before it and after it.

The crowd, **after they had enjoyed the exciting game,** applauded the winners.

When an adverb clause follows an independent clause, no comma is needed.

We hurried out of the arena **before the parking lot became congested.**

CONNECT TO WRITER'S CRAFT

You can improve your writing by using subordinating conjunctions to show a clear relationship between two ideas.

> I worked all summer. I did not get the athletic scholarship.

> I worked all summer **because** I did not get the athletic scholarship.

> The MVP is a skilled ball player. He is not a skilled speaker.

> **Although** the MVP is a skilled ball player, he is not a skilled speaker.

If you do not clarify the relationship between ideas, your reader must guess at the connection and may guess incorrectly!

PRACTICE YOUR SKILLS

● Check Your Understanding
Recognizing Adverb Clauses as Modifiers

Contemporary Life

Write each adverb clause. Then beside it write the word or words the adverb clause modifies.

1. When a thunderstorm strikes on a hot day, hail may fall.
2. We sloshed through puddles after the storm ended.
3. We went back inside so that we could find our umbrellas.
4. After the snowstorm ended, we shoveled the walk and the driveway.
5. As soon as you build the snowman, call me.
6. We left for the ice-skating lesson later than we had planned.
7. We can share the snowboard if each of us pays half.
8. Put the snow chains on your tires after you read the directions.
9. Because Cheryl wanted skis, she worked at the sports store until she saved enough money.
10. Before she skied down the steep hill, she watched the more experienced skiers.

● Connect to the Writing Process: Editing
Punctuating Adverb Clauses

Contemporary Life

Write the following sentences, adding a comma or commas where needed. If no comma is needed, write C for correct.

11. When the thunderstorm began we ran for shelter.
12. We stayed beneath the trees as long as the rain continued.
13. All day long the downhill skiing champion walked as though she had injured her leg.
14. Because Judy practiced faithfully she did well in the figure skating competition.

15. John after he completed his bachelor's degree in architecture started an ice arena design company.

16. He worked on a design for an Olympic-sized ice arena until he was satisfied with every detail.

17. Even though we were cold we played hockey on the frozen lake for an hour.

18. The mayor of Denver left after he had cut the ribbon at the opening of the new ski resort.

19. I placed a padded cover over my car so that the hail could not damage the paint.

20. Even though I had taken this precaution the hail dented the bumper.

Elliptical Clauses

Words in an adverb clause are sometimes omitted to streamline a sentence and to prevent unnecessary repetition. Even though the words are omitted, they are still understood to be there. An adverb clause in which words are missing is called an **elliptical clause.** Notice in the following examples that the elliptical clauses begin with *than* or *as* and are missing only the verb.

Alvin visits the zoo more often **than I.** (The completed elliptical clause reads "than I *do.*")

A hippopotamus may weigh as much **as a medium-sized truck.** (The completed elliptical clause reads "as a medium-sized truck *weighs.*")

Sometimes the subject and the verb, or just part of the verb phrase, may be omitted in an elliptical clause.

I collected more donations to the wildlife fund this weekend **than last weekend.** (The completed elliptical clause reads "than *I collected* last weekend.")

When sighted, the zebra had already begun to run. (The completed elliptical clause reads "When *it was* sighted.")

You can learn more about using the correct case of a pronoun in an elliptical clause on pages L148–L152.

CONNECT TO WRITER'S CRAFT

You may more easily remember what an elliptical clause is if you are familiar with using the mark of punctuation called the **ellipses**. An ellipses is a series of three dots that indicate where the writer has omitted words, usually in a quotation. Just as an **elliptical clause** omits words that the reader understands to be there, an ellipses indicates an omission of words that the reader understands to be in the original.

PRACTICE YOUR SKILLS

● Check Your Understanding
Recognizing Elliptical Clauses

Science Topic **Write each elliptical clause and then complete it.**

1. At five and a half feet tall, the black rhinoceros is as tall as many people.

2. The white rhinoceros stands about six inches shorter than the black rhino.

3. Most rhinoceroses are taller than the hippopotamus.

4. The hippopotamus weighs the same as the rhinoceros.

5. When told that the rhinoceros is not a meat-eater, many people are surprised.

6. While searching for leaves, twigs, and fruits for food, a rhinoceros stirs up insects from the grass.

7. Egrets, while riding on the backs of rhinoceroses, eat these insects.

8. The white rhino is more sociable than the black rhino.

9. Although timid, the white rhino will defend itself when threatened.

10. There are thousands fewer rhinoceroses in Africa today than a decade ago.

● Connect to the Writing Process: Prewriting
Freewriting Using Adverb Clauses

Many species of animals and plants become extinct every year, and usually the cause for extinction is a human cause. Here is a list of a few of the animals that are endangered:

black rhinoceros	brown pelican
gorilla	California condor
Amazon River dolphin	Peruvian penguin
Asian elephant	king salmon
Hawaiian monk seal	Florida manatee
short-tailed albatross	woodland caribou
Idaho spring snail	Wyoming toad
Kirtland's warbler	pallid sturgeon

For ten minutes freewrite about endangered species. Write your thoughts, feelings, questions, and ideas. If you run out of ideas, look over the list of subordinating conjunctions on page L142, and write the first clause that comes to mind.

Communicate Your Ideas

APPLY TO WRITING

Informative Report: *Adverb Clauses*

Write a brief report informing your classmates and teacher about an endangered species. To begin, use your freewriting from the above exercise. A trip to a library or a search session on the Internet will help you find additional facts. You may also be able to talk to personnel at a local zoo or an environmental group. After studying several strong sources, write your report, making sure to use a variety of adverb clauses and elliptical clauses to form informative, varied sentences.

Adjective Clauses

An **adjective clause** is a subordinate clause that is used as an adjective to modify a noun or a pronoun.

An adjective clause is used as a single adjective or an adjective phrase. In the following examples, the single adjective, the adjective phrase, and the adjective clause all modify *fire*.

SINGLE ADJECTIVE	The **intense** fire destroyed the building.
ADJECTIVE PHRASE	The fire **with billowing flames and thick smoke** destroyed the building.
ADJECTIVE CLAUSE	The fire, **which raged out of control**, destroyed the building.

Like a single adjective, an adjective clause answers the question *Which one(s)?* or *What kind?*

WHICH ONE(S)?	The firefighters **who volunteered their time last night** became heroes.
WHAT KIND?	They saved a historic building **that was constructed of valuable hardwoods**.

Relative Pronouns

A relative pronoun usually begins an adjective clause. A **relative pronoun** relates an adjective clause to its antecedent. The relative adverbs *where* and *when* also introduce adjective clauses.

RELATIVE PRONOUNS				
who	whom	whose	which	that

Lakeview's firefighters, **who sponsor a fundraiser each summer**, have not raised enough money for new hoses.

Charles Daly moved here from Miami, **where he had worked as a mechanic at a fire station**.

The relative pronoun *that* is sometimes omitted from an adjective clause; nevertheless, it is still understood to be in the clause.

Playing with matches is something **everyone should avoid.**
(***That*** *everyone should avoid* is the complete adjective clause.)

PRACTICE YOUR SKILLS

● Check Your Understanding
Recognizing Adjective Clauses as Modifiers

General Interest **Write each adjective clause. Then beside it write the word it modifies.**

1. Firefighting is a dangerous job that requires a commitment to public service.

2. Fire hoses, which carry 2,000 gallons of water per minute, will test the user's strength and dexterity.

3. Fire hydrants, where firefighters access critical water supplies, must never be blocked by parked cars.

4. Firefighters, who often carry unconscious people down stairs, must develop strong muscles.

5. Their coworkers, whom they trust with their lives every day, often become close friends for many years.

6. Did you hear about the conference that will update us on firefighting technology?

7. These conferences, workshops, and seminars are events every firefighter should attend.

8. Jerry, whose high school diploma hangs on the wall, passed the firefighter's examination.

9. Some colleges offer fire science programs, which attract many firefighters who are already on the job.

Functions of a Relative Pronoun

A relative pronoun functions in several ways in a sentence. It usually introduces an adjective clause and refers to another noun or pronoun in the sentence. A relative pronoun also has a function within the adjective clause itself. It can be used as a subject, direct object, or object of a preposition. A relative pronoun can also show possession.

SUBJECT	Robert Frost, **who read a poem at President Kennedy's inauguration**, lived from 1874 to 1963. (*Who* is the subject of *read*.)
DIRECT OBJECT	The poems **you like** were written by Emily Dickinson. (The understood relative pronoun *that* is the direct object of *like: you like that . . . .*)
OBJECT OF A PREPOSITION	The volume **in which I found Frost's biography** is quite interesting. (*Which* is the object of the preposition *in*.)
POSSESSION	Carl Sandburg is an American poet **whose father emigrated from Sweden**. (*Whose* shows possession of *father*.)

PUNCTUATION WITH ADJECTIVE CLAUSES

No punctuation is used with an adjective clause that contains information essential to identify a person, place, or thing in the sentence.

A comma or commas, however, should set off an adjective clause that is nonessential.
- A clause is nonessential if it can be removed from the sentence without changing the basic meaning of the sentence.
- An adjective clause is usually nonessential if it modifies a proper noun.

The relative pronoun *that* usually begins an essential clause, and *which* often begins a nonessential clause.

ESSENTIAL	The author **who was Poet Laureate of the United States from 1993–1994** was Rita Dove. (No commas are used because the clause is needed to identify which author.)
NONESSENTIAL	Rita Dove, **who was Poet Laureate of the United States from 1993 to 1994**, received the Heinz Award in the Arts and Humanities in 1996. (Commas are used because the clause can be removed from the sentence.)

PRACTICE YOUR SKILLS

 Check Your Understanding
Determining the Function of a Relative Pronoun

Literature Topic

Write each adjective clause. Then label the use of each relative pronoun, using the following abbreviations. If an adjective clause begins with an understood *that*, write *(that)* and then write how *that* is used.

subject = *subj.*   object of a preposition = *o.p.*
direct object = *d.o.*   possession = *poss.*

1. Robert Frost, whose poetry was awarded the Pulitzer Prize, first published his poems at age thirty-eight.

2. The poet who dressed entirely in white is Emily Dickinson.

3. The poem from which I get my inspiration is "The Road Not Taken" by Frost.

4. The poem you memorized has only six lines.

5. The lines "The fog comes / on little cat feet," which comprise the poem's first stanza, create a vivid image in my mind.

6. Carl Sandburg, who wrote this short poem, lived from 1878 to 1967.

7. The African American poet about whom I wrote my essay is Rita Dove.

8. The recordings of her poetry that I heard were on the Internet.

9. Wallace Stevens, who wrote "The Emperor of Ice Cream," dropped out of Harvard and then later went to law school.

10. The students whose essays are the most interesting are the students who felt a true connection with the poets they studied.

● Connect to the Writing Process: Editing
Punctuating Adjective Clauses

Literature Topic — **Write the sentences, adding commas where needed. If no commas are needed, write C for correct.**

11. Emily Dickinson who lived in Amherst, Massachusetts was considered a recluse later in life.

12. This intelligent woman whose poems fascinate millions of readers often gave sweets to neighborhood children.

13. The poet would tie the treats to a string that she lowered from her window.

14. Adults who visited in the parlor almost never saw Emily there.

15. The poems which she wrote all her life are about nature, religion, and personal emotions.

16. The person to whom she turned for advice was Thomas Wentworth Higginson who was a literary critic.

17. Her poems which do not have titles are numbered for purposes of organization.

18. Mabel Todd who lived near the Dickinsons became friends with Emily.

19. The friendship the two women shared was established through notes, poems, and flowers.

20. Todd met Dickinson face-to-face on only one occasion which was Emily Dickinson's funeral!

APPLY TO WRITING

Writer's Craft: *Analyzing the Use of Adjective Clauses*

As you have learned, an adjective clause usually is next to the word it modifies. However, poets often rearrange thoughts to create particular effects. In each stanza in this poem are two adjective clauses that modify the same word. Read the poem and then follow the instructions below.

> Who is the East?
> The Yellow Man
> Who may be Purple if He can
> That carries in the Sun.
>
> Who is the West?
> The Purple Man
> Who may be Yellow if He can
> That lets Him out again.
>
> —Emily Dickinson

- Write each adjective clause. Beside it, write the word it modifies.
- How do the adjective clauses make the poet's description more vivid?
- For the reader, what is the overall effect of Dickinson's use of these adjective clauses?

Misplaced Modifiers

To avoid confusion, place an adjective clause as near as possible to the word it describes. Like a phrase, a clause placed too far away from the word it modifies can cause confusion and is called a **misplaced modifier.**

MISPLACED	Tim discovered a park near his new house that included a pond and walking trail.
CORRECT	Near his new house, Tim discovered a park **that included a pond and walking trail**.
MISPLACED	Dennis ran to take the meat off the grill, which was burned to a crisp.
CORRECT	Dennis ran to take the meat, **which was burned to a crisp**, off the grill.

You can learn more about misplaced and dangling modifiers on pages L120–L122.

PRACTICE YOUR SKILLS

 Check Your Understanding
Identifying Misplaced Modifiers

Contemporary Life — **Write *MM* for misplaced modifier if the underlined modifier is used incorrectly in the sentence. If the modifier is used correctly, write C.**

1. Monique packed a picnic basket full of tasty food <u>that was made of straw</u>.

2. Monique's best friend loaded the car with blankets, sunscreen, and a volleyball <u>who was also going on the picnic</u>.

3. I showed the lawn chairs to the girls <u>that I had just bought</u>.

4. My neighbor offered to drive us in his car <u>whom I had invited on the picnic</u>.

5. The car belongs to my neighbor, <u>which has the convertible top</u>.

6. The trunk of the car could barely contain all of our picnic supplies, <u>which was the size of a suitcase</u>.

7. We spread a cloth over the table <u>that had a red-and-white checkered pattern</u>.

8. Some ducks, <u>which were cute and fluffy</u>, begged for food.

9. Ed and I tossed a large disk across the grassy clearing <u>that was made of black plastic</u>.

10. We feasted on food <u>that was tasty</u> and enjoyed each other's company.

Connect to the Writing Process: Revising
Correcting Misplaced Modifiers

11.–18. Rewrite the incorrect sentences from the preceding exercise, correcting each misplaced modifier. Use a comma or commas where needed.

▶ Noun Clauses

A **noun clause** is a subordinate clause that is used as a noun.

A noun clause is used in the same ways a single noun can be used. The examples show some of the uses.

SUBJECT	**What Jenny planned** was a river cruise.
DIRECT OBJECT	Julian knows **that the current is swift**.
INDIRECT OBJECT	Give **whoever arrives** a life jacket.
OBJECT OF A PREPOSITION	People are often surprised by **what they find on the river bottom**.
PREDICATE NOMINATIVE	A challenging trip down the rapids is **what I want right now**.

The following list contains words that often introduce a noun clause. Remember, though, that *who, whom, whose, which,* and *that* can also be used as relative pronouns to introduce adjective clauses.

COMMON INTRODUCTORY WORDS FOR NOUN CLAUSES				
how	what	where	who	whomever
if	whatever	whether	whoever	whose
that	when	which	whom	why

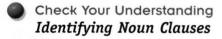

It would be impossible to communicate some ideas without using noun clauses—just try it! Suppose you tell the editor of the yearbook staff, "Send **whomever** this brochure." You have spoken in a complete sentence, yet vital information is missing.

> Send **whoever paid ten dollars** this brochure.
> Send **whoever is on the committee** this brochure.

Noun clauses add clarity and variety to your writing and speaking, whether that communication be a personal letter, a set of instructions, or a business report.

PRACTICE YOUR SKILLS

Check Your Understanding
Identifying Noun Clauses

General Interest **Write the noun clause in each sentence.**

1. How people live in other countries interests many people.
2. A trip to the ancient monuments of Egypt is what the historians requested.
3. That the tour included the Nile River and Alexandria was pleasing news.
4. The tour guide gave the best seats to whoever arrived first.
5. Did you know that the Nile is the longest river in the world?

6. The tour guide said that the Amazon River in Brazil is the second longest river.

7. Give whomever you wish a list of the longest rivers in each country.

8. Does anyone in class know how a stream becomes a river?

9. Tell me whatever you know.

10. Where the Rio Grande flows is the border between Texas and Mexico.

● Check Your Understanding
Determining the Uses of Noun Clauses

Science Topic **Write each noun clause. Then label the use of each one, using the following abbreviations.**

subject = *subj.* object of a preposition = *o.p.*
direct object = *d.o.* predicate nominative = *p.n.*
indirect object = *i.o.*

11. Did you know that heart disease kills people every day?

12. How people can learn about heart health interests me.

13. That a cardiologist can implant donor or artificial hearts is impressive.

14. Nutritionists tell whoever will listen facts about the heart.

15. People are often surprised by what they learn from these experts.

16. Few have heard that every 20 seconds a person in the United States suffers a heart attack.

17. Healthful foods and an exercise program are what people need.

18. That walking is good exercise is well documented in medical journals.

19. A sedentary lifestyle is what people should avoid.

20. Good eating habits can be taught to whoever is willing to learn.

Using Noun Clauses in Sentences

Use each noun clause in a complete sentence. Then write how you used the noun clause, using the following abbreviations.

subject = *subj.*   object of a preposition = *o.p.*
direct object = *d.o.*   predicate nominative = *p.n.*
indirect object = *i.o.*

21. why exercise is essential

22. whoever is interested

23. that medical school is worth the time and money

24. what they learn during these years

25. whoever registers for a cholesterol test

26. where she will be doing her internship

27. if I can get loans for tuition payments

28. how the application process works

29. whomever you admire

30. that a medical degree is yours for life

Communicate Your Ideas

APPLY TO WRITING

Career Profile: *Noun Clauses*

You and your classmates will create a catalog of career profiles that will assist students in choosing and planning their careers. First, choose a career for your profile. Interview people in your chosen career to find out the required education, the years of schooling involved, typical job duties, the average pay rate, and any other information that will help students decide whether this career is what they want. Write a draft of the profile. Use noun clauses to make your writing clear and specific. Then edit your work for grammar, spelling, and punctuation, and write your final draft.

Science Topic **Write the subordinate clauses in the following sentences. Then label the use of each one, using the following abbreviations.**

adverb = *adv.*   noun = *n.*
adjective = *adj.*

1. When the earth, moon, and sun are in line, an eclipse occurs.

2. What most people associate with Saturn are the rings around the planet.

3. Our science teacher, Mrs. Jeffries, told us that Mercury is the planet closest to the sun.

4. The planet that is furthest from the sun is Pluto.

5. As I built my model of the solar system, I consulted at least three reference books.

6. A thick dictionary with diagrams and charts is what helped me the most.

7. Although the sun shone brightly, the weather forecasters maintained that the weekend would be rainy.

8. A planetarium, which contains a working model of the solar system, offers students a chance to see the planets in motion.

9. Mars is the planet that is notable for its red color.

10. I became more interested in the solar system when I learned that Mars is both a planet and the name of the Roman god of war.

Kinds of Sentence Structure

A sentence can be simple, compound, complex, or compound-complex, depending on the number and the kind of clauses in it.

A **simple sentence** consists of one independent clause.

> World War II airplanes fascinate me.

A simple sentence can have a compound subject, a compound verb, or both. In the examples below, the subject is underlined once and the verb is underlined twice.

> Balloons and blimps can carry passengers.
> The airplane and the tank crashed and burned.

A **compound sentence** consists of two or more independent clauses.

A compound sentence should be composed of only closely related independent clauses joined by a coordinating conjunction such as *and, but, for, nor, or, so,* or *yet.*

> ┌────── independent clause ──────┐ ┌independent clause┐
> I ran to the airport terminal, but I missed my plane.
>
> ┌─ independent clause ─┐ ┌──── independent clause ────┐
> The pilot has arrived, the flight attendants are checking
>
> ┌──────────── independent clause ────────────┐
> tickets, and the passengers may now board.

You can learn about punctuating a compound sentence on pages L441–L442.

A **complex sentence** consists of one independent clause and one or more subordinate clauses.

A complex sentence consists of one independent clause and one or more subordinate clauses that are connected by a subordinating conjunction such as *because, that,* or *if.*

```
┌─────── independent clause ───────┐┌─ subordinate clause ─┐
We bought a vacation package that included airfare.
```

```
┌ independent clause ┐┌──────── subordinate clause ────────┐
We flew to Florida because we had tickets to a theme park
┌─── subordinate clause ───┐
that was ready to open.
```

You can find a list of subordinating conjunctions on page L142. You can learn about punctuating complex sentences on pages L143 and L150–L151.

A **compound-complex sentence** consists of two or more independent clauses and one or more subordinate clauses.

Conjunctions and punctuation in compound-complex sentences are used in the same way as they are used in compound sentences and in complex sentences.

```
┌──────── independent clause ────────┐      ┌── independent ──
I have dreamed of becoming a pilot, but I have not taken
┌── clause ──┐┌──────── subordinate clause ────────┐
flying lessons because I am saving the necessary money.
```

CONNECT TO WRITER'S CRAFT

A paragraph with all simple sentences becomes dull and monotonous to read. On the other hand, a paragraph with all complex or compound-complex sentences can be confusing. A paragraph that includes a combination of different kinds of sentences is by far the most interesting. Notice the combination of the different kinds of sentences in the following paragraph.

The plane began its descent to the airport. Passengers looked out the windows, but all they could see was whiteness. The plane bumped through the turbulent air. When the plane was almost over the runway, it finally broke free of the clouds. After landing the plane safely, the pilot turned off the seat-belt sign.

PRACTICE YOUR SKILLS

● Check Your Understanding
Classifying Sentences

Science Topic **Label each sentence *simple, compound, complex,* or *compound-complex*.**

1. In 1984, Byron Lichtenberg, who is a biomedical engineer, became a member of a spacecraft crew.

2. Lichtenberg discovered that dealing with zero gravity was difficult.

3. The other two astronauts were able to control their movements, but at first Lichtenberg kept bouncing off the walls.

4. Lichtenberg found that eating was not easy either.

5. He ate with only a spoon because he had to hold onto his food with his other hand.

6. Once he tried to make a sandwich, but this task was much harder than he had expected.

7. The beef and cheese floated around, but then he clamped them together with the bread.

8. Peanuts were the most fun to eat.

9. When Lichtenberg tried to pour them down his throat, they escaped and floated around the cabin.

10. Eventually he chased them down like a cat and mouse.

● Connect to the Writing Process: Revising
Combining Sentences

Combine the first five pairs of sentences into compound sentences. Then combine the next three pairs into complex sentences. Combine the last two pairs into compound-complex sentences.

11. Mythology associates the winged horse Pegasus with lightning. The modern era associates Pegasus with poetic inspiration.

12. An airplane has wings like a bird. They do not flap like a bird's wings.

13. Wings are associated with Christian angels. They have also been associated with spirits and demons of ancient cultures.

14. Wings can symbolize physical flight above the earth. They can represent rising high above earthly cares and concerns.

15. Fairies are seen as dainty creatures. They are drawn with the wings of butterflies and dragonflies.

16. Wings work in pairs. One is not enough for successful flight.

17. Humans do not have wings. They must fly in spacecraft and aircraft.

18. The Wright brothers made their first flight in 1903. Flying developed relatively quickly.

19. The afternoon was clear and sunny. I felt like flying a kite. I had made the kite from a special kit.

20. I tried to fly the kite in a park. I could not keep it in the air. The kite string kept tangling in the sycamore trees.

Communicate Your Ideas

APPLY TO WRITING

Plan of Action: *Kinds of Sentence Structure*

For high school graduation, you are given a voucher for a free airline ticket to a destination of your choice. You must write down a tentative itinerary to leave with family members before you go. Write a plan of action for this trip. Describe where you are going, where you'll stay, and what you plan to do. In addition to simple sentences, make sure you use compound sentences, complex sentences, and compound-complex sentences to vary your writing. Be prepared to identify each kind of sentence.

Clause Fragments

Even though a subordinate clause has both a subject and a verb, it does not express a complete thought. Therefore, it cannot stand alone as a sentence. When it stands alone, a **clause fragment** results. To correct a clause fragment, add or change words to express a complete thought or attach the clause to a related sentence.

Adverb Clause Fragment	**Whenever I have the opportunity.** I enjoy learning about animals.
Corrected	Whenever I have the opportunity, I enjoy learning about animals.
Noun Clause Fragment	**That a cow has four stomachs called the rumen, reticulum, omasum, and abomasum.** I know.
Corrected	I know that a cow has four stomachs called the rumen, reticulum, omasum, and abomasum.
Adjective Clause Fragment	At the workshop she visited booths. **That featured veterinary information.**
Corrected	At the workshop she visited booths that featured veterinary information.

You can learn about other kinds of sentence fragments on pages L68–L71 and L123–L125.

CONNECT TO SPEAKING AND WRITING

When someone asks you a question that begins with the word *why,* you probably begin your answer with the word *because.*

Why did you visit the career fair? **Because** I wanted to learn more about job opportunities.

Sentences that begin with *because* are often fragments. While acceptable in conversation, they should be avoided in writing.

● Check Your Understanding
Identifying Clause Fragments

Science Topic **Write S if the word group is a sentence. Write F if the word group is a clause fragment.**

1. Ruminants are animals that chew their cud.

2. As soon as I heard about them.

3. Because I had never seen a moose up close.

4. That the oryx has long, pointed horns that point upward.

5. Whoever drew the picture of the kudu's long spiral horns.

6. I liked the chamois, whose soft skin is sometimes used as a "chamois cloth."

7. That I would never use a real leather chamois cloth again.

8. Until you know the difference between a bison and a musk ox.

9. So that I could also see the striped-backed duikers.

10. When I saw the gazelles.

11. After she saw the picture of a unicorn.

12. Does the Loch Ness monster really exist?

13. Before the American bald eagle was taken from the endangered list.

14. The alligator that made its home in the swamp.

15. Despite the differences between an alligator and a crocodile, many people cannot tell them apart.

● Connect to the Writing Process: Revising
Correcting Clause Fragments

16.–26. Correct each clause fragment you identified in the preceding exercise by either adding or changing words to express a complete thought.

APPLY TO WRITING
Description: *Complete Sentences*

You have created a Website in honor of your beloved pet. You have already scanned in a photograph of Fluffy/ Spike/Fishy, and now you must write an engaging description of him/her. Write a paragraph describing what makes your pet so lovable or cute or interesting. If you don't have a pet, write about a pet you used to have or make one up. Use a variety of clauses, but make sure you don't have any fragments.

Run-on Sentences

A **run-on sentence** is two or more sentences that are written as one sentence and are separated by a comma or no mark of punctuation at all.

Run-on sentences result either from writing too fast or from the mistaken idea that very long sentences sound more scholarly. A run-on sentence is usually written in either of the following two ways.

WITH A COMMA	Horticulturists grow beautiful plants, they often organize garden shows for interested audiences.
WITH NO PUNCTUATION	In the winter some trees lose their leaves others do not.

▶ Ways to Correct Run-on Sentences

A run-on sentence can be corrected in several ways. (1) It can be written as two separate sentences. (2) It can be written as a compound sentence with a comma and a conjunction or with a semicolon. (3) It can be written as a complex sentence by changing one part of the run-on sentence into a subordinate clause.

RUN-ON SENTENCE	This botanical garden covers over four acres, it is the second largest in the state.
SEPARATE SENTENCES	This botanical garden covers over four acres. It is the second largest in the state.
COMPOUND SENTENCE	This botanical garden covers over four acres, **and** it is the second largest in the state. (with a comma and a conjunction)

This botanical garden covers over four acres; it is the second largest in the state.
(with a semicolon)

COMPLEX SENTENCE

This botanical garden, **which covers over four acres,** is the second largest in the state.
(adjective clause)

Since this botanical garden covers over four acres, it is the second largest in the state.
(adverb clause)

PRACTICE YOUR SKILLS

● Check Your Understanding
Identifying Run-on Sentences

Science Topic **Label each group of words as *RO* for run-on or *S* for sentence.**

1. Many plants have poisonous leaves or fruits, these cause skin irritation or sickness.

2. The belladonna has a beautiful name and poisonous berries, it is also called deadly nightshade.

3. Holly, commonly used for holiday decoration, has poisonous leaves and berries.

4. Another seasonal flower, the lily of the valley, has berries too these should not be eaten by anyone either.

5. Many people love rhubarb pie, they do not know that rhubarb leaves should not be eaten.

6. Like most people, I cannot touch poison ivy, it gives me a rash.

7. Digitalis is a plant used in some medicines the leaves are poisonous when eaten.

8. As a child I learned not to touch the nettle, I learned the hard way.

9. Children and pets don't know the dangers of poisonous plants, some will innocently eat them and become sick or die.

10. English ivy foliage is not poisonous, but the berries are.

● Connect to the Writing Process: Editing
Correcting Run-on Sentences

11.–18. Rewrite the run-on sentences you identified in the preceding exercise as separate sentences, compound sentences, or complex sentences. Use conjunctions and punctuation as needed.

Communicate Your Ideas

APPLY TO WRITING

Personal Narrative: *Complete Sentences*

As you finish high school and prepare for graduation, you may find yourself remembering certain events in your senior year with emotions such as happiness, regret, humor, or anger. Write a personal narrative about one of these memories for your Senior Scrapbook. Use different kinds of sentences for variety. Remember that run-on sentences usually occur when you are focused on getting ideas down on paper in a first draft. Therefore, be sure to edit your work for run-on sentences and then prepare a final copy.

Diagraming Sentences

Each clause—whether independent or subordinate—is diagramed on a separate baseline like a simple sentence.

Compound Sentences   Each independent clause is diagramed like a simple sentence. The clauses are joined at the verbs with a broken line on which the conjunction is written.

The cafeteria food is good, but I still take my lunch.

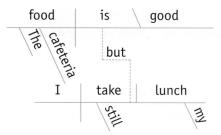

Complex Sentences   An adverb or an adjective clause in a complex sentence is diagramed beneath the independent clause it modifies. The following diagram contains an adverb clause. The subordinating conjunction goes on a broken line that connects the verb in the adverb clause to the modified verb, adverb, or adjective in the independent clause.

Before I begin my article, I must do more research.

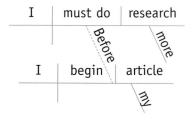

The relative pronoun in an adjective clause is connected by a broken line to the noun or the pronoun the clause modifies.

We recently bought a clock that chimes on the hour.

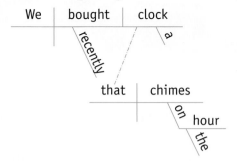

A noun clause is diagramed on a pedestal in the same position as a single noun with the same function, such as a direct object.

Tell us what you want for your birthday.

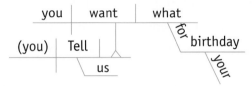

Compound-Complex Sentences   To diagram these sentences, apply rules for diagraming compound and complex sentences.

PRACTICE YOUR SKILLS

Diagraming Sentences

Diagram the following sentences or copy them. If you copy them, draw one line under each subject and two lines under each verb. Then put parentheses around each subordinate clause and label each one *adverb*, *adjective*, or *noun*.

1. An earthquake begins when underground rocks move.
2. This movement creates waves of energy which travel up to the surface.
3. Because earthquakes often cause severe damage, architects now can build earthquake-proof buildings.
4. Thousands of earthquakes occur during a year, but only a few are large ones.
5. What scientists still cannot do is predict earthquakes.

Identifying Clauses

Write each subordinate clause. Then label each one *adverb, adjective,* or *noun.*

1. Although many tornadoes occur throughout the United States, they are quite rare west of the Rockies.
2. Several champion ice-hockey teams have come from Canada, where ice-skating is a very popular sport.
3. I heard that trucks can no longer travel on Grove Street.
4. Wrap that meat in foil before you put it into the freezer.
5. Since I will have a test in Spanish, I went to the language lab.
6. The microphone that he used had a cord attached to it.
7. If you take a trip to Mount Vernon, you will be taken back two centuries into the past.
8. Parachutists often fall a considerable distance before they pull the cord that opens the parachute.
9. Someone once said that an egotist is a person who is "me-deep" in conversation.
10. My mother, who seemed happy and relieved, reported that she had found a new apartment for us.
11. Don ran when he saw a huge bull approaching him.
12. Whoever is qualified for the job will have an interview.
13. Early schoolhouses were always red because red paint was the cheapest paint available.
14. The oldest fossils date back to a time when seas covered large areas that have long since become dry land.
15. Since I wasn't there, I honestly don't know what happened.

Classifying Sentences

Label each sentence *simple, compound, complex,* or *compound-complex*.

1. John Paul Jones moved to America to avoid a trial that involved his handling of a mutiny.
2. Although he was born in Scotland, he became a hero of the American Revolution.
3. He battled British ships off the coast of North America.
4. His most famous victory occurred in 1779 aboard the *Bonhomme Richard*.
5. His ship was badly damaged, but Jones refused to give up.
6. He was urged to surrender, but he called out, "Sir, I have not yet begun to fight," words that have gone down in history.
7. Jones was only in his early 30s when he captured the British warships *Drake* and *Serapis*.
8. After the war American shipping became vulnerable to attacks by pirates.
9. Thomas Jefferson suggested that John Paul Jones could destroy the pirates.
10. He mentioned this in a letter to James Monroe, but nothing came of it.

Using Sentence Structure

Write five sentences that follow the directions below. (The sentences may come in any order.) Write about an unrecognized hero or a topic of your choice.

1. Write a simple sentence.
2. Write a complex sentence with an introductory adverb clause.
3. Write a complex sentence with an adjective clause.
4. Write a compound sentence.
5. Write a complex sentence with a noun clause.

Label each sentence and check its punctuation.

Language and *Self-Expression*

Leo and Diane Dillon attended New York City's Parsons School of Design and School of Visual Arts. They have collaborated on many picture books for children. The illustrations for this one, Verna Aardema's retelling of *Why Mosquitoes Buzz in People's Ears,* won the Caldecott Medal in 1976.

Folktales of this kind are designed to explain natural phenomena. They might tell, for example, "How the Leopard Got His Spots" or "Why the Elephant Has a Trunk." Think of a natural occurrence among animals that you could "explain" through a folktale. Write a tale that features animals who talk and interact. Use your knowledge of clauses to add interest to your writing.

Prewriting Begin with your title. Then outline your story, working backward as shown here:

Why Mosquitoes Buzz in People's Ears

I.
II.
III.
IV.   Today, mosquitoes buzz in people's ears.

Drafting Refer to your outline as you draft your folktale. Begin with a paragraph that introduces your main characters and setting. Continue with the problem that is to be solved. End with a solution that "explains" the phenomenon mentioned in your title.

Revising Read your folktale critically, looking for ideas that do not flow smoothly or that seem extraneous. Cut and add material as needed.

Editing Review your folktale, looking for errors in grammar, capitalization, punctuation, and spelling. Make any corrections that are necessary.

Publishing Prepare and illustrate a final copy of your folktale. Publish it by sharing it with your class.

Another Look

A **clause** is a group of words that has a subject and a verb.

Types of Clauses
An **independent (or main) clause** can usually stand alone as a sentence because it expresses a complete thought. *(page L139)*
A **subordinate (or dependent) clause** cannot stand alone as a sentence, because it does not express a complete thought. *(page L139)*

Uses of Subordinate Clauses
An **adverb clause** is a subordinate clause that is used like an adverb to modify a verb, an adjective, or an adverb. *(page L141)*
An adverb clause usually begins with a **subordinating conjunction**. *(page L142)*
An **adjective clause** is a subordinate clause that is used like an adjective to modify a noun or pronoun. *(page L148)*
An adjective clause usually begins with a **relative pronoun**. *(page L148)*
A **noun clause** is a subordinate clause that is used as a noun. *(page L155)*

Kinds of Sentence Structure
A **simple sentence** consists of one independent clause. *(page L160)*
A **compound sentence** consists of two or more independent clauses. *(page L160)*
A **complex sentence** consists of one independent clause and one or more subordinate clauses. *(page L160)*
A **compound-complex sentence** consists of two or more independent clauses and one or more subordinate clauses. *(page L161)*

Other Information About Clauses
Punctuating adverb clauses *(page L143)*
Punctuating adjective clauses *(page L150)*
Recognizing elliptical clauses *(page L145)*
Avoiding misplaced modifiers *(page L153)*
Avoiding clause fragments *(page L164)*

Posttest

Directions
Write the letter of the term that correctly identifies each sentence or underlined part of a sentence.

EXAMPLE
1. *Stream of consciousness* refers to the free flow of thoughts through a character's mind.
   1 **A** simple sentence
     B compound sentence
     C complex sentence
     D compound-complex sentence

ANSWER
1 **A**

1. James Joyce was a great master of stream of consciousness.

2. Joyce, however, owed much to a French novelist who had used the technique much earlier.

3. Edouard Dujardin experimented with the technique in 1887 when he published *The Laurels Are Cut Down*.

4. His novel is rarely read today, but it influenced many writers.

5. Dujardin defined his *interior monologue* as "an unspoken discourse without a hearer present. . . ."

6. Some critics distinguish interior monologue from stream of consciousness; they feel that there is a clear difference.

7. Although both include a character's thoughts and feelings, interior monologue indicates nothing in the way of a narrator.

8. Joyce used both in *Ulysses,* which is one of his finest works.

9. If you read Virginia Woolf's work, you will see many examples of stream-of-consciousness writing.

10. *To the Lighthouse* alternates between the thoughts of Mr. Ramsay, whose mind works rationally and dispassionately, and those of his wife, a creative, intuitive person.

1 A simple sentence
   B compound sentence
   C complex sentence
   D compound-complex
      sentence

2 A simple sentence
   B compound sentence
   C complex sentence
   D compound-complex
      sentence

3 A simple sentence
   B compound sentence
   C complex sentence
   D compound-complex
      sentence

4 A simple sentence
   B compound sentence
   C complex sentence
   D compound-complex
      sentence

5 A simple sentence
   B compound sentence
   C complex sentence
   D compound-complex
      sentence

6 A independent clause
   B adverb clause
   C adjective clause
   D noun clause

7 A independent clause
   B adverb clause
   C adjective clause
   D noun clause

8 A independent clause
   B adverb clause
   C adjective clause
   D noun clause

9 A independent clause
   B adverb clause
   C adjective clause
   D noun clause

10 A independent clause
   B adverb clause
   C adjective clause
   D noun clause

CHAPTER 5

Using Verbs

· ·

Directions
Read the passage and choose the word or group of words that belongs in each underlined space. Write the letter of the correct answer.

EXAMPLE   **1.** Modern dance __(1)__ its origins in ancient sacred and ceremonial dance.

    1 **A** will have
       B have
       C have been
       D has

ANSWER   **1 D**

   In prehistoric times, dancing __(1)__ an early form of artistic expression. Along the shores of the Mediterranean Sea, decorative carvings found in Egyptian tombs __(2)__ that dances __(3)__ during funerals and parades as well as in religious rituals. Dancing always __(4)__ an important part in Greek celebrations. The Romans, too, __(5)__ ceremonial dancing to Italy from Greece, still use it in theatrical performances.

   During the Middle Ages dance continued __(6)__ an important role in both courtly and village life. The peasants especially __(7)__ performing sword dances, Maypole dances, chain dances, and circle dances. Change, however, __(8)__ in the air. Professional performances __(9)__ as *balletti* originated in the Renaissance and within a few years __(10)__ over all of Europe.

1   **A**   have been
    B   were
    C   was
    D   will be

2   **A**   reveal
    B   revealed
    C   are revealing
    D   do reveal

3   **A**   will have been
        performed
    B   have been performed
    C   perform
    D   were performed

4   **A**   has played
    B   have played
    C   is played
    D   were played

5   **A**   have brought
    B   having brought
    C   bringing
    D   had brought

6   **A**   played
    B   to play
    C   did play
    D   having been played

7   **A**   have enjoyed
    B   will enjoy
    C   enjoy
    D   enjoyed

8   **A**   were
    B   is
    C   was
    D   has been

9   **A**   known
    B   were known
    C   knew
    D   having been known

10 **A**   sweep
    B   swept
    C   had swept
    D   sweeping

Pierre-Auguste Renoir. *Le Moulin de la Galette,* 1876.
Oil on canvas, 68 by 51 inches. Musée d'Orsay, Paris.

Describe What is happening in the foreground of the painting? What is happening in the middle ground and background?

Analyze At what time of day does the action in the painting take place? How do you know? What do you think the woman bending over in the center foreground is doing? How do the people respond to her? What do you think the light splotches in the painting mean?

Interpret If you wrote art reviews for a newspaper, what would you report about Renoir's technique? What headline might you write for a review?

Judge Would you prefer to see a photo of this scene, read a review of the painting, or study the painting? Why?

At the end of this chapter, you will use the artwork to stimulate ideas for writing.

The Principal Parts of Verbs

This is the first chapter on usage. The next three chapters will show you how to use pronouns correctly, how to make a verb agree with its subject, and how to determine which form of a modifier to use. These chapters on using the grammar that you have learned are extremely important. Knowing grammar without knowing proper usage is like buying a new car and leaving it parked in the driveway because you never learned to drive!

This first chapter covers verbs. Why should you know what a verb is? If you know which word in a sentence is a verb, you can consciously substitute a specific, colorful verb for a dull, general one. Once you have chosen a particular verb, however, you must know which form of that verb to use. In this chapter you will learn to use the correct forms of verbs.

The four basic forms of a verb are called its principal parts. The six tenses of a verb are formed from these principal parts.

The **principal parts** of a verb are the present, the present participle, the past, and the past participle.

Notice that helping verbs are needed with the present participle and the past participle when they are used as the main verb of the sentence.

PRESENT	I usually **eat** lunch after drama class.
PRESENT PARTICIPLE	I *am* **eating** lunch earlier this week.
PAST	I **ate** lunch an hour ago.
PAST PARTICIPLE	I *have* already **eaten** lunch.

Regular and Irregular Verbs

Verbs are sometimes classified in two categories: regular verbs and irregular verbs. How a verb forms its past and past participle will determine how it is classified.

A **regular verb** forms its past and past participle by adding *–ed* or *–d* to the present.

An **irregular verb** does not form its past and past participle by adding *–ed* or *–d* to the present.

Regular Verbs

Most verbs are classified as regular verbs because they form their past and past participle in the same way—by adding *–ed* or *–d* to the present. Following are the four principal parts of the regular verbs *talk*, *use*, *equip*, and *commit*. Notice that the present participle is formed by adding *–ing* to the present form, and as the rule says, the past participle is formed by adding *–ed* or *–d* to the present form.

REGULAR VERBS			
Present	**Present Participle**	**Past**	**Past Participle**
talk	(is) talking	talked	(have) talked
use	(is) using	used	(have) used
equip	(is) equipping	equipped	(have) equipped
commit	(is) committing	committed	(have) committed

When endings such as *–ing* and *–ed* are added to some verbs like *use*, *equip*, and *commit*, the spelling changes. If you are unsure of the spelling of a verb form, look it up in the dictionary.

CONNECT TO SPEAKING AND WRITING

Some verb forms are easier to write than to say. Be careful not to drop the *–ed* or *–d* from such frequently used verb forms as *asked*, *helped*, *looked*, *seemed*, *supposed*, *talked*, *used*, and *walked* when you are speaking, especially in formal situations.

INCORRECT   This was **suppose** to be an ancient pottery exhibit.

CORRECT   This was **supposed** to be an ancient pottery exhibit.

PRACTICE YOUR SKILLS

● Check Your Understanding
Determining the Principal Parts of Regular Verbs

Art
Topic
Write each verb form. Beside it, label its principal part: *present, present participle, past,* or *past participle.* (Do not include any helping verbs.)

1. I sketched too many portraits.
2. Thelma is running for Art Club president.
3. I have committed to summer art classes.
4. I like watercolors.
5. Trish is mixing tempera paints.
6. She has searched for the perfect still life.
7. Tonya and Kyle are arranging fruit in a stained glass bowl.
8. The fruit looks beautiful.
9. Everyone else painted fruit yesterday.
10. I have signed up for a class in stained glass.
11. Louis C. Tiffany greatly impacted the Art Nouveau movement with his stained glass.
12. He started his career as a landscape artist.
13. Tiffany experimented with color and texture.
14. He incorporated beautiful images of nature in glass.
15. Studio artists have sketched patterns for each product.

Irregular Verbs

Some common verbs are classified as irregular because they form their past and past participle in different ways and do not add *–ed* or *–d* to the present. The irregular verbs have been divided into groups according to the way they form their past and past participle.

Remember that *is* is not part of the present participle and *have* is not part of the past participle. They have been added to the following lists of irregular verbs, however, to remind you that all present and past participles must have a form of one of these helping verbs when they are used as a verb in a sentence.

Group 1   These irregular verbs have the same form for the present, the past, and the past participle.

PRESENT	PRESENT PART.	PAST	PAST PART.
burst	(is) bursting	burst	(have) burst
cost	(is) costing	cost	(have) cost
hit	(is) hitting	hit	(have) hit
hurt	(is) hurting	hurt	(have) hurt
let	(is) letting	let	(have) let
put	(is) putting	put	(have) put

Group 2   These irregular verbs have the same form for the past and the past participle.

PRESENT	PRESENT PART.	PAST	PAST PART.
bring	(is) bringing	brought	(have) brought
buy	(is) buying	bought	(have) bought
catch	(is) catching	caught	(have) caught
feel	(is) feeling	felt	(have) felt
find	(is) finding	found	(have) found
get	(is) getting	got	(have) got or gotten
hold	(is) holding	held	(have) held
keep	(is) keeping	kept	(have) kept
lead	(is) leading	led	(have) led
leave	(is) leaving	left	(have) left
lose	(is) losing	lost	(have) lost
make	(is) making	made	(have) made
say	(is) saying	said	(have) said
sell	(is) selling	sold	(have) sold
send	(is) sending	sent	(have) sent
teach	(is) teaching	taught	(have) taught
tell	(is) telling	told	(have) told
win	(is) winning	won	(have) won

PRACTICE YOUR SKILLS

● Check Your Understanding
Using the Correct Verb Form

History Topic **Write the past or the past participle of each underlined verb.**

1. In 1836, the Mexican General Santa Anna <u>lead</u> his army to the Alamo.

2. He had <u>bring</u> with him an army of thousands.

3. He <u>find</u> fewer than 200 Texas soldiers at the mission.

4. These volunteer freedom fighters had <u>put</u> their lives at risk for their beliefs.

5. After 13 days of battle, every soldier in the Alamo had <u>lose</u> his life.

6. Despite the bloodshed, they had <u>make</u> history.

7. Santa Anna had <u>win</u> the battle but at great cost.

8. One of Santa Anna's colonials <u>say</u> they couldn't afford many more "victories" like the Alamo.

9. The next month Santa Anna was <u>catch</u> at the Battle of San Jacinto.

10. Santa Anna had <u>tell</u> everyone he was "the Napoleon of the West."

● Check Your Understanding
Determining the Principal Parts of Irregular Verbs

Make four columns on your paper. Label them *Present, Present Participle, Past,* and *Past Participle*. Then write the four principal parts of the following verbs.

11. buy
12. keep
13. let
14. put
15. hurt

16. tell
17. sell
18. get
19. teach
20. leave

Rewrite the following paragraph, correcting the verb forms.
(You will correct 8 forms in all.)

Francis Scott Key, author of "The Star-Spangled Banner,"
hold a degree from St. John's College. He make his living as
a lawyer. In 1814, he finded himself aboard a British ship
within sight of the British attack on Fort McHenry in
Baltimore. He had leaved Fort McHenry but could clearly
see the bombs. Many bursted in the air above, and others
hitted the fort. Key felt such strong emotions about the
battle that he wrote "The Star-Spangled Banner." After the
war, he get a job as United States District Attorney. In
1843, he contracted pleurisy, which costed him his life.

● Connect to the Writing Process: Drafting
Using Verb Forms in Sentences

**Write sentences about a career you would like to have. Follow
each direction.**

1. Use the past participle of *find*, and name your career.
2. Ask about it using the past participle of *make*.
3. Write a command using the present tense of *leave*.
4. Include a description using the past participle of *said*.
5. Write a command using the present tense of *lead*.
6. Use the past participle of *sent* in a sentence.
7. Exclaim using the present participle of *catch*.
8. Include the present tense of *put* in a command.
9. Use the past participle of *kept* in a sentence.
10. Use the present participle of *bring* in a sentence.

Group 3 These irregular verbs form the past participle by adding *-n* to the past.

PRESENT	PRESENT PART.	PAST	PAST PART.
break	(is) breaking	broke	(have) broken
choose	(is) choosing	chose	(have) chosen
freeze	(is) freezing	froze	(have) frozen
speak	(is) speaking	spoke	(have) spoken
steal	(is) stealing	stole	(have) stolen

Group 4 These irregular verbs form the past participle by adding *-n* to the present.

PRESENT	PRESENT PART.	PAST	PAST PART.
blow	(is) blowing	blew	(have) blown
draw	(is) drawing	drew	(have) drawn
drive	(is) driving	drove	(have) driven
give	(is) giving	gave	(have) given
grow	(is) growing	grew	(have) grown
know	(is) knowing	knew	(have) known
see	(is) seeing	saw	(have) seen
take	(is) taking	took	(have) taken
throw	(is) throwing	threw	(have) thrown

PRACTICE YOUR SKILLS

● **Check Your Understanding**
  Using the Correct Verb Form

Contemporary Life **Write the past or the past participle of each underlined verb.**

1. Willis has <u>throw</u> three balls through the hoop.

2. Brian <u>steal</u> two bases during the sixth inning.

3. Every day at camp, we <u>take</u> polo lessons.

4. Last night we <u>see</u> the team's most exciting game ever.

5. Mom <u>drive</u> us home after the game.

6. Chris asked if we had <u>choose</u> a captain yet.

7. Last fall I <u>break</u> my arm playing softball.

8. My arm has <u>grow</u> stronger with the help of exercise.

9. Tori <u>know</u> how to play softball before she came to camp.

10. A strong, cold wind <u>blow</u> down the goals last night.

11. The canoes in the water nearly <u>freeze</u> in the ice storm.

12. I thought I had <u>speak</u> to you about the canoes.

13. The counselors had <u>take</u> the canoes to a boathouse.

14. Mia <u>give</u> her old tennis racket to her young camper.

15. Our team <u>draw</u> a poster for our counselor.

Check Your Understanding
Determining the Correct Verb Form

Contemporary Life **Write the correct form of each underlined verb. If the verb is correct, write C.** Remember that all the action took place the previous summer.

16. I <u>buy</u> a bonsai tree at Bao's Bonsai Garden last summer.

17. I had <u>see</u> this quaint little nursery before.

18. I had <u>take</u> the opportunity and had <u>speak</u> to Bao.

19. I could not <u>forget</u> about owning a beautiful bonsai.

20. Monday, I <u>get</u> up early and <u>make</u> my way to Bao's store.

21. I <u>choose</u> a tiny, perfect tree.

22. Bao <u>give</u> me a tree-care guide.

23. She <u>say</u> most people have never <u>grow</u> a bonsai before.

24. She had <u>draw</u> pictures of how to trim the tree's roots.

25. Also, she had <u>make</u> a chart of pruning and watering schedules for the tree.

26. I <u>know</u> I would need fertilizer and other supplies.

27. I <u>take</u> a basket and then <u>choose</u> pruning shears and a wide, flat pot for the tree I had <u>buy</u>.

28. I <u>feel</u> satisfied with my new purchases.

29. I <u>leave</u> the store a happy customer.

30. I have faithfully <u>take</u> care of my miniature tree.

Using Verb Forms

Rewrite the following paragraph, changing the present-tense verbs to the past tense and the past-tense verbs to the past participle. (You will change 21 verb forms in all.)

June bursts into the room and makes an announcement. She says she had saw a kit for a window-sill herb garden. She had drove to the farmer's market and had sold some fresh vegetables she had grew in her large garden. Afterwards, she grows interested in the other booths. She takes a stroll down the aisles. She finds the herb kit and knows she wants it. It costs only a few dollars, and so she gives the seller her money. She puts her new purchase in the trunk and then finds her car keys in her large bag. She feels happy about the herb-garden project. She takes the shortcut across the pasture and drives quickly home.

June takes the kit into her garage. She breaks its seal. She found a calendar schedule for the garden in the directions.

Group 5   These irregular verbs form the past and the past participle by changing a vowel.

PRESENT	PRESENT PART.	PAST	PAST PART.
begin	(is) beginning	began	(have) begun
drink	(is) drinking	drank	(have) drunk
ring	(is) ringing	rang	(have) rung
shrink	(is) shrinking	shrank	(have) shrunk
sing	(is) singing	sang	(have) sung
sink	(is) sinking	sank	(have) sunk
swim	(is) swimming	swam	(have) swum

Group 6 These irregular verbs form the past and the past participle in other ways.

PRESENT	PRESENT PART.	PAST	PAST PART.
come	(is) coming	came	(have) come
do	(is) doing	did	(have) done
eat	(is) eating	ate	(have) eaten
fall	(is) falling	fell	(have) fallen
go	(is) going	went	(have) gone
ride	(is) riding	rode	(have) ridden
run	(is) running	ran	(have) run
tear	(is) tearing	tore	(have) torn
wear	(is) wearing	wore	(have) worn
write	(is) writing	wrote	(have) written

CONNECT TO SPEAKING AND WRITING

If you've been around young children much, you know they have difficulty using irregular verbs. They are apt to say proudly, "I **putted** my toys away" or to complain loudly, "She **drinked** my juice." You can help children learn the correct form by rephrasing their statements: "Good! You **put** your toys away," or "She **drank** your juice?"

PRACTICE YOUR SKILLS

● Check Your Understanding
Using the Correct Verb Form

General
Interest **Write the past or the past participle of each underlined verb.**

1. Thousands of people go to the rodeo.
2. Many come from far away.
3. They wear their best boots and a new hat.
4. Cowboys had begin practicing for the bull rides long ago.
5. These daring men and women had fall many times.

6. Some had even <u>tear</u> ligaments or muscles.

7. Nevertheless, they had <u>come</u> to the rodeo ready to ride.

8. In another show talented vocalists <u>sing</u> country songs.

9. I ate and <u>drink</u> until I thought my waistband <u>shrink</u>.

10. I enjoyed what Rachel <u>do</u>.

11. She <u>ride</u> her pony and <u>ring</u> the starting bell for the race.

12. She had <u>write</u> to the rodeo organizers ahead of time.

13. Also, she had <u>go</u> to fill out an application.

14. She got the job and <u>begin</u> work on the first rodeo day.

15. I had accidentally <u>sink</u> my trailer in the mud and could not bring my pony.

● Check Your Understanding
Supplying the Correct Verb Form

Contemporary Life **Complete each pair of sentences by supplying the past or the past participle of the verb in parentheses at the beginning of the sentence.**

16. (begin) The school play ▧ 15 minutes ago. It should have ▧ a half hour ago.

17. (do) Have you ▧ your homework? I ▧ mine at school.

18. (run) Matthew ▧ for Student Council president last year. He should have ▧ again this year.

19. (drink) We ▧ some ice water after cheerleading practice. We should never have ▧ it fast.

20. (go) Have you ▧ to a pep rally yet? Yes, I ▧ to one Friday.

21. (write) I ▧ my essay last night. Have you ▧ yours?

22. (swim) Kelly ▧ the fastest today. I have ▧ faster than her many times.

23. (sing) Have you ever ▧ in school choir before? Once I ▧ a solo in our chorus concert.

24. (eat) I just ▧ lunch in the cafeteria. Have you ▧ yet?

25. (ride) The basketball team ▧ to the last game in the new bus. They had ▧ in rusty old buses all season.

Correcting Verb Forms

Rewrite the following paragraphs, using past and past participle verb forms. (You will change 23 verb forms in all.)

Brandy comes to my school last month. Before, she had went to another school. I speak to her before homeroom because I know what it's like to be new. I find Brandy knows sign language. She teaches me some before class. I see her again at lunch and get up from my seat. She sees me and comes over. She had already ate her lunch, but she drinks a soda while I eat. We write down ideas for a sign language club. By the end of lunch period, we had make much progress.

Later we send a copy of our plans to the class president. He chooses to support our idea. He speaks to the student council, and they draw up a plan for the club. Brandy and I go to several planning sessions. We also begin telling other students about the sign language club. The club has became my favorite school activity.

Communicate Your Ideas

APPLY TO WRITING

Persuasive Letter: *Verb Forms*

A new student is transferring to your homeroom, and you want to convince him or her to join your favorite school activity. Using past and past participle verb forms, write a letter to the new student, describing what your group has done this year. Try to convince him or her to join.

Six Problem Verbs

Some verbs present problems, not because they are regular or irregular, but because their meanings are easily confused. Always make sure, therefore, that you have chosen the verb that correctly expresses what you want to say or write.

lie and lay   *Lie* means "to rest or recline." *Lie* is never followed by a direct object. *Lay* means "to put or set (something) down." *Lay* is usually followed by a direct object.

You can learn more about direct objects on pages L72–L77.

PRESENT	PRESENT PART.	PAST	PAST PART.
lie	(is) lying	lay	(have) lain
lay	(is) laying	laid	(have) laid

LIE

Her party dresses **lie** on the floor of the guest bedroom.

They are **lying** in a heap now.

They **lay** there last weekend, too.

They **have lain** in the guest bedroom for weeks.

LAY

Lay the servers' aprons on the table.
(You lay what? *Aprons* is the direct object.)
Harry **is laying** the aprons on the table.
Shoshana **laid** the aprons on the table last night.
Usually **I have laid** the aprons on the table.

CONNECT TO SPEAKING AND WRITING

When *lie* means "to tell a falsehood," the principal parts are *lie, is lying, lied,* and *(have) lied.* Be sure to include enough information to make the meaning clear because some of the principal parts are the same as those for *to lie,* meaning "to rest or recline."

CONFUSING	Jesse never *lies* about.
CORRECT	Jesse never *lies* about his chores.

rise* and *raise   *Rise* means "to move upward" or "to get up."
Rise is never followed by a direct object. *Raise* means "to lift
(something) up," "to increase," or "to grow something." *Raise* is
usually followed by a direct object.

PRESENT	PRESENT PART.	PAST	PAST PART.
rise	(is) rising	rose	(have) risen
raise	(is) raising	raised	(have) raised

RISE   **Rise** early for the breakfast shift.
Marianne **is rising** early for her new job.
Marianne **rose** at sunrise yesterday.
She **has risen** early for several weeks.

RAISE   **Raise** the cattle for the restaurant supplier.
(You raise what? *Cattle* is the direct object.)
He **is raising** the cattle for beef.
He **raised** cattle for the beef suppliers.
He **has raised** cattle for two decades.

sit* and *set   *Sit* means "to rest in an upright position." *Sit* is
never followed by a direct object. *Set* means "to put or place
(something)." *Set* is usually followed by a direct object.

PRESENT	PRESENT PART.	PAST	PAST PART.
sit	(is) sitting	sat	(have) sat
set	(is) setting	set	(have) set

SIT   **Sit** near me at the awards banquet.
She **is sitting** at the head table.
She **sat** there near Tim.
She **has** never **sat** near Tim before tonight.

SET   **Set** the awards on the podium.
(You set what? *Awards* is the direct object.)
He **is setting** the awards on the podium.
He **set** the awards on the podium this morning.
He **has set** the awards on the podium every year.

You can learn more about other confusing verbs on pages L352–L387.

PRACTICE YOUR SKILLS

● Check Your Understanding
Using the Correct Verb Form

Contemporary Life **Write the correct verb form from the choices provided.**

1. (lie/lay) I will ■ on the sofa for a rest before the party.
2. (sitting/setting) Why are you ■ on the sofa?
3. (sat/set) Charlie has ■ the record for hosting the most parties in a summer.
4. (rise/raise) Tell Jane she must ■ funds to buy the cake.
5. (lain/laid) You have ■ on that sofa for too long.
6. (sit/set) Perry, will you ■ the fine china on the table?
7. (lying/laying) Shelly is ■ a napkin across her lap.
8. (rising/raising) I am ■ to the challenge of entertaining.
9. (sat/set) That shy girl has ■ in the corner all evening.
10. (rise/raise) If you want to play charades, ■ your hand.

● Connect to the Writing Process: Editing
Correcting Verb Form

Contemporary Life **Write each sentence, correcting the verb form. If the verb form is correct, write C.**

11. Sherm's father has rose enough money for a restaurant.
12. At the opening gala, I will set next to Keisha.
13. She is laying her clothes out for the gala, now.
14. Keisha's mother has sat a cool glass of water on the side table for me.
15. Prices at restaurants are rising.
16. I lie my nice jacket over the chair.
17. The waiter is sitting the dessert tray on the table.
18. Let's raise and go get dessert.
19. You shouldn't leave your purse laying there.
20. Don't forget where we are sitting.

APPLY TO WRITING

News Article: *Problem Verbs*

You are a journalist who covers the social events in a small town. Write a news article that describes the latest social news, whether it be a wedding, fund raiser, park dedication, restaurant opening, or some other community event. Use each of the following problem verbs at least once: *lie, lay, rise, raise, sit, set.*

QuickCheck Mixed Practice

Sports Topic

Write the past or the past participle of each verb in parentheses.

1. For over seven decades, the Harlem Globetrotters have (bring) an unusual dimension to basketball.

2. In 1926, the Globetrotters (begin) as a serious team.

3. They (play) some of their first games in the Savoy Ballroom in Chicago.

4. When the dance hall (fall) on hard times, the team (go) on the road.

5. Since that time the Globetrotters have never (leave) the touring circuit.

6. Abe Saperstein, who (form) the first team, always (choose) the best players he could find.

7. As a result, his team eventually (get) so good that no one (want) to play them.

8. That's when Saperstein (make) an important decision.

9. He (break) from tradition and (add) comedy routines.

10. Ever since, the Globetrotters have (be) as famous for their humor as for their basketball skills.

Verb Tense

Knowing the four principal parts of a verb, you can easily form the six tenses: the present, past, future, present perfect, past perfect, and future perfect.

The time expressed by a verb is called the tense of a verb.

In the following examples, the six tenses of *drive* are used to express action at different times.

PRESENT	Bart **drives** Tad to school.
PAST	Bart **drove** Tad to school yesterday.
FUTURE	Bart **will drive** Tad to school tomorrow.
PRESENT PERFECT	Bart **has driven** Tad to school all month.
PAST PERFECT	Bart **had** never **driven** Tad to school before February.
FUTURE PERFECT	By May, Bart **will have driven** Tad to school for four months.

Uses of the Tenses

The six basic tenses—three simple tenses and three perfect tenses—and their various forms have particular uses. Clearly communicating your ideas will sometimes depend upon knowing the distinctions among these tenses. As you review the various uses, remember that all of the tenses are formed from the four principal parts of a verb and the helping verbs *have, has, had, will,* and *shall.*

Present tense is the first of the three simple tenses. It is used mainly to express (1) an action that is going on now, (2) an action that happens regularly, or (3) an action that is usually constant or the same. To form the present tense, use the present form (the first principal part of the verb) or add *–s* or *–es* to the present form.

PRESENT TENSE **Look** at this scuba suit. (current action)

I **dig** for treasure each weekend.

(regular action)

Geology class **interests** me.

(constant action)

Occasionally you will also use the present tense in two other ways. Use the **historical present tense** when you want to relate a past action as if it were happening in the present. Also, when you write about literature, you can use the present tense.

HISTORY Christopher Columbus **encourages** his sailors daily.

LITERATURE In *Beowulf*, the poet **tells** of Grendel's underwater lair.

Past tense is used to express an action that already took place or was completed in the past. To form the past tense of a regular verb, add *–ed* or *–d* to the present form. To form the past of an irregular verb, check a dictionary for the past form or look for it on pages L183–L190.

PAST TENSE I **organized** the artifacts last week.
I **wrote** about my findings.

Future tense is used to express an action that will take place in the future. To form the future tense, use the helping verb *shall* or *will* with the present form. In formal English, *shall* is used with *I* and *we*, and *will* is used with *you, he, she, it,* or *they*. In informal speech, however, *shall* and *will* are used interchangeably with *I* and *we*—except *shall* is still always used with *I* and *we* for questions.

FUTURE TENSE I **shall organize** the artifacts tomorrow.
Leonore **will write** about the shipwreck.

You can learn more about shall *and* will *on page L378.*

Another way to express a future action is to use a present-tense verb with an adverb or group of words that indicate a future time.

FUTURE ACTION   Leonore **presents** her report to the committee tomorrow.

Present perfect tense is the first of three perfect tenses. It has two uses: (1) to express an action that was completed at some indefinite time in the past and (2) to express an action that started in the past and is still going on. To form the present perfect tense, add *has* or *have* to the past participle.

PRESENT PERFECT TENSE   I **have organized** several boxes of artifacts.

(action completed over an indefinite time)

She **has written** the reports for more than five years.

(action that is still going on)

Past perfect tense expresses an action that took place before some other action. To form the past perfect tense, add *had* to the past participle.

PAST PERFECT TENSE   I **had organized** the artifacts before I read the instructions.

Leonore **had written** the report by the time I arrived.

Future perfect tense expresses an action that will take place before another future action or time. To form the future perfect tense, add *shall have* or *will have* to the past participle.

FUTURE PERFECT TENSE   I **shall have organized** fifty artifacts by tonight.

By next semester, Leonore **will have written** six reports.

Verb Conjugation

A **conjugation** lists all the singular and plural forms of a verb in its various tenses. A conjugation of the irregular verb *eat* follows.

CONJUGATION OF *EAT*

FOUR PRINCIPAL PARTS: eat, eating, ate, eaten

SIMPLE TENSES

Present

SINGULAR	PLURAL
I eat	we eat
you eat	you eat
he, she, it eats	they eat

Past

SINGULAR	PLURAL
I ate	we ate
you ate	you ate
he, she, it ate	they ate

Future

SINGULAR	PLURAL
I shall/will eat	we shall/will eat
you will eat	you will eat
he, she, it will eat	they will eat

PERFECT TENSES

Present Perfect

SINGULAR	PLURAL
I have eaten	we have eaten
you have eaten	you have eaten
he, she, it has eaten	they have eaten

Past Perfect

SINGULAR	PLURAL
I had eaten	we had eaten
you had eaten	you had eaten
he, she, it had eaten	they had eaten

Future Perfect

SINGULAR	PLURAL
I shall/will have eaten	we shall/will have eaten
you will have eaten	you will have eaten
he, she, it will have eaten	they will have eaten

The present participle is used to conjugate only the progressive forms of a verb. You can learn more about the progressive forms of verbs on pages L212–L213.

Since the principal parts of the verb *be* are highly irregular, the conjugation of that verb is very different from other irregular verbs.

CONJUGATION OF *BE*

FOUR PRINCIPAL PARTS: am, being, was, been

SIMPLE TENSES

Present

SINGULAR	PLURAL
I am	we are
you are	you are
he, she, it is	they are

Past

SINGULAR	PLURAL
I was	we were
you were	you were
he, she, it was	they were

Future

SINGULAR	PLURAL
I shall/will be	we shall/will be
you will be	you will be
he, she, it will be	they will be

PERFECT TENSES

Present Perfect

SINGULAR	PLURAL
I have been	we have been
you have been	you have been
he, she, it has been	they have been

Past Perfect	
SINGULAR	**PLURAL**
I had been	we had been
you had been	you had been
he, she, it had been	they had been

Future Perfect	
SINGULAR	**PLURAL**
I shall/will have been	we shall/will have been
you will have been	you will have been
he, she, it will have been	they will have been

CONNECT TO SPEAKING AND WRITING

While most people develop an "ear" for proper verb conjugation, people in some careers use their knowledge of verb conjugation on a daily basis. These careers include language teacher, spokesperson, linguist, journalist, speech writer, translator, editor, copy editor, fiction writer, and proofreader. You can probably think of other careers as well.

PRACTICE YOUR SKILLS

● Check Your Understanding

Identifying Verb Tenses

Science Topic **Write the tense of each underlined verb.**

1. An underwater archaeologist <u>studies</u> shipwrecks and artifacts from watery graves.

2. Archaeologists <u>have found</u> underwater treasures such as jewels, precious metals, and even medical instruments.

3. Radioactive material in the Garigiano River <u>made</u> underwater searches there dangerous.

4. Many students of archaeology <u>will have completed</u> an archaeological dig by graduation.

5. Students <u>will learn</u> about certain underwater worms.

6. These worms <u>eat</u> the wooden parts of a shipwreck.

7. Bodies of water with less salt <u>have provided</u> wooden artifacts in the best condition.

8. Riverbeds and lake bottoms in Europe <u>hold</u> much of the world's riches.

9. After World War II, divers <u>found</u> ammunition beneath old battle sites.

10. The United States government <u>had passed</u> a law about archaeological findings.

11. Underwater archaeologists cannot <u>steal</u> or <u>destroy</u> their discoveries.

12. Officials <u>will monitor</u> the dive teams and their projects.

13. Many fields of science <u>incorporate</u> underwater archaeology.

14. Biologists, geologists, and chemists <u>have studied</u> underwater excavations.

15. Students everywhere <u>will have learned</u> valuable information about past civilizations from these digs.

● Check Your Understanding
Choosing the Correct Tense

General Interest **Write the correct form of the verb in parentheses. Beside it, identify its tense using the following abbreviations:**

present = *pres.*	present perfect = *pres. p.*
past = *past*	past perfect = *past p.*
future = *fut.*	future perfect = *fut. p.*

16. In a few years, I (shall train/have trained) as a forensic pathologist in the state medical examiner's office.

17. By then I (will have achieved/achieved) the same career goals as my role model, Aunt Maya.

18. In college Maya (studies/studied) forensic anthropology.

19. This science (applied/applies) physical anthropology to the legal process.

20. She (has become/became) an expert in her field over the past five years.

21. A forensic pathologist (helped/helps) solve murders.

22. Now Maya (took/has taken) a job as forensic pathologist.

23. I often (ask/had asked) her questions about her job.

24. She once (determines/determined) the age and gender of a victim by studying the bones.

25. I (have asked/ask) Maya for a letter of recommendation for my college application.

● **Connect to the Writing Process:** Drafting
Writing Answers to Questions

Write an answer to each question. Then underline the verb you used and identify its tense.

26. Did Mr. Lewis finish college last year?

27. Will you choose a career in education?

28. Why did Bettina attend the study-skills workshop?

29. Will this topic work for a college admissions essay?

30. Have you done your student teaching yet?

31. Where will you take the teacher-certification test?

32. Which friend will be your college roommate?

33. Did I pass the English test?

34. Will you be my lab partner?

35. When had you written that history report?

Communicate Your Ideas

APPLY TO WRITING

Thank-You Note: *Verb Tenses*

Write a thank-you note to a teacher or coach who has made an impact on you. If the person taught you in a previous year, write in past tense. If she or he currently teaches you, write in present tense. Include a description of a time in the past when the teacher was especially helpful. Also include a description of how the knowledge you gained will help you in the future. After you complete your note, check that you used the correct verb tenses.

QuickCheck — Mixed Practice

Social Studies — **Write each verb and label its tense using the following abbreviations:**

present = *pres.* present perfect = *pres. p.*
past = *past* past perfect = *past p.*
future = *fut.* future perfect = *fut. p.*

1. After this week I will have learned about several cultural holidays.

2. I look forward to next May.

3. I had heard about Cinco de Mayo before this week.

4. Some friends excitedly described this Mexican holiday.

5. Now I have learned more information about the Cinco de Mayo celebration.

6. Spanish speakers will translate the name as Fifth of May.

7. On this date in 1862, a Mexican army defeated a French army at the Battle of Puebla.

8. The French eventually occupied Mexico after all.

9. Nevertheless, this battle has become a symbol of Mexican unity and pride.

10. By the early 1800s, Mexico had faced another enemy.

11. Mexico won its independence from Spain in 1810.

12. This holiday is *Diez y Seis de Septiembre* (Sixteenth of September).

13. Mexican-American communities throughout the United States have celebrated both of these holidays for many years.

14. The festivities include parades, *mariachi* music, dancing, and feasting.

15. By year's end, my friends and I shall have enjoyed all of these activities.

Problems Using Tenses

Knowing the tenses of verbs and their uses will eliminate most of the verb errors you may have been making. There are, however, a few special problems you should keep in mind when you edit your writing.

The tense of the verbs you use depends on the meaning you want to express.

Past Tenses

If you want to express two past events that happened at the same time, use the past tense for both. Sometimes, however, you will want to tell about an action that happened before another action in the past. In such a situation, use the past perfect to express the action that happened first.

Past/Past	⌐ past ⌐ ⌐ past ⌐ When the author **arrived**, we **cheered**. (Both events happened at the same time.)
Past/ Past Perfect	⌐past⌐ past perfect I **wrote** the play after I **had gone** to Broadway. (I went to Broadway before I wrote the play.)

CONNECT TO SPEAKING AND WRITING

A common error in speaking is to use the words *would have* in a clause starting with *if* when that clause expresses the earlier of two past actions. You should instead use the past perfect tense to express the earlier action.

Incorrect	If John **would have studied**, he might have passed the literature test.
Correct	If John **had studied**, he might have passed the literature test. (The past perfect shows that studying would have come before passing the test.)

Present and Past Tenses

To express an exact meaning, occasionally you will have to use a combination of present and past tense verbs.

PRESENT/PAST	*present* *past* Kelly **knows** that I **borrowed** her book yesterday. (*Knows* is in the present tense because it describes action that is happening now, but *borrowed* is in the past tense because it happened at a definite time in the past.)
PAST/PRESENT PERFECT	*past* Ever since I **discovered** *Wuthering Heights*, *present perfect* I **have read** that book every night. (*Discovered* is in the past tense because it occurred at a definite time in the past, but *have read* is in the present perfect because it started in the past and is still going on.)

PRACTICE YOUR SKILLS

● Check Your Understanding
Identifying Combinations of Tenses

Literature Topic
Write the tense of each underlined verb. Be prepared to explain why the tense is correct.

present = *pres.*	present perfect = *pres. p.*
past = *past*	past perfect = *past p.*
future = *fut.*	future perfect = *fut. p.*

1. I went to class and I received a copy of *Canterbury Tales.*

2. I smiled because I had heard of the tales before.

3. I hope we read "The Pardoner's Tale."

4. My classmates discovered that Geoffrey Chaucer had written the tales in verse form.

5. Chaucer began *Canterbury Tales* after he had penned *Troilus and Criseide.*

Past Participles

Like verbs, participles have present and past tenses to express specific time.

PARTICIPLES OF *EAT*	
PRESENT PARTICIPLE	eating
PAST PARTICIPLE	eaten

Use *having* with a past participle in a participial phrase to show that one action was completed before another one.

INCORRECT **Applying** for the job, she waited for the manager's phone call.
(The use of *applying*, the present participle, implies illogically that she was still applying while she waited for the phone call.)

CORRECT **Having applied** for the job, she waited for the manager's phone call.
(The use of *having* with the past participle *applied* shows that she applied for the job *before* she waited for the phone call.)

You can learn more about participial phrases on pages L108–L111.

Present and Perfect Infinitives

Like participles, infinitives also have different forms.

INFINITIVES OF *EAT*	
PRESENT INFINITIVE	to eat
PERFECT INFINITIVE	to have eaten

To express an action that takes place *after* another action, use the present infinitive, but to express an action that takes place *before* another action, use the perfect infinitive.

PRESENT INFINITIVE	For a year I waited **to apply** for a job on the school newspaper.	
	(The applying came *after* the waiting.)	
PERFECT INFINITIVE	I feel very happy **to have applied** for a job in journalism.	
	(The applying came *before* the feeling of happiness.)	

You can learn more about infinitives on pages L115–L119.

PRACTICE YOUR SKILLS

● Check Your Understanding
Identifying Correct Tenses of Participles and Infinitives

Art Topic **If the tense of the underlined participle or infinitive is incorrect, write *I*. If the sentence is correct, write *C*.**

1. I feel happy to view Leonardo Da Vinci's *Mona Lisa.*
2. He feels confident to write to the Duke of Milan.
3. Having explained his credentials as designer, inventor, and artist, he was hired.
4. For months he strove to have honored the Duke's father with the consignment of a great sculpture.
5. Having drawn the sculpture, Da Vinci sought materials.
6. Da Vinci is pleased to design a colossal horse.
7. Creating the design, he named it *Il Cavallo,* meaning "The Horse" in Italian.
8. Designing the statue, Da Vinci soon built a clay model.
9. Having attacked Milan, French forces threatened the safety of everyone.
10. French archers are jubilant to have destroyed the clay model with arrows.

11. Sacrificing the bronze for the war, the dream ended.

12. The rest of his life, da Vinci waited rebuilding it.

13. He feels sad to have missed his opportunity.

14. Having read about *Il Cavallo*, Charles Dent pursued Da Vinci's dream.

15. Having founded an organization, he raised funds.

16. The organization feels confident to hire the artist, Nina Akamu.

17. Having completed the design, Akamu cast the statue.

18. Having required 15 tons of bronze, it stood 24 feet tall.

19. The people of Milan are happy to have received *Il Cavallo*.

20. Shipping the horse 500 years late, Da Vinci's dream and Charles Dent's dream came true.

● Connect to the Writing Process: Editing
Correcting the Tenses of Participles and Infinitives

> **21.–30. Rewrite the incorrect sentences in the preceding exercise, correcting the tenses of the participles and infinitives.**

● Connect to the Writing Process: Editing
Correcting Tenses

Each sentence in the paragraphs contains an improper shift in tense. Write each sentence, using the correct tense. (You will correct tenses 9 times in all.)

Yesterday I went to an art exhibit, and I have enjoyed it very much. Having heard of the Art Guys, I want to see some of their work. I have never seen so many unusual sculptures and displays before, and I will want to tell you about one of them.

The artists had designed one room to be entertaining people. When I walked into the room, I hear jets flying overhead. As I looked up, I am noticing that they had hung televisions pointing straight down from the ceiling. Each television was playing a video of jets that had been flying in the sky.

I am glad to go to the exhibit. I intended to return soon.

Communicate Your Ideas

APPLY TO WRITING
Description: *Verb Tenses*

The Art Guys. *Phantom Neighborhood,* 1990.
Concrete steps, varying dimensions.

You are in Buffalo Bayou Park in Houston, Texas, and you see the mysterious steps shown in this photo. A passing tourist asks you why they are there. Write an explanation for this tourist. Describe the past, present, and future purpose of the steps. Try to incorporate all the verb tenses you have been studying. Then edit your work for improper shifts in tense.

Progressive and Emphatic Verb Forms

In addition to the six basic tenses, every verb has six progressive forms and an emphatic form for the present and past tenses.

Progressive Forms

The **progressive forms** are used to express continuing or ongoing action. To write the progressive forms, add a present or perfect tense of the verb *be* to the present participle. Notice in the following examples that all of the progressive forms end in *–ing*.

PRESENT PROGRESSIVE	I am eating.
PAST PROGRESSIVE	I was eating.
FUTURE PROGRESSIVE	I will (shall) be eating.
PRESENT PERFECT PROGRESSIVE	I have been eating.
PAST PERFECT PROGRESSIVE	I had been eating.
FUTURE PERFECT PROGRESSIVE	I will (shall) have been eating.

The **present progressive** form shows an ongoing action that is taking place now.

I **am playing** volleyball now.

Occasionally the present progressive can also show action in the future when the sentence contains an adverb or a phrase that indicates the future—such as *tomorrow* or *next month*.

I **am playing** volleyball after school tomorrow.

The **past progressive** form shows an ongoing action that took place in the past.

I **was playing** volleyball when the rain began.

The **future progressive** form shows an ongoing action that will take place in the future.

I **will be playing** volleyball when you have your party.

The **present perfect progressive** form shows an ongoing action that is continuing in the present.

> I **have been playing** volleyball for the past two and a half years.

The **past perfect progressive** form shows an ongoing action in the past that was interrupted by another past action.

> I **had been playing** volleyball when Coach Williams asked me to play basketball instead.

The **future perfect progressive** form shows a future ongoing action that will have taken place by a stated future time.

> By next summer I **will have been playing** volleyball for over three years.

Emphatic Forms

The **emphatic forms** of the present and past tenses of verbs are mainly used to show emphasis or force. To write the present emphatic, add *do* or *does* to the present tense of a verb. To write the past emphatic, add *did* to the present tense.

> PRESENT   I **eat** lunch every day at twelve o'clock.
>
> PRESENT EMPHATIC   I **do eat** lunch every day at twelve o'clock.
>
> PAST   I **ate** lunch yesterday.
>
> PAST EMPHATIC   I **did eat** lunch yesterday.

The emphatic forms are also used in some questions and negative statements.

> QUESTIONS   **Do** you **eat** lunch every day?
> NEGATIVE STATEMENT I **did** not **eat** lunch Monday.

CONNECT TO WRITER'S CRAFT

Do you remember *Green Eggs and Ham* by Dr. Seuss? You probably never realized that one of the things that makes the story fun to listen to is the emphatic verb forms.

> **Do** you **like** green eggs and ham?
> I **do** not **like** them, Sam-I-am. I **do** not **like** green eggs and ham.
>
> I **do** not **like** them in a house. I **do** not **like** them with a mouse. I **do** not **like** them here or there. I **do** not **like** them anywhere.
>
> —*Dr. Seuss*, Green Eggs and Ham

PRACTICE YOUR SKILLS

● Check Your Understanding
Identifying Progressive and Emphatic Forms

Contemporary Life   **Write the progressive or emphatic form in each sentence. Beside it write *P* for *progressive* or *E* for *emphatic*.**

1. Did you go to the swim meet?

2. I will be buying season tickets tomorrow.

3. I have been saving my money all month.

4. Coach Chang didn't know about the new uniforms.

5. He will have been looking for the old uniforms for two hours.

6. He does look frantic.

7. I am going to the football game.

8. I shall be sitting at the fifty yard line.

9. I had been running track until I sprained my ankle.

10. I didn't have a sports bandage for my ankle.

11. Stephanie is jogging tomorrow afternoon.

12. She does love that activity.

13. She will have been jogging for one hour by dark.

14. Jon has been timing her laps.

15. Marcos will be lifting weights two days a week.

16. I did lift weights this morning.

17. Sarah is meeting Cleo at the gym this afternoon.

18. Do you like to lift weights?

19. Sarah was stretching when the music started.

20. By July Pablo will have been biking for one year.

21. He does ride five miles every day.

22. Conrad will be training with Pablo next month.

23. They have been planning a bike tour.

24. Next summer they will have graduated from college.

25. They will be touring the United States afterward.

● Connect to the Writing Process: Drafting
Using Emphatic Verbs

26.–30. Brainstorm for five ideas that you emphatically agree or disagree with. Write an emphatic statement expressing each of these ideas. Underline the emphatic form of the verb in each statement.

Communicate Your Ideas

APPLY TO WRITING

Opinion Essay: *Progressive and Emphatic Forms*

Choose one of the emphatic statements you wrote in the above exercise. Write an opinion piece to share with your classmates. State your opinion on the topic, and describe an event that helped you develop this opinion. Use progressive and emphatic verb forms to express your ideas. Be prepared to identify the two verb forms.

QuickCheck Mixed Practice

General Interest **Write the tense of each underlined verb.**

1. In health class we <u>are learning</u> about vegetarian diets.
2. I have always <u>wanted</u> to learn about this topic.
3. In college Ms. Summers <u>had taken</u> a nutrition class.
4. Afterward she <u>designed</u> a lesson plan on vegetarian diets.
5. The class <u>was taking</u> careful notes.
6. We <u>will be planning</u> a vegetarian banquet for our class on Friday.
7. *Vegans*, or strict vegetarians, <u>do</u> not <u>consume</u> meat or animal products of any kind.
8. By the end of the school year, Ms. Summers <u>will have been following</u> a vegan diet for ten years.
9. I <u>am</u> not <u>feeling</u> comfortable with the vegan diet.
10. *Lactovegetarians* always <u>have eaten</u> milk, cheese, and other dairy products.
11. Lactovegetarians <u>don't eat</u> meats, poultry, or eggs.
12. My friend Kandie <u>resolved</u> to be a lactovegetarian.
13. By the end of class, she <u>had changed</u> her mind.
14. An *ovolactovegetarian* <u>will eat</u> eggs and dairy products.
15. An ovolactovegetarian <u>does</u> not <u>eat</u> meats or poultry.
16. Having learned about vegetarian diets, I <u>plan</u> to be a part-time vegetarian.
17. I <u>have been analyzing</u> my diet.
18. I felt I <u>had been consuming</u> too much red meat.
19. I <u>will design</u> my meals around fruits and vegetables.
20. In addition to these fruits and vegetables, I <u>am planning</u> to eat meat once or twice a week.

Active and Passive Voice

All verbs have tense, but some action verbs also have voice. Transitive verbs can be in the active voice or the passive voice.

> The **active voice** indicates that the subject is performing the action.

> The **passive voice** indicates that the action of the verb is being performed upon the subject.

Notice in the following examples that the verb in the active voice has a direct object, making it a transitive verb. However, the verb in the passive voice does not have a direct object.

	d.o.
ACTIVE VOICE	Horace **found** a silver dollar.
PASSIVE VOICE	A silver dollar **was found** by Horace.
	(no direct object)

	d.o.
ACTIVE VOICE	Marie **sent** the money by courier.
PASSIVE VOICE	The money **was sent** by courier.
	(no direct object)

You can learn about transitive verbs on pages L16–L17.

Changing a verb from the active voice to the passive voice, you automatically turn the direct object into the subject. In the previous example, *money* was the direct object when the verb was active, but it became the subject when the verb became passive. Notice also that verbs in the passive voice consist of some form of the verb *be* plus a past participle—such as *was found* and *was sent*.

In addition to a direct object, some transitive verbs can also have an indirect object. When such a verb and its objects are changed to the passive voice, either of the two objects can become the subject of the sentence. The other object remains an object and is called a **retained object.**

	i.o.	d.o.

ACTIVE VOICE   The judges gave each **winner** fifty **dollars**.

r.o.

PASSIVE VOICE   Each winner was given fifty **dollars** by
the judges.

r.o.

PASSIVE VOICE   Fifty dollars was given each **winner** by
the judges.

PRACTICE YOUR SKILLS

● Check Your Understanding
Identifying Active and Passive Voice

General Interest **Write the verb in each sentence. Then label each one *A*
for *active* or *P* for *passive*.**

1. The early American colonists used currencies from
several different countries.

2. America once issued a five-cent bill.

3. The first Continental coin was designed by Benjamin
Franklin.

4. The dies for that coin were engraved by Abel Buell.

5. Tobacco was used as money in Virginia and Maryland.

6. Martha Washington may have donated several of her
silver forks and spoons for the minting of a series
of half dimes.

7. The buffalo nickel was designed by James Earle Fraser,
a famous sculptor.

8. Fraser's model for the nickel had been borrowed from
the Bronx Zoo.

9. Nickels contain mostly copper.

10. The average United States dollar bill has a life span
of less than one year.

⦿ Use of Voice in Writing

Because verbs in the active voice are more forceful and have greater impact than verbs in the passive voice, you should use the active voice as much as possible. The passive voice, however, should be used in the following situations: (1) when the doer of the action is unknown or unimportant and (2) when you want to emphasize the receiver of the action or to emphasize the results.

> The extra tickets **were sold** at a profit.
>
> (doer unknown or unimportant)
>
> The crumbling currency **was made** during the Civil War.
>
> (emphasis on the results)

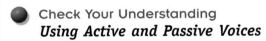

CONNECT TO SPEAKING AND WRITING

Newspaper headlines must convey in a few words what the article's main focus is. The writers use active or passive voice, depending on what they want to highlight. When you read the active-voice headline **"Workers Strike at Factory,"** you know that the article will focus on the workers. However, when you read the passive-voice headline **"Factory Is Closed by Strike,"** you know the article will focus on the factory.

PRACTICE YOUR SKILLS

⦿ Check Your Understanding
Using Active and Passive Voices

Literature Topic | **Write the verb in each sentence. Then label each one A for *active* or P for *passive*.**

1. An interesting novel was given to my class by our literature teacher.

2. *Robinson Crusoe* was written by Daniel Defoe.

3. In the story, Robinson Crusoe is shipwrecked on an island.

4. Later, the character Friday befriends Crusoe.

5. This novel was published in 1719.

6. It is judged by scholars to be one of the first English novels ever written.

7. Before this time period, stories were written in verse form by authors.

8. Defoe was born in London in 1660.

9. His father named him Daniel Foe.

10. Around 1695, the name was changed to Defoe by Daniel.

● Connect to the Writing Process: Revising
Using Active and Passive Voice

11.–18. Rewrite the passive-voice sentences in the preceding exercise, changing the passive voice to the active voice if appropriate. If a sentence is better in the passive voice, write C.

● Connect to the Writing Process: Drafting
Using Active and Passive Voice in Sentences

Write sentences that follow the directions below.

19. In an active-voice statement, name a book you have read.

20. Write a passive-voice statement that tells the name of the author.

21. Write a passive-voice statement that tells when the book was published.

22. Use an active-voice statement to describe the main character.

23. Write a passive-voice statement that describes the setting.

24. Write an active-voice statement that states the conflict.

25. Identify the solution in a passive-voice statement.

26. Write an active-voice statement that tells your opinion of the book.

APPLY TO WRITING

Writer's Craft: *Analyzing the Use of Voice*

In *Robinson Crusoe*, Defoe shows Crusoe fighting for his life in the water after the shipwreck. Read the following passage, and then follow the instructions.

> The wave that came upon me again, buried me at once 20 or 30 foot deep in its own body; and I could feel my self carried with a mighty force and swiftness towards the shore a very great way; but I held my breath, and assisted my self to swim still forward with all my might. I was ready to burst with holding my breath, when, as I felt my self rising up, so to my immediate relief, I found my head and hands shoot out above the surface of the water; and tho' it was not two seconds of time that I could keep my self so, yet it relieved me greatly, gave me breath and new courage. I was covered again with water a good while, but not so long but I held it out;...
>
> —*Daniel Defoe,* Robinson Crusoe

- Write each verb and label it *active, passive,* or *linking.*
- Now look at the verbs in active voice. What is the effect of expressing these actions in active voice instead of passive voice?
- What is performing the action of the verb in passive voice?
- What is the effect on the reader of using passive voice to express the action?

Mood

The mood of a verb is the way in which the verb expresses an idea. In English there are three moods: indicative, imperative, and subjunctive.

The **indicative mood** is used to state a fact or to ask a question.

The **imperative mood** is used to give a command or to make a request.

Since the indicative mood is used to state facts or ask questions, it is used most often in both writing and speaking.

INDICATIVE	A national park **makes** a good vacation spot. What **makes** camping so much fun?
IMPERATIVE	**Look** at this brochure on Yellowstone National Park. **Consider** a trip to Mesa Verde.

The **subjunctive mood** is used to express (1) a condition contrary to fact, which begins with words such as *if, as if*, or *as though*, (2) a wish, and (3) a command or a request after the word *that*.

CONTRARY TO FACT	If I **were** you, I'd pack a water bottle. (I am not you.) If Karla **were** here, she could go with us. (She is not here.)
A WISH	I wish I **were** a better skier. I wish that **were** our flight.
COMMAND/ REQUEST BEGINNING WITH *THAT*	I demand *that* we **be** given a better camp site. (If not in the subjunctive mood, the subject and verb would be *we are given.)*

> She ordered *that* nobody **hike** without proper boots.
>
> (If not in the subjunctive mood, the subject and verb would be *nobody hikes.*)

In English, the subjunctive verb forms differ from the indicative forms in only two situations.

The **present subjunctive** uses the base form of the verb for all persons and numbers, including the third-person singular, but indicative verbs use the *–s* form.

INDICATIVE	My camp fire **is** small.
SUBJUNCTIVE	The park ranger suggested that all fires **be** small.

In the present subjunctive, the verb *to be* is always *be.*

> He recommended that all canoe trips **be** in the afternoon.

The **past subjunctive** form of the verb *to be* is *were* for all persons and numbers.

> If my grandfather **were** here, he would enjoy the horseback riding.

Although the subjunctive mood is not used much today, it still shows up in a number of idiomatic expressions such as the following.

SUBJUNCTIVE EXPRESSIONS	**Be** that as it may, . . .
	Far **be** it from me to . . .

CONNECT TO SPEAKING AND WRITING

The subjunctive voice is a persuasive tool. It can be used to soften a suggestion or strengthen a command.

I wish I were going to the park.

I demand that she take me to the park.

PRACTICE YOUR SKILLS

● Check Your Understanding
Using the Subjunctive Mood

General
Interest **Write the correct form of the verb in parentheses.**

1. I wish I (was, were) brave enough to ski the steep slopes.

2. Tom talks as if he (was, were) the hike leader.

3. I wish Earl (was, were) here.

4. If I (was, were) you, I'd wear a life jacket.

5. I suggest that you (be, are) at the dock in an hour.

6. Lisa wished she (was, were) at the beach right now.

7. Marnie requested that he (be, is) in the boat.

8. After ten minutes in the sun, my skin felt as though it (was, were) already burned.

9. Cheryl asked that we (be, are) ready at noon.

10. If Todd (was, were) here, he would want to surf.

● Connect to the Writing Process: Revising
Using Subjunctive and Indicative Mood in Sentences

Write each sentence using either the subjunctive or the indicative mood of the verb form. Then write *S* for *subjunctive* or *I* for *indicative*.

11. Yosemite National Park (be) a national treasure.

12. If I (be) you, I'd hike up Bridalveil Falls.

13. I wish I (be) a mountain climber.

14. I demand that we (allow) to climb El Capitan.

15. If I (be) you, I would not climb El Capitan.

16. That mountain (be) 7,569 feet high.

17. I wish I (rappel) up its flat face.

18. The ranger requested that we all (be) in before dark.

19. Far (be) it from me to disagree with you.

20. The Merced River (flow) through Yosemite Valley.

21. The terrain (offer) meadows and steep mountains.

22. Yosemite Falls (drop) 1,430 feet into the valley.

23. I expect that we (give) a beautiful campsite.

24. Mirror Lake (reflect) the beautiful mountains.

25. Chipmunks (scamper) along the mountain trails.

Connect to the Writing Process: Drafting
Writing Sentences

Write sentences that follow the directions below.

26. Include an indicative-mood verb that makes a statement.

27. Include an indicative-mood verb that asks a question.

28. Include a verb in the imperative mood.

29. Include a subjunctive-mood verb that is used to express an idea contrary to fact.

30. Include a subjunctive-mood verb that is used to express a wish.

31. Include a subjunctive-mood verb that is used to make a request.

Communicate Your Ideas

APPLY TO WRITING

Campaign Speech: *Voice and Mood*

You have been nominated to run for Student Advisor to the Principal. Write a campaign speech describing what you would do for your fellow students if you were elected. What kinds of issues would you raise with the principal if you were to talk with him or her? What do you wish were different at your school? Use the subjunctive mood to express these thoughts.

Using the Correct Verb Form

Write the past or past participle of each verb in parentheses.

1. We (speak) to her before she (drive) to New York.

2. I should have (know) his name because we both (grow) up in Park Ridge.

3. She (write) to the manufacturer after the boat had (sink) for the second time.

4. Grandmother (make) two blueberry pies and (take) them to the fair.

5. I (begin) thinking about entering the race because I have (ride) bicycles for ten years.

6. He has (begin) a letter that he should have (write) months ago.

7. Yesterday I (rise) about 6:00 A.M. and (run) around the reservoir.

8. Since I have (hear) his opinion many times, I have (give) the matter a great deal of thought.

9. Paolo has just (catch) the baseball and has (throw) it to first.

10. After I (do) most of my homework, I (go) for a walk.

Correcting Verb Tenses

Write the correct form of any incorrect verb in each sentence.

1. Ever since 1787, the bald eagle was America's national bird.

2. If that dog was mine, I would take better care of him.

3. Mike just realized that he left his books in Leroy's car.

4. Since the senator has been reelected, Pam is happy to work on her campaign.

5. Because Karen sleep late, she missed the bus again.

6. Since I was young, I was afraid of bees.
7. As the buzzers sounded, the quarterback has thrown a pass into the end zone.
8. I wish I was already graduated from high school.
9. Raymond noticed that he saw the same red car pass by our house twice.
10. Dad knows I have worked hard yesterday.

Determining Active and Passive Voice

Write the verb in each sentence and label it *active* or *passive*. Then rewrite any sentence in the passive voice that should be in the active voice.

1. Because of the severe ice storm, the school was closed for the day.
2. An interesting experiment was performed by us in chemistry.
3. In 1863, Lincoln made Thanksgiving a national holiday.
4. Great interest in space exploration has been shown by the United States.
5. The SATs were taken by many seniors on Saturday.

Writing Sentences

Write five sentences that follow the directions below.

1. Write a sentence with a perfect participle and a verb in the future tense.
2. Write a sentence in the subjunctive mood.
3. Write an imperative sentence. Use one verb in the present tense along with an infinitive.
4. Write a sentence with one verb in the passive voice and another in the active voice.
5. Write a sentence using both the verb *rise* and the verb *sit* in the past tense.

Language and *Self-Expression*

Auguste Renoir was one of the leaders of the Impressionist school of painting. The Impressionists were interested in showing the play of light and shadow that often defined the subjects they painted. Since light changes so quickly, an Impressionist painting actually portrays a subject as it appears only at one particular moment.

The play of light and shadow affects lives as well. You may have heard these expressions—somewhat changeable depending on the subject—"She lights up my life" and "A shadow passed over my heart." Write a brief essay about the way that light and/or shadow (literally or figuratively) affects your life. Be sure to use verbs correctly as you write.

Prewriting Brainstorm moments of special happiness and deep sadness you have experienced. List them briefly.

Drafting Choose one example of happiness and one of sadness. Then write a thesis statement for your essay. Write your first paragraph about your moment of happiness. Concentrate on the feeling of light, or elation, that made the moment glow. Then write a paragraph on your moment of sadness. Focus on the darkness or heaviness cast by the shadow. End your essay by reflecting on the two experiences.

Revising Reread your draft. Do the sentences flow naturally from one to the next? Do they all relate to your two "light and shadow" experiences?

Editing Review your work, this time concentrating on grammar, mechanics, and especially usage. Be sure your verb tenses are correct. Check your spelling as well.

Publishing Make a clean copy of your essay. Publish your work by joining a classmate and taking turns reading to each other.

Another Look

A **regular verb** forms its past and past participle by adding –*ed* or –*d* to the present.

An **irregular verb** does not form its past and past participle by adding –*ed* or –*d* to the present.

Tense is the time expressed by a verb.

The three **simple tenses** are present, past, and future. *(pages L197–L199)*
The three **perfect tenses** are present perfect, past perfect, and future perfect. *(page L199)*

Voice
The **active voice** indicates that the subject is performing the action. *(page L217)*
The **passive voice** indicates that the action of the verb is being performed upon the subject. *(page L217)*

Mood
The **indicative mood** is used to state a fact or to ask a question. *(page L222)*
The **imperative mood** is used to give a command or to make a request. *(page L222)*
The **subjunctive mood** is used to express a condition contrary to fact that begins with words such as *if, as if,* or *as though;* a wish; and a command or a request after the word *that.* *(page L222)*

Other Information About the Use of Verbs
Using the problem verbs *lie, lay; sit, set;* and *rise, raise* *(pages L193–L196)*
Conjugating an irregular verb *(page L200)*
Conjugating the verb *be* *(page L201)*
Using present and past participles *(page L208)*
Using present and perfect infinitives *(pages L208–L209)*
Using progressive and emphatic verb forms *(pages L212–L216)*

Directions
Read the passage and choose the word or group of words that belongs in each underlined space. Write the letter of the correct answer.

EXAMPLE **1.** Colleges and universities __(1)__ people for many kinds of professional careers.

    1 **A** prepare

       B had prepared

       C will have been preparing

       D prepares

ANSWER **1** **A**

    Did you know that modern universities __(1)__ from schools that originated in Europe during the Middle Ages? Such schools __(2)__ their name from the Latin word *universitas,* meaning "a group of people assembled for a common purpose." In early English schools, colleges __(3)__ within universities to provide living quarters and dining rooms for various groups of students. Such students __(4)__ members of a college and a university at the same time. Today, however, both colleges and universities __(5)__ teaching institutions.

    My friend Paul __(6)__ to attend a small liberal-arts college. However, I __(7)__ a university with several colleges, or branches, each offering course work in a different discipline. Freshmen and sophomores must take certain basic courses before __(8)__ on a major field of interest. If it __(9)__ not for this regulation, students might choose majors that are not suited to them. __(10)__ for two years to select a major, for example, my sister Tawnee knew she really wanted to major in chemistry even though she had also been interested in physics and engineering.

1 **A** develop
   B will have developed
   C developed
   D develops

2 **A** took
   B has taken
   C taking
   D were taking

3 **A** form
   B have been formed
   C will be formed
   D were formed

4 **A** were becoming
   B have become
   C become
   D became

5 **A** were
   B are
   C will be
   D was

6 **A** choose
   B chosen
   C were chosen
   D chose

7 **A** have selected
   B will have selected
   C selecting
   D to select

8 **A** decide
   B decided
   C deciding
   D having been decided

9 **A** was
   B were
   C have been
   D is

10 **A** Waiting
   B To wait
   C Having waited
   D Waited

CHAPTER 6

Using Pronouns

Pretest

Directions
Read the passage and choose the pronoun that belongs in each underlined space. Write the letter of the correct answer.

EXAMPLE

1. Wilbur Wright once said, "Since we were children, Orville and __(1)__ have always done things together."

   1 A me
      B I
      C us
      D my

ANSWER   **1 B**

 __(1)__ are Wilbur and Orville Wright? As everyone knows, these men from Dayton, Ohio, became famous when __(2)__ invented __(3)__ most famous invention, the airplane. Before 1900, most people could not even imagine __(4)__ flying through the air like a bird! Of course, it took two extraordinary individuals to create such an inconceivable machine. Each of the brothers brought __(5)__ own unique talents and qualities to the collaboration. Wilbur, __(6)__ few knew well because of his quietness, was the visionary of the two. __(7)__ was the one __(8)__ first dreamed of flying. Orville, on the other hand, was more mechanically minded than __(9)__ . It was also Orville's enthusiasm that carried __(10)__ throughout the long years preceding their first flight at Kitty Hawk, North Carolina.

1	**A**	Who	**6**	**A**	whoever
	B	Whom		**B**	whomever
	C	Whose		**C**	who
	D	Whomever		**D**	whom
2	**A**	them	**7**	**A**	He
	B	they		**B**	Him
	C	theirs		**C**	His
	D	their		**D**	Their
3	**A**	them	**8**	**A**	who
	B	they		**B**	whom
	C	theirs		**C**	whose
	D	their		**D**	whoever
4	**A**	them	**9**	**A**	he
	B	they		**B**	him
	C	theirs		**C**	their
	D	their		**D**	them
5	**A**	his	**10**	**A**	they
	B	his or her		**B**	them
	C	their		**C**	their
	D	theirs		**D**	he

Glenna Goodacre. *Vietnam Women's Memorial*, 1993.
Bronze cast, height 92 inches. National Mall, Washington, D.C.

Describe Identify the figures in the sculpture. What is the central character doing? Are the figures depicted realistically or impressionistically?

Analyze What expression do you see on the face of the woman? What bond do you think is there between the soldier and the woman looking down at him? Give reasons for your answer.

Interpret Who do you think would come closer to the real spirit of the sculpture, a writer of fiction or a writer of nonfiction? Why?

Judge Would you rather read a newspaper article about the scene or study the sculpture? Why?

At the end of this chapter, you will use the sculpture as a visual aid for writing.

The Cases of Personal Pronouns

As a child you learned that the colors of traffic lights are signals to motorists and pedestrians. You also learned another set of signals. You learned, for example, that you should use the pronoun *he* in one situation, *him* in another situation and *his* in still another situation.

He, him, and *his* send out different signals because they indicate the case of a pronoun. A pronoun has a different form and a different function for each case. When you use a particular form of a pronoun, therefore, you are signaling to a reader or a listener how that pronoun is being used in a sentence. (Nouns change form only in the possessive case. For example, *girl* becomes *girl's* in the possessive case.)

Case is the form of a noun or a pronoun that indicates its use in a sentence.

English has three cases: the nominative case, the objective case, and the possessive case. Many pronouns change form for each of the cases. Notice, though, that *you* and *it* are the same in both the nominative and the objective cases.

NOMINATIVE CASE
(Used for subjects and predicate nominatives)
SINGULAR   I, you, he, she, it
PLURAL   we, you, they

OBJECTIVE CASE
(Used for direct objects, indirect objects, objects of prepositions, and objects of verbals)
SINGULAR   me, you, him, her, it
PLURAL   us, you, them

POSSESSIVE CASE
(Used to show ownership or possession)
SINGULAR   my, mine, your, yours, his, her, hers, its
PLURAL   our, ours, your, yours, their, theirs

The Nominative Case

I, you, he, she, it, we, and *they* are the personal pronouns in the nominative case.

The **nominative case** is used for subjects and predicate nominatives.

Pronouns as Subjects

A pronoun can be used as a subject of an independent clause or a dependent clause.

INDEPENDENT CLAUSE	**We** applied for jobs in the campus bookstore.
DEPENDENT CLAUSE	As soon as **he** had filled out the application, the boss hired him.

The case of a pronoun that is part of a compound subject is sometimes not as obvious as a single-subject pronoun. That is why it is important to double-check any pronoun in a compound subject to make sure that it is in the nominative case. To do this, say the nominative and the objective pronouns separately—to find out which one is correct.

Jason and (he, him) cashed the paychecks.
He cashed the paychecks.
Him cashed the paychecks.

The nominative case *he* is the correct form to use.

> Jason and **he** cashed the paychecks.

This method of checking for the correct case also works if both subjects are pronouns.

> He and (she, her) worked at the campus bookstore.
> **She** worked at the campus bookstore.
> **Her** worked at the campus bookstore.

The nominative case *she* is the correct form to use.

> He and **she** worked at the campus bookstore.

Pronouns as Predicate Nominatives

A predicate nominative follows a linking verb and identifies, renames, or explains the subject.

> That was **I** who won the scholarship.

The preceding example probably sounds extremely formal—or even incorrect—to you. However, while *That was me* or *It's me* is common usage in conversation, it should be avoided in written work.

> It was **she.**   That is **he.**   The winners are **they.**

To decide whether the pronoun in a compound predicate nominative is in the correct case, turn the sentence around to make the predicate nominative the subject. Then say the nominative and the objective pronouns separately to find out which one is correct.

> The finalists for the essay award are Ben and (she, her).
> Ben and (she, her) are the finalists for the essay award.
> **She** is a finalist.
> **Her** is a finalist.
> The finalists for the essay award are Ben and **she.**

Sometimes the wording of a sentence becomes awkward when pronouns or compound pronouns are used as predicate nominatives. You can avoid this awkwardness by turning the sentence around.

| Awkward | The financial aid officer is **she.** |
| Turned Around | **She** is the financial aid officer. |

| Awkward | The financial aid recipients are Di and **he.** |
| Turned Around | Di and **he** are the financial aid recipients. |

You can learn more about predicate nominatives on pages L77–L81. Also, you can find lists of common linking verbs on page L21.

Nominative Case Pronouns Followed by Appositives

An **appositive** is a noun or a pronoun that renames or identifies another noun or pronoun in the sentence. Occasionally when *we* is used as a subject or a predicate nominative, a noun or a pronoun functions as the appositive of *we*. The noun appositive that follows *we* never affects the case of *we*. The best way to check whether you have used the correct pronoun is to drop the appositive mentally from the sentence.

We *language specialists* thoroughly enjoy our jobs.
(We thoroughly enjoy our jobs.)

The newest college students on campus are **we** *freshmen*.
(The newest college students on campus are we.)

CONNECT TO SPEAKING AND WRITING

An appositive is an excellent tool for clarifying information for the reader or listener.

| Vague | We completed our applications. |
| More Specific | We students completed our applications. |

Nominative Case Pronouns as Appositives

An appositive is in the same case as the noun or pronoun to which it refers. Occasionally a pronoun itself will be part of an appositive to a subject or a predicate nominative. Then the pronoun should be in the nominative case.

> The exchange students, *Yuri* and ***he***, work in the language lab.

Yuri and *he* are appositives to the subject *students*. Since the subject is in the nominative case, an appositive to the subject is also in the nominative case.

PRACTICE YOUR SKILLS

  Check Your Understanding
Using Pronouns in the Nominative Case

Contemporary Life | **Write the correct form of the pronoun in parentheses.**

1. The students concerned about the cost of college are (we, us) seniors.
2. Several financial aid advisors, Victor and (they, them), spoke to us.
3. Todd and (him, he) described the best ideas.
4. Neither Ava nor (me, I) is worried about college fees.
5. Of all our classmates, (her, she) and (I, me) are the ones who immediately took the advisors' suggestions.
6. It was (me, I) who learned about college work-study.
7. It was (she, her) who got the application forms.
8. The recipients of grant money are Ava and (I, me).
9. Maddy and (he, him) will apply for athletic scholarships.
10. The champions of our track meet are (them, they).
11. It wasn't (me, I) who applied for an academic scholarship at the university.

12. Suzanne believes that both (she, her) and Jake will be awarded scholarships.

13. The valedictorian and salutatorian of our class are (them, they).

14. (We, Us) students from lower-income families applied for need-based financial aid.

15. Trisha said that (her, she) and Tyrone would apply for guaranteed student loans.

16. The twins, Angela and (she, her), have already applied for loans.

17. The persons responsible for paying back the loans are (them, they).

18. The students awarded scholarships by the English department are Miguel and (her, she).

19. The recipient of the journalism scholarship is either Jenny or (he, him).

20. The graduates ready for our freshman year in college are (we, us) financial aid applicants.

● Connect to the Writing Process: Editing
Using the Nominative Case

If an underlined pronoun is in the wrong case, write it correctly. If it is in the correct case, write C.

21. Mom said that Monica and <u>him</u> would get summer jobs.

22. The new burger chefs are Ben and <u>her</u>.

23. <u>We</u> workers are saving our money for college.

24. Last summer, Juan and <u>him</u> saved enough for tuition.

25. Gloria and <u>me</u> will live in the dorms to save money.

26. The people awarded the internships are Holly and <u>she</u>.

27. Their parents and <u>them</u> are visiting the campus soon.

28. The students who most appreciate their education are <u>us</u> workers.

29. Two friends, Amy and <u>him</u>, pay their own expenses.

30. The new lab assistants are <u>her</u> and <u>me</u>.

Writing Sentences

Write a sentence for each of the following groups of words. Use one group as a compound subject, one as a compound predicate nominative, and one as a compound appositive. Then label each one.

31. you and I   **32.** he and she   **33.** Julio and they

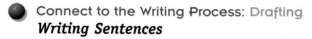
Communicate Your Ideas

APPLY TO WRITING

Plan of Action: *Nominative Case Pronouns*

　　　Look at the picture of the student working. She might be saving money to help pay for her college education.

　　　How do you plan to pay for your college expenses? Write a plan of action that you can share with other seniors. Include details such as where you want to work and how you will balance work and school, what forms of financial aid you will apply for, and what you will do to cut down on expenses. Remember to use nominative case pronouns correctly.

Contemporary Life **If an underlined pronoun is in the wrong case, write it correctly. If it is in the correct case, write C.**

1. <u>Me</u> and <u>him</u> went to the zoo last weekend.

2. The tour guides are <u>them</u>.

3. <u>Us</u> animal lovers never tire of observing the zoo's inhabitants.

4. The ticket-takers, Arnold and <u>she</u>, are in our high-school biology class.

5. <u>Them</u> and <u>us</u> sometimes help feed the lambs in the petting zoo.

6. It was <u>me</u> who noticed the new reptile exhibit.

7. The reptile caretakers, Lynn and <u>her</u>, told us about the heat lamps.

8. Lynn said, "The luckiest employees here are <u>we</u> snake handlers!"

9. Petra and <u>him</u> watched the poison arrow frogs.

10. This frog sweats poison when <u>he</u> senses danger.

11. <u>They</u>, the frogs, live in South America.

12. One of this frog's enemies is <u>us</u> humans.

13. My friend Jeremy and <u>him</u> enjoy visiting the lions.

14. Monique and <u>her</u>, two of my good friends, found us by the orangutans.

15. <u>We</u> students watched the orangutans eat fruit.

The Objective Case

Me, you, him, her, it, us, and *them* are the personal pronouns in the objective case.

The **objective case** is used for direct objects, indirect objects, objects of prepositions, and objects of verbals.

Pronouns as Direct and Indirect Objects

A pronoun that is used as a direct object will follow an action verb and answer the question *Whom?* A pronoun that is used as an indirect object will answer the question *To whom?* or *For whom?* after the direct object.

DIRECT OBJECTS
Dad will drive **us** to work.
The optician will assist **her** now.

INDIRECT OBJECTS

                                    i.o.   d.o.
The cashier gave **me** a receipt.

            i.o.   d.o.
Give **him** those eyeglass frames.

To check for the correct case of a compound direct object, say the nominative and the objective case pronouns separately.

Jason saw the Dyers and (they, them) at the optical store.
Jason saw **they** at the optical store.
Jason saw **them** at the optical store.

The objective case *them* is the correct form to use.

Jason saw the Dyers and **them** at the optical store.

Compound indirect objects can be checked in the same way.

           i.o.   i.o   d.o.
Fred gave Beth and (I, me) new sunglasses.
Fred gave **I** new sunglasses.
Fred gave **me** new sunglasses.

The objective case *me* is the correct form to use.

           i.o.   i.o   d.o.
Fred gave Beth and **me** new sunglasses.

You can learn more about direct objects and indirect objects on pages L72–L77.

Pronouns as Objects of Prepositions

A prepositional phrase begins with a preposition and ends with a noun or a pronoun called the **object of a preposition.** As the following examples show, a pronoun that is used as an object of a preposition is in the objective case.

> You can ride to work with **us.**
> (*With us* is the prepositional phrase.)
>
> Is this lab coat for **me?**
> (*For me* is the prepositional phrase.)
>
> The patient gave his insurance card to **you.**
> (*To you* is the prepositional phrase.)

You can check to see that a pronoun in a compound object of a preposition is in the objective case by saying the nominative and objective case pronouns separately.

> The ophthalmologist wrote prescriptions for David and (she, her).
>
> The ophthalmologist wrote prescriptions for **she.**
>
> The ophthalmologist wrote prescriptions for **her.**

The objective case *her* is the correct form to use.

> The ophthalmologist wrote prescriptions for David and **her.**

You might have noticed that sometimes people will use nominative case pronouns after the preposition *between* in an effort to sound formal or correct. However, all pronouns used as objects of a preposition should be in the objective case.

> INCORRECT   The sales agreement was *between* **he** *and* **I.**
> CORRECT   The sales agreement was *between* **him** *and* **me.**

You can learn more about objects of prepositions on page L97. Also, you can find a list of common prepositions on pages L37–L38.

PRACTICE YOUR SKILLS

● Check Your Understanding
Using Pronouns as Objects

Contemporary Life **Write the correct form of the pronoun in parentheses. Then write how the pronoun is used, using the following abbreviations.**

direct object = *d.o.*   indirect object = *i.o.*
object of a preposition = *o.p.*

1. Like you and (I, me), Yvonne is looking for a job.
2. The manager hired Tim and (I, me) as opticians.
3. Dad called Megan and (he, him) to tell them about our jobs as interns.
4. We should talk to Rebecca and (she, her), our coworkers.
5. For four hours I waited on Mr. Stuart and (they, them), my best customers.
6. Give the customer and (we, us) copies of the receipt.
7. Between you and (I, me), I plan to become the assistant manager.
8. Mrs. Samuelson will pay (they, them) or (we, us) fifteen dollars to repair her antique spectacles.
9. Would you like to go to the training seminar with Tom and (we, us)?
10. Why did you disagree with the experienced lens cutter and (he, him)?
11. Ask Janice or (she, her) about the schedule.
12. You should clean these ground lenses for the Kents and (they, them).
13. Ms. Randolph gave Alma and (I, me) a large tip.
14. We will notify Andrea or (she, her) when your eyeglasses are ready.
15. After school yesterday Neal showed (he, him) and (she, her) the new sunglasses I sold him.

16. No employees work on Sunday except Jacqueline and (he, him).

17. Please bring Brent Morgan and (she, her) some eyeglass frames to try on.

18. This break room is for the receptionist and (we, us).

19. Danielle will meet Scott and (they, them) after work.

20. Leave your key to the store with Heather or (she, her).

Pronouns as Objects of Verbals

Because participles, gerunds, and infinitives are verb forms, they can take objects. The direct object of a verbal is in the objective case.

PARTICIPIAL PHRASE	*Seeing* **her** *in the restaurant,* Jeff asks the tennis star for her autograph. (The phrase is *seeing her in the restaurant. Her* is the object of the participle *seeing*.)
GERUND PHRASE	I don't recall *seeing* **him** *at practice.* (The phrase is *seeing him at practice. Him* is the object of the gerund *seeing*.)
INFINITIVE PHRASE	I want *to watch* **them** *soon,* but I am very busy. (The phrase is *to watch them soon. Them* is the object of the infinitive *to watch*.)

A pronoun in a compound object of a verbal can be checked by saying the nominative and objective case pronouns separately.

I hope to see Bill and (she, her) at the game.
I hope to see **she** at the game.
I hope to see **her** at the game.
I hope to see Bill and **her** at the game.

You can learn more about verbals on pages L107–L119.

Objective Case Pronouns Followed by Appositives

An appositive of *us* does not affect the case of *us*. To check whether you have used the correct pronoun, mentally drop the appositive from the sentence.

> Give **us** *fans* those season tickets.
> (Give *us* those season tickets. *Us* is used as an indirect object, and *fans* is the appositive.)

Objective Case Pronouns as Appositives

Occasionally a pronoun itself is part of an appositive to a direct object, an indirect object, or an object of a preposition. Then the pronoun should be in the objective case.

> d.o.
> We found two volunteers, *Gladys* and **him,** to work at the refreshment stand.
> (*Gladys* and *him* are the appositives to the direct object *volunteers*. Since a direct object is in the objective case, an appositive to the direct object is also in the objective case.)

PRACTICE YOUR SKILLS

● Check Your Understanding
Using Objective Case Pronouns

Contemporary Life | **Write the correct form of the pronoun in parentheses.**

1. Making (he, him) the shortstop was a wise decision.

2. The principal asked (we, us) athletes for our opinion on the new gymnasium.

3. Finding (he, him) in the weight room, the coach helped the bodybuilder.

4. Be sure to tell Carrie and (she, her) about the basketball game after school.

5. At the awards ceremony, the coach gave special recognition to two athletes, Pedro and (he, him).

6. It was a great disappointment to (we, us) fans when Mason struck out.

7. Alex tried in vain to find Sarah and (he, him) in the crowded stadium.

8. I don't recall seeing Nat and (they, them) at the soccer game last week.

9. They interviewed two of my favorite baseball players, Mark and (he, him), for the evening newscast.

10. Watching Liz and (they, them) on the field, Mom was very proud.

11. We asked several baseball players, Andy and (they, them), to help out with Little League.

12. I remember helping Terrence and (she, her) learn to spike a volleyball.

13. I don't want to coach Sammy and (they, them) in the drizzling rain.

14. Meeting the pro wrestler and (him, he) in person was a memorable event.

15. Giving the boys and (she, her) our tickets, we went back home.

16. We asked the coach to give (we, us) runners some time to warm up.

17. I found two alumni, Troy and (him, he), to speak at the sports banquet.

18. Coach Hernandez tried not to mislead the captain and (they, them) about their chances of winning.

19. When we got to P.E. class we begged, "Give (us, we) hard workers a day off!"

20. During homeroom the principal announced the Mr. and Ms. Fitness winners, Alex and (she, her).

Using Objective Case Pronouns

If an underlined pronoun is in the wrong case, write it correctly. If it is in the correct case, write C.

21. Please save seats for <u>he</u> and Sharon.

22. Will you show Marcia and <u>I</u> your canoe over the holiday weekend?

23. Dad had warned you and <u>she</u> about that thin ice!

24. The assistant coach explained the plays to <u>we</u> quarterbacks.

25. Will Roger be able to drive <u>us</u> home after the game?

26. We saw the performances of the two finalists, Pat and <u>he</u>.

27. He should never have taken <u>her</u> and the dog rafting.

28. We saw Dad watching our cousin and <u>they</u> on the balance beams.

29. Mom sent Harold and <u>I</u> to summer basketball camp.

30. Be sure to call <u>we</u> parents when you get to the ball park.

Connect to the Writing Process: Drafting
Writing Sentences

Write sentences that follow the instructions.

31. Use *it* as a direct object.

32. Use *us* as a direct object followed by an appositive.

33. Use *her* as an indirect object.

34. Use *Beth and him* as an object of a preposition.

35. Use *me* in a participial phrase as the object of a verbal.

36. Use *you* in a gerund phrase as the object of a gerund.

37. Use *them* in an infinitive phrase as the object of an infinitive.

38. Use *Luke and her* as an appositive.

APPLY TO WRITING

Descriptive Account: *Objective Case Pronouns*

Study the photograph of two ethnic Albanian refugees who fled Kosovo in 1999. Imagine that you are either the man or the child in this photo. You have been violently driven out of your home and out of your country, and as you sit on a bus with other refugees, a reporter snaps your picture. The reporter then asks you to tell him what has happened to you and how it has made you feel.

Create an account of events and write a description for the reporter. You may want to look up newspaper articles about Kosovo's Albanian refugees to get ideas and factual information. In your account, use objective case pronouns in the various ways you have learned in this section. Then work with a writing partner to edit mistakes in pronoun usage. Finally, write the revised copy.

QuickCheck Mixed Practice

Contemporary Life **Write each underlined pronoun that is incorrectly used; beside it, write the correct objective case pronoun.**

1. Taking <u>they</u> to the counter, I paid for the guitar picks with my allowance.

2. Dad bought new CDs by our favorite rock group for Leslie and <u>I</u>.

3. Photographing <u>she</u> and <u>he</u> during their concert is my job.

4. The ticket agents sold <u>we</u> country-western fans discount tickets.

5. I wanted to invite the new band members, Steve and <u>they</u>, to the party.

6. Mr. Vernon trained Valerie and <u>he</u> on the cello.

7. I forgot to wish the drummers, <u>she</u> and Emily, good luck on their audition.

8. After telling my brother and <u>they</u> about my new baby grand piano, I invited them over to see it.

9. I laughed when Peter said, "Take <u>we</u> groupies backstage!"

10. We asked two people, <u>he</u> and Kathy, to take turns driving the tour bus.

The Possessive Case

My, mine, your, yours, his, her, hers, its, our, ours, their, and *theirs* are the personal pronouns in the possessive case.

The **possessive case** is used to show ownership or possession.

Possessive case pronouns are most often used before a noun or by themselves.

BEFORE A NOUN	This is **my** poem.
BY THEMSELVES	These are **mine**, but which are **his**?

Be careful not to confuse certain possessive pronouns with contractions. A personal pronoun in the possessive case never includes an apostrophe. *Its, your, their,* and *theirs* are possessive pronouns. However, *it's, you're, they're,* and *there's* are contractions.

CONNECT TO SPEAKING AND WRITING

Context clues help a listener determine whether a speaker is using a possessive pronoun or a contraction.

POSSESSIVE PRONOUN	**Their** poems are in the class binder.
CONTRACTION	**They're** proud of the original poems.

Possessive Pronouns with Gerunds

As you may recall, a gerund is a verb form ending in *–ing* that is used in all the ways a noun is used. If a pronoun comes directly in front of a gerund, it should be in the possessive case—in just the same way a possessive pronoun would come in front of a regular noun.

gerund
We were pleased at ***his*** *writing the story.*
(The whole gerund phrase is *his writing the story*. It is used as an object of the preposition *at*. Since *writing* is a gerund, it is preceded by a possessive pronoun: *his writing.*)

gerund
A big surprise was ***their*** *publishing his story.*
(The whole gerund phrase is *their publishing his story*. It is used as a predicate nominative. Since *publishing* is a gerund, it is preceded by a possessive pronoun: *their publishing.*)

A common error is to put a nominative or objective case pronoun before a gerund—instead of a possessive case pronoun.

> INCORRECT   We were pleased at **him** writing the story.
> INCORRECT   A big surprise was **they** publishing his story.

Another possible error is confusing a gerund with a participle because both are verb forms that end in *–ing*. However, since a participle is used as an adjective, it would never be preceded by a possessive pronoun.

> GERUND   The children enjoyed ***our*** *reading to them.*
> (The gerund phrase is the direct object. The children enjoyed what? *Our reading to them.* Since *reading* is a gerund, it is preceded by a possessive pronoun.)
>
> PARTICIPLE   We baby-sat the children and watched ***them*** *reading to one another.*
> (*Them* is a direct object in this sentence. We watched whom? *Them.* Since *them* is a direct object, it is in the objective case. The participial phrase is used as an adjective to describe *them.*)

You can learn more about gerunds on pages L112–L115. You can find out more about participles on pages L107–L111.

PRACTICE YOUR SKILLS

● Check Your Understanding
Using Pronouns in the Possessive Case

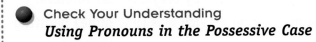

Contemporary Life   **Write the correct pronoun in parentheses.**

1. (Theirs, There's) is the remodeled bookstore on Pier 21.

2. We were surprised at (them, their) buying the building.

3. (Him, His) renovating it was a smart business move.

4. This shelf and (its, it's) hardware are covered in rust.

5. Is there any chance of (you, your) getting a job at the Recycled Books and More store?

6. That shipment of used books must be (ours, our's).

7. Dan was surprised at (me, my) knowing so much about bookbinding.

8. I hadn't heard about (him, his) getting hired as assistant manager.

9. We all appreciated (you, your) explaining the employee insurance benefits to us.

10. My parents are pleased at (me, my) learning the bookstore business.

11. The idea of buying used textbooks for the store was (hers, her's).

12. (Him, His) stocking the shelves with the recycled textbooks was my suggestion.

13. The job of buying used CDs for the music section is (their's, theirs).

14. (Her, She) finding the true crime section of the store took five minutes.

15. These paperbacks are (your's, yours), but the hardbacks are mine.

16. We were grateful for (they're, their) bringing in old grocery bags for their book purchases.

17. During (our, ours) first week of business, we made a nice profit.

18. (His, Him) cleaning the entire Recycled Books and More store each night saves money on janitorial services.

19. Another money-saving service was (my, mine) painting the walls.

20. We are all so happy about (them, their) making a success of the store.

21. I donated (my, mine) box of mystery books.

22. Jeanne spent (her, hers) morning sorting books.

23. We listened to (you, your) return policies.

24. (Your, You're) knowledge about books is awesome.

25. (Her, She) shopping at garage sales is a good idea.

● **Connect to the Writing Process:** Revising
Using Possessive Pronouns

Write each sentence, replacing the possessive nouns with possessive pronouns.

26. The National Book Foundation awards the National Book Award each year for The National Book Foundation's choice of best fiction in the United States.

27. In 1951, William Faulkner won the National Book Award for William Faulkner's *The Collected Stories*.

28. Alice Walker won the National Book Award in 1983 for Alice Walker's novel *The Color Purple*.

29. Authors in the British Commonwealth of Nations are eligible to win the British Commonwealth of Nations' Booker Prize for the authors' full-length novels.

30. In 1992, Michael Ondaatje and Barry Unsworth were each awarded the Booker Prize for Michael Ondaatje's and Barry Unsworth's novels *The English Patient* and *Sacred Hunger*.

31. Ondaatje later agreed to let Ondaatje's novel be made into a film that received much critical acclaim and several Academy Award nominations.

32. Since Nobel Prizes are awarded internationally, writers in any country may be given the award for the writers' literary work.

33. An author who receives the Nobel Prize in literature receives the award for the author's entire body of work up to that point.

34. Authors who receive the Pulitzer Prize in literature are given the honor for the authors' novels about American life, even though they may have written other books.

35. Joseph Pulitzer established the Pulitzer Prize through Joseph Pulitzer's endowment to Columbia University.

APPLY TO WRITING

Poetry: *Possessive Pronouns*

Read the following lines taken from Li Po's "Ballad of Ch'ang-Kan" and then follow the instructions below.

> My hair barely covered my forehead then.
> My play was plucking flowers by the gate.
> You would come on your bamboo horse,
> Riding circles round my bench, and pitching
>   green plums.
> Growing up together here, in Ch'ang-kan.
> Two little ones; no thought of what would come.
> At fourteen I became your wife,
> Blushing and timid, unable to smile,
> Bowing my head, face to dark wall.
> You called a thousand times, without one answer.
> At fifteen I made up my face,
> And swore that our dust and ashes should be one. . . .
>
> —*Li Po*, "Ballad of Ch'ang-Kan"

- List the possessive pronouns in the order in which they are used.

- Referring to your list, notice that the choice of possessive pronouns changes from the beginning of the poem to the end. What does the progression tell you about the speaker's attitude toward her listener?

- Next to every pronoun on your list, write a possessive noun that might replace that possessive pronoun within the poem. Read aloud the poem using the possessive nouns.

- What would happen if the poet had used possessive nouns instead of possessive pronouns? How would possessive nouns change your response to the poem?

General
Interest
Write each pronoun that is in the wrong case. Then write it correctly. If a sentence is correct, write C.

1. Mr. Ayers, the librarian, showed Alicia and I some books about holidays.

2. Them will be enjoyable to read.

3. I listened to Mr. Ayers and she discussing Kwanzaa.

4. Tell we listeners about the seven principles of Kwanzaa.

5. Him and me are planning a Kwanzaa celebration.

6. Notifying them of the plans will take time.

7. The sets for the Christmas play were painted by two people, Carmen and I.

8. In the car, dressed in red and green, were Ben and her.

9. Everyone was glad to hear of me joining the choir.

10. We latke lovers will serve crispy latkes to our guests during Hanukkah.

11. Kyle and them enjoy the eight days of Hanukkah.

12. Is there any chance of you lending me your extra silver menorah?

13. He found two teachers, Mr. Kendall and she, who will chaperone the Holiday Dazzle Dance.

14. Ask the food committee, Sue and he, about traditional holiday foods.

15. The best dancers in the class are Beverly and him.

16. For the slow dance, Tiffany played the violin with the other instrumentalists, John and they.

17. Taking him by the hand, Lauren led him onto the dance floor.

18. This winter vacation will give we guys a chance to work on restoring Oliver's 1934 Buick.

19. Give your ticket to Ted, Maya, or he.

20. Please find us something to eat.

Pronoun Problems

Has anyone at the other end of the telephone ever said to you, "Whom may I say is calling"? The next time you hear that expression, you will know that the speaker has just made a pronoun error. This section will cover the cases of the pronouns *who* and *whoever,* pronouns in comparisons, and reflexive and intensive pronouns.

 ## Who or Whom?

The correct case of *who* is determined by how the pronoun is used in a question or a clause.

Like personal pronouns, the pronouns *who* and *whoever* change their forms—depending upon how they are used within a sentence.

WHO AND WHOEVER	
NOMINATIVE CASE	who, whoever
OBJECTIVE CASE	whom, whomever
POSSESSIVE CASE	whose

Who and *whoever* and their related pronouns are used in questions and in subordinate clauses.

In questions *who* and *whoever* and their related pronouns are frequently used. The case you should use depends upon how the pronoun is used.

NOMINATIVE CASE **Who** volunteered for Meals on Wheels? (subject)

OBJECTIVE CASE **Whom** did you assist at the shelter? (direct object)

To **whom** did you donate the shoes? (object of the preposition *to*)

When deciding which case to use, turn a question around to its natural order.

QUESTION **Whom** did you assist?
NATURAL ORDER You did assist **whom.**

CONNECT TO SPEAKING AND WRITING

In casual conversation you might hear people say, **"Who** did you invite?" instead of **"Whom** did you invite?" This informal usage is accepted in most casual settings; however, in your formal written work, you should use *whom.*

In clauses forms of *who* and *whoever* and their related pronouns are also used. The case you use depends, once again, upon how the pronoun is used in an adjective or noun clause. The following examples show how forms of *who* are used in adjective clauses.

NOMINATIVE CASE Eva is a girl **who enjoys helping others.**
(*Who* is the subject of *enjoys.*)

OBJECTIVE CASE Mr. Jenkins is the man **whom the community theater group consulted.**
(*Whom* is the direct object of *consulted.* The theater group consulted whom.)

Peg is the health aide **from whom I learned about candystripers.**
(*Whom* is the object of the preposition *from. From* is part of the clause.)

The following examples show how forms of *who* and *whoever* are used in noun clauses.

NOMINATIVE CASE **Whoever collects clothing for the charity drive** will receive a free lunch.
(*Whoever* is the subject of *collects.*)

Jerry didn't know **who the new volunteer was.**
(*Who* is a predicate nominative. The volunteer was who.)

OBJECTIVE CASE	Invite **whomever you want.**
	(*Whomever* is the direct object of *want*. You want whomever.)
	At the soup kitchen, Ray gives help to **whomever he sees.**
	(The entire clause is the object of the preposition *to*. *Whomever* is the direct object of *sees*.)

Sometimes an interrupting expression such as *I believe, we know, do you suppose,* and *I hope* appears in a question or a clause. Mentally drop this expression to avoid any confusion.

Who *do you suppose* will win the fundraiser raffle?
(Who will win the fundraiser raffle? *Who* is the subject of *will win.*)

Otis, **who** *I think* is a volunteer at the YMCA, is a senior.
(Otis, who is a volunteer at the YMCA, is a senior. *Who* is the subject of *is.*)

You can learn more about adjective and noun clauses on pages L148–L159.

PRACTICE YOUR SKILLS

● Check Your Understanding
Using Who *and Its Related Pronouns*

Contemporary Life **Write each form of *who* or *whom* that is used incorrectly. If a sentence is correct, write C.**

1. Whom may I say is volunteering for the campus cleanup on Saturday?

2. I met Roth, who is a community service director.

3. Tell whoever you see about the neighborhood playground project.

4. Did they say whom the sponsors of Paint the Playground Day are?

5. With who did you work at the park?

6. Who did you nominate as volunteer of the year?

7. Do you know who the event director is?

8. The school board will give 50 dollars to whomever organizes a school-improvement event.

9. With whom did you travel recently to the Volunteer America conference?

10. Mr. Davis is the social worker who we know from the homeless shelter.

11. Aaron usually likes whoever he works for.

12. From who should we request a new supply of the drug education materials?

13. It was Marshall whom we all agree did the most to establish the free art school for kids.

14. Whom did he think should join our active environmentalist group?

15. Do you know whom the director of the YMCA is?

● Connect to the Writing Process: Editing
Using Forms of Who *and* Whom

16.–27. Rewrite the incorrect sentences in the preceding exercise, using the correct form of *who* or *whom*. Then, using the following abbreviations, write how each pronoun is used.

subject = *subj.*   predicate nominative = *p.n.*
direct object = *d.o.*   object of a preposition = *o.p.*

● Connect to the Writing Process: Drafting
Writing Sentences with Who *and* Whom

Write sentences that follow the instructions, using the correct forms of *who* and *whom*.

28. as a subject

29. as a direct object

30. in a question

31. as the object of a preposition

32. to introduce an adjective clause

33. to begin a noun clause

Pronouns in Comparisons

Pronouns are often used in comparisons. A problem sometimes arises when a comparison is made but not said or written out completely. The result is an elliptical clause.

An **elliptical clause** is a subordinate clause that begins with *than* or *as.*

Although words are omitted from an elliptical clause, they are still understood to be in the clause.

Mr. Lee coached Eric more **than I.**
Mr. Lee coached Eric more **than me.**

Depending upon what meaning is intended, both of the preceding examples are correct.

Mr. Lee coached Eric more **than I coached Eric.**

(*I* is correct because it is the subject of *coached.*)

Mr. Lee coached Eric more **than he coached me.**

(*Me* is correct because it is the direct object of *coached.*)

In an elliptical clause, use the form of the pronoun you would use if the clause were completed.

To decide which pronoun to use in an elliptical clause, mentally complete the clause. Then choose the form of the pronoun that expresses the meaning you want.

An elliptical clause, however, can sometimes correctly express only one meaning.

Do you think David Greene shoots hoops as well as (I, me)?

Do you think David Greene shoots hoops as well **as I shoot hoops?**

You can learn more about elliptical clauses on pages L145–L147.

PRACTICE YOUR SKILLS

● Check Your Understanding
Using Pronouns in Elliptical Clauses

Contemporary Life **Write each pronoun that is used incorrectly in an elliptical clause. If a sentence is correct, write C.**

1. Amy ran more laps than me.
2. In the tryouts I think Susannah did better than her.
3. When coaching Little League, Barry has more patience than him.
4. Andrea is as experienced a gymnast as me.
5. Martha likes the softball uniforms more than us.
6. At the track meet, Anna earned more ribbons than me.
7. Coach Ferguson trained that player better than he.
8. Ben is not as tall as her, but he runs much faster.
9. My sister was always better in sports than me.
10. Mary cheered for Doug more than him.

● Connect to the Writing Process: Editing
Using Pronouns in Comparisons

11.–20. Referring to the preceding sentences, complete each elliptical clause, using the correct pronoun. If a clause can be completed two ways, write them both.

● Connect to the Writing Process: Drafting
Using Elliptical Clauses in Sentences

Write sentences that follow the instructions. Then underline the elliptical clause in each sentence.

21. Write a comparison that includes *than I.*
22. Write a comparison that includes *than they.*
23. Write a comparison that ends with *as he.*
24. Write a comparison that ends with *as they.*
25. Write a comparison that ends with *than she.*

Reflexive and Intensive Pronouns

Because reflexive and intensive pronouns end in *–self* or *–selves,* they are easy to recognize. These pronouns are often used for emphasis.

REFLEXIVE AND INTENSIVE PRONOUNS	
SINGULAR	myself, yourself, himself, herself, itself
PLURAL	ourselves, yourself, themselves

Reflexive pronouns always refer back to a previous noun or pronoun in the sentence.

> REFLEXIVE
> PRONOUNS
>
> Tiffany voted for **herself**.
>
> They saw **themselves** as rivals.

Intensive pronouns are used to emphasize a noun or another pronoun in the sentence.

> INTENSIVE
> PRONOUNS
>
> Ben **himself** was elected homecoming king.
>
> They **themselves** decorated the gym.

Never use reflexive or intensive pronouns by themselves. They always have to have an antecedent in the same sentence.

> INCORRECT
> Laura and **myself** are the only candidates.
> (*Myself* has no antecedent in the sentence.)
>
> CORRECT
> Laura and **I** are the only delegates.

CONNECT TO SPEAKING AND WRITING

In daily conversation, you may hear *theirself* used as a reflexive or intensive pronoun. For example, a friend may say, "When they laughed in class, they couldn't help theirself." *Theirself,* however, is not a word; you should always use *themselves* instead. Similarly, you would never say, "He cut hisself." Instead, you would say "He cut *himself*."

PRACTICE YOUR SKILLS

● Check Your Understanding
Using Reflexive and Intensive Pronouns

Contemporary Life · **Write the reflexive and intensive pronouns in the following sentences. Then write *I* if the pronoun is incorrect and *C* if the pronoun is correct.**

1. The nominees for homecoming queen are Amber Stockton and myself.

2. I can see myself in the crown already.

3. I noticed themselves in the top row of the bleachers.

4. The football team and ourselves marched onto the field.

5. The quarterback bought hisself a new tux.

6. The former homecoming queen will perform the crowning herself.

7. When last year's homecoming king arrived, the announcer said, "Himself is here."

8. I myself did not see himself.

9. The band of my corsage had tangled itself on my ring.

10. The girls in the court admired theirself in the mirrors.

● Connect to the Writing Process: Editing
Replacing Reflexive and Intensive Pronouns

11.–17. **Write the pronoun that correctly replaces the incorrect pronoun in each sentence in the preceding exercise.**

● Connect to the Writing Process: Drafting
Using Reflexive and Intensive Pronouns in Sentences

Write sentences that follow the instructions.

18. Include *myself* in a compound subject.

19. Use *herself* to emphasize a noun.

20. Use *himself* to refer back to a noun.

21. Use *themselves* to emphasize another pronoun.

22. Include *yourself* with an antecedent.

APPLY TO WRITING

Friendly Letter: *Pronouns*

One of your friends is in the hospital, and you want to cheer him or her up. Write an amusing letter, describing your recent school experiences. (Feel free to embellish them.) Use the pronouns you studied in this section: the *who/whom* pronouns, pronouns in comparisons, and reflexive and intensive pronouns. Edit your letter for mistakes in pronoun usage, and then write the final copy.

 QuickCheck Mixed Practice

Contemporary Life **Write each pronoun that is used incorrectly. Then write it correctly. If a sentence is correct, write C.**

1. I answered the telephone by saying, "Whom may I say is calling?"

2. A salesperson asked to speak to whomever was "the lady of the house."

3. If they could hear theirself talk, salespeople wouldn't say things like that.

4. This is the kind of telemarketer whom I believe should be banned.

5. Maria and I have spoken to more salespeople than her.

6. Do you think she is more sympathetic to pushy salespeople than I?

7. Whom do you think buys useless junk?

8. Wayne, who everyone knows is too trusting, buys whatever a salesperson shows I22.

9. No one has more encyclopedias than him.

10. Maria and myself use the encyclopedias at school.

Pronouns and Their Antecedents

A pronoun's **antecedent** is the word that the pronoun refers to or replaces. A pronoun and its antecedent must agree in number and gender since they both are referring to the same person, place, or thing.

Number is the term used to indicate whether a noun or a pronoun is singular (one) or plural (more than one). **Gender** is the term used to indicate whether a noun or a pronoun is masculine, feminine, or neuter.

GENDER			
MASCULINE	he	him	his
FEMININE	she	her	hers
NEUTER	it	its	

To make a pronoun agree with its antecedent, first find the antecedent. Then determine its number and gender. Making a pronoun agree with a single-word antecedent usually is not a problem.

> **Nancy** must plant **her** vegetable garden soon.
> (*Nancy* is singular and feminine; therefore, *her* is correct because it also is singular and feminine.)
>
> **Members** of the landscape team presented **their** ideas at a special meeting.
> (*Members* is plural; therefore, *their* is plural.)

If the antecedent of a pronoun is more than one word, you need to remember two rules.

If two or more singular antecedents are joined by *or, nor, either/or,* or *neither/nor,* use a singular pronoun to refer to them.

All the conjunctions listed in this rule indicate a choice—one *or* the other. In the following example, Harold *or* Cliff gave me his shovel—not both of them. As a result the pronoun must be singular.

> Either Harold or Cliff gave me **his** shovel.

When one antecedent is singular and the other is plural, the pronoun agrees with the closer antecedent.

> Neither Sue nor the other two gardeners planted **their** begonias in the proper soil.
>
> Neither my brothers nor my father brought **his** rake.

If two or more singular antecedents are joined by *and* or *both/and*, use a plural pronoun to refer to them.

The conjunctions *and* and *both/and* indicate more than one. In the following example, both Greta and Mavis—two people—planted their spring flowers too early. Because the antecedent is plural, the plural pronoun must be used.

> Both Greta and Mavis planted **their** spring flowers too early.

The gender of most antecedents is obvious. *Harold* and *Cliff* are masculine; *Greta* and *Mavis* are feminine. The gender of some antecedents, however, is not as obvious. Standard English solves the agreement problem in such cases by using the phrase *his or her* to refer to antecedents of unknown gender.

> Each horticulturist should photograph **his or her** prize roses.

Overusing *his or her* in a short passage can make writing sound awkward. You can often avoid this problem by rewriting such sentences, using plural forms.

> All horticulturists should photograph **their** prize roses.

You can learn more about pronouns and antecedents on pages L9–L15.

PRACTICE YOUR SKILLS

● Check Your Understanding

Making Pronouns Agree with Their Antecedents

General **Write the pronoun that correctly completes**
Interest **each sentence.**

1. Every American should know what ■ state flower is.

2. Texans see ■ state flower, the bluebonnet, bloom in March and April.

3. Both Florida and Delaware have fruit blossoms as ■ state flowers.

4. Florida claims the orange blossom as ■ flower, and Delaware claims the peach blossom.

5. Each member of the Women's Garden Club in Rhode Island makes sure that ■ grows the state flower, the violet, in ■ garden.

6. In Nevada some residents are allergic to ■ state flower, sagebrush.

7. Iris and Lily know that ■ mothers named ■ after Tennessee's and Utah's flowers.

8. Maine residents know that the pine cone is ■ state flower.

9. Either Jonah or Carl left ■ picture of the North Carolina dogwood on the table.

10. Neither my aunts nor my uncle realized that ■ home state, Alaska, has the forget-me-not as ■ flower.

11. School children in Kansas can easily draw ■ state flower, the sunflower.

12. Both Nebraska and Kentucky have adopted goldenrod as ■ flower.

13. Hawaii's foliage is as lush and exotic as ■ state flower, the red hibiscus.

14. An Oklahoma native decorates ■ home at Christmas time with the state flower, the mistletoe.

15. The men on the road crew in Wyoming decided that ■ would not mow down the Indian paintbrush.

Rewrite the paragraphs, correcting errors in pronoun and antecedent agreement.

A gardener should test their soil to see if they should add fertilizer or compost. A local garden center should have testing kits on their shelves. If the gardener's soil is too alkaline or acidic, they can buy additives to mix into them. Smart gardeners develop soil that crumbles easily in its hands. Sometimes they have to add sand, clay, or compost to create rich soil. Both my neighbor, Mrs. Kent, and I turn ~~their~~ soil with a shovel and mix in other soil types.

I learned that soil which sticks together when you press it probably has too much clay in them. Clumpy, sticky clay packs too tightly around a plant's roots, and they cannot drain properly. Conversely, a loose and sandy soil loses his nutrients and the plants can't get what it will need to thrive. Loam is the best kind of soil because she is not too sticky or sandy. Either leaves or manure will provide their nutrients to any soil you mix them into. A gardening center stocks bags of compost and fertilizer on their shelves.

▶ Indefinite Pronouns as Antecedents

Based on their number, the common indefinite pronouns have been divided into the following three groups.

COMMON INDEFINITE PRONOUNS	
SINGULAR	anybody, anyone, each, either, everybody, everyone, neither, nobody, no one, one, somebody, someone
PLURAL	both, few, many, several
SINGULAR/PLURAL	all, any, most, none, some

A personal pronoun must be singular if its antecedent is one of the singular indefinite pronouns.

> **Each** of the girls is bathing **her** puppy.

A personal pronoun must be plural if its antecedent is one of the plural indefinite pronouns.

> **Both** of the brothers donated **their** time to the humane society.

If the antecedent of a personal pronoun is one of the singular/plural indefinite pronouns, the personal pronoun agrees in number and gender with the object of the preposition that follows the indefinite pronoun.

> **Some** of the dog *food* has ants in **it**. (singular)

> **Some** of the cat *owners* have declawed **their** pets. (plural)

Sometimes the gender of a singular indefinite pronoun is not indicated by other words in the sentence. Standard English solves this problem by using *his or her* to refer to antecedents of unknown gender. You can also rewrite the sentence, using the plural form.

> **Each** of the riders must register **his or her** horse by Monday.

> **All** of the riders must register **their** horses by Monday.

● Check Your Understanding
Making Pronouns Agree

Science Topic   **Write the pronoun that correctly completes each sentence.**

1. Neither of the squirrels has had ▤ dinner of sunflower seeds and strawberries.

2. All of the parakeets had green feathers on ▤ wings.

3. Both of my parrots recently learned to say ▤ names.

4. Most of the lizards sat cozily beneath ▤ heat lamps.

5. Each of the Siamese fighting fish must have ▤ own bowl in which to swim.

6. If any of these shells will work, put ▤ in the hermit crab's case.

7. Several of my cats have torn apart ▤ cat toys.

8. One of the boys said that ▤ would groom my poodle.

9. Most of the floor of the rabbits' cage had alfalfa on ▤.

10. Either of the women should place broccoli in ▤ turtle's food dish.

11. Each hamster sleeps in ▤ corner during the day.

12. Most of the cages have wheels in ▤.

13. Each of the water bottles has vitamins in ▤.

14. Some of the guinea pigs ate ▤ carrots.

15. Neither the finches nor the parakeets built ▤ nests.

● Connect to the Writing Process: Prewriting
Using Pronouns and Antecedents

You have just learned that a product you use nearly every day (shampoo, lipstick, allergy medication, etc.) is tested on animals. Take five minutes to list your opinions, questions, and ideas about product-testing on animals. Use pronouns and antecedents in your statements and check for agreement in number and gender.

Communicate Your Ideas

APPLY TO WRITING

Persuasive Essay: *Pronouns and Antecedents*

Refer to the prewriting you generated in the preceding exercise, and write a persuasive essay about testing products on animals. Convince your classmates to see the issue as you do. For example, do you believe testing on animals is never okay? Is it acceptable when developing life-saving medicine but unacceptable when developing a new kind of mascara? Use specific examples to illustrate your opinions. Check for pronoun and antecedent agreement before you write your final copy.

✔ QuickCheck Mixed Practice

Contemporary Life **Write a pronoun that correctly completes each sentence.**

1. Participants in the auto show should bring ▦ vehicles to the lot by Saturday.

2. All of my sisters received cars on ▦ sixteenth birthdays.

3. Both Ray and Otis forgot ▦ keys today.

4. Most of these abandoned vehicles will never be claimed by ▦ owners.

5. Somebody who owns the red convertible has left ▦ car unlocked.

6. Some of the girls are riding to the game with ▦ friends.

7. Many of the boys in shop class have already rebuilt ▦ carburetors.

8. Susan and Julie asked ▦ father for a ride to the library.

9. Neither of my brothers could find ▦ spare tire.

10. Several of my friends drive ▦ cars to school every day.

Unclear, Missing, or Confusing Antecedents

Not only does a pronoun have to agree in number and gender with its antecedent, but that antecedent must also be very clear. If an antecedent is hard to determine or if it is missing entirely, then your writing will become confusing or even misleading. As a result, as part of your editing, you should look for unclear, missing, or confusing antecedents.

Every personal pronoun should clearly refer to a specific antecedent.

Unclear Antecedents

Although words such as *it, they, this,* and *that* might vaguely refer to antecedents within a piece of writing, you still should substitute specific antecedents to avoid any confusion or misunderstanding.

UNCLEAR	Chuck is a tour guide, but none of his friends chose **it** as a career.
	(The antecedent of *it* is not clear. The context of the sentence only suggests that the pronoun *it* refers to guiding tours as a profession.)
CLEAR	Chuck is a tour guide, but none of his friends chose **guiding tours** as a career.
UNCLEAR	The recreation director pulled the bell cords, and **they** rang out loudly.
	(Although the antecedent of *they* is not clear, the context of the sentence suggests that the antecedent is *bells*.)
CLEAR	The recreation director pulled the bell cords, and the **bells** rang out loudly.

UNCLEAR	I spent the summer at a horse ranch. **This** convinced me I wanted to become a veterinarian.
	(This has no clear antecedent, but it suggests the experience of being at the horse ranch.)
CLEAR	I spent the summer at a horse ranch. **This experience** convinced me I wanted to become a veterinarian.

You may have noticed that sometimes the pronoun *you* is incorrectly used in a sentence because *you* does not refer to the person being spoken to. In many cases, the *you* is actually referring to the person who is speaking. As a result, the pronoun *you* does not have a clear antecedent either.

| UNCLEAR | I work at the YMCA recreation center because **you** can be outdoors all summer. |
| CLEAR | I work at the YMCA recreation center because **I** can be outdoors all summer. |

⬤ Missing Antecedents

Occasionally pronouns are written without any antecedents at all. To correct this kind of mistake, you most often have to rewrite the sentence and replace the pronoun with a noun.

MISSING	In the book **it** shows how to re-string a guitar.
	*(The antecedent of *it* is missing.)*
CLEAR	The **book** shows how to re-string a guitar.
MISSING	In the spring **they** are offering public recitals at the music academy.
	*(The antecedent of *they* is missing.)*
CLEAR	In the spring **the music academy** is offering public recitals.

Confusing Antecedents

The problem with some other pronouns is that they have more than one possible antecedent. As a result, readers can easily confuse the sentence's meaning. To correct this mistake, you must rewrite the sentence and replace the pronoun with a specific noun.

CONFUSING	As Paulo was showing Mike the boat, **he** fell into the water. (Who fell in, Paulo or Mike?)
CLEAR	As Paulo was showing Mike the boat, **Mike** fell into the water.
CONFUSING	Rita had oars in both hands, but now **they** have disappeared. (What disappeared, the oars or her hands?)
CLEAR	Rita had oars in both hands, but now **the oars** have disappeared.

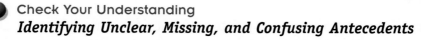

PRACTICE YOUR SKILLS

Check Your Understanding
Identifying Unclear, Missing, and Confusing Antecedents

Contemporary Life **Write *I* if the sentence contains a pronoun-antecedent error and *C* if the sentence is correct.**

1. When Jane told Shawna about the new jet skis, she was very excited.
2. After my father and grandfather stowed the gear, he said, "All aboard!"
3. The Virgin Islands are our destination, and you can snorkel there.
4. I could hardly see the jellyfish and stingray underwater because it was cloudy.
5. Later I told Michelle and Marla about our trip, and they said it sounded enjoyable.

6. Wearing flippers on both feet, Geoffrey jumped into the water and then they fell off.

7. I packed a sun hat and tanning lotion, and it spilled inside my bag.

8. I asked Erica or Joanne to lend me a towel, and they both offered me one.

9. After I took the fish off the hooks, I threw them into the water.

10. When the boat hit the rock, it was a disaster.

● Connect to the Writing Process: Revising
Correcting Antecedent Problems

11.–18. Rewrite the sentences from the preceding exercise, correcting unclear, missing, or confusing antecedents.

● Connect to the Writing Process: Revising
Correcting Unclear, Missing, and Confusing Antecedents

Rewrite the paragraphs, using clear pronouns and antecedents.

I bought a large supply of oil paints, knowing I would enjoy it. On the flyer it said beginners were welcome. Later, when I saw the colors in my paintings, I decided I didn't like them. I had seen Minnie and Leo mixing reds and blues, so I copied them. In the directions it had said to experiment with color, but I don't like it when you feel completely lost when you're doing a new project.

I tried to create an impressionist painting of flowers in vases, but they looked like cartoon creatures from outer space. This taught me new respect for Renoír, Monet, and other painters of impressionist works. They make it look easy, but it is actually difficult.

Despite my trouble with paints and brushwork, it was not completely disappointing. If I hold a simple pen in my hand, it serves me well. When I showed my pen-and-ink sketches to Minnie and Leo, they were sitting by the windows. They admired my sketches, and that encouraged me to create more.

Communicate Your Ideas

APPLY TO WRITING
Fantasy: *Antecedents*

Study the photograph and think, "adventure."

Create a fantasy adventure involving you and your best friend. First write freely, creating an imaginary world of strange surroundings and bizarre creatures. (For ideas, think of science-fiction movies like *Star Wars* or fantasy stories like *Gulliver's Travels*.) Next, write some action scenes: How did you and your friend get to this peculiar place? What is your first obstacle? How do you overcome it?

Now write the first draft. Use pronouns and antecedents carefully. Include vivid details and references to the senses when describing the land and its inhabitants. Then edit your story and check for unclear, missing, or confusing antecedents; make corrections. Write a final copy and read your story to a friend.

QuickCheck Mixed Practice

Contemporary Life **Rewrite each sentence, correcting unclear, missing, or confusing antecedents.**

1. On the map of South Padre Island, it shows where the best swimming areas are.

2. Clark and Billy bought hamburgers for the swimmers and then ate them.

3. When my friends and I tossed cheese puffs to the seagulls, they flew through the air.

4. It says "No Diving" on the sign at the end of the dock.

5. Shari and Shane do not want sunburns, so they used plenty of sunblock.

6. In the morning I watched the sun rise over the water. That stayed in my mind all day.

7. We placed our tent and ice chest near the sand dunes, and later they were gone.

8. Hunter swam just beneath the water's surface with a plastic shark fin on his back. This backfired when I kicked him with my sharp toenails.

9. I had no idea that when you throw a foam cup into the campfire, it melts.

10. As the surfboard skimmed the water, it reflected the bright sun.

Using Pronouns in the Correct Case

Write the correct form of the pronoun in parentheses.

1. Mrs. Winters asked my friend Raymond to mow the lawn (himself, herself).

2. (Who, Whom) do you think will win the award for best singer?

3. Roy knows more about both folk music and country music than (she, her).

4. Was it Ken or (she, her) who saved that man's life at the beach yesterday?

5. Daniel, (who, whom) the coach promoted from junior varsity, has become one of Reading's best players.

6. The mayor promised three seniors, Carla, Al, and (he, him), summer jobs at City Hall.

7. Is Spencer older than (she, her)?

8. Show your pass to (whoever, whomever) is at the entrance to the estate.

9. Three of (we, us) boys volunteered to help load the moving van for Mr. Rodriguez.

10. Both Mom and Dad were surprised at (me, my) offering to clean the garage.

11. (Who, Whom) did you visit in Albany?

12. Neither the blue jay nor the sparrow abandoned (its, their) nest during the storm.

13. The only ones in the store were Kim and (he, him).

14. Both Lynn and Donna brought (her, their) umbrellas to the baseball game.

15. When am I going to ride in (your, you're) new car?

Editing for Pronoun Problems

Find at least one error in each sentence below. Write the sentences correctly.

1. With who are you going to the senior prom?
2. Daniel talks to Beth more than she talks to he.
3. Whom do you suppose will replace Mrs. Bennett?
4. E-mailing Antoine probably would be much easier than phoning himself.
5. Our friend Barbara asked whom the man in the blue seersucker suit was.

Making Pronouns Agree with Antecedents

Write the pronoun that correctly completes each sentence.

1. All the girls on the softball team packed ■ gear into the minivan.
2. Every duck in the pond had a piece of bread in ■ beak.
3. Neither Jeremiah nor Vincenzo submitted ■ history report on time.
4. One of the girls must have sold ■ bicycle.
5. Dogs perspire through ■ paw pads.

Writing Sentences

Write five sentences that follow the directions below.

1. Write a sentence using a form of the word *you* preceding a gerund.
2. Write a sentence with two pronouns in an appositive that agrees with the subject.
3. Write a sentence that correctly uses the word *whomever*.
4. Write a sentence that includes an elliptical clause.
5. Write a sentence using a form of *we* followed by an appositive.

Language and *Self-Expression*

Glenna Goodacre was deeply impressed by the suffering, the heroism, and the kindness shown by members of the armed forces during the Vietnam War. She was especially proud of the work done by women both as officers and as medical and support personnel.

Sometimes a realistic sculpture can evoke emotional responses that paintings and photographs cannot quite summon. Walking around a sculpture, touching the tears on a face, or tracing the folds in a shirt brings out the reality and raw emotional appeal of its subject. Think about the people portrayed in this sculpture and imagine their hope and their sorrow. Write a paragraph that describes both the sculpture and your feelings about it.

Prewriting Brainstorm or use a word web to list objects and emotions associated with war. For example, you may use objects evident in the sculpture. Choose the ones that affect you most deeply. Then list your choices in some logical order, such as from the top to the bottom of the sculpture, or from the left to the right.

Drafting Write your description and your feelings in the order in which you listed them in the prewriting activity. Conclude your description by giving your feelings about the sculpture as a whole.

Revising Read your paragraph as a critic would read it, searching for elements that are spatially incorrect or that do not fit together smoothly. Add transitions, rearrange ideas, and build toward a single effect.

Editing Read your work again, this time looking for errors in grammar, spelling, and usage. Check that all of the pronouns you used are correct.

Publishing Make a clean copy of your paragraph. If you wish, photocopy the picture of the sculpture and enlarge it to show the details you focused on.

Another Look

Case is the form of a noun or a pronoun that indicates its use in a sentence.

Cases of Personal Pronouns
The **nominative case** is used for subjects and predicate nominatives. *(page L236)*
The **objective case** is used for direct objects, indirect objects, objects of prepositions, and objects of verbals. *(page L242)*
The **possessive case** is used to show ownership or possession. *(page L251)*

Who and Whom
The correct case of *who* is determined by how the pronoun is used in a question or a clause. *(page L258)*

Pronouns in Comparisons
An **elliptical clause** is a subordinate clause that begins with *than* or *as*. *(page L262)*

Reflexive and Intensive Pronouns
Both reflexive and intensive pronouns end in *–self* or *–selves*. *(page L264)*
A **reflexive pronoun** always refers to a previous noun or pronoun in a sentence. *(page L264)*
An **intensive pronoun** emphasizes a noun or another pronoun in a sentence. *(page L264)*

Pronouns and Their Antecedents
If two or more singular antecedents are joined by *or, nor, either/or,* or *neither/nor,* use a **singular** pronoun to refer to them. *(page L267)*
If two or more singular antecedents are joined by *and* or *both/and,* use a **plural** pronoun to refer to them. *(page L268)*
Every personal pronoun should clearly refer to a specific antecedent. *(page L274)*

Other Information About the Use of Pronouns
Using indefinite pronouns as antecedents *(pages L270–L273)*
Avoiding unclear, missing, or confusing antecedents *(pages L274–L279)*

Posttest

Directions

Read the passage and choose the pronoun that belongs in each underlined space. Write the letter of the correct answer.

EXAMPLE

1. Walt Disney's wife once said, "I didn't want Walt to make a feature film, but he didn't listen to __(1)__ ."

    1 A I

    B me

    C my

    D mine

ANSWER

1 B

Most young people today have seen __(1)__ fair share of full-length animated movies, such as *The Lion King* or *A Bug's Life*. In fact, you probably remember __(2)__ seeing movies such as *Cinderella* and *Toy Story* when you were younger. However, before 1937, a full-length cartoon feature had never been made. It was Walt Disney, of course, __(3)__ produced the first one, *Snow White and the Seven Dwarfs*.

Back then, no one thought __(4)__ idea would succeed. For example, Walt's brother and business partner Roy O. Disney, who was more conservative than __(5)__ , feared financial ruin. Nevertheless, Walt was confident that __(6)__ watched it would love it, and Walt wanted to show __(7)__ and everyone else that he was right.

For three years each of the animators worked hard on __(8)__ drawings of Snow White. Walt gave __(9)__ high standards to follow, but all of the difficult work eventually paid off. When the movie ended its first showing, the members of the audience rose from __(10)__ seats and cheered wildly.

1 **A** they
   B them
   C their
   D theirs

2 **A** you
   B your
   C yours
   D their

3 **A** who
   B whom
   C whoever
   D whoever

4 **A** he
   B him
   C his
   D himself

5 **A** he
   B him
   C his
   D their

6 **A** who
   B whoever
   C whom
   D whoever

7 **A** he
   B his
   C him
   D their

8 **A** their
   B theirs
   C his
   D him

9 **A** him
   B his
   C they
   D them

10 **A** they
   B them
   C their
   D theirs

CHAPTER 7

Subject and Verb Agreement

Directions

Write the letter of the best way to write the underlined verb(s) in each sentence. If the underlined part contains no error, write *D*.

EXAMPLE

1. Hurricanes <u>arises</u> in warm water and travel across the ocean.

    1 **A** arised

    B arise

    C arose

    D No error

ANSWER

1 **B**

1. Storm trackers track hurricanes and <u>map</u> their locations.
2. The data compiled by storm trackers <u>are</u> both extensive and important.
3. Each year a few storms <u>was defined</u> as *major hurricanes*.
4. Hurricanes in the eastern U.S. <u>has caused</u> great damage.
5. Each of the hurricanes <u>seem</u> worse than the one before.
6. One hundred miles inland <u>are</u> a common distance for a storm to travel.
7. Both of these storms <u>is</u> very dangerous.
8. An area struck by either of these storms often <u>suffer</u> great damage.
9. Neither storms nor other bad weather <u>are avoided</u> by a move to another state.
10. The media <u>inform</u> us that storms occur everywhere.

1 **A** maps
   B is mapping
   C has mapped
   D No error

2 **A** is
   B has proven
   C was proven
   D No error

3 **A** has been defined
   B are defined
   C were defined
   D No error

4 **A** was caused
   B is causing
   C have caused
   D No error

5 **A** seems
   B have seemed
   C do seem
   D No error

6 **A** is
   B seem
   C were
   D No error

7 **A** seems
   B are
   C be
   D No error

8 **A** suffers
   B has suffered
   C suffering
   D No error

9 **A** were avoided
   B be avoided
   C is avoided
   D No error

10 **A** has informed
   B was informing
   C informing
   D No error

Painter of Micali. *Hydria with Running Figures,* date unknown. Museo Gregoriano Etrusco, Rome.

Describe   What is depicted in this Etruscan vase painting inspired by Greek black-figured art? What are the figures wearing? What technique does the artist use to create a sense of movement?

Analyze   Notice the vase has two handles. What do you think the vase was used for? Do you think it had more of a functional or decorative use?

Interpret   Would you consider the painting on the vase great art? Why or why not?

Judge   What advantage might the artwork—and the vase itself—have over a written description of the scene? Suppose the image were unavailable and all you had was a description. Who do you think would do the best job of describing it—a novelist, a writer of nonfiction prose, or a poet? Why?

At the end of this chapter, you will use the artwork as a visual aid for writing.

Agreement of Subjects and Verbs

How many times have you seen the "perfect" pair of jeans, tried them on, and then discovered to your great disappointment that they were either too loose or too short? "Perfect" as they are, you cannot wear them because they do not fit. In a way, subjects and verbs are like people and jeans. Some fit together; others do not. When words do fit together, they are said to be in **agreement.** This chapter will review the different types of subjects and verbs. Then it will show you which agree and which do not.

A verb must agree with its subject in number.

Number determines whether a word is singular (one) or plural (more than one). A subject and a verb agree when they have the same number.

To understand agreement, you must know the singular and plural forms of nouns, pronouns, and verbs. The plurals of most nouns are formed by adding –s or –es to the singular form. Some nouns, however, form their plurals irregularly. For example, *children* is the plural of *child*. Certain pronouns also form their plurals by changing form.

NOUNS		PRONOUNS	
Singular	**Plural**	**Singular**	**Plural**
lion	lions	I	we
fox	foxes	you	you
goose	geese	he, she, it	they

Verbs also have singular and plural forms, but only present tense verbs change endings. The third-person singular of present tense verbs ends in –s or –es. However, most plural forms of present tense verbs do not end in –s or –es. Notice that *I* and *you* take the plural form of the verb.

| THIRD PERSON SINGULAR | (He, She, It) **sits.** |
| OTHERS | (I, You, We, They) **sit.** |

In the following box are the singular and the plural forms of the irregular verbs *be, have,* and *do* in the present tense. Notice that *be* also has irregular forms for both the singular and the plural in the past tense.

PRESENT TENSE	PAST TENSE
Singular	**Singular**
I **am, have, do**	I **was**
you **are, have, do**	you **were**
he, she, it **is, has, does**	he, she, it **was**
Plural	**Plural**
we **are, have, do**	we **were**
you **are, have, do**	you **were**
they **are, have, do**	they **were**

Since a subject and a verb both have number, they must agree in a sentence.

A singular subject takes a singular verb.

A plural subject takes a plural verb.

The lion pounces.	The lions pounce.
The fox hides.	The foxes hide.
The goose flies.	The geese fly.
It is a hawk.	They are hawks.

Be, have, and *do* are often used as helping verbs. When they are, they must agree in number with the subject.

The first helping verb must agree in number with its subject.

Pamela **is** studying primates in science class.

The baby gorillas **were** found in the jungle.

The birds **have** flown away.

Mark **does** have a pet cockatoo.

You can learn more about regular and irregular verbs on pages L181–L192.

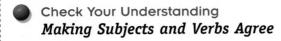

CONNECT TO WRITER'S CRAFT

        Mark Twain is one writer who is known for breaking rules of grammar in the dialogue of his characters. For example, Huckleberry Finn tells the reader that when "Mr. Mark Twain" wrote *Tom Sawyer,*

> "There was things which he stretched, but mainly he told the truth."

You probably noticed that the correct grammar is "There *were* things that he stretched." Twain's misuse of subject and verb agreement is one aspect of **local color writing.** With this type of writing, authors write sentences exactly as the people in a particular region would speak them.

PRACTICE YOUR SKILLS

● Check Your Understanding
Making Subjects and Verbs Agree

Science Topic **Write the correct form of the verb in parentheses.**

1. Alex (is, are) a 22-year-old gray parrot.

2. Trainers (talks, talk) to Alex every day.

3. Irene Pepperberg (train, trains) Alex to speak and reason.

4. The teacher (hold, holds) a tray of wood, plastic, and wool items.

5. She (asks, ask) Alex, "How many wood?"

6. Alex (respond, responds) with the correct number of wooden objects.

7. As a reward, Irene (gives, give) a wooden object to Alex to play with.

8. Sometimes Alex (want, wants) a treat instead of a toy.

9. On these occasions, the parrot (say, says), "Wanna nut."

10. Some scientists (believes, believe) that gray parrots (rival, rivals) dolphins and apes in intelligence.

● Connect to the Writing Process: Editing
Correcting Subject and Verb Agreement

Edit the sentences in the following paragraphs for subject-verb agreement. If a subject and verb do not agree in number, write the sentence correctly.

Koko were born in 1971. She are a black gorilla, and she weigh about 280 pounds. Her handlers has taught her to understand over 2,000 words of American Sign Language. The teachers shows Koko how to form the words, or they molds Koko's hands into the proper shape. The techniques is very similar to teaching sign language to a human. Koko speak to people using over 1,000 signs. Koko's gorilla friend Michael also have learned some sign language—over 500 signs. Sometimes, the two gorillas communicates with each other in this way.

Koko were able to name her own pet kitten, whom she called All Ball. Her favorite color are red, and her favorite toys is rubber alligators. She love to watch *Wild Kingdom* on television, and she also like films about children and animals, such as *Free Willy*. Koko's caregivers at the Gorilla Foundation has noticed that the gorilla's favorite book are *The Three Little Kittens*.

Also, a computer company were able to make a special computer for Koko. When she touch icons on the screen, the computer "speak" the word the icon represent. Koko also recognize the letters in her own name. Fans has wanted to send E-mail to Koko, but the gorilla's computer are not online.

 Interrupting Words

Often a subject and a verb are side by side in a sentence. When they are, agreement between them is usually easy to recognize. Many times, however, a phrase or a clause modifying the subject separates it from the verb. In such sentences a mistake in agreement may occur. The error that might happen is to make the verb agree with the word closest to it—rather than with its subject. To avoid making this mistake in agreement, first find the subject and then make the verb agree with it.

The agreement of a verb with its subject is not changed by any interrupting words.

Notice in each of the following examples that the subject and the verb agree in number—regardless of any interrupting words.

PREPOSITIONAL PHRASE
The <u>games</u> on the computer **were** installed yesterday afternoon.
(The plural helping verb *were* agrees with the plural subject *games,* even though the singular noun *computer* is closer to the verb.)

PARTICIPIAL PHRASE	The <u>monitor</u>, covered with notes, <u>is</u> mine. (*Is* agrees with *monitor,* not *notes.*)
NEGATIVE STATEMENTS	The program <u>architects</u>, not their manager, <u>design</u> the project. (*Design* agrees with *architects,* not *manager.*)
ADJECTIVE CLAUSES	Computer <u>programs</u> that compose music <u>are</u> a form of artificial intelligence. (*Are* agrees with *programs,* not *music.*)

A compound preposition—such as *in addition to, as well as, along with,* and *together with*—will often interrupt a subject and a verb. Make sure the verb always agrees with the subject, not the object of the compound preposition.

<u>Gail</u>, together with her sisters, **is** <u>starting</u> a computer software company.
(*Is* agrees with *Gail,* not *sisters.*)

The <u>boys</u>, as well as my uncle, **are** <u>installing</u> the satellite dish.
(*Are* agrees with *boys,* not *uncle.*)

PRACTICE YOUR SKILLS

● Check Your Understanding
Making Interrupted Subjects and Verbs Agree

Contemporary Life **Write the subject in each sentence. Next to each subject, write the form of the verb in parentheses that agrees with it.**

1. Many students at the science fair (was, were) honored for their technological creations.

2. The inventions, arranged on a table, (includes, include) telephones, speakers, and other electronics.

3. The cost of each project (averages, average) one hundred dollars.

4. Tyrone Purdy, unlike other students, (has, have) a parent who is a scientist.

5. Dr. Purdy, so helpful to us students, (hands, hand) out the awards while a photographer takes pictures.

6. The telephone that "speaks" the names of callers (is, are) my favorite invention.

7. The pager-on-a-necklace, including ports for phone jacks and printers, (wins, win) an award as well.

8. The underwater fisher's camera, not the musical earrings, (was, were) the first-place winner.

9. The lucky students who won first, second, and third place (was, were) given scholarships for college.

10. The second-place winner, as well as several other participants, (plan, plans) to attend M.I.T.

● Connect to the Writing Process: Editing
Using Subject and Verb Agreement

Write each verb that does not agree with its subject. Beside the verb, write its correct form.

Scientists who work at universities and laboratories regularly invents amazing items. Their expensive inventions, often funded by grants, introduces creative applications for technology. Scientists at the Massachusetts Institute of Technology Media Lab was able to create "intelligent clothes." For example, a television reporter, together with journalists of all kinds, are now able to stay ahead of the competition by wearing gloves! The reporter wear a glove equipped with a video camera in the palm. A pair of special glasses show the image being recorded.

These scientists at M.I.T. has created other wearable technology. People who travel to a foreign country has the option of wearing a translation vest. These vests, not a foreign language dictionary, is what will translate the tourists' speech. A speaker, wearing the vest, talk normally. Microphones built into the vest records the spoken words, and speakers at shoulder level relays the translation.

Also, pool players can wear smart caps. The camera on the hat analyze the position of the balls. Then the special software, which is loaded in these caps, identify the easiest shot. Special eyeglasses (like the reporter's glasses) shows the pool player how to line up winning shots.

Communicate Your Ideas

APPLY TO WRITING

Description: *Subject and Verb Agreement*

Your class is planning a Science Fair of the Future, and the theme is "wearable hardware." As a sample exhibit idea, you are shown the photograph on the preceding page of a pair of shoes that converts the wearer's steps into music. Wearing them, you could create your own dance music or analyze your jogging stride.

Write a description of your own idea for a "wearable hardware" creation. Describe what its purpose is, how it works, and where a person will wear it. Edit your writing for agreement between subjects and verbs. Make any necessary corrections, and then write the final copy.

 **QuickCheck** Mixed Practice

General Interest **Write the subject in each sentence. Then write the form of the underlined verb that agrees with the subject. If the verb is correct, write C.**

1. This lawn, covered with weeds, <u>need</u> Rodney's attention and expertise.

2. Rodney, one of my neighbors, <u>own</u> a lawn care and landscaping business.

3. His customers <u>is impressed</u> by his knowledge and skill.

4. Rodney <u>have told</u> me how he learned the business.

5. Informative books, not luck, <u>explains</u> his success.

6. In their high school, students who have money <u>buys</u> clothes and CDs.

7. Rodney, as well as his brothers, <u>was</u> not able to buy these things.

8. The books in the library <u>was</u> the key to their small business success.

9. The brothers, immersed in study, <u>was</u> able to learn lawn care and irrigation techniques.

10. Now, their accounts in the bank <u>hold</u> plenty of money for what the brothers need or want.

Common Agreement Problems

When you edit your writing, look for the following common agreement problems.

Compound Subjects

When you make two or more subjects agree with a verb, you should remember two rules.

When subjects are joined by *or, nor, either/or*, or *neither/nor*, the verb agrees with the closer subject.

> Either <u>Joe</u> or <u>Lola</u> <u>buys</u> vegetables at the Vine Street Farmers' Market.
> (*Buys* agrees with the closer subject *Lola*.)
>
> A <u>ladybug</u> or an <u>earthworm</u> <u>is</u> a helpful creature for a vegetable garden.
> (*Is* agrees with the closer subject *earthworm*.)

The same rule applies when one subject is singular and the other subject is plural.

> Neither the <u>trowel</u> nor our <u>shovels</u> <u>were</u> in sight.
> (*Were* agrees with the closer subject *shovels*—even though *trowel* is singular.)

When compound subjects are joined by other conjunctions, however, a different rule applies.

When subjects are joined by *and* or *both/and*, the verb is plural.

These conjunctions always indicate more than one. Since more than one is plural, the verb must be plural also.

The mulch and the fertilizer are in the barn.

(Two items—the *mulch* and the *fertilizer*—are in the barn. The verb must be plural to agree with both of them.)

Both the rakes and that wheelbarrow **were** left in the rain.

(Even though *wheelbarrow* is singular, the verb is still plural because the wheelbarrow and the rakes—together—were left in the rain.)

The second rule has certain exceptions. Two subjects joined by *and* occasionally refer to only one person or one thing. In such a case, the verb must be singular.

Fruit and cheese is my mom's favorite dessert.

(*Fruit and cheese* is considered one item.)

Strawberries and cream is also very good.

(*Strawberries and cream* is considered one item.)

Another exception involves the words *every* and *each*. If one of these words comes before a compound subject that is joined by *and,* each subject is considered separately. As a result, the verb must be singular to agree with a singular subject.

Every barn and fence receives a fresh coat of paint.

Each pond and creek brims with rainwater.

CONNECT TO WRITER'S CRAFT

If you take a look at the next sales circular that arrives in your mailbox, you will see how subject and verb agreement can make the difference between your getting a good buy or not.

Lawn Mower or Rototiller, Only $449.99!
Lawn Mower and Rototiller, Only $449.99!

In both instances, the ad omitted the verb—*is* in the first ad, *are* in the second—but you should be able to supply the verb that agrees with the subject.

PRACTICE YOUR SKILLS

● Check Your Understanding
Making Verbs Agree with Compound Subjects

Horticulture Topic **Write the correct form of the verb in parentheses.**

1. Wheat and corn (grows, grow) well in Washington.
2. For some reason neither snails nor slugs (crawl, crawls) over crushed eggshells.
3. Each flower garden and vegetable plot (was, were) sprinkled with eggshells.
4. Either chicken wire or a wooden fence (form, forms) a good garden enclosure.
5. On a busy farm, every man, woman, and child (is, are) given duties.
6. Bacon and eggs (are, is) many farmers' favorite breakfast food.
7. Neither chemical fertilizers nor chemical pesticides (is, are) used in organic gardens.
8. Every horticulturist and gardener (know, knows) that lavender repels insects in the garden and moths in the closet.
9. Peanuts or potatoes (grow, grows) on many of Oklahoma's farms.
10. Both cantaloupe and spinach (flourishes, flourish) in southwest Texas along the border of Mexico.

● Connect to the Writing Process: Revising
Making Compound Subjects and Verbs Agree

Write each sentence, replacing each subject with a compound subject. Use a variety of joining words, such as *either/or*, *both/and*, and *or*. Then change the verb form if necessary, making it agree with the compound subject.

11. Fruit is on sale at the market.
12. Each stump was cleared from the new garden plot.
13. Jelly is the peanut farmer's favorite sandwich.

14. Grapefruit is commonly grown in Florida.
15. The flowerpots are in the shed.
16. Every morning is a good time to water the bean patch.
17. The blackbird was not afraid of the scarecrow.
18. The squirrel was able to get into my garden despite the chain link fence.
19. Water is necessary for every plant's survival.
20. Each cherry was picked with care.

● Indefinite Pronouns as Subjects

A verb must agree in number with an indefinite pronoun used as a subject.

The indefinite pronouns in the following chart have been grouped according to number.

COMMON INDEFINITE PRONOUNS	
SINGULAR	another, anybody, anyone, anything, each, either, everybody, everyone, everything, much, neither, nobody, no one, one, somebody, someone, something
PLURAL	both, few, many, others, several
SINGULAR/PLURAL	all, any, most, none, some

A singular verb agrees with a singular indefinite pronoun, and a plural verb agrees with a plural indefinite pronoun.

SINGULAR   One of my golf balls is muddy.

PLURAL   Many of my golf balls are muddy.

The number of an indefinite pronoun in the singular/plural group is determined by the object of the prepositional phrase that follows it.

SINGULAR   <u>Some</u> of the equipment <u>is</u> on sale.

OR PLURAL   <u>Most</u> of the barbells <u>are</u> on sale.

PRACTICE YOUR SKILLS

● Check Your Understanding
Making Verbs Agree with Indefinite Pronoun Subjects

Contemporary Life

Write the subject in each sentence. Next to it, write the form of the verb in parentheses that agrees with the subject.

1. All of the players (has, have) received their letters.

2. Everybody at the pep rally (are, is) wearing the school colors, green and gold.

3. Both of the teams (wear, wears) green jerseys.

4. Most of the opposing team (have, has) the flu.

5. Neither of those footballs (is, are) mine.

6. Some of the basketball fans (has, have) arrived.

7. Others (plans, plan) to be here soon.

8. Everyone, including the band, (was, were) thirsty during halftime.

9. Any of the game plan (is, are) open to revision.

10. Another of my teammates (has, have) become severely dehydrated.

11. Several of the rackets (was, were) damaged.

12. All of the field (is, are) artificial grass.

13. Something left in one of these gymnasium lockers (smell, smells) horrible.

14. Each of those skates (needs, need) new blades.

15. Anything (is, are) possible with a team this dedicated.

16. Some of the court (was, were) being resurfaced.

17. Many of those helmets (fits, fit) too tightly.

18. One of my sisters (has, have) just made the track team.

19. None of my baseball bats (is, are) aluminum.

20. Few of the cracked hockey masks (gives, give) the players much protection.

● Connect to the Writing Process: Revising
Making Verbs and Indefinite Pronouns Agree

Rewrite each sentence twice. First, add a prepositional phrase with a plural object. Second, add a prepositional phrase with a singular object. Be sure to check that all subjects and verbs agree.

21. Some have finished the marathon.

22. Any are welcome.

23. None is accused of cheating.

24. Most train all day.

25. All is in the locker.

● Subjects in Inverted Order

A sentence is said to be in **inverted order** when the verb or part of the verb phrase comes before the subject. Even though a verb may precede a subject, it still must agree with the subject in number.

The subject and the verb of an inverted sentence must agree in number.

There are several types of inverted sentences. When you are looking for the subject in an inverted sentence, turn the sentence around to its natural order. To have the sentence make sense, you must occasionally drop *here* or *there* when putting the sentence into its natural order.

INVERTED ORDER	In the valley is a babbling brook.
	(A babbling *brook is* in the valley.)
QUESTION	Was the mountain visible in the fog?
	(The *mountain was* visible in the fog.)
SENTENCES BEGINNING WITH *HERE* OR *THERE*	Here are the hiking trails.
	(The hiking *trails are* here.)
	There is a waterfall on the edge of the cliff.
	(Drop *there*. A *waterfall is* on the edge of the cliff.)

You can learn more about sentences written in inverted order on pages 62–64.

PRACTICE YOUR SKILLS

● Check Your Understanding
Making Subjects and Verbs in Inverted Order Agree

Geography Topic **Write the subject in each sentence. Next to it write the form of the verb in parentheses that agrees with the subject.**

1. Along the Tennessee-North Carolina border (run, runs) a mountain range.

2. (Has, Have) you ever heard anyone talk about the Great Smoky Mountains?

3. There (is, are) a park called Great Smoky Mountain National Park on the highest peak.

4. (Do, Does) they know that the Great Basin between the Sierra Nevada and Wasatch Range in the western United States has no outlet to the sea?

5. Here (is, are) colorful, current maps of the five Great Lakes: Superior, Michigan, Huron, Erie, and Ontario.

6. (Were, Was) souvenir shops selling pieces of the Berlin Wall after it was brought down?

7. Across western Australia (stretches, stretch) the sands of the Great Sandy Desert.

8. (Is, Are) the tour scheduled to visit the Greater Antilles, a group of islands in the West Indies?

9. There (is, are) a seaport called Great Yarmouth on the eastern coast of England in Norfolk.

10. Off the northeast coast of Australia (lies, lie) the Great Barrier Reef, a coral reef 1,250 miles long.

● Connect to the Writing Process: Prewriting
Brainstorming: Sentences in Inverted Order

Referring to the preceding exercise, choose one of the geographical locations that interests you. Using sentences in inverted order, write down your thoughts and questions about this place. For example, you might write, "In the Great Smoky Mountains is a great hiking trail" or "Where is Australia located?" Then save your sentences for the following activity.

Communicate Your Ideas

APPLY TO WRITING

Oral Presentation: *Common Agreement Problems*

Using the prewriting you generated in the preceding exercise, write an oral presentation for your classmates. Answer the questions you have about the location, explain where the place is in relation to the United States, and describe other information that your classmates would find interesting. You will probably need to use reference sources such as maps and encyclopedias to gather information. When you finish, be sure to edit your presentation for agreement between subjects and verbs, paying special attention to compound subjects, indefinite pronouns as subjects, and subjects in inverted order.

QuickCheck Mixed Practice

Write each sentence, using the correct present tense form of the verb in parentheses.

1. (is) Both Sherlock Holmes and Dr. Watson ■ characters in a popular series of mystery stories.

2. (read) Many of the world's mystery fans ■ these stories by Arthur Conan Doyle.

3. (investigate) Throughout London and the surrounding countryside, Holmes ■ murders and thefts.

4. (is) There ■ cases such as the murderous "speckled band" and the disappearance of a horse called Silver Blaze.

5. (find) Across a windowsill, Hilton Cubitt ■ drawings of little stick-figure men.

6. (is) Neither Hilton nor the police ■ able to solve the mystery of the dancing men.

7. (is) All of the "dancing" hieroglyphics ■ interpreted by Holmes.

8. (chop) Someone ■ off a man's thumb in the story, "The Engineer's Thumb."

9. (is) "Where ■ we to find the photograph?" Holmes asks in "A Scandal in Bohemia."

10. (solve) No one ■ the mystery of the Musgrave Ritual until Holmes steps in.

11. (appear) The villain Colonel Moran ■ in "The Adventure of the Empty House."

12. (include) Some of Sherlock Holmes' talents ■ boxing and swordsmanship.

13. (analyze) Three characteristics Holmes ■ about suspects are nails, sleeves, and stride.

14. (Do) ■ Holmes know a great deal about chemistry?

15. (is) There ■ cases in which Holmes depends on his great knowledge of literature.

Other Agreement Problems

There are several other situations in which agreement between a subject and a verb may present a problem.

Collective Nouns

You may recall that a **collective noun** names a group of people or things. A collective noun may be either singular or plural—depending on how it is used in a sentence.

COMMON COLLECTIVE NOUNS			
band	congregation	flock	orchestra
class	crew	gang	swarm
committee	crowd	herd	team
colony	family	league	tribe

Use a singular verb with a collective-noun subject that is treated as a unit. Use a plural verb with a collective-noun subject that is treated as individual parts.

> The class **is** presently holding elections.
> (The class is working together as a whole unit in this sentence. As a result, the verb is singular.)
>
> The class **are** casting their ballots today.
> (The members of the class are acting independently—each one casting a ballot. As a result, the verb is plural.)

CONNECT TO SPEAKING AND WRITING

In informal language, collective nouns are often used with singular verbs. It sounds awkward to use plural verbs. Therefore when you discuss a collective noun as separate parts, practice using plural verbs to master agreement.

The band **are** voting for a new Drum Major.

Words Expressing Amounts or Times

Subjects that express amounts, measurements, weights, or times usually are considered to be a single unit. However, they often have plural forms.

A subject that expresses an amount, a measurement, a weight, or a time is usually considered singular and takes a singular verb.

QUANTITY	**Ten dollars** is the amount of my campaign contribution. (one amount of money)
	Five miles is the distance from my house to City Hall. (one unit of distance)
	Two pounds is the weight of this box of campaign buttons. (one unit of weight)
TIME	**Six months is** needed to prepare the candidates. (one period of time)
	Thirty minutes is how long the legislator spoke. (one period of time)

If an amount, measurement, weight, or time is treated in its individual parts, then the verb must be plural.

Two pounds of pencils **were** lost.

Ten dollars were in the treasurer's hand.

Six months have passed since the election.

When the subject is a fraction or a percent, the verb agrees with the object of the prepositional phrase that follows the subject.

SINGULAR	**One third** of my salary goes to taxes.
PLURAL	**One fourth** of the seniors are old enough to vote.

The Number of, A Number of

Although these expressions are very similar, one expression takes a singular verb and one takes a plural verb.

> Use a singular verb with *the number of* and a plural verb with *a number of.*

The number of students touring the White House is surprising. (singular)

A number of high school students intend to go into city government. (plural)

CONNECT TO WRITER'S CRAFT

Be sure to choose the correct expression for your writing purpose. **A number of tourists visit yearly** focuses on the action of the **tourists**. **The number of tourists escalates yearly** focuses on the action of the **number**.

Singular Nouns That Have Plural Forms

Even though a word ends in *-s*, it may not take a plural verb. Some nouns are plural in form but singular in meaning because they name a single thing—one area of knowledge or one type of disease, for example.

SINGULAR NOUNS WITH PLURAL FORMS			
civics	economics	gymnastics	mathematics
measles	molasses	mumps	news
physics	social studies	the United States	

> Use a singular verb with certain subjects that are plural in form but singular in meaning.

Civics is the study of citizens' rights and responsibilities.
The local news covers the mayor's weekly activities.

A second group of similar nouns are usually plural, as their form indicates. A third group can be either singular or plural—depending on how they are used in a sentence. If you are confused about a particular noun, it sometimes helps to check the dictionary.

SIMILAR NOUNS	
USUALLY PLURAL	barracks, data, eyeglasses, media, pliers, scissors, shears, slacks, thanks, trousers
SINGULAR/PLURAL	acoustics, athletics, headquarters, ethics, politics, tactics

Your eyeglasses **were** found in the courtroom. (plural)

The headquarters for the United Nations **is** located in New York City. (singular—an administrative center)

The headquarters **are** located on the outskirts of the town. (plural—a group of buildings)

Notice that if the word *pair* precedes a word that is usually plural, the verb is nevertheless singular because the verb then agrees with the singular noun *pair*.

SINGULAR   That pair of scissors is dull.

PLURAL   Those scissors are dull.

CONNECT TO SPEAKING AND WRITING

Although *data* and *media* are both plural nouns, many people use them as singular nouns in informal speech. However, in your formal speaking and writing, it is best to use *data* and *media* as plural nouns; their singular forms are *datum* and *medium*.

SINGULAR   My favorite medium of communication is the newspaper.

PLURAL   Various media are radio, television, and print.

SINGULAR   This datum is not the result I expected.

PLURAL   The data I collected are accurate.

PRACTICE YOUR SKILLS

● Check Your Understanding
Making Subjects and Verbs Agree

General Interest **Write the correct form of the verb in parentheses.**

1. A large number of the candidates (is, are) female.

2. Campaigning for school government (takes, take) up most of my sister's spare time.

3. Two thirds of the people in town (does, do) not vote.

4. Ten minutes (was, were) not a long wait to vote.

5. Sixty percent of the student body (has, have) voted in student government elections.

6. Three miles (is, are) the distance from here to the governor's mansion.

7. The jury (was, were) in complete disagreement throughout the deliberations.

8. The headquarters for Steve's campaign for class president (is, are) the corner pizza parlor.

9. The city government news (is, are) broadcast at five o'clock.

10. Almost three fourths of the apples in the basket (was, were) used in pies at the mayor's reception dinner.

● Connect to the Writing Process: Editing
Correcting Subject and Verb Agreement Problems

Write the subject and the correct verb form. If a sentence is correct, write C.

11. A swarm of reporters want to question the politician.

12. "Mumps are preventable with a vaccine," said the new county health commissioner.

13. Approximately four dollars was paid for each nominee's campaign poster.

14. The number of candidates for Student Council is surprisingly large.

15. The committee was arguing about the details of the voting procedure.

16. A group of students from the twelfth grade are ready to vote.

17. That pair of red suspenders look good on the senator.

18. Economics are Kevin's major at the University of Florida in Gainesville.

19. The media are distorting the candidate's remarks.

20. A number of students is planning for political careers.

Doesn't or Don't?

Doesn't and *don't* are contractions. When checking for agreement with a subject, say the two words of a contraction separately. Also keep in mind which contractions are singular and which are plural.

CONTRACTIONS	
SINGULAR	doesn't, hasn't, isn't, wasn't
PLURAL	don't, haven't, aren't, weren't

The verb part of a contraction must agree in number with the subject.

This cold weather **does**n't bother me at all.
These rainstorms **do**n't alter my plans.

Subjects with Linking Verbs

A predicate nominative follows a linking verb and identifies, renames, or explains the subject. Occasionally, however, a subject and its predicate nominative will not have the same number. The verb, nevertheless, agrees with the subject.

A verb agrees with the subject of a sentence, not with the predicate nominative.

Hail is small pieces of ice in a thunderstorm.

(The singular verb *is* agrees with the singular subject *hail*—even though the predicate nominative *pieces* is plural.)

Small pieces of ice in a thunderstorm are hail.

(*Are* agrees with the plural subject *pieces*—not with the singular predicate nominative *hail*.)

CONNECT TO SPEAKING AND WRITING

When writing, avoid creating sentences in which the subject and the predicate nominative do not agree in number.

| INCORRECT | Hailstones are a small **piece** of ice. |
| CORRECT | Hailstones are small **pieces** of ice. |

You can find lists of linking verbs on page L21.

Titles

Some titles may seem plural because they are composed of several words. A title, nevertheless, is the name of only one book, poem, play, work of art, country, or the like. As a result, a title is singular and takes a singular verb. Most multiword names of businesses and organizations are also considered singular.

A title is singular and takes a singular verb.

BOOK	*Great Expectations* is a novel by Charles Dickens.
POEM	"The Planters" is a poem by Margaret Atwood.
PLAY	*Death of a Salesman* is my favorite play.
WORK OF ART	*Midsummer* is an oil painting by Albert Joseph Moore.

COUNTRY	The Netherlands <u>is</u> an interesting vacation destination.
COMPANY	Barrett's Book Barn **is** having a sale on mystery novels.

PRACTICE YOUR SKILLS

● Check Your Understanding
Making Subjects and Verbs Agree

General Interest **Write the correct form of the verb in parentheses.**

1. Snowy ski slopes (is, are) a great attraction in Colorado.

2. He (doesn't, don't) know the way through the fog.

3. *The Iceman Cometh,* a play with four acts, (is, are) Eugene O'Neill's most celebrated work.

4. These rain boots (is, are) the perfect gift.

5. Ick! The snow (feel, feels) slushy and grainy.

6. (Doesn't, Don't) the weather bureau issue tornado warnings?

7. A tornado spinning across fields (look, looks) violent.

8. *Human Figure with Two Birds* (was, were) created from scrap wood, black paper, emery paper, and oil paints by Max Ernst.

9. Car Havens (is, are) the store for snow tires.

10. (Doesn't, Don't) daylight saving time start tonight?

● Connect to the Writing Process: Drafting
Writing Sentences in Which Subjects and Verbs Agree

Write sentences, following the directions indicated. Be sure that the subject and verb agree.

11. Use *doesn't.*

12. Use *don't.*

13. Use a linking verb.

14. Use the title of a book.

15. Use the title of a company.

16. Use the title of a poem.

Who, Which, and That

Who, which, and *that* are often used as relative pronouns to begin an adjective clause. When one of these words is the subject of the clause, the number of its verb will depend upon the number of the pronoun's antecedent.

> **In an adjective clause in which the relative pronoun *who,* *which,* or *that* is used as the subject, the verb agrees with the antecedent of the relative pronoun.**

Bobby read a nonfiction **book** that was a thousand pages long.
(The antecedent of *that* is *book.* Since *book* is singular, *was* is also singular.)

Find the titles of three **books** that deal with space exploration.
(The antecedent of *that* is *books.* Since *books* is plural, *deal* is also plural.)

If an adjective clause is preceded by the expression *one of,* the verb in the clause is usually plural.

Alfred, Lord Tennyson is *one of* the **poets** who **were** appointed poet laureate of England.
(The antecedent of *who* is *poets,* not *one.*)

You can learn more about adjective clauses on pages L148–L153.

PRACTICE YOUR SKILLS

Check Your Understanding
Making Verbs Agree with Relative Pronouns

Literature Topic **Write the correct form of the verb in parentheses.**

1. Did you see the film that (was, were) adapted from Charlotte Brontë's *Jane Eyre?*

2. Jane Eyre and Mr. Rochester, who (is, are) the primary characters, grow to love each other.

3. A mysterious, ghostlike woman, who (is, are) locked in the attic, sets Jane's room afire.

4. *Wide Sargasso Sea,* which (were, was) written by Jean Rhys, creates a story for this mysterious woman.

5. *Shirley* is one of the novels that (was, were) written by Charlotte Brontë.

6. This author had two sisters who (was, were) writers.

7. *Wuthering Heights* is the novel that (was, were) published under Emily Brontë's pen name, Ellis Bell.

8. This is a story that (contain, contains) love and hate, riches and poverty, curses and ghosts.

9. The poems that the sisters wrote (was, were) published as *Poems by Currer, Ellis,* and *Acton Bell.*

10. Anne Brontë's novel *The Tenant of Wildfell Hall,* which (is, are) one of her two novels, was published in 1848.

Connect to the Writing Process: Editing
Using Subject and Verb Agreement

Write the correct form of the verb in parentheses.

11. (is) Miss Marple and Hercule Poirot, who ▨ Agatha Christie's most famous creations, both solve crimes.

12. (is) These fictional characters, which ▨ beloved by many, are featured in separate mystery series.

13. (discover) Jane Marple is an old woman who ▨ murders and other crimes in unexpected places.

14. (is) *The Murder at the Vicarage,* which ▨ her first adventure, chronicles a murder investigation.

15. (occur) The victim of the murder that ▨ at the vicarage is the unlikable Colonel Protheroe.

16. (live) Two suspects are the vicar and his wife, who ▨ in the vicarage.

17. (emerge) Other suspects who ▨ are the victim's wife, Mrs. Protheroe, and her lover, Lawrence Redding.

18. (has) Miss Marple discovers seven people who ▨ a motive for the murder.

19. (elude) The identity of the murderer, which  the police, is revealed by the demure Miss Marple.

20. (feature) A number of short stories ▇ Miss Marple.

Communicate Your Ideas

APPLY TO WRITING

Character Essay: **Subject and Verb Agreement**

You have decided to write a detective story for a mystery magazine. Write a letter to your literary agent, K. B. Anderson, asking if she thinks your detective is marketable. Describe your detective. What are his or her quirks? What types of mysteries does he or she solve? Where does he or she live? Pay attention to making subjects and verbs agree.

QuickCheck Mixed Practice

Science Topic **Write the verbs that do not agree with their subjects. Then write those verbs correctly.**

What does you know about trees? Do you know that the leaves on a tree has several functions? One of these functions are to make food for the tree. Carbon dioxide from the air is taken in by the leaves. Water and minerals from the soil is taken in by the roots. The chlorophyll in leaves absorbs energy from the sun and then change the carbon dioxide and water into glucose, food.

Leaves also give off enormous quantities of water. Some of the water that flow from the roots to the leaves are used to make food. Most of the rest of the water in leaves evaporate through tiny holes on the surface of the leaves.

Correcting Errors with Modifiers

Write the correct form of each verb in parentheses.

1. New Orleans—with its ornate grillwork, marvelous food, and fascinating history—(attracts, attract) many tourists from around the world.

2. One of my presents (was, were) a gift certificate from the huge video store on Madison Avenue.

3. (Was, Were) many world records broken in the 1984 Olympics in Los Angeles?

4. Both the hockey team and the baseball team (has, have) won state championships this year.

5. Mathematics (is, are) a special kind of language.

6. (Is, Are) ten dollars too much for that thin paperback book?

7. My uncle, not my cousins, (was, were) visiting at the end of August.

8. A grouping of millions of stars (is, are) called a galaxy.

9. Ham and eggs (makes, make) a hearty breakfast for our family.

10. In the basket (was, were) two apples, a pear, and a bunch of grapes.

11. (Doesn't, Don't) Richard play on the varsity basketball team anymore?

12. There (is, are) more than 19 species of buzzards.

13. Neither the center nor the guard (knows, know) that play well.

14. A gift and a card (was, were) on the table.

15. All of today's newspaper (is, are) wet.

Correcting Errors with Subject-Verb Agreement

Write the following sentences, correcting each mistake. If a sentence is correct, write C after the number.

1. Either a bookcase or some shelves is needed.
2. Two–thirds of the students has voted.
3. Has all the applicants been interviewed?
4. This week there have been several warm days.
5. Don't the movie start at 5:30?
6. Neither of these reports has any footnotes.
7. Barry's voice and acting ability is exceptional.
8. The number of boys who have jobs are growing.
9. Most of those cantaloupes are too soft.
10. Sam, along with members of his family, are here.
11. Both Kansas and Missouri has a Kansas City.
12. Pancakes and sausage are my favorite breakfast.
13. None of those buses stops at the mall.
14. Everyone, including the musicians, were lined up for the final curtain call.
15. Throughout the West is the ruins of once prosperous mining towns.

Writing Sentences

Write five sentences that follow the directions below.

1. Write a sentence in which the subject is a number of miles.
2. Write a sentence with a collective noun as a subject. Write the sentence so that the members of the group act independently.
3. Write a question that begins with *doesn't* or *don't*.
4. Write a sentence in which the subject and the verb are separated by a participial phrase.
5. Write a sentence that contains a subordinate clause beginning with *that*. Make the subject in the independent clause singular.

Language and *Self-Expression*

Painter of Micali. *Hydria with Running Figures,* date unknown.
Museo Gregoriano Etrusco, Rome.

Artist unknown, Greek. *Women Gathering Fruit,* ca. 5th century B.C.
Red-figured cup. Musée Vivenel, Compiègne, France.

Archaeologists consider red-figure pottery, such as the artwork pictured on the right, the product of a more advanced Greek culture than that of the black-figure period. In what ways might a culture advance enough for the differences to be reflected in its art? Write a short essay using both pieces to compare and contrast the different periods to which they belong.

Prewriting Make a two-column list of the differences you see in the artworks. If a graphic organizer would be a greater help, use a Venn Diagram.

Drafting Begin the first paragraph with a topic sentence stating that you will both compare and contrast the two works. Include the similarities if you mentioned comparison first. Then begin your second paragraph with a transitional expression to lead into your contrasts. End your essay with a concluding statement.

Revising Reread your work, several times if necessary. Be sure your sentences flow.

Editing Be sure that all your subjects and verbs agree. Also check grammar, spelling, and mechanics.

Publishing Once all corrections have been made, write or print out a clean copy of your essay. You might publish it by sharing it with your class.

Another Look

Agreement of Subjects and Verbs

A verb must agree with its subject in number. *(page L289)*
A singular subject takes a singular verb. *(page L290)*
A plural subject takes a plural verb. *(page L290)*
The first helping verb must agree in number with its subject. *(page L290)*
The agreement of a verb with its subject is not changed by any
  interrupting words. *(page L293)*

Common Agreement Problems

When subjects are joined by *or, nor, either/or,* or *neither/nor,* the verb
  agrees with the closer subject. *(page L298)*
When subjects are joined by *and* or *both/and,* the verb is plural.
  (page L298)
A verb must agree in number with an indefinite pronoun used as a
  subject. *(page L301)*
The subject and the verb of an inverted sentence must agree in number.
  (page L303)

Other Agreement Problems

Use a singular verb with a collective-noun subject that is thought of as a
  unit. Use a plural verb with a collective-noun subject that is treated as
  individual parts. *(page L307)*
A subject that expresses an amount, a measurement, a weight, or a time
  is usually considered singular and takes a singular verb. *(page L308)*
Use a singular verb with *the number of* and a plural verb with *a number of.*
  (page L309)
Use a singular verb with certain subjects that are plural in form but
  singular in meaning. *(page L309)*
The verb part of a contraction must agree in number with the subject.
  (page L312)
A verb agrees with the subject of a sentence, not with the predicate
  nominative. *(page L312)*
A title is singular and takes a singular verb. *(page L313)*
In an adjective clause in which the relative pronoun *who, which,* or *that*
  is used as the subject, the verb agrees with the antecedent of the
  relative pronoun. *(page L315)*

Posttest

Directions
Write the letter of the best way to write the underlined verb(s) in each sentence. If the underlined part contains no error, write _D_.

EXAMPLE

1. Some of the detergent <u>was spilled</u> on the floor.

    1   **A**   were spilled

          B   have been spilled

          C   are spilled

          D   No error

ANSWER   **1**   **D**

1. There are some traffic signs that <u>is understood</u> in all countries.

2. Two fifths of Dad's salary <u>go</u> into the family savings account every month.

3. The number of honor students <u>are growing</u> year by year at our school.

4. Neither my brother nor his friends <u>wants</u> to dance.

5. Amy, not her friends, <u>supports</u> my position on this issue.

6. Long grain white rice, along with cheese and pine nuts, <u>are</u> my favorite side dish.

7. <u>Has</u> the audience <u>been seated</u>?

8. Some of the dishes in the dining room cabinet <u>has been broken</u>.

9. The orchestra <u>has put</u> away all their equipment.

10. A number of students in this class <u>has</u> consistently <u>appeared</u> on the honor roll.

1 **A** was understood
   B has been understood
   C are understood
   D No error

2 **A** have gone
   B goes
   C were going
   D No error

3 **A** were growing
   B is growing
   C have been growing
   D No error

4 **A** want
   B has wanted
   C does want
   D No error

5 **A** support
   B have supported
   C were supporting
   D No error

6 **A** were
   B have
   C is
   D No error

7 **A** Have been seated?
   B Were seated?
   C Were being seated?
   D No error

8 **A** have been broken
   B was broken
   C be broken
   D No error

9 **A** was putting
   B is putting
   C have put
   D No error

10 **A** is appearing
   B have appeared
   C was appearing
   D No error

CHAPTER 8

Using Adjectives and Adverbs

 **Pretest**

Directions
Read the passage and choose the word or group of words that belongs in each numbered, underlined space. Write the letter of the correct answer.

Example

1. You __(1)__ to be a weather forecaster to predict weather.

    1 **A**   don't never have

        B   don't have

        C   don't hardle have

        D   don't scarcely have

Answer   **1** **B**

In 1803, Luke Howard, an English scientist, devised the basic system of cloud classification. This system of ten kinds of clouds still works __(1)__ even today. In fact, for over 200 years, his cloud classification system remains better than __(2)__ system. The __(3)__ clouds are nimbostratus clouds, which are called rain clouds. They are often __(4)__ than other clouds, and they __(5)__ exceed even a mile up into the sky. Because these clouds often produce rain or snow, they look __(6)__ to people with outdoor plans. __(7)__ threatening are stratus clouds. The rain in these clouds is always less than __(8)__ clouds. Stratus clouds are __(9)__ because they only produce drizzle or mist. The __(10)__ clouds of all, of course, are the cumulus clouds, which are called fair-weather clouds.

1
A well
B good
C better
D best

2
A any
B a
C any other
D this

3
A closer and most familiar
B closest and more familiar
C closer and more familiar
D closest and most familiar

4
A darker
B most darker
C more darker
D more darkerer

5
A don't never
B don't ever
C don't hardly
D don't barely

6
A bad
B badly
C more bad
D more badly

7
A Little
B Less
C Lesser
D Least

8
A other
B in other
C the rain in other
D the rain in

9
A nice
B nicer
C more nicer
D most nicest

10
A most best
B best
C bestest
D most better

Vincent van Gogh. *Enclosed Field with Rising Sun,* 1889.
Oil on canvas, 27⅔ by 35½ inches. Private collection.

Describe What kinds of lines does van Gogh use to depict the vegetation in the field? What kinds does he use for the sun and its rays? What do you see in the upper right of the canvas, just beyond the field's enclosure?

Analyze Even though van Gogh is more an impressionist than a realist painter, how are the lines in his painting true-to-life? In what ways are the colors he uses realistic?

Interpret What kind of order would a writer use to describe this painting? Why? If you were writing a description, where would you begin and end?

Judge How is this painting different from a photograph of the same field? Which would give you more detail? Which would offer you more emotion? If you had a choice, which would you prefer to depict this scene? Why?

At the end of this chapter, you will use the artwork to stimulate ideas for writing.

Comparison of Adjectives and Adverbs

Everyone has preferences. You may feel, for example, that meat loaf tastes *good* and spaghetti tastes *better;* but a thick, juicy steak tastes the *best* of all. Adjectives and adverbs have more than one form to express such preferences. This chapter will review the different forms of comparison, as well as some problems you might have with making comparisons.

The three forms that most adjectives and adverbs take to show the degrees of comparison are the positive, the comparative, and the superlative.

Most modifiers show the degree of comparison by changing form.

The basic form of an adjective or an adverb is the **positive degree.** It is used when no comparison is being made—when you simply are making a statement about a person or a thing.

ADJECTIVE	This route to the track meet is **quick**.
ADVERB	Brad can run **fast**.

When two people, things, or actions are being compared, the **comparative degree** is used. Notice that *–er* has been added to *quick* and *fast*.

ADJECTIVE	Of the two routes to the track meet, this one is **quicker**.
ADVERB	Of the two runners, Brad can run **faster**.

When more than two people, things, or actions are being compared, the **superlative degree** is used. Notice that *–est* has been added to *quick* and *fast*.

ADJECTIVE	Of the three routes to the track meet, this one is **quickest**.
ADVERB	Of all the runners in the race, Brad can run **fastest**.

You can learn more about adjectives and adverbs on pages L24–L36.

Regular and Irregular Comparison

Most adjectives and adverbs form their comparative and superlative degrees in the same way, following a few simple rules. A few modifiers, however, form their comparative and superlative degrees irregularly.

Regular Comparison

The comparative and superlative forms of most adjectives and adverbs are determined by the number of syllables in them.

> Add *–er* to form the comparative degree and *–est* to form the superlative degree of one-syllable modifiers.

ONE-SYLLABLE MODIFIERS		
Positive	**Comparative**	**Superlative**
young	younger	youngest
hot	hotter	hottest
soon	sooner	soonest
green	greener	greenest

You probably have noticed that a spelling change sometimes occurs when an ending is added to a modifier. If you are not sure how to form the comparative or superlative degree of a modifier, check the dictionary.

Most two-syllable words form their comparative degree by adding *–er* and their superlative degree by adding *–est*. Some of these words, however, use *more* and *most* because the words would sound awkward—or be impossible to pronounce—if *–er* or *–est* were added. You would never say, for example, "carefuler" or "famouser." *More* and *most* are also used with all adverbs that end in *–ly*.

> Use *–er* or *more* to form the comparative degree and *–est* or *most* to form the superlative degree of two-syllable modifiers.

TWO-SYLLABLE MODIFIERS		
Positive	**Comparative**	**Superlative**
graceful	more graceful	most graceful
early	earlier	earliest
slowly	more slowly	most slowly

Use *more* to form the comparative degree and *most* to form the superlative degree of modifiers with three or more syllables.

MODIFIERS WITH THREE OR MORE SYLLABLES		
Positive	**Comparative**	**Superlative**
dangerous	more dangerous	most dangerous
rapidly	more rapidly	most rapidly
furious	more furious	most furious

Less and *least* are used to form negative comparisons.

NEGATIVE COMPARISONS		
Positive	**Comparative**	**Superlative**
tasty	less tasty	least tasty
steadily	less steadily	least steadily

Irregular Comparison

A few adjectives and adverbs change form completely for the comparative and superlative degrees.

IRREGULAR MODIFIERS		
Positive	**Comparative**	**Superlative**
bad/badly/ill	worse	worst
good/well	better	best
little	less	least
many/much	more	most

The endings *–er* and *–est* should never be added to the comparative and superlative forms of the irregular modifiers on the preceding page. For example, you should never use "worser" as the comparative form of *bad*.

PRACTICE YOUR SKILLS

● Check Your Understanding
Forming the Comparison of Modifiers

Write each modifier. Beside it, write its comparative and superlative forms.

1. weak	**6.** light	**11.** little
2. hurriedly	**7.** different	**12.** quickly
3. good	**8.** bad	**13.** clever
4. horrible	**9.** great	**14.** many
5. busy	**10.** unsafe	**15.** swift

● Check Your Understanding
Using the Correct Form of Comparison

Contemporary Life **Write the correct form of the modifier in parentheses.**

16. Of the three boys, Colin devised the (better, best) game plan.

17. Rita's, not Amy's, kite flew (higher, highest).

18. Jan swam across the pool (more, most) rapidly than Ty.

19. Which sport do you like (better, best): football, basketball, or tennis?

20. Which has the (more, most) photogenic mascot, our high school or theirs?

21. Of your two friends who play soccer, which one is (more, most) athletic?

22. Which city has the (larger, largest) sports arena: Dallas or San Francisco?

23. Since there are two acceptable candidates for team captain, the coach has to choose the (better, best) one.

24. I don't know which I like (less, least), running laps or doing push-ups.

25. Alex is the (louder, loudest) of all the fans.

● Connect to the Writing Process: Editing
Using Comparisons

Write each incorrect modifier. Beside it, write the correct form.

On October 17, 1989, baseball fans attended what would become their more memorable game ever. On this fateful day, over 62,000 fans packed Candlestick Park for the third game of the World Series. As the game wore on, the fans became most excited, stomping their feet and doing the wave. At 5:04 P.M., a Richter-magnitude 7.1 earthquake struck. At first, fans did not suspect anything dangerouser than the bleachers' shaking from stomping feet. Then they realized that an event most life-threatening than rumbling bleachers had occurred: an earthquake had shaken the entire San Francisco Bay area. This 20-second earthquake was the baddest quake in years. Its shocks reached San Francisco from the epicenter, 60 miles to the south. Six years earlier, in 1983, Candlestick Park had been examined and then reinforced to a more high level of structural integrity. The 1989 Loma Prieta Earthquake, therefore, did not cause extensiver damage to the ballpark than could be repaired in about a week. Ten days after the earthquake, the World Series continued in Candlestick Park.

Connect to the Writing Process: Prewriting
Brainstorming Comparisons

Consider the sports featured in the following photographs or a sport you like more. Brainstorm a list of comparisons explaining why this sport is superior. Use regular and irregular comparisons.

Communicate Your Ideas

APPLY TO WRITING
Persuasive Essay: *Regular and Irregular Comparisons*

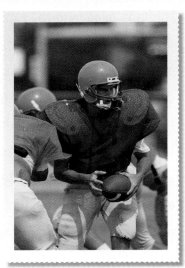

A graduate of your school has donated $5,000 to the athletic department. Your principal has announced an essay contest, and the winner will determine how the $5,000 is used.

Write a persuasive essay describing why your chosen sport is more deserving of the money than any other. Referring to the list you brainstormed, write the first draft. Include facts, examples, and details to support your major points. Then after you revise your essay, edit it, correcting any errors in regular and irregular comparisons.

General
Interest **Write the correct form of the modifier in parentheses.**

1. Which is (longer, longest), a yard or a meter?

2. Which one—George, Thomas, or Ken—ran (faster, fastest) in the 100-meter dash?

3. Since there were two liters of juice in the refrigerator, I drank the (older, oldest) one first.

4. Leroy's essay on the metric system was (more, most) informative than Maria's.

5. Who do you think is the (heavier, heaviest) person, the 50-kilo Lewis or the 50-pound James?

6. Which is (shorter, shortest): the centimeter, the millimeter, or the inch?

7. I think the inch is the (more, most) useful unit of measure.

8. Which costs (less, least), the ruler or the yardstick?

9. Of the centipede and the millipede, which has (more, most) legs?

10. The races include the one-kilometer, the two-kilometer, and the five-kilometer; I think the two-kilometer race would be (better, best) for you.

11. Jesse Owens jumped (farther, farthest) than Luz Long of Germany, a total of 26¾ feet, to win an Olympic gold medal for long jump in 1936.

12. Owens ran the 200-meter dash (faster, fastest) than all other runners to win gold again.

13. Kenny Brack averaged 153.176 mph per lap as the (better, best) of all drivers in the Indy 500 in 1999.

14. The track at Indianapolis is a 2½ mile oval on which the curves are (more, most) dangerous than the straight-away lengths.

15. Do you think a race-car driver is (less, least) fit than a long-distance runner?

⊙ Problems with Comparisons

When you edit your work, look for the following problems that can result when adjectives and adverbs are used with comparisons.

Double Comparisons

Use only one method of forming the comparative and superlative degrees at a time. Using both methods simultaneously results in a **double comparison**.

Do not use both *–er* and *more* to form the comparative degree, or both *–est* and *most* to form the superlative degree of modifiers.

DOUBLE COMPARISON	That snake is **more longer** than this one.
CORRECT	That snake is **longer** than this one.
DOUBLE COMPARISON	This is the **most loudest** parrot.
CORRECT	This is the **loudest** parrot.

Illogical Comparisons

When you write a comparison, be sure you compare two or more similar things. When you compare different things, the comparison becomes illogical.

Compare only items of a similar kind.

ILLOGICAL COMPARISON	A dachshund's **legs** are shorter than most other **dogs.**
	(*Legs* are being compared with *dogs.*)
LOGICAL COMPARISON	A dachshund's **legs** are shorter than other dogs' **legs.**
	(*Legs* are now being compared with *legs.*)

LOGICAL COMPARISON	A dachshund's **legs** are shorter than most other **dogs'.**
	(With the possessive *dogs'*, legs is understood; therefore, *legs* are being compared with *legs*.)
LOGICAL COMPARISON	A dachshund's **legs** are shorter than **those** of other dogs.
	(The demonstrative pronoun *those* takes the place of *legs;* therefore, *legs* are being compared with *legs*.)
ILLOGICAL COMPARISON	Roy's **puppy** looked different from the **picture.**
	(*Puppy* is being compared with a picture.)
LOGICAL COMPARISON	Roy's **puppy** looked different from the **puppy** in the picture.
	(Now Roy's *puppy* is being compared with a *puppy* in a picture.)

You can learn about using an apostrophe with possessives on pages L471–L479.

Other and *Else* in Comparisons

Very often, one or more people or things will be compared with other people or things in the same group. When you make such a comparison, however, be sure you do not appear to compare a person or a thing with itself.

Add *other* or *else* when comparing a member of a group with the rest of the group.

INCORRECT	In today's show Greased Lightning has won more awards than any horse.
	(Since Greased Lightning is a horse in the show, it is being compared with itself.)
CORRECT	In today's show Greased Lightning has won more awards than any **other** horse.
	(*Greased Lightning* is now being compared only with the *other* horses.)

INCORRECT	The pet store manager, Mandy, knows more about fish than anyone in the store. *(Since Mandy is in the store, she is being compared with herself.)*
CORRECT	The pet store manager, Mandy, knows more about fish than anyone **else** in the store. *(Mandy is now being compared only with the other people in the store.)*

CONNECT TO SPEAKING AND WRITING

The next time you listen to advertisements on the radio or television, notice the misleading manner in which many product "comparisons" are made. For example, some advertisers will give you the first half of a comparison but not the second half.

> Our pizza is Number One because it has more toppings.
> (It has more toppings than what?)

When you hear or read an advertisement that only partially completes a comparison, finish the comparison and then decide for yourself if the product is a superior one!

PRACTICE YOUR SKILLS

Check Your Understanding
Identifying Mistakes with Comparisons

General Interest **Using the following abbreviations, write the type of each mistake. If a sentence is correct, write C.**

double comparison = *d.c.*   illogical comparison = *i.c.*
needs *other* or *else* in comparison = *o.e.*

1. Fifi jumps higher and farther than any dog in the show.

2. A properly fed animal will perform more better than one indulged with unhealthy snacks.

3. Nathan has more pets than anyone on the obedience school staff.

4. Though not the prettiest canines, pit bulls are perhaps more popular watchdogs than any dog.

5. I think a rabbit's fur is more softer than even a cat's fur.

6. The beauty of this stray mutt is greater than the purebred Great Dane.

7. Andrew is fairer than any other judge on the regional cat show panel.

8. The African elephant probably has larger eyes than any animal in the world.

9. This dog-walkers' club is the most wonderful idea of the summer!

10. Chu is kinder to animals than anyone in his family.

Connect to the Writing Process: Editing
Correcting Mistakes with Comparisons

11.–18. Write the incorrect sentences in the preceding exercise, correcting the mistakes in the use of comparisons.

Connect to the Writing Process: Drafting
Drafting: Writing Comparisons

Write a sentence that includes a comparison for each direction.

19. Compare one owl to several owls.

20. Compare your two favorite animals.

21. Use *other* in a comparison.

22. Include *else* in a comparison.

23. Write a product ad for a pet product.

24. Compare a famous animal to other animals of the same species.

25. Compare two different kinds of fish.

26. Write an ad for a pet you would like to sell.

Comparison of Adjectives and Adverbs **L337**

APPLY TO WRITING
Evaluation: *Comparisons*

Henri Rousseau. *Tropical Storm with a Tiger (Surprise),* 1891.
Oil on canvas, 51⅛ by 31³/₁₆ inches. National Gallery, London.

Wang Yani. *Little Monkeys and Mummy,*
1980.
Ink and pigment on paper, 15 by 21 inches.

You are a judge in an art contest, and you must decide which one of these works of art deserves first place. Write your evaluation of the two paintings for the awards committee. Compare strengths and weaknesses in use of color, use of space, originality, meaningfulness of content, and any other elements you choose to evaluate. After writing the first draft, edit your work for mistakes in using comparisons. Then write the final copy.

QuickCheck Mixed Practice

Art Topic **Write each sentence, correcting the mistakes in comparisons. If a sentence is correct, write C.**

1. Primary colors like blue and red are more purer than secondary colors like purple and orange.

2. Yellow and green can be seen more readily by the human eye than any colors.

3. Isn't hot pink much more brighter than pastel pink?

4. These greens and yellows are more cheerful than black and silver.

5. Yellow, red, and orange hues are the most brightest colors of all.

6. That double rainbow was more vivid than any rainbow I have seen.

7. Does a rainbow exhibit more colors than a sunset?

8. Yellow is more analogous to yellow-green than to orange.

9. Colors that are opposite each other on the color wheel are more complementary than those next to each other.

10. Except for water, the sky contains more hues of blue and white than any part of nature.

11. Turquoise is the most universal color for people to wear.

12. Which is paler: orange, peach, or rust?

13. Purple is more quicker associated with royalty than red.

14. Blend white with any color to soften it.

15. A prism is a better tool than anything for refracting white light into the colors of a rainbow.

Problems with Modifiers

You should be aware of the following usage problems with adjectives and adverbs.

Adjective or Adverb?

Although adjectives and adverbs are both modifiers, they are very different in many other ways. You learned in the grammar section of this book that an adjective describes a noun or pronoun. You also learned that an adjective usually comes before the noun or pronoun it describes, or it follows a linking verb. Adjectives are usually easy for you to recognize because they answer the following questions.

WHICH ONE?	That recipe is **easy.**
WHAT KIND?	This lemonade tastes **sweet.**
HOW MANY?	I have **three** cookies.
HOW MUCH?	I need **more** butter for this frosting.

Remember that some verbs—such as *feel, smell,* and *taste*—can be either linking verbs or action verbs. When they are used as linking verbs, they are often followed by an adjective.

LINKING VERB	The milk **smelled** sour.
	(*Smelled* links *milk* and *sour*—sour milk.)
ACTION VERB	I **smelled** the milk.
	(*Smelled* is used as an action verb.)

If you are not sure whether a verb is being used as a linking verb or as an action verb, substitute the verb *is*. If the sentence makes sense, the verb is a linking verb. If it does not make sense, the verb is an action verb.

You can find a list of common linking verbs and a list of additional linking verbs on page L21.

Like adjectives, adverbs are modifiers. Adverbs describe verbs, adjectives, and other adverbs. Because adverbs can be placed almost anywhere in a sentence, ask the following questions to find them.

WHERE?	Place the carved roast **here.**
WHEN?	**Yesterday** I made butterscotch pudding.
HOW?	**Briskly** whisk the eggs.
TO WHAT EXTENT?	Please don't stir the muffin batter **too long.**
	I'll have another of those **wonderfully** tasty crab puffs!

Because so many adverbs end in *–ly,* they are usually easy to recognize. Remember, however, that a few adjectives—such as *early* and *lively*—also end in *–ly.*

ADVERB	He cooks breakfast **daily.**
	(*Daily* tells when he cooks breakfast.)
ADJECTIVE	His **daily** ritual includes a healthful breakfast.
	(*Daily* tells what kind of ritual it is.)

You may have noticed that a few words—such as *first, hard, high, late,* and *long*—do not change form whether they are used as an adjective or an adverb.

ADVERB	Eat **first** and then wash the pans.
	(*First* tells when you should eat.)
ADJECTIVE	His **first** omelet was a success.
	(*First* tells which omelet was successful.)

Good or *Well?*

Good is always an adjective. *Well* is usually used as an adverb. *Well* is used as an adjective, however, when it means "in good health" or "satisfactory."

ADJECTIVE	Sally is a **good** cook.
ADVERB	Sally cooks **well.**
ADJECTIVE	Sally doesn't feel **well** today. (in good health)

Bad or *Badly?*

Bad is an adjective and often follows a linking verb. *Badly* is used as an adverb.

ADJECTIVE	This egg smells **bad.**
ADVERB	Oh! I've **badly** jammed the garbage disposal.

CONNECT TO SPEAKING AND WRITING

In casual conversation, it is acceptable to use *bad* or *badly* after the verb *feel*. In formal writing, however, always use *bad* as an adjective and *badly* as an adverb.

| IN WRITING | I feel **bad** about taking the last cookie. |
| IN CONVERSATION | I feel **badly** about taking the last cookie. |

Double Negatives

Some words are considered negatives. In most sentences two negatives, called a **double negative**, should not be used together.

Avoid using a double negative.

COMMON NEGATIVES	
but (meaning "only")	none
barely	no one
hardly	not (and its contraction *n't*)
neither	nothing
never	only
no	scarcely

DOUBLE NEGATIVE	Sue doesn't have **no** choice in this meal.
CORRECT	Sue doesn't have any choice in this meal.
DOUBLE NEGATIVE	There isn't **hardly** any reason to eat now.
CORRECT	There isn't any reason to eat now.
CORRECT	There is **hardly** any reason to eat now.

PRACTICE YOUR SKILLS

● Check Your Understanding
Identifying Mistakes in the Use of Modifiers

Contemporary Life

Using the following abbreviations, write the type of each mistake. If a sentence is correct, write C.

adjective or adverb = *a. a.*   *good* or *well* = *g. w.*
bad or *badly* = *b. b.*   double negative = *d. n.*

1. Everyone did good on the home economics final exam.
2. Jeff looked hungry at the feast the class cooked.
3. Liza did quite well in baking crab puffs.
4. No one knew nothing about making chocolate mousse.
5. Those who arrived to class early got the best utensils.
6. "The early bird gets the worm!" shouted Shelly, grabbing the best of the three mixers.
7. Don't feel bad if your first piecrust is a little tough.
8. That marmalade tastes bitterly.
9. There ain't no reason why you can't help wash dishes.
10. That fish casserole smells rather strongly.
11. I don't have hardly any sugar left.
12. Gareth felt bad about burning the cinnamon rolls.
13. Because of Don's confusing directions, we could not hardly make a successful soufflé.
14. Don't you think this frosted cake looks well?
15. After eating your cooking, I don't feel good.

16. We had not worked hardly a minute before someone broke a pie plate.

17. Mix the butter, sugar, and eggs together very well.

18. When Julie said she didn't want no dessert, I said I didn't want none neither.

19. My stomach never hurt as bad as it did when I ate that bad egg.

20. How good did you sterilize that surface where the poultry had lain?

● **Connect to the Writing Process:** Editing
Correcting Mistakes in Comparisons

21.–34. Write the incorrect sentences in the preceding exercise, correcting each mistake in comparisons.

CONNECT TO WRITER'S CRAFT

Inexperienced writers often use comparisons that have become clichés through overuse. Similes such as "black as night," "flat as a pancake," and "thin as a rail" have been used so often that they no longer create any special image in a reader's mind. As you develop your writing skills, practice writing comparisons that are fresh, surprising, and vivid. The extra thought is worth the results! ●

Communicate Your Ideas

APPLY TO WRITING

Description: *Similes*

From the list of trite similes on the following page, choose one that you often read or hear. (If you know of a different simile you'd rather use, that is fine.) Think of a new way to write this simile. Then write a description for your classmates, explaining how the two things in your new comparison are similar. Edit your writing, making sure you have used the correct forms of any adjectives and adverbs.

- quick as a wink
- soft as a baby's breath
- sharp as a tack
- slow as molasses
- green as grass
- pure as the driven snow

QuickCheck Mixed Practice

Science Topic **Write the following paragraphs, correcting each error in the use of comparisons.**

Venus has been called Earth's twin. Second in distance from the sun, Venus comes more nearer to Earth than any planet. Venus's diameter, density, mass, and gravity are all close to Earth. Venus's year is about three fifths as long as Earth's. Venus's rotation, however, is from east to west, while Earth and most planets rotate from west to east.

Venus is masked by dense clouds. Astronomers knew hardly nothing about Venus's atmosphere and surface until radar and unpiloted spacecraft penetrated the clouds. Despite Venus's clouds, the surface gets much more hotter than Earth. The temperature on Venus can reach 460°C.

Because Venus is more closer to the sun than Earth is, you can see it only when you face in the general direction of the sun. During most of the daytime, the sun shines too vivid to allow you to see Venus. When Venus is east of the sun, however, the sun sets before it. Then Venus can be seen clear in the twilight of the western sky.

Correcting Errors with Modifiers

Write the following sentences, correcting each error. If a sentence is correct, write _C_ after the number.

1. We couldn't go swimming this morning because there wasn't no lifeguard on duty.
2. Which tastes worse, that bitter cough medicine or warm milk?
3. Today I feel the bestest I have felt in over a week.
4. Why haven't you never learned to swim?
5. After her argument with her brother Michael, Marsha felt badly.
6. Rich can paint both figures and landscapes better than anyone I know.
7. How was China's early civilization different from Egypt?
8. Avery's sweater and pants match well.
9. Next week I won't have ~~no~~ time to work at the Brewsters' music shop.
10. I think Yori's acting ability is better than Jason.
11. Which would you like best, a cruise or an overland trip to Alaska?
12. Steven Mitchell is the most wittiest reporter on the school newspaper.
13. The cheetah is different from members of the cat family because it can't hide its claws.
14. That shirt comes in blue, green, or yellow; I think blue would look better on you.
15. The fog is so thick this morning that I couldn't see nothing.

Editing for Correct Use of Modifiers

Read the following paragraphs. Then find and write the eight errors in the use of adjectives or adverbs. Beside each error write the correct form.

Mercury is the planet most nearest the sun. Its diameter is about one-third that of Earth. Because of its smaller size, Mercury's gravity is also much weaker than Earth. One hundred kilograms on Earth, for example, would weigh only about 37 kilograms on Mercury.

Scientists knew hardly nothing about the surface of Mercury until *Mariner 10,* an unpiloted spacecraft, made flyby observations in 1974 and 1975. The photographs it took of Mercury turned out good. They showed that Mercury's surface was similar to the moon. Mercury's rocky landscape is marked by broad plains, a few large ringed basins, and highlands studded with more smaller craters. The plains were formed by lava. The basins and most of the craters were formed when rock masses from space collided forceful with Mercury. The most largest basin has a diameter of 1,300 kilometers and is ringed by mountains 2 kilometers high.

Writing Sentences

Write five sentences that follow the directions below.

1. Write a sentence using the superlative degree of *good* and the comparative degree of *little*.
2. Write a sentence using the word *taste* first as an action verb and then as a linking verb.
3. Write a sentence using both *bad* and *badly*.
4. Write a sentence about a river, lake, or ocean. Use a positive adverb and a comparative adjective.
5. Write a sentence using *well* as an adjective.

Language and *Self-Expression*

Vincent van Gogh was a man with a passion for art and the natural world. When he looked at landscapes, he saw a kind of raw beauty which he translated into heavy brushstrokes of bright, clear colors.

Each of us sees the natural world from a different point of view. Imagine that you are studying a landscape you saw some time ago, perhaps as a child. Write a paragraph about the scene, but not about what you *see.* Instead, explain *how it made you feel.*

Prewriting Think about the landscape. Make a two-column list, one column for the actual things you saw—buildings, trees, people—and another for the emotions you felt when you observed them.

Drafting Begin with a sentence that puts you at the center of your view. Then "look" at individual people and objects and explain how you reacted to them, individually or together. Use your list to guide you. End the paragraph by summing up the experience with a single, clear emotion.

Revising Study your paragraph. Be sure the description moves from the view to the way you felt when you observed it. Check your adjectives and adverbs. Are they vivid? Do they express what you really remember?

Editing Read your work again. This time, look for errors in spelling, mechanics, and usage. Have you used the appropriate forms of adjectives and adverbs?

Publishing Make a clean copy of your paragraph. If you wish, share your work with a classmate or with the members of a small group. Keep in mind that your family, too, might be interested in your work—especially if they were present at the scene you remember.

Another Look

Most modifiers show **degrees of comparison** by changing form.

Regular and Irregular Comparisons

Add *–er* to form the **comparative degree** and *–est* to form the **superlative degree** of one-syllable modifiers. *(page L328)*

Use *–er* or *more* to form the **comparative degree** and *–est* or *most* to form the **superlative degree** of two-syllable modifiers. *(page L328)*

Add *more* to form the **comparative degree** and *most* to form the **superlative degree** of modifiers with three or more syllables. *(page L329)*

Double, Illogical, and Other Comparisons

Do not use both *–er* and *more* to form the comparative degree, or both *–est* and *most* to form the superlative degree. *(page L334)*

Compare only items of a similar kind. *(page L334)*

Add *other* or *else* when comparing a member of a group with the rest of the group. *(page L335)*

Avoid using a double negative. *(page L342)*

Special Cases

Good is always an adjective. *Well* is usually used as an adverb. *Well* is used as an adjective only when it means "in good health" or "satisfactory." *(pages L341–L342)*

Bad is an adjective and often follows a linking verb. *Badly* is an adverb. *(page L342)*

Other Information About the Comparison of Modifiers

Using irregular modifiers *(page L329)*

Distinguishing between adjectives and adverbs *(pages L340–L341)*

Avoiding double negatives *(page L342)*

Directions

Read the passage and choose the word or group of words that belongs in each numbered, underlined space. Write the letter of the correct answer.

EXAMPLE	**1.** The funnel of a tornado is one of the __(1)__ sights ever!

1 A scarier

B most scariest

C scariest

D more scarier

ANSWER   **1 C**

Weather forecasters are __(1)__ today than they were even 25 years ago. __(2)__ have a hard time understanding why. Because of satellites and other technological advances, forecasters have __(3)__ information available to them than their predecessors did. Nevertheless, their predictions of violent storms like tornadoes remain __(4)__ . Tornadoes, by far, are more destructive than __(5)__ storm on Earth! They are __(6)__ on the plain states than __(7)__ in the U.S. In 1925, one of the __(8)__ tornadoes of all times killed 700 people in only three and a half hours! Tornadoes cause so much destruction because their winds are stronger __(9)__ storms! Listen __(10)__ to this advice: If a tornado is approaching, go to a cellar or a closet far away from the outside walls of your house!

1 **A** more smarter
   B smarter
   C smartest
   D most smarter

2 **A** No one scarcely would
   B No one hardly would
   C No one wouldn't
   D No one would

3 **A** more
   B most
   C morer
   D much

4 **A** badly
   B more badly
   C bad
   D more badder

5 **A** any
   B a
   C any other
   D this

6 **A** more common
   B more commoner
   C most common
   D most commoner

7 **A** anywhere
   B anywhere else
   C everywhere
   D nowhere

8 **A** bad
   B badly
   C worse
   D worst

9 **A** than other
   B than those of other
   C than all other
   D than most

10 **A** good
   B better
   C well
   D most well

A Writer's Glossary of Usage

Part of the growing process is learning that some behavior is appropriate and some is not. Everyone quickly learns as a child, for example, that throwing food on the floor is definitely not acceptable or appropriate behavior.

As children grow older, most learning becomes more complicated. No longer is everything either good or bad, right or wrong. Some behavior is appropriate in some situations but inappropriate in others. Using your fingers, for example, to eat fried chicken may be appropriate behavior at home, but it may become inappropriate at a fancy restaurant.

Different expressions of the English language are somewhat like certain types of behavior; they may be appropriate with one audience but not with another. Using contractions in your conversations, for example, is standard and acceptable, but using contractions in a research paper is not appropriate.

Professor Higgins in *My Fair Lady* prided himself on his ability to name the towns where people were born by analyzing their dialects. **Dialect** is a regional variety of language that includes grammar, vocabulary, and pronunciation. Like the English, Americans have different dialects. The accents and expressions of people from parts of Texas, for example, are quite different from the accents and expressions of people from parts of Massachusetts. In spite of these variations in dialect, though, people from Texas and people from Massachusetts can easily understand and communicate with each other.

The place of your birth, however, is not the only influence on the way you speak. Your ethnic and educational backgrounds, as well as other factors, also contribute to the particular way you speak. All of these combined factors add a richness and a vibrant diversity to the English language. These factors have also created the need for different levels of expression. Traditionally these levels are recognized as standard and nonstandard English.

Standard English is used in public by almost all professional people—such as writers, television and radio personalities, government officials, and other notable figures. Standard English uses all the rules and conventions of usage that are accepted most widely by English-speaking people throughout the world. (They are the same rules and conventions that are taught in this text.) The use of standard English varies, nevertheless, in formal and informal situations.

Formal English, which follows the conventional rules of grammar, usage, and mechanics, is the standard for all written work. It is used mainly in such written work as formal reports, essays, scholarly writings, research papers, and business letters. Formal English may include some words that are not normally used in everyday conversation and frequently may employ long sentences with complex structures. To maintain a formal tone of writing, most writers avoid contractions, colloquialisms, and certain other common verbal expressions. The following example of formal English is an excerpt from one of Carson McCullers' essays.

> Whether in the pastoral joys of country life or in the labyrinthine city, we Americans are always seeking. We wander, question. But the answer waits in each separate heart—the answer of our own identity and the way by which we can master loneliness and feel that at last we belong.
>
> —*Carson McCullers,* The Mortgaged Heart

Informal English does not mean "inferior English." Just like formal English, informal English follows the rules and the conventions of standard English; however, it follows them less rigidly. It includes some words and expressions, such as contractions, that would sound out of place in formal writing. English-speaking people around the world generally use informal English in their everyday conversation. It is also used in magazines, newspapers, advertising, and much of the fiction that is written today. The following example of informal English is a diary entry that was written by Admiral Byrd during one of his expeditions to Antarctica.

> Something—I don't know what—is getting me down. I've been strangely irritable all day, and since supper I have been depressed. . . . This would not seem important if I could only put my finger on the trouble, but I can't find any single thing to account for the mood. Yet it has been there; and tonight, for the first time, I must admit that the problem of keeping my mind on an even keel is a serious one.
>
> —*Richard Byrd*, Alone

Nonstandard English, which is suitable in certain instances, incorporates the many variations produced by regional dialects, slang, and colloquial expressions. However, it should be used in limited situations and only if the use of standard English, as set forth in the preceding section, is not required. Since nonstandard English lacks uniformity from one section of the country to the next and from year to year, you should always use standard English when you write. Some fiction authors use nonstandard English, however, to recreate the conversation of people from a particular locale or time period. This, for example, was Eudora Welty's purpose when she wrote the following passage.

> "This is what come to me to do," she said. "I going to the store and buy my child a little windmill they sells, made out of paper. He going to find it hard to believe there such a thing in the world. I'll march myself back where he waiting, holding it straight up in this hand."
>
> —*Eudora Welty*, "The Worn Path"

Some of the entries in the following glossary of usage make reference to standard and nonstandard English, the terms discussed in the previous section. Since the glossary has been arranged alphabetically, you can use it easily.

a, an Use *a* before a word beginning with a consonant sound. Use *an* before a word beginning with a vowel sound. Always keep in mind that this rule applies to sounds, not letters. For example, *an hour ago* is correct because the *h* is silent.

> He finished painting **a** home on our block.
> Then he asked for **an** honest evaluation of his work.

accept, except *Accept* is a verb that means "to receive with consent." *Except* is usually a preposition that means "but" or "other than." *Acceptance* and *exception* are the noun forms.

> The players will **accept** all the new rules **except** one.

adapt, adopt Both of these words are verbs. *Adapt* means "to adjust." *Adopt* means "to take as your own." *Adaption*, *adaptation*, and *adoption* are the noun forms.

> We can **adapt** to our new environment if we **adopt** some new habits.

advice, advise *Advice* is a noun that means "a recommendation." *Advise* is a verb that means "to recommend."

> What **advice** would you give to a freshman?
> I would **advise** any freshman to get involved in school activities.

affect, effect *Affect* is a verb that means "to influence" or "to act upon." *Effect* is usually a noun that means "a result" or "an influence." As a verb, *effect* means "to accomplish" or "to produce."

> Eastern Kansas was seriously **affected** by the storm.
> The **effects** of the storm cost the state millions of dollars.
> The fear of mud slides **effected** detours.

ain't This contraction is nonstandard and should be avoided in your writing.

> NONSTANDARD   This **ain't** her first choice.
> FORMAL   This **is not** her first choice.
> INFORMAL   This **isn't** her first choice.

all ready, already *All ready* means "completely ready." *Already* means "previously."

> Are the children **all ready** to go?
> Yes, they have **already** changed their clothes.

all together, altogether *All together* means "in a group." *Altogether* means "wholly" or "thoroughly."

> The members of our group were **all together** at the concert.
> The concert was **altogether** enjoyable.

allusion, illusion Both of these words are nouns. An *allusion* is "an implied or indirect reference; a hint." An *illusion* is "something that deceives or misleads."

> During the showing of the film, I noticed many biblical and mythological **allusions.**

> I also learned that movement in motion pictures is created by an optical **illusion.**

a lot These two words are often written as one word. There is no such word as "alot." *A lot* should be avoided in formal writing. (Do not confuse *a lot* with *allot*, which is a verb that means "to distribute by shares.")

> INFORMAL   Do you miss them **a lot?**
> FORMAL   Do you miss them **very much?**
>   I hope they will **allot** the chores equally.

among, between Both of these words are prepositions. *Among* is used when referring to three or more people or things. *Between* is usually used when referring to two people or things.

> The senator moved **among** the people in the crowd.
> He divided his time **between** shaking hands and speaking.

amount, number *Amount* refers to a quantity. *Number* refers to things that can be counted.

> A small **number** of students raised a large **amount** of money for the athletic program.

PRACTICE YOUR SKILLS

● Check Your Understanding
Finding the Correct Word

Literature Topic — **Write the word in parentheses that correctly (formally) completes each sentence.**

1. The (affect, effect) of the recent Globe Theater restoration has been to heighten interest (a lot, considerably) in this (all ready, already) well-known Elizabethan theater.

2. The Globe, which opened in 1599, was also known as "The Wooden O," (a, an) (allusion, illusion) to its shape.

3. A view of the building from above gives the spectator the (allusion, illusion) of a large "O."

4. Built to accommodate a large (amount, number) of people, the Globe could hold approximately three thousand people (all together, altogether).

5. William Shakespeare was (among, between) the five actors who (all together, altogether) owned half interest in the theater.

6. Although the exact (amount, number) of performances (ain't, isn't) known, Shakespeare's plays were often enacted at the Globe.

7. In 1613, the (affect, effect) of a malfunctioning cannon during a performance was the burning down of the theater.

8. Acting on good (advice, advise), the owners rebuilt the Globe in the same fashion (accept, except) for a tiled roof instead of a thatched one.

9. By 1642, however, the strict religious beliefs (adapted, adopted) by the Puritans had (all ready, already) adversely (affected, effected) the success of the Globe.

10. It, along with great (amounts, numbers) of theaters in England, was closed (all together, altogether) because of Puritan opposition to drama.

Recognizing Correct Usage

Rewrite the following paragraphs, changing the words that are used incorrectly.

Adoption to the theatrical conventions of the Elizabethan era had a affect on the design of the Globe. For example, the adoption of an trapdoor in the center of the stage provided for the entrance and exit into "Hell." Two pillars, located among the two sides of the stage held up "Heaven." At the rear of the stage was a gallery that was already if needed for musicians or for a balcony scene. The stage itself extended out about thirty feet all together into the courtyard. Since the yard was an open area, the weather sometimes effected performances.

In this area there were a lot of spectators who were called groundlings. To be admitted, groundlings paid the amount of one penny. They stood through an entire performance and could move around accept when it was too crowded. Although often disruptive, the conduct of the groundlings was altogether accepted by the actors for economic reasons. The people who sat among the seven galleries upstairs had to pay the number of two pence for their seats.

---

any more, anymore Do not use *any more* for *anymore*. *Any more* refers to quantity. The adverb *anymore* means "from now on" or "at present."

Is there **any more** lettuce in the garden?
No, I don't raise lettuce **anymore.**

anywhere, everywhere, nowhere, somewhere Do not add *s* to any of these words.

NONSTANDARD	Melanie wants to travel **everywheres.**
STANDARD	Melanie wants to travel **everywhere.**

as far as This expression is sometimes confused with "all the farther," which is nonstandard English.

NONSTANDARD	Is a mile **all the farther** you can walk?
STANDARD	Is a mile **as far as** you can walk?

at Do not use *at* after where.

NONSTANDARD	Let me know **where** the keys are **at.**
STANDARD	Let me know **where** the keys are.

a while, awhile *A while* is an expression made up of an article and a noun. It must be used after the prepositions *for* and *in*. *Awhile* is an adverb and is not used after a preposition.

You won't get your test results for **a while.**
I think you should wait **awhile** before calling again.

bad, badly *Bad* is an adjective and often follows a linking verb. *Badly* is used as an adverb and often follows an action verb. In the first two examples, *felt* is a linking verb.

NONSTANDARD	My sister felt **badly** about missing us.
STANDARD	My sister felt **bad** about missing us.
STANDARD	She was so upset that she burned the dinner **badly.**

You can learn more about using adjectives and adverbs on pages L24–L36 and pages L327–L345.

because Do not use *because* after *the reason*. Use one or the other.

NONSTANDARD	**The reason** he joined the exercise class was **because** he wanted to feel more energetic.

| STANDARD | He joined the exercise class **because he** wanted to feel more energetic. |
| STANDARD | **The reason** he joined the exercise class was **that** he wanted to feel more energetic. |

being as, being that These expressions should be replaced with *because* or *since*.

| NONSTANDARD | **Being as** it rained on Saturday, I didn't run. |
| STANDARD | **Since** it rained on Saturday, I didn't run. |

beside, besides *Beside* is always a preposition that means "by the side of." As a preposition, *besides* means "in addition to." As an adverb, *besides* means "also" or "moreover."

Sit **beside** me at the PTA meeting. (by the side of)

Besides meeting the teachers, we also will tour the new facilities. (in addition to)

The school has a swimming pool, tennis courts, and an indoor track **besides.** (also)

both Never use *the* before *both*.

| NONSTANDARD | We saw **the both** of you at the mall. |
| STANDARD | We saw **both** of you at the mall. |

both, each *Both* refers to two persons or objects together, but *each* refers to an individual person or object.

Both office buildings were designed by the same architect; however, **each** building is quite different.

bring, take *Bring* indicates motion toward the speaker. *Take* indicates motion away from the speaker.

Bring me a stamp and then **take** this letter to the mailbox.

PRACTICE YOUR SKILLS

● Check Your Understanding
Finding the Correct Word

Contemporary Life **Write the word in parentheses that correctly completes each sentence.**

1. (Beside, Besides) the preliminary audition, those trying out for a high school musical usually have to attend a callback audition.

2. Although (both, each) of them are essential to the casting process, (both, each) has a different procedure.

3. (Both, The both) require student performance but with certain important differences.

4. For example, when going to the preliminary audition, students usually may (bring, take) their own music or may use a selection from the musical.

5. At the callback audition, students do not have a choice (any more, anymore), (being as, since) the musical theater team decides which selections it wishes to hear each student perform.

6. Similarly, for (a while, awhile), students have the option to read for any part they choose; however, at the callback, no matter how (bad, badly) they may want a particular role, the choice may not be theirs.

7. Even if permitted to read their favorite part, students may be asked to read dialogue from several other parts (beside, besides).

8. In the preliminary, to prevent students from feeling (bad, badly), they usually perform only in front of the drama director, choreographer, and musical director.

9. At callback, other students who are waiting to audition again are (everywhere, everywheres) while an individual is auditioning.

10. After (a while, awhile) students get used to having others (beside, besides) them while they're performing, thus helping to prevent the actors from having (any more, anymore) stage fright.

Rewrite the following paragraphs, changing the words that are used incorrectly.

A musical theater team would assure you that nowheres is teamwork required any more than in a musical production. Collaboration begins with the drama director, choreographer, and musical director being that they must model cooperative behavior for their students. Even though they bring individual expertise to the production, together they take responsibility for evaluating, casting, encouraging, and critiquing the performers. After a while, students begin to understand how bad teamwork is needed to coordinate the details.

In many high schools, the students go all the farther promoting ticket sales, distributing posters, and coordinating costumes. Many productions even have two student stage managers, the both of whom share responsibilities. In other words, although both are involved with the smooth operation of every scene, each stage manager has particular duties. For example, one might instruct a performer where to stand at while the other might place props besides a piece of scenery. Beside being stage managers, students often operate both the lighting and sound equipment. Ultimately, the reason a production is successful is because each person contributes to the whole.

APPLY TO WRITING

Explanatory Writing: *Correct Usage*

The concept of collaboration, working together to create a desired result, may be applied in many subject areas. You have probably worked together at one time or another in your classes to produce a collaborative assignment. Some students prefer working together while others prefer doing independent work. Compose an original paragraph explaining your personal preference concerning collaborative assignments. In your explanation include at least five of the following words.

- *advice/advise*
- *affect/effect*
- *all together/altogether*
- *among/between*
- *both/each*

can, may *Can* expresses ability. *May* expresses possibility or permission.

> **Can** you see the third line of the eye chart?
> **May** I try one more time?

can't help but In this expression use a gerund instead of *but*.

> NONSTANDARD I **can't help but** notice your new haircut.
> STANDARD I **can't help** noticing your new haircut.

capital, capitol A *capital* is the chief city of a state. Also, names are written with *capital* letters, people invest *capital*, and a person can receive *capital* punishment. A *capitol* is the building in which the legislature meets.

> The name of the **capital** of Florida is written in **capital** letters on the **capitol** building in Tallahassee.

coarse, course *Coarse* is an adjective that means "loose or rough in texture" or "crude and unrefined." *Course* is a noun that means "a way of acting or proceeding" or "a path, road, or route." Also, people play golf on a *course*; an appetizer is one *course* of a meal; and students take *courses* in school. *Course* is also the word used in the parenthetical expression *of course*.

> Many people heard his **coarse** remarks after the tennis match.
> What **course** of action would you take to stop his behavior?

continual, continuous Both of these words are adjectives. *Continual* means "frequently repeated." *Continuous* means "uninterrupted."

> The **continual** bolts of lightning frightened me.
> The rain was **continuous** for over ten hours.

different from Use this form instead of *different than*. *Different than*, however, can be used informally when it is followed by a clause.

> INFORMAL   My sweater is **different than** the one Gram knitted for Maureen.
> FORMAL   My sweater is **different from** the one Gram knitted for Maureen.
> STANDARD   Her jacket is **different from** mine, also.

discover, invent Both of these words are verbs. *Discover* means "to find or get knowledge of for the first time." *Invent* means "to create or produce for the first time." Something that is discovered has always existed but it was unknown. Something that is invented has never existed before. The noun forms of these words are *discovery* and *invention*.

> I learned that Isaac Newton **discovered** the law of gravity and that Benjamin Franklin **invented** bifocal glasses.

doesn't, don't *Doesn't* is singular and should be used only with singular nouns and the personal pronouns *he, she,* and *it. Don't* is plural and should be used with plural nouns and the personal pronouns *I, you, we,* and *they*.

| NONSTANDARD | He **don't** need any help. |
| STANDARD | He **doesn't** need any help. |

| NONSTANDARD | An apple a day **don't** keep the doctor away. |
| STANDARD | An apple a day **doesn't** keep the doctor away. |

done *Done* is the past participle of the verb *do*. So, when *done* is used as a verb, it must be used with one or more helping verbs.

| NONSTANDARD | Eli **done** exactly what the doctor told him. |
| STANDARD | Eli **has done** exactly what the doctor told him. |

double negative Words such as *hardly, never, no, not* and *nobody* are considered negatives. Do not use two negatives to express one negative meaning.

NONSTANDARD	He doesn**'t hardly** have any spare time.
STANDARD	He doesn**'t** have any spare time.
STANDARD	He **never** has any spare time.

You can learn more about the use of negatives on pages L342–L343.

emigrate, immigrate Both of these words are verbs. *Emigrate* means "to leave a country to settle elsewhere." *Immigrate* means "to enter a foreign country to live there." A person emigrates *from* a country and immigrates *to* another country. *Emigrant* and *immigrant* are the noun forms.

Kin Fujii **emigrated** from Japan ten years ago.
Did he **immigrate** to this country for economic reasons?

etc. *Etc.* is an abbreviation for a Latin phrase, *et cetera,* that means "and other things." Never use the word *and* with *etc.* If you do, what you are really saying is "and and other things." It is best, however, not to use this abbreviation at all in formal writing.

| INFORMAL | For the salad we need grapes, oranges, **etc.** |
| FORMAL | For the salad we need grapes, oranges, **and other fruits.** |

farther, further *Farther* refers to distance. *Further* means "additional" or "to a greater degree or extent."

> How much **farther** will we travel tonight?
> The tour guide will give us **further** instructions shortly.

fewer, less *Fewer* is plural and refers to things that can be counted. *Less* is singular and refers to quantities and qualities that cannot be counted.

> I scored **fewer** points in basketball this year than last year.
> You should place **less** importance on the mistakes you make.

former, latter *Former* is the first of two people or things. *Latter* is the second of two people or things. (Use *first* and *last* when referring to three or more.)

> For the main course, we had a choice of roast beef or pork chops. We learned that the portions for the **former** would be larger than the portions for the **latter.**

Practice Your Skills

 Check Your Understanding
Finding the Correct Word

History Topic **Write the word in parentheses that correctly completes each sentence.**

1. One of the most dramatic occurrences of the Great Depression (can, may) be the Dust Bowl.

2. The (former, latter) affected the entire nation; the (former, latter) affected only the Great Plains states.

3. During the 1930s, no (fewer, less) than a million people were uprooted from their land and charted their (coarse, course) to California.

4. The combination of fear and hope they experienced (doesn't, don't) seem a great deal (different from, different than) that felt by the (emigrants, immigrants) to America at the turn of the 19th century.

5. Of (coarse, course), the exodus to California was a result of a (continual, continuous) drought that plagued the Great Plains.

6. Unknowingly, many farmers (done, had done) irreversible damage to the land by uprooting the natural sod that provided drought protection for the soil.

7. The drought gave rise to (farther, further) problems as enormous quantities of dust swirled across the plains forcing the farmers (farther, further) away from home.

8. The name "Okie" was (discovered, invented) to describe the migrating people even though many came from other states besides Oklahoma.

9. Today we (can hardly, can't hardly) imagine the endless line of homeless people traveling away from the plains in search of a new life.

10. Many (discovered, invented) that the stories of abundant jobs had been (discovered, invented) by wealthy landowners looking for cheap labor.

Connect to the Writing Process: Revising
Recognizing Correct Usage

Rewrite the following paragraphs, changing the words that are used incorrectly.

Born in Salinas, California, John Steinbeck had an opportunity to discover the continuous plight of migrant workers. By living among them, he gained farther knowledge of them and their working conditions. He had done his research thoroughly; from those experiences, he discovered the characters for several of his works. Some critics considered his characters to be course and common. Others, however, felt Steinbeck had special empathy for the lonely, the mistreated, the poor, and others who suffered.

Readers can't help but recognize this continuous theme in works such as *Tortilla Flat, Of Mice and Men,* and *The Grapes of Wrath.*

No other account of the Dust Bowl migration has had more impact than John Steinbeck's *The Grapes of Wrath.* Although some consider this work a social protest, it can more accurately be described as a work of art. In 1940, the film version of the novel was well received even though the ending was different than the novel's. Steinbeck received no less than the Pulitzer Prize for this novel in the same year. Its artistic value hasn't never decreased; in fact, it has increased over the years. His literary acclaim spread farther when he received the Nobel Prize for his life's work in 1962.

good, well *Good* is an adjective and often follows a linking verb. *Well* is an adverb and often follows an action verb. However, when *well* means "in good health" or "satisfactory," it is used as an adjective.

> Do you feel **good** this morning? (adjective)
> Yes, I work **well** in the morning. (adverb)
> Pat doesn't feel **well.** ("in good health")

You can learn more about using adjectives and adverbs on pages L327–L345.

had of Do not use *of* after *had.*

> NONSTANDARD   I would have taken my umbrella if I **had of** listened to the weather forecast.
>
> STANDARD   I would have taken my umbrella if I **had** listened to the weather forecast.

have, of Never substitute *of* for the verb *have.* When speaking, many people make a contraction of *have.* For example, someone might say, "We should've left sooner." Because 've sounds like *of*, *of* is often incorrectly substituted for *have*.

| NONSTANDARD | You should **of** roasted the potatoes. |
| STANDARD | You should **have** roasted the potatoes. |

hear, here *Hear* is a verb that means "to perceive by listening." *Here* is an adverb that means "in this place."

If you stand over **here**, can you **hear** the phone ring?

hole, whole *Hole* is an opening in something. *Whole* means "complete or entire."

The **whole** time I watched the **hole,** no animal went in.

imply, infer Both of these words are verbs. *Imply* means "to suggest" or "to hint." *Infer* means "to draw a conclusion by reasoning or from evidence." A speaker implies; a listener infers. *Implication* and *inference* are the noun forms.

Grandmother **implied** that she might be visiting soon.
We **inferred** from what she said that she was excited.

in, into Use *into* when you want to express motion from one place to another.

The mixture **in** the bowl should be put **into** the blender.

irregardless Do not substitute this word for *regardless*.

| NONSTANDARD | **Irregardless** of anything you say, I still think he was telling the truth. |
| STANDARD | **Regardless** of anything you say, I still think he was telling the truth. |

CONNECT TO SPEAKING AND WRITING

Both the prefix *ir–* and the ending *–less* are negative. Since the use of a double negative should not be used to express one negative meaning, *irregardless* should not be used in speaking or writing.

its, it's *Its* is a possessive pronoun. *It's* is a contraction for *it is*.

> The committee will announce **its** findings on Friday.
> **It's** going to be a controversial report.

kind, sort, type These words are singular and should be preceded by *this* or *that*. *Kinds, sorts,* and *types* are plural and should be preceded by *these* or *those*.

> Joan likes **that type** of book bag.
> Joan likes **those types** of book bags.

kind of, sort of Never substitute these expressions for *rather* or *somewhat* in formal writing.

> NONSTANDARD   Calculus was **sort of** difficult for me.
> STANDARD   Calculus was **rather** difficult for me.

CONNECT TO SPEAKING AND WRITING

Practice using the words *rather* and *somewhat* during informal conversations. Practicing their use will help you to use them correctly when you write formally.

knew, new *Knew*, the past tense of the verb *know*, means "was acquainted with." *New* is an adjective that means "recently made" or "just found."

> We **knew** all along that a **new** gym would be built.

learn, teach Both of these words are verbs. *Learn* means "to acquire knowledge." *Teach* means "to instruct."

> NONSTANDARD   Who **learned** you how to water-ski?
> STANDARD   Who **taught** you how to water-ski?
> STANDARD   I **learned** how to water-ski from my sister.

leave, let Both of these words are verbs. *Leave* means "to depart." *Let* means "to allow" or "to permit."

NONSTANDARD	**Leave** me fix dinner before the game.
STANDARD	**Let** me fix dinner before the game.
STANDARD	I want to **leave** early to get a good seat.

PRACTICE YOUR SKILLS

● Check Your Understanding
Finding the Correct Word

General Interest **Write the word in parentheses that correctly completes each sentence.**

1. Environmental issues, ranging from ocean pollution to a (hole, whole) in the ozone layer, plague the (hole, whole) world.

2. As our population grows, these (type, types) of issues will increase.

3. We (hear, here) horror stories every day about companies that pollute (irregardless, regardless) of environmental regulations.

4. (Its, It's) not unusual to have specials on TV that warn us about the damaging (implications, inferences) of air and water pollution.

5. (Its, It's) importance is (kind of, rather) difficult to (learn, teach) the public.

6. From the indifference displayed by many, we can only (imply, infer) that some people don't care about (learning, teaching).

7. Community projects, such as going (in, into) the streams to remove trash, (let, leave) us have an opportunity to help.

8. Promoting recognition (in, into) the community of environmentally safe products works (good, well).

9. More (knew, new) and innovative approaches are needed to make people feel (good, well) about their involvement.

10. We could (have, of) made more rapid progress if we had known how to increase public support.

Answer each question using the correct form of the appropriate word in parentheses.

11. How did you find out about the library at your school? (learn, teach)

12. Were you already acquainted with the different options for foreign language clubs? (new, knew)

13. Which subject interests you? (sort of, somewhat)

14. Is journalism an option at your school? (hear, here)

15. Who allowed your class to attend the workshop? (leave, let)

● Connect to the Writing Process: Revising
Recognizing Correct Usage

Rewrite the following paragraph, changing the words that are used incorrectly.

One woman who new well how to raise public awareness was writer and scientist Rachel Carson. She is a well example of how it's possible to combine our interests with our learning to produce results. Drawn to nature as a child, she later wrote about it's wonders and also managed to learn a hole generation about environmental dangers. Also, she put a hole in the accepted theory in the 1920s that science was a profession kind of ill-suited for women. Irregardless of her gender, she earned a master's degree in zoology from Johns Hopkins University and went in the field of aquatic biology. With *The Sea Around Us*, she opened up a new world to the reading public. However, from the inferences in *The Silent Spring* about the harmful effects of pesticides, the public implied the threat to our environment.

APPLY TO WRITING

Analysis of a Photograph

Rachel Carson's love of nature led her to write *The Sea Around Us.* This photograph of the California coastline illustrates the power and beauty of the sea. Imagine that you are seated on the shore and want to preserve the memory of the moment. Using at least six of the following words, describe the photograph in detail and explain what you think the photographer wanted to accomplish.

- *can/may*
- *continual/continuous*
- *farther/further*
- *hole/whole*
- *kind/sort/type*
- *learn/teach*

lie, lay *Lie* means "to rest or recline." *Lie* is never followed by a direct object. Its principal parts are *lie, lying, lay,* and *lain. Lay* means "to put or set (something) down." *Lay* is usually followed by a direct object. Its principal parts are *lay, laying, laid,* and *laid.*

Don't **lie** down now.
The workers will **lay** the new carpet in your room.

You can learn more about using the verbs lie *and* lay *on pages L193–L196.*

like, as *Like* can be used as a preposition to introduce a prepositional phrase. *As* is usually a subordinating conjunction that introduces an adverb clause. Although *like* is sometimes used informally as a conjunction, it should be avoided in formal situations.

INFORMAL	The room is perfect just **like** it is. (clause)
FORMAL	The room is perfect just **as** it is.
FORMAL	The wallpaper is gray-striped **like** mine. (prepositional phrase)

loose, lose *Loose* is usually an adjective that means "not tight." *Lose* is a verb that means "to misplace" or "not to have any longer."

Your tooth is very **loose**.
I hope you don't **lose** it before class pictures are taken.

may be, maybe *May be* is a form of the verb *be*. *Maybe* is an adverb that means "perhaps."

The chance of a lifetime **may be** in this envelope.
Maybe we have won the expense-paid vacation to Greece.

most, almost *Most* is a noun, a pronoun, or an adjective that modifies a noun or a pronoun. *Almost*, which means "nearly," is an adverb. Do not substitute *most* for *almost*.

NONSTANDARD	Did you type **most** all of your term paper?
STANDARD	Did you type **almost** all of your term paper?
STANDARD	I spent **most** of the weekend on the computer.

nor, or Use *neither* with *nor* and *either* with *or*.

Neither Fred **nor** Jane is coming to the party.
They are going to **either** the movies **or** the concert.

of Prepositions such as *inside, outside,* and *off* should not be followed by *of*.

NONSTANDARD	The ball rolled **off of** the chair.
STANDARD	The ball rolled **off** the chair.

ought Never use *have* or *had* with *ought*.

NONSTANDARD	Ben **hadn't ought** to drive so fast.
STANDARD	Ben **ought not** to drive so fast.

passed, past *Passed* is the past tense of the verb *pass*. As a noun *past* means "a time gone by." As an adjective *past* means "just gone" or "elapsed." As a preposition *past* means "beyond."

In the **past** she always **passed** her courses with *A's*.
(*past* as a noun)

For the **past** several mornings, I have walked **past** the park on my way to school.
(*past* as an adjective and then as a preposition)

precede, proceed Both of these words are verbs. *Precede* means "to be, go, or come ahead of something else." *Proceed* means "to move along a course," "to advance," or "to continue after a pause or an interruption."

One guide will **precede** our group down the mountain.
Proceed down the steep mountain with great caution.

principal, principle As an adjective *principal* means "main" or "chief." As a noun *principal* means "the head of a school" or "a leader." *Principle* is a noun that is synonymous with *law, truth, doctrine,* or *code of conduct.*

The **principal** reason he stayed in school was because of the advice given by the **principal** at Atlantic High.

Roberto decided to stick by the **principles** his parents had instilled in him.

respectfully, respectively *Respectfully* is related to the noun *respect*, which means "high regard or esteem." *Respectively* means "in the order given."

Respectfully, the guide inquired about my destination.
I replied that it would be London and Paris, **respectively**.

rise, raise *Rise* means "to move upward" or "to get up." *Rise* is never followed by a direct object. Its principal parts are *rise, rising, rose,* and *risen. Raise* means "to lift up," "to increase," or "to grow something." *Raise* is usually followed by a direct object. Its principal parts are *raise, raising, raised,* and *raised.*

> The spectators always **rise** when the judge enters the courtroom.
>
> They wondered if the attorney would **raise** the same issue that he brought up yesterday.

You can learn more about using the verbs rise *and* raise *on pages L194–L196.*

PRACTICE YOUR SKILLS

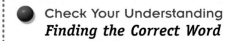 Check Your Understanding
Finding the Correct Word

Literature Topic — **Write the word in parentheses that correctly completes each sentence.**

1. (Almost, Most) all people agree that poetry (may be, maybe) described in a variety of ways.

2. Neither poets (nor, or) readers of poetry agree on how it (had ought, ought) to be defined.

3. Words, of (coarse, course), are the (principal, principle) components of poetry.

4. This fact (raises, rises) the question as to why one poem isn't basically (as, like) another.

5. However, in the usage and pattern of those words (lays, lies) the uniqueness of each poem.

6. In the (passed, past) some argued that a poem (ain't, isn't) true poetry unless it (passed, past) certain criteria—namely, the use of elevated language.

7. In the late 1800s, Walt Whitman (preceded, proceeded) to use the language of the common people.

8. The (loose, lose) style of Whitman's poetry, known as free verse, did not cause it to (loose, lose) a rhythmical quality.

9. His style (lay, laid) to rest the idea that poetry could not move (outside, outside of) the fixed forms of tradition.

10. Whitman has been (respectfully, respectively) praised as the "poet of the common man" and the "father of modern poetry."

● Connect to the Writing Process: Revising
Recognizing Correct Usage

Rewrite the following paragraphs, changing the words that are used incorrectly.

Sonnets, revered in the passed, continue to be a principal part of poetry. The names of two major forms, Petrarchan and Shakespearean, proceed from their extensive use by Petrarch and Shakespeare. These are known also as either the Italian sonnet or the English sonnet, respectfully. Although each contains fourteen lines, they loose their similarity in most other elements.

Ballads, another fixed form, are based in principal on songs that tell a story; they may be one of the oldest forms of poetry. Proceeding the others, the first stanza typically ought to present the characters and the problem; the rest of the stanzas proceed to solve the dilemma presented by the first.

In contrast, the intent of the five-line limerick, whose name comes from a city in Ireland, is to amuse. May be the varied forms of poems ensure that poetry doesn't ever loose its universal appeal.

says, said Do not use *says*, the present tense of the verb *say*, when you should use the past tense, *said*.

NONSTANDARD	Then she **says**, "I want to go with you."
STANDARD	Then she **said**, "I want to go with you."

–self, –selves A reflexive or an intensive pronoun that ends in *–self* or *–selves* should not be used as a subject. (Never use "hisself" or "theirselves.")

NONSTANDARD	Ken and **myself** were chosen.
STANDARD	Ken and **I** were chosen.
NONSTANDARD	They made **theirselves** sandwiches.
STANDARD	They made **themselves** sandwiches.

shall, will Formal English uses *shall* with first-person pronouns and *will* with second- and third-person pronouns. Today, however, *shall* and *will* are used interchangeably with *I* and *we*, except that *shall* is usually still used with first-person pronouns for questions.

Shall I meet you at the mall?
Will you meet me at the mall?

sit, set *Sit* means "to rest in an upright position." *Sit* is never followed by a direct object. Its principal parts are *sit, sitting, sat,* and *sat*. *Set* means "to put or place (something)." *Set* is usually followed by a direct object. Its principal parts are *set, setting, set* and *set*.

Sit down and rest for a while.
I'll **set** the dishes on the shelf.

You can learn more about using the verbs sit *and* set *on pages L194–L196.*

some, somewhat *Some* is either a pronoun or an adjective that modifies a noun or a pronoun. *Somewhat* is an adverb.

NONSTANDARD	School enrollment has declined **some.**
STANDARD	School enrollment has declined **somewhat.**

than, then *Than* is usually a subordinating conjunction and is used for comparisons. *Then* is an adverb that means "at that time" or "next."

> I didn't think I would finish sooner **than** you.
> Finish your homework and **then** call me.

that, which, who These words are often used as relative pronouns to introduce adjective clauses. *That* refers to animals and things and usually begins an essential clause. *Which* refers to animals and things. *Who* refers to people.

> The ad **that** was posted on the board sounds interesting.
> That ad, **which** also runs on radio, will attract many people.
> Anyone **who** responds to the ad may fill out an application.

their, there, they're *Their* is a possessive pronoun. *There* is usually an adverb, and sometimes it will begin an inverted sentence. *They're* is a contraction for *they are*.

> **Their** car is parked over **there**, ready for the trip.
> **They're** leaving for Mobile tomorrow.

theirs, there's *Theirs* is a possessive pronoun. *There's* is a contraction for *there is*.

> **There's** an easy solution to my problem, but what about **theirs?**

them, those Never use *them* as a subject or an adjective.

> NONSTANDARD **Them** are from whose garden? (subject)
> STANDARD **Those** are from whose garden?
>
> NONSTANDARD Rachel grew **them** tomatoes. (adjective)
> STANDARD Rachel grew **those** tomatoes.

this here, that there Avoid using *here* and *there* in addition to *this* and *that*.

NONSTANDARD	**That there** sunset looks beautiful.
STANDARD	**That** sunset looks beautiful.
NONSTANDARD	**This here** saddle is mine.
STANDARD	**This** saddle is mine.

this, that, these, those *This* and *that* are singular and should modify singular nouns. *These* and *those* are plural and should modify plural nouns.

| NONSTANDARD | Does the Sport Shop sell **those** kind of bats? |
| STANDARD | Does the Sport Shop sell **that** kind of bat? |

threw, through *Threw* is the past tense of the verb *throw*. *Through* is a preposition that means "in one side and out the other."

I hope no one **threw** Sunday's newspaper away.
Look **through** the stack of papers on the table.

PRACTICE YOUR SKILLS

● Check Your Understanding
Finding the Correct Word

Sports Topic **Write the word in parentheses that correctly completes each sentence.**

1. It would be classified as an understatement if someone (said, says) that interest in soccer had increased (some, somewhat) in the United States.

2. In fact, most (shall, will) agree the sport has gone (threw, through) an amazing transformation.

3. Actually soccer has increased in popularity more (than, then) any other sport.

4. (This, This here) transformation began taking place in the 1950s; before (than, then), it was simply known as the favorite sport of Europe and South America.

5. The 1994 World Cup held in the United States (set, sit) in motion a nationwide interest.

6. At the matches, fans (threw, through) (theirselves, themselves) energetically into the excitement.

7. (These sort of, This sort of) excitement spilled over to playgrounds, recreation centers, and schools.

8. Many spectators (setting, sitting) in the stands had to learn the rules of soccer.

9. (These, These sort of) rules are actually much simpler (than, then) rules for American football.

10. (Shall, Will) we some day find that soccer has become the national sport of the United States?

Connecting to the Writing Process: Revising
Recognizing Correct Usage

Rewrite the sentences below, changing the words that are used incorrectly. Write a brief explanation for each change.

11. There has been a growing trend for U.S. schools to include soccer in they're athletic programs.

12. Their often set up to include teams for both young men and women there.

13. Theirs is an enviable task because theirs such an increased interest in this country.

14. Soccer is a game which requires stamina from its players, that must train rigorously.

15. Agility, that is another needed skill, poses a challenge for those which aspire to be competent soccer players.

---

to, too, two *To* is a preposition. *To* also begins an infinitive. *Too* is an adverb that modifies an adjective or another adverb. *Two* is a number.

> **Two** more people are **too** many **to** take in our car.
> We hurried **to** the picnic area before it got **too** crowded.

try to Use *try to* instead of *try and*, which is nonstandard.

> NONSTANDARD   Please **try and** be there on time.
> STANDARD   Please **try to** be there on time.

use to, used to Be sure to add the *–d* to *use*.

NONSTANDARD	I **use to** paint with watercolors.
STANDARD	I **used to** paint with watercolors.

way, ways Do not substitute *ways* for *way* when referring to a distance.

NONSTANDARD	Aren't you a long **ways** from home?
STANDARD	Aren't you a long **way** from home?

weak, week *Weak* is an adjective that means "not strong" or "likely to break." *Week* is a noun that means "a time period of seven days."

For the first **week** after your surgery, you'll feel quite **weak**.

what Do not substitute *what* for *that*.

NONSTANDARD	The car **what** you bought was too expensive.
STANDARD	The car **that** you bought was too expensive.

when, where Do not use *when* or *where* directly after a linking verb in a definition.

NONSTANDARD	In the North, October is **when** you should plant tulip bulbs.
STANDARD	In the North, October is the **month when** you should plant tulip bulbs.
NONSTANDARD	The Hall of Mirrors is **where** the Treaty of Versailles was signed.
STANDARD	The Hall of Mirrors is the **room where** the Treaty of Versailles was signed.
NONSTANDARD	A harvest is **when** the farmers bring in their crops.
STANDARD	A harvest is **the time when** the farmers bring in their crops.

where Do not substitute *where* for *that*.

> NONSTANDARD   I read **where** bowling is the number one participant sport in the United States.
>
> STANDARD   I read **that** bowling is the number one participant sport in the United States.

who, whom *Who*, a pronoun in the nominative case, is used either as a subject or a predicate nominative. *Whom*, a pronoun in the objective case, is used mainly as a direct object, an indirect object, or an object of a preposition.

> **Who** is waving at you?
> (subject)
>
> It is Howard, **whom** I have known all my life.
> (direct object of the verb *have known* in the adjective clause)
>
> To **whom** will you give permission to drive?
> (object of the preposition *to*)

CONNECT TO WRITER'S CRAFT

Except when using nonstandard English for special effect, professional writers use standard English even in the titles of their works. Notice the correct usage of *who* in the nominative case and *whom* in the objective case in the following titles.

> For **Whom** the Bell Tolls by Ernest Hemingway
> The Man **Who** Came to Dinner by Moss Hart

whose, who's *Whose* is a possessive pronoun. *Who's* is a contraction for *who is*.

> **Whose** suitcase is that?
> It belongs to the man **who's** walking this way.

your, you're *Your* is a possessive pronoun. *You're* is a contraction for *you are*.

> **You're** sure you put **your** baseball glove in the car?

PRACTICE YOUR SKILLS

● Check Your Understanding
Finding the Correct Word

Contemporary Life — **Write the word in parentheses that correctly completes each sentence.**

1. (Your, You're) senior year is one of the most important and memorable ones, (to, too, two).

2. Many (who, whom) previously thought they had a long (way, ways) to go before graduation realize that the time is rapidly approaching.

3. It is essential that you (try and, try to) keep a focus on the goals (that, what) you have set.

4. (Your, You're) certain (to, too, two) discover that all decisions about (your, you're) future need careful consideration.

5. (Whose, Who's) qualified to help with college or career decisions should determine (whose, who) help you seek.

6. If you should find yourself (weak, week) in a certain subject, find out (who, whom) can provide tutoring.

7. When in doubt, remember that (to, too, two) excellent sources from (who, whom) you can seek advice are your parents and guidance counselors.

8. If you are (use to, used to) letting decisions slide, (try and, try to) practice self-discipline.

9. Every (weak, week) that you procrastinate could affect your career.

10. (Too, To, Two) much depends on what (your, you're) planning for the future.

11. (Who, Whom) should you contact about touring a local college campus?

12. Confirm (that, what) the college-prep classes you took are transferable for credit.

13. Enjoy (your, you're) last year of school; the senior activities are fun, (to, two, too).

14. (Try to, Try and) save (your, you're) graduation programs, pictures, and memorabilia for a class scrapbook.

15. A class reunion is (where, the event at which) you could share your scrapbook with old friends.

16. You will not believe how (bad, badly) you will want to see your classmates after ten years.

17. At the reunion, (anywhere, anywheres) you look will be a familiar face.

18. Look carefully for your homecoming king and queen, because (the both, both) of them will have changed a great deal.

● Connecting to the Writing Process: Revising
Recognizing Correct Usage

Rewrite the following paragraph, changing the words that are used incorrectly.

Be sure to participate in senior activities leading up too you're graduation; they're two special to miss. The memories what you accumulate will last a lifetime. One event, the junior-senior prom, is where the junior class honors graduating seniors. The king and queen are the couple who juniors and seniors recognize symbolically at the dance. The academic awards program is designed to try to give recognition to those who are deserving. The yearbook signing is when seniors write final messages to one another. You're sure to have teachers, too, who wish to add congratulatory notes. This informal party, usually held the last weak of school, is a special memory before the formal activities of graduation actually begin.

APPLY TO WRITING

Personal Response: *Correct Usage*

The following words of George Will, a *Washington Post* columnist, are an excerpt from his column and the advice he offered his daughter's graduating class. Examine this excerpt and then read the instructions on the following page.

Well, we live and learn. Indeed, the happiest people live to learn. They live for the delightful astonishments that never stop coming to those who never stop learning.

So, said the columnist to the Class of '99: Go through life with, figuratively speaking, a crick in your neck from looking back at the path by which humanity got to today. It is a path littered with true stories that astonish. Understand that happiness is a talent, one that immunizes you against being bored. Boredom is sinful because, as a character says in a Saul Bellow novel, "Boredom is the shriek of unused capacities."

—*George Will,* "Will's Way"

Using any ten of the glossary words from *lie/lay* through *your/you're*, write a personal response to George Will's commencement advice. Underline the words you chose, checking that you used the correct form.

QuickCheck Mixed Practice

Write the word in parentheses that correctly completes each sentence.

Contemporary Life

1. While the rituals of (passed, past) high school graduations may have changed (some, somewhat), the excitement and solemnity of the occasion have not.

2. The importance of graduation is reflected in the (amount, number) of preparations made during the (preceding, proceeding) (weak, week).

3. The salutatorian and valedictorian usually make (farther, further) revisions to (their, they're) speeches.

4. A proper fit of the mortarboard is essential; if (it's, its) (to, too, two) (loose, lose), you might (loose, lose) it.

5. (To, Too, Two) achieve the full (affect, effect) and ensure that it fits (good, well), try on the robe, also.

6. Graduation practices are held to (learn, teach) graduates how to walk (all together, altogether) in the processional march.

7. At practice the coordinator (can, may) even (raise, rise) the issue of when and how to (raise, rise) at the proper time.

8. The coordinator also (learns, teaches) you how to properly adjust the tassel after receiving (you're, your) diploma.

9. Special instructions that (lay, lie) out important details are available (beside, besides) the stage.

10. As these preparations (infer, imply), the (hole, whole) ceremony is carefully planned.

CHAPTER 9

Capital Letters

Directions
Read the passage and decide which word or words should be capitalized in each underlined part. Write the letter of the correct answer. If the underlined part contains no error, write *D*.

EXAMPLE   The <u>south pole is an icy continent</u>
                                    (1)

             <u>called antarctica</u>.

     1 **A**   Continent, Antarctica
        B   Icy
        C   South Pole, Antarctica
        D   No error

ANSWER   **1 C**

On the <u>continent of Antarctica, the sun shines for half a</u>
                                    (1)
<u>year</u>. I don't know if <u>i could endure the other six months of</u>
                                    (2)
<u>darkness, although</u> the experience would be interesting.

<u>human populations do not live in Antarctica</u>, but penguins
                    (3)
and seals do. Can you picture yourself writing letters that

begin, "<u>dear mom, Here I am</u> on a <u>giant glacier far from</u>
                    (4)   **(5)**
<u>civilization</u>"?

1   **A**   Sun
    B   Continent
    C   Year
    D   No error

2   **A**   I
    B   Although
    C   Darkness
    D   No error

3   **A**   Populations
    B   Human
    C   Human, Populations
    D   No error

4   **A**   Dear
    B   Mom
    C   Dear Mom,
    D   No error

5   **A**   Giant
    B   Glacier
    C   Civilization
    D   No error

James Rosenquist. *Telephone Explosion*, 1983.
Oil on canvas, 78 by 66 inches. Courtesy of SBC Communications Inc. ©James
Rosenquist/Licensed by VAGA, New York, NY.

Describe List specific objects you recognize in this painting.

Analyze What area of the painting do you notice first? Why do you think this area attracts your attention first?

Interpret What do you think the artist, James Rosenquist, is saying with this painting?

Judge If you could change one aspect of this painting, what would it be? How would your modification change the painting's message?

At the end of this chapter, you will use the artwork to stimulate ideas for writing.

Capitalization

Until the advent of printing in the fifteenth century, words were written in all capital letters, and no punctuation was used. When scribes wrote, they ran words TOGETHERLIKETHIS.

Fortunately along with the printing press came specific uses for capitalization and the introduction of punctuation. As a result, not only could people read faster, but they could also understand more easily what they read. The correct use of capitalization and punctuation will add clarity to your writing and prevent any misunderstanding of your meaning.

When lowercase letters were first introduced, capital letters were used only in special situations. Today, however, a capital letter marks the beginning of certain constructions and emphasizes the importance of certain words. This chapter will review the uses of capitalization.

First Words and the Pronoun *I*

Capitalization is used to draw attention to the beginning of a sentence, a direct quotation, and a line of poetry. The pronoun *I* is always capitalized, regardless of its position in a sentence or line of poetry.

Sentences and Poetry

Capital letters draw a reader's attention to the beginning of a sentence or of a new line of poetry.

Capitalize the first word of a sentence and of a line of poetry.

SENTENCE	**T**eenagers in our community have become increasingly involved in poetry readings.

POETRY	The panther is like a leopard, Except it hasn't been peppered. Should you behold a panther crouch, Prepare to say Ouch. Better yet, if called by a panther, Don't anther.

—Ogden Nash

When only two or three lines of poetry are quoted, they can be written with a slash (/) between each line. Each new line after a slash begins with a capital letter.

"God in His wisdom made the fly / And then forgot to tell us why."

—Ogden Nash

Capitalize the first word when a direct quotation is used.

Marvin asked, "**D**o you understand this essay by Orwell?"

You can learn more about capitalization in direct quotations on pages L506–L507.

Some poets, especially modern poets, deliberately misuse or eliminate capital letters. If you are quoting a poem in your writing, copy it exactly as the poet has written it. Emily Dickinson, for example, sometimes capitalized common nouns for emphasis or to make them seem like people with feelings and actions.

The Sky is low—the Clouds are mean,

. . .

A Narrow Wind complains all Day

. . .

William Carlos Williams, on the other hand, wrote entire poems without using a single capital letter.

> so much depends
> upon
>
> a red wheel
> barrow
>
> glazed with rain
> water
>
> beside the white
> chickens
>
> —"The Red Wheelbarrow"

These unusual ways of using capitalization contribute to the beauty and meaning of the poems. When you quote poetry in your writing, duplicate the author's capitalization, even if it "breaks the rules."

Parts of a Letter

The first word in a salutation, or greeting of a letter, and the first word in the closing of a letter are capitalized.

Capitalize the first word in the greeting and the first word in the closing of a letter.

PARTS OF A LETTER		
GREETINGS	Dear Sir or Madam:	Attention Subscriber:
	To Whom It May Concern:	My dearest Jimmy,
CLOSINGS	Sincerely yours,	Best regards,
	Your friend,	Cordially,

In some informal letters, people write a word in all capital letters to show emphasis—especially in E-mail messages, where many browsers do not permit formatting such as italics and boldface.

You will NOT believe what I did at school today.

I can't think of ANY way to make my presentation more creative.

Outlines

Capital letters draw the reader's attention to the beginning of each heading in an outline.

Capitalize the first word of each item in an outline and the letters that begin major subsections of the outline.

    I. **A**rgument for a student bookstore-café
        A. **E**ncourages reading for relaxation
        B. **P**rovides space for poetry readings
        C. **P**rovides school supplies and snacks

Formal Resolutions

Some formal resolutions are constructed as clauses instead of sentences; nevertheless, the first word of the resolution is usually capitalized.

Capitalize the first word in a formal resolution that follows the word *Resolved.*

    Resolved: **T**hat this school should build a bookstore-café for the use of all students.

Some Formal Statements

Formal statements are sometimes introduced with phrases ending in colons, such as *The decision is this:* and *The question was this:*. In these situations, the formal statement usually begins with a capital letter.

Capitalize the first word of a formal statement that follows a colon.

The question was this: **C**ould we afford to pay a speaker as prestigious as Maya Angelou?

The committee issued the following statement: **D**onations to the guest speaker's fund are needed.

You can learn more about using colons on pages L491–L495.

The Pronoun *I*

The pronoun *I* is always capitalized, no matter its position in a sentence or a line of poetry.

Capitalize the pronoun *I*, both alone and in contractions.

I'm sure **I** saw her in English class.
I don't know if **I**'ll want to read my poem aloud.

The first word of a direct quotation is also capitalized. You can learn more about capitalization with quotations on pages L506–L507.

CONNECT TO WRITER'S CRAFT

When writing a narrative in first-person, such as an autobiography, use the pronoun *I* sparingly unless you are striving for self-emphasis.

SELF-EMPHASIS   **I** write poetry, **I** critique books, and **I** teach literature classes.

SUBJECT EMPHASIS   **I** write poetry, critique books, and teach literature classes.

PRACTICE YOUR SKILLS

● Check Your Understanding
Using Capitalization with First Words and I

Literature Topic   **Choose the item in each pair that is capitalized correctly. Then write the letter of each correct item.**

1. a. I sign all my letters "yours sincerely."

   b. I sign all my letters "Yours sincerely."

2. a. Resolved: That the first day of spring be Poetry Day at our school.

   b. Resolved: that the first day of spring be Poetry Day at our school.

3. a. I. Ideas for Poetry Day
     A. Guest poet
     B. Public reading
     C. Contest

   b. I. Ideas for Poetry Day
     A. guest poet
     B. public reading
     C. contest

4. a. For Cynthia's birthday I'm getting her *Sonnets from the Portuguese* by Elizabeth Barrett Browning.

   b. For Cynthia's birthday i'm getting her *Sonnets from the Portuguese* by Elizabeth Barrett Browning.

5. a. We have been assigned to write to an author whose work we enjoy. perhaps I will write to John Fowles.

   b. We have been assigned to write to an author whose work we enjoy. Perhaps I will write to John Fowles.

6. a. Should I begin this letter with "Dear Sir" or "Dear Mr. Fowles"?

   b. Should I begin this letter with "Dear sir" or "Dear Mr. Fowles"?

7. a. The question is this: can you read this entire novel by midterm?

   b. The question is this: Can you read this entire novel by midterm?

8. a. "'beauty is truth, truth beauty,'—that is all
ye know on earth, and all ye need to know."

—John Keats

b. "'Beauty is truth, truth beauty,'—that is all
Ye know on earth, and all ye need to know."

—John Keats

9. a. Who wrote these lines: "That's my last Duchess
painted on the wall, / looking as if she were
alive. . . . "?

b. Who wrote these lines: "That's my last Duchess
painted on the wall, / Looking as if she were
alive. . . . "?

10. a. Now that i've studied Robert Browning, I know he
wrote "My Last Duchess."

b. Now that I've studied Robert Browning, I know he
wrote "My Last Duchess."

● Connect to the Writing Process: Editing
Using Capitalization

Write each item using correct capitalization.

11. T. S. Eliot's character J. Alfred Prufrock says, "I should
have been a pair of ragged claws / scuttling across the
floors of silent seas."

12. II. The early life of George Orwell
    A. born in India
    B. birth name Eric Blair
    C. private school in England

13. in "Shooting an Elephant" Orwell writes, "in Moulmein,
in Lower Burma, I was hated by large numbers of
people—the only time in my life that I have been
important enough for this to happen to me."

14. the narrator in O'Brien's "Sister Imelda" makes the
following statement: "in our deepest moments, we say
the most inadequate things."

15. this summer I'm going to read *Fahrenheit 451* by Ray
Bradbury and then try to write my own futuristic
short story.

16. Byron wrote the following to his publisher:

"Sept 15th. 1817
dear sir—
i enclose a sheet for correction if ever you get to
another edition . . . ."

17. Resolved: that "Mutability" by Shelley be the official
poem of the senior class.

18. In *Heart of Darkness,* Conrad writes: "no, it is
impossible; it is impossible to convey the life-sensation
of any given epoch of one's existence—that which
makes its truth, its meaning—its subtle and
penetrating essence. it is impossible. we live, as we
dream—alone. . . . "

Communicate Your Ideas

APPLY TO WRITING

Analyzing Poetry: *Capitalization*

Study the use of capitalization in this poem. Then answer
the items that follow.

The Bustle in a House
    The Morning after Death
Is solemnest of industries
Enacted upon Earth,—

The sweeping up the Heart
And putting Love away
We shall not want to use again
Until Eternity.

–Emily Dickinson

- List all the words that Dickinson capitalizes.
- What rule of capitalization does Dickinson
  follow correctly?
- What words are capitalized that normally would not be?
  How does this affect the reader?

- Try writing the poem without the unusual capitalization, and then read it. What words do you skim over now that you previously noticed because of capitalization?

Proper Nouns

Beginning a noun with a capital letter tells a reader that it is a **proper noun**—that it names a particular person, place, or thing.

Capitalize proper nouns and their abbreviations.

Proper nouns may be divided into the following groups.

Names of particular persons and animals should be capitalized. Also capitalize the initials that stand for people's names.

NAMES	
PERSONS	James, Jocelyn **W**eiss, Allison **R**. **F**errara
ANIMALS	**R**ex, **F**elix, **S**pot, **D**ancer, **T**hunderbolt

Surnames that begin with *De, Mc, Mac, O',* or *St.* usually contain two capital letters. However, since such names do vary, it is always best to ask individuals how their names are spelled and capitalized.

NAMES WITH TWO CAPITAL LETTERS				
DeJong	**Mc**Guire	**Mac**Innis	**O'H**ara	**St. J**ames

Capitalize a descriptive name, title, or nickname that is used as a proper noun or as part of a proper noun.

DESCRIPTIVE NAMES		
Calamity **J**ane	**H**onest **A**be	the **C**ornhusker **S**tate

Capitalize abbreviations that follow a person's name.

Stephanie Wong, **M.D.**, will be tonight's guest speaker.

Capitalize common nouns that are clearly personified.

> "O Memory! thou fond deceiver."
>
> —*Oliver Goldsmith*

Geographical names, including the names of particular places, bodies of water, and celestial bodies should be capitalized.

GEOGRAPHICAL NAMES	
STREETS, HIGHWAYS	Tremont Street (St.), Meridian Turnpike (Tpk.), Route (Rt.) 77, Montgomery Freeway (Frwy.), Interstate Highway 35 (I-35), Charleton Boulevard (Blvd.), Sunshine Highway (Hwy.), Michigan Avenue (Ave.), Thirty-second Street (The second part of a hyphenated numbered street is not capitalized.)
CITIES, STATES	Rapid City, South Dakota (SD); Terre Haute, Indiana (IN); Washington, D.C.
TOWNSHIPS, COUNTIES, PARISHES	Pottsville Township, Broward County, New Hope Parish
COUNTRIES	Saudi Arabia, Thailand, Ireland, Canada
SECTIONS OF A COUNTRY	the Northwest, New England, the South, the Sun Belt (Words that are used as sections of the country are often preceded by *the.* Compass directions do not begin with a capital letter: *Go east on Route 23.*)
CONTINENTS	South America, Africa, Australia
WORLD REGIONS	Northern Hemisphere, South Pole, the Far East
ISLANDS	Long Island, the Philippine Islands

MOUNTAINS	Mount (**Mt.**) Hood, the Allegheny Mountains (**Mts.**), the White Mountains
PARKS	Bryce Canyon National Park
BODIES OF WATER	Pacific Ocean, South China Sea, Persian Gulf, Merrimack River, Cedar Lake
STARS	Sirius, Nova Hercules, North Star
CONSTELLATIONS	Big Dipper, Ursa Minor, Orion
PLANETS	Venus, Neptune, Saturn, Earth (Do not capitalize *sun* or *moon*. Also do not capitalize *earth* preceded by *the*.)

You can learn more about proper nouns on pages L6–L9.

Words such as *street, mountain, river, island,* and *county* are capitalized only when they are part of a proper noun.

> Which lake is larger, Lake Superior or Lake Michigan?
> Which county is central, Travis County or Randall County?

PRACTICE YOUR SKILLS

● Check Your Understanding
Using Capital Letters

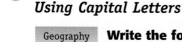 **Write the following items, using capital letters where needed.**

1. the columbia river
2. jackson park
3. the milky way
4. fifty-third st.
5. a trip to the southwest
6. the city of louisville
7. the earth and mars
8. mountains in the east
9. the gulf of suez
10. madrid, spain
11. north on hayes highway
12. his horse dusty
13. alfred moses, jr.
14. the state of ohio
15. lake victoria
16. the bluegrass state
17. newport news, va
18. a country in africa

Using Capital Letters

History Topic **Correctly write each word that should be capitalized.**

19. Woodrow Wilson, born in staunton, va, had a pet ram named old ike.

20. William J. Clinton and his family moved into the White House with their pet cat named socks.

21. Before they were known as the rocky mountains, they were called the stony mountains.

22. The first woman to swim the english channel in both directions was Florence Chadwick of california.

23. Old North Church-Christ Church, built in 1723, is the oldest church in boston.

24. It is the place where the signal lantern for the midnight ride of paul revere was hung.

25. Henry wadsworth longfellow wrote a poem about the famous ride.

26. The capital of texas was changed 15 times before austin was finally chosen.

27. mt. st. helens, a volcano in the state of Washington, erupted in 1980.

28. Address your letter to the President of the United States, 1600 pennsylvania ave., washington, dc 20500-0001.

● Connect to the Writing Process: Drafting
Writing Sentences with Proper Nouns

Use each of the following items in a sentence, correctly capitalizing each word that should be capitalized. Correct any words that are incorrectly capitalized.

29. the nile river

30. a trip to the united kingdom

31. a Cruise to nassau in the caribbean

32. a Dog named cimarron lee

33. at the corner of citrus ave. and Thirty-First st.

34. ursa major, a Constellation

35. a party in central park

APPLY TO WRITING

Invitation: *Proper Nouns*

Write an invitation to a famous novelist or poet. Explain that your school district is planning a Reader's Theater and would like for him or her personally to read original poetry or excerpts. Determine the theme of the Reader's Theater for the writer. Then ask him or her to contact you. Also, provide directions to your school from the nearest airport. Include major highways, cities and towns, and states. When you finish, edit your invitation for mistakes in capitalization, and then write the final copy.

Names of groups, including the names of organizations, businesses, institutions, government bodies, political parties, and teams, should be capitalized.

NAMES OF GROUPS	
ORGANIZATIONS	the **A**merican **R**ed **C**ross, the **B**oy **S**couts of **A**merica, the **A**ir **N**ational **G**uard
BUSINESSES	**F**ly **N**ow **A**irlines, **T**he **G**old and **S**ilver **C**ompany, **H**awthorne's **G**reenery, **T**aft **S&L**
INSTITUTIONS	**H**awthorne **H**igh **S**chool, **L**akeview **H**ospital, the **U**niversity (**U**niv.) of **P**ennsylvania, **N**ew **Y**ork **U**niversity (**NYU**) (Words such as *school, hospital,* and *university* are not capitalized unless they are part of a proper noun.)

GOVERNMENT BODIES OR AGENCIES	the **United States Supreme Court, C**ongress, the **Senate**, the **Veterans Administration,** the **House of Commons, Parliament, NASA**
POLITICAL PARTIES	the **Democratic party, a Republican**
TEAMS	the **Boston Bruins**, the **Seattle Seahawks,** the **Houston Rockets**, the **Ames Little League**

Specific time periods, events, and documents, including the days of the week, months of the year, civil holidays, and special events are capitalized. Also capitalize the names of historical events, periods, and documents.

TIME PERIODS, EVENTS, AND DOCUMENTS	
DAYS, MONTHS	**Tuesday (Tues.), Wednesday (Wed.), February (Feb.), December (Dec.)** (Do not capitalize the seasons of the year—such as summer and winter—unless they are part of a proper noun: **B**rooks **S**ummer Fair.)
HOLIDAYS	**Memorial D**ay, **Thanksgiving, President's D**ay
SPECIAL EVENTS	the **Orange Bowl Parade**, the **Olympics**, the **Boston Marathon**
HISTORICAL EVENTS	the **Trojan War**, the **Boston Tea Party**, the **Louisiana Purchase, D-Day**
TIME PERIODS	the **Middle Ages**, the **Age of Reason**, the **Great Depression, Reconstruction**
TIME ABBREVIATIONS	**A.M./P.M., B.C./A.D.**
DOCUMENTS	the **Truman Doctrine**, the **Treaty of Paris**, the **First Amendment**, the **Civil Rights Act**

Prepositions are not usually capitalized in proper nouns.

Names of nationalities, races, languages, and religions, including religious holidays and references, are capitalized.

NATIONALITIES, RACES, LANGUAGES, AND RELIGIONS	
NATIONALITIES AND RACES	Chinese, Mexican, Norwegian, Canadian, Irish, Dutch, Portugese, Caucasian, Asian, African, Cherokee
LANGUAGES AND COMPUTER LANGUAGES	Spanish, Greek, Russian, Latin, Arabic, C++, Hyper Text Markup Language (**HTML**), Cobol, Java
RELIGIONS	Roman Catholism, Judaism, Lutheranism, Islam
RELIGIOUS HOLIDAYS AND REFERENCES	Purim, Kwanzaa, Christmas, Ramadan, the Bible, the New Testament, the Torah, the Koran, Buddha, God (Do not capitalize *god* when it refers to a polytheistic god.)

CONNECT TO WRITER'S CRAFT

You may have noticed that some writers capitalize the pronouns *he* and *him* when referring to God. Other writers do not capitalize these pronouns.

God told Pharaoh to let **H**is people go.
God told Pharaoh to let **h**is people go.

Also, religious writers sometimes capitalize *thy, thine,* and *thou* (archaic words for *your, yours,* and *you*) when they use pronouns in direct address to God. Whatever decision you make regarding capitalization of such pronouns, you should be consistent.

Other proper nouns should also be capitalized.

OTHER PROPER NOUNS	
AWARDS	the Nobel Prize, the Davis Cup
BRAND NAMES	a Trifect computer, Peaches soap (The product itself is not capitalized.)

STRUCTURES, MEMORIALS, MONUMENTS	Golden Gate Bridge, Sears Tower, Vietnam Memorial, Washington Monument, Mount Rushmore
SHIPS, TRAINS, AIRCRAFT, SPACECRAFT	*SS Minnow, Orient Express, Spirit of St. Louis, Apollo 13, Challenger*
TECHNOLOGICAL TERMS	Internet, Web, World Wide Web, Website, Web page, Web art
NAMES OF COURSES	Chemistry II, Drafting I, Drawing 101

Unnumbered courses such as *history, science,* and *art* are not capitalized. Language courses such as *Spanish* and *English,* however, are always capitalized (even when unnumbered) because the name of a language is always capitalized. Also, do not capitalize class names such as *freshman* or *senior* unless they are part of a proper noun: *Senior Class Picnic.*

PRACTICE YOUR SKILLS

 Check Your Understanding
Capitalizing Proper Nouns

 General Interest **Write the following items, using capital letters only where needed.**

1. math and spanish
2. the eiffel tower in paris
3. turkey on thanksgiving
4. dec.
5. the stone age
6. computer sciences corp.
7. the god zeus
8. computer book on java
9. harvard college
10. spring and summer
11. the supreme court
12. friday
13. allah, the islamic name of god
14. a jewish rabbi
15. website on the internet
16. a.m.
17. wise eyes sunglasses
18. political science 1302
19. new york police department
20. argus architects, inc.

Using Capital Letters

General Interest **Correctly write each word that should begin with a capital letter.**

21. Edith Wharton won a pulitzer prize for her fiction.

22. John Adams was a member of the federalist party.

23. Dolley Madison was voted a seat in the house of representatives on january 9, 1844.

24. When my sister graduated from purdue university, she got a job with a computer company.

25. Did you visit mount vernon, george washington's home?

26. Ty Cobb of the detroit tigers made 4,191 base hits during his career.

27. Last year, when I was a junior, I enjoyed french, creative writing, art II, and mechanical drawing.

28. J. R. Andrews was captain of the *derwent,* which sailed between sydney and london in the 1880s and 1890s.

29. Stephanie Louise Kwolek, a scientist, was inducted into the national inventors hall of fame on july 22, 1995.

30. Do you think any inventor will ever be as well known as Thomas alva Edison?

● Connect to the Writing Process: Editing
Capitalizing Proper Nouns

Rewrite the following sentences, capitalizing the proper nouns and using lowercase for words that are incorrectly capitalized.

31. A famous tourist attraction in italy is the Leaning Tower of pisa.

32. This Tower continues to lean each year.

33. The Cathedral of notre dame is a very famous Cathedral in Paris, france.

34. It is located on the Île de la Cité, a small Island of the Seine river.

35. The phrase *Notre dame* means "our lady" in french.

Communicate Your Ideas

APPLY TO WRITING
Autobiography: *Proper Nouns*

Why is it important to learn about one's cultural heritage?
Write your own autobiography to present orally to your
class. Describe an aspect of your cultural heritage that has
contributed to who you are, whether for good or for bad.
Use correct capitalization when writing names, time
periods, events, languages, and so on. Edit your use of
capitalization carefully before writing the final copy.

✓ QuickCheck Mixed Practice

General Interest **Correctly write each word that should begin with a capital letter.**

1. In an average year, santa fe, new mexico, receives 17
   more inches of snow than fairbanks, alaska.

2. The first college for women, which opened in 1834, was
   wheaton college in norton, massachusetts.

3. andrew jackson fought in the revolutionary war when
   he was only thirteen years old.

4. the largest natural history museum in the world is the
   american museum of natural history.

5. The closest planet to the sun, mercury, is about one
   third the size of earth.

6. John glenn's space capsule, *friendship 7,* was picked up
   by the recovery ship *noah.*

7. The people of philadelphia first celebrated the fourth of
   july a year after the declaration of independence had
   been adopted by the continental congress.

8. In 1888 in new york, george eastman invented a box
   camera that held rolled film.

9. The philadelphia eagles started playing in the national football league in 1933.
10. The last state to join the union before alaska and hawaii was arizona, which was admitted on valentine's day in 1912.
11. Charles Lindbergh flew the *spirit of st. louis* solo from the U.S. to Paris in May, 1927.
12. Gold was discovered by accident at sutter's mill in California on January 24, 1848.
13. The statue of liberty was a gift from the french to celebrate the first centennial of independence in the U.S.
14. The *titanic* sank on April 14, 1912.
15. Toni Morrison won the 1993 nobel prize in literature for her six visionary and poetic novels.

Proper Adjectives

Because proper adjectives are formed from proper nouns, they should be capitalized—as proper nouns are.

Capitalize most proper adjectives.

PROPER NOUNS AND ADJECTIVES	
PROPER NOUNS	Spain, Idaho
PROPER ADJECTIVES	Spanish rice, Idaho potatoes

When adjectives are formed from the words that refer to the compass directions, such as *east,* no capital letters are used.

The wind was blowing from an **e**asterly direction.

Some proper adjectives derived from proper nouns are so familiar that they are no longer capitalized.

COMMONPLACE PROPER ADJECTIVES		
china plates	pasteurized milk	quixotic vision

When a proper adjective is part of a hyphenated adjective, capitalize only the part that is a proper adjective. Sometimes, however, both parts of a hyphenated adjective are proper adjectives.

HYPHENATED PROPER ADJECTIVES	
all-American team	trans-Siberian journey
Indo-European languages	African-American literature

PRACTICE YOUR SKILLS

● Check Your Understanding
Capitalizing Proper Adjectives

Sports Topic **Correctly write each word that should begin with a capital letter. If a sentence is correct, write C.**

1. The olympic Athletes first competed in Greece.

2. Also popular were the Isthmian Games, which were held near the Isthmus of Corinth.

3. Baseball is often called the all-american game.

4. Nemesio Guillot began cuban baseball in 1866.

5. Guillot taught his fellow Cubans to play the game after learning it from Americans in the U.S.

6. American soccer is equivalent to the latin-american game of football.

7. In 1959, Rong Guotuan won a gold medal in table tennis, becoming the first athlete in chinese history to be a world champion.

8. Some activities we enjoy today—swimming, equestrian sports, rowing—were also popular ancient egyptian sports.

9. Cricket, tennis, and kabaddi (a combination of wrestling and rugby) are popular indian athletic activities.

10. A relatively cold climate encourages canadian youngsters to play ice hockey.

● Connect to the Writing Process: Drafting
Writing Sentences: Using Proper Adjectives

Use each of the following proper nouns as a proper adjective in a sentence, capitalizing the adjective correctly.

11. hawaii

12. italy

13. freud

14. democrat

15. shakespeare

16. trans-europe

17. victoria

18. texas

19. spain

20. hippocrates (hint: doctors' oath)

● Connect to the Writing Process: Editing
Capitalizing Proper Nouns and Adjectives

Write each sentence, capitalizing the nouns and adjectives correctly. If a sentence is correct, write C.

21. A republican senator spoke at assembly today.

22. The friday afternoon traffic near my school is heavy.

23. "An anglophile loves all things english," said my english teacher, Miss Gilbert.

24. Should I use roman numerals or arabic numerals?

25. I received a french dictionary for graduation.

26. Our class is going to hike in the appalachian mountains.

27. The history teacher showed us pre-columbian artifacts.

28. She also told us that the first non-indian visitor to arizona arrived in 1539.

29. In french class I learned that many of the numerous french-speaking people in canada live in quebec.

30. I plan to sign up for History 101 and beginning German.

Titles

Capital letters signal the importance of titles of persons and works of art.

Capitalize the titles of persons and works of art.

Titles with Names of People

Capitalize a title showing office, rank, or profession when it comes before a person's name.

BEFORE A NAME	Is **Judge** Abraham Goodell in his chambers this morning?
USED ALONE	Who was the **judge** at the recent grand larceny trial?
BEFORE A NAME	I worked on **Senator** Sheridan Ames's re-election campaign.
USED ALONE	The **senator** from our district is running for re-election.

Do not capitalize the prefix *ex–* or the suffix *–elect* when either is connected to a title.

The patriotic parade honored **ex**-Senator Hillmann and Governor-**e**lect Baray.

Titles Used Alone

Capitalize a title that is used alone when it is substituted for a person's name in direct address or when it is used as a name. The titles for the current United States President and Vice President, for the Chief Justice, and for the Queen of England are almost always capitalized when they are being substituted for the person's name.

USED AS A NAME	How is the patient in room 114 this evening, **D**octor?
NOT USED AS A NAME	The **d**octor will speak to you before she leaves.
HIGH GOVERNMENT OFFICIAL	The **P**resident and the **V**ice **P**resident will attend the summit meeting next month.

Remember that *president* and *vice president* are capitalized when they stand alone only if they refer to the *current* president and vice president.

> Was John F. Kennedy the youngest **p**resident ever to hold office?

Titles Showing Family Relationships

Capitalize a title showing a family relationship when it comes before a person's name, when it is used as a name, or when it is substituted for a person's name.

BEFORE A NAME	When did **U**ncle Ron and **A**unt Mary leave?
USED AS A NAME	Please tell **M**om that she has a visitor.
DIRECT ADDRESS	I'll help you paint the porch, **D**ad.

Titles showing family relationships should not be capitalized when they are preceded by a possessive noun or pronoun—unless they are considered part of a person's name.

NO CAPITAL	My **a**unt lives in California.
	Aaron is taking Phil's **s**ister to the prom.
CAPITAL	When does your **U**ncle Ralph get home from work?
	(*Uncle* is considered part of Ralph's name.)

Titles of Written Works and Other Works of Art

Capitalize the first word, the last word, and all important words that are used in the following titles: books, stories, poems, newspapers and newspaper articles, magazines and magazine articles, movies, plays, television series, musical songs and compositions, and works of art. Short prepositions, coordinating conjunctions, and articles should not be capitalized unless they are the first or last words in a title.

TITLES OF WORKS	
BOOKS AND PARTS OF BOOKS	*Pride and Prejudice, Dictionary of Desktop Publishing,* **C**hapter 11, **V**ol. V, **N**o. 4, **P**art IV
SHORT STORIES	"**O**dor of **C**hrysanthemums"
POEMS	"**T**he **R**oad **N**ot **T**aken"
NEWSPAPERS AND NEWSPAPER ARTICLES	the *Chicago Tribune* (The word *the* before the title of a newspaper is usually not capitalized.), "**N**ew **C**ity **P**ark **O**pens," "**A** **D**ay in the **L**ife of **O**ur **M**ayor"
MAGAZINES AND MAGAZINE ARTICLES	*Discover Magazine, Newsweek,* "**T**en **C**olleges **E**very **S**enior **S**hould **K**now **A**bout"
MOVIES	*Men in Black, Gone with the Wind*
PLAYS	*Hamlet, The Importance of Being Earnest*
TELEVISION SERIES	*Dawson's Creek, Dateline, Tom and Jerry*
MUSICAL SONGS AND COMPOSITIONS	"**A**mazing **G**race," "**T**he **S**tar-**S**pangled **B**anner," "**V**iolin **C**oncerto in **E** **M**inor"
WORKS OF ART	*Water Lilies* (painting by Claude Monet), *Sleeping Muse* (sculpture by Constantin Brancusi), *McPherson's Woods* (photograph by Matthew Brady)

You can learn about punctuating titles on pages L501–L504.

PRACTICE YOUR SKILLS

● Check Your Understanding
Capitalizing Titles

Contemporary Life **Correctly write each word that should begin with a capital letter. If an item is correct, write C.**

1. justice ruth bader ginsburg
2. *I never saw another butterfly,* a play by Celeste Raspunti
3. my science professor
4. *uncle tom's cabin,* a novel by Harriet Beecher Stowe
5. my best friend's uncle sam
6. *felicity,* a series on television
7. *the thinker,* a sculpture by Auguste Rodin
8. the *albuquerque journal*
9. "the forgotten city," a poem by William Carlos Williams
10. ex-speaker of the house of representatives
11. *tv guide*
12. "what a wonderful world," a song by Louis Armstrong
13. *Blizzard of one,* poetry by Mark Strand
14. *teen sports illustrated*
15. Will you lend me five dollars, dad?
16. the *lincoln statue* by Vinnie Reams
17. "the dog and the wolf," a fable by Aesop
18. *a tale of two cities,* a book by Charles Dickens
19. dr. martin luther king, jr.
20. "dance of the sugar plum fairy," from the ballet *the nutcracker suite*
21. my grandfather harry's farm
22. Former president carter is active in public service.
23. The doctor sent Lena to the hospital.
24. *Muhammed Ali: The World's Greatest Champion,* a biography by John Tessitore
25. *much ado about nothing,* a play by William Shakespeare

APPLY TO WRITING

Descriptive Newspaper Article: *Capitalization*

This is a photo of the Laughing Roosevelt Bear, which was crafted in 1907 to display President Roosevelt's toothy grin. The advertisement for the bear read, "The Laughing Teddy Bear laughs and shows his teeth at critics."

Choose a current public figure with a title—in politics, law, medicine, education, for example—and then choose a "mascot" for this person (like the teddy bear for Teddy Roosevelt). Write a newspaper article describing this public figure and his or her distinctive characteristics, and then describe how the animal or toy mirrors these characteristics. Be sure to give your article a title.

Edit your writing for correct capitalization of proper nouns, proper adjectives, and titles. Then write the final copy. If possible, find or draw a picture of the mascot to accompany your article.

General Interest **Correctly write each word that should begin with a capital letter. Then answer each question, if you can!**

1. was alan b. shepard, jr., or john glenn the first american to orbit the earth?

2. was it the pilgrims or the puritans who landed at plymouth rock in 1620?

3. which is the most westerly state in the u.s., alaska or hawaii?

4. who is the author of *great expectations,* a novel written during queen victoria's reign in england?

5. in what country were the first olympic games held?

6. was william mckinley or theodore roosevelt the first president elected in the twentieth century?

7. who was the first american president elected in the twenty-first century?

8. what was the name of dorothy's dog in *the wizard of oz?*

9. is the geyser old faithful in wyoming or nevada?

10. "i want to hold your hand" was the first american number-one single of what british group?

11. did world war II end in 1942 or 1945?

12. is the cy young award given in baseball or football?

13. is sacramento or los angeles the capital of california?

14. general lee surrendered to general grant at the appomattox court house. in what state did this occur?

15. did clark kent work for the *metropolis journal* or the *daily planet?*

16. what was the russian equivalent of the u.s. central intelligence agency?

17. is the lincoln memorial or the washington monument the tallest structure in washington, d.c.?

18. is the astrodome in chicago or houston?

Using Capital Letters Correctly

Correctly write each word that should begin with a capital letter.

1. dalia's address is 43 thirty-third street, kokomo, indiana.
2. school usually starts on the wednesday after labor day.
3. the mediterranean sea is one of the most polluted seas on earth.
4. mount desert island, off the coast of maine, was discovered in 1604 by champlain, a french explorer.
5. have you any tickets for the chicago white sox game on saturday?
6. when i was a junior, my favorite course was biology, but this year i like english best.
7. the oscar weighs 7 pounds and is 10 inches high.
8. minnesota is called the land of 10,000 lakes, but it actually contains more than 11,000 lakes.
9. there really was a molly pitcher, but her real name was mary hayes mccauley.
10. during the battle of monmouth, she carried water in a pitcher to thirsty american soldiers.
11. when my parents went to canada last summer, they visited the small nova scotian town where mother was born.
12. have you ever read elizabeth jennings's poem "in memory of anyone unknown to me"?
13. last month the vice president represented the president on a tour of the far east.
14. the *andrea doria* collided with a swedish ship off the coast of nantucket in 1956.
15. i enjoy watching the television series *masterpiece theatre*.

Editing for the Correct Use of Capital Letters

Correctly write each word that should begin with a capital letter. Do not include words that are already capitalized.

How did the state of idaho get its name? Some believe it is a shoshoni indian word meaning "gem of the mountains." The idaho state historical society, though, insists that the state's name does not have any meaning. It was first coined by a mining lobbyist in 1860 as a good name for a new territory in the pikes peak mining country. However, just before congress voted in washington, d.c., the hoax was discovered. That territory was then named colorado. The word *idaho*, nevertheless, kept popping up in the pacific northwest. For example, a steamboat that carried prospectors up and down the columbia river was named the *idaho*. As a result, three years later the name was again suggested to congress; but this time it was accepted.

Writing Sentences

At the library find a fact that pertains to each of the following topics. Each fact should include a proper noun, a proper adjective, or a title.

Write a sentence that includes . . .

1. a fact about a famous bridge.
2. a fact about a holiday.
3. a fact about a state capital.
4. a fact about an English poet.
5. a fact about basketball.

Language and *Self-Expression*

If you created a work of art focused on a method of communication, what would that method be? Would you choose the telephone, as Rosenquist did? An E-mail message? Face-to-face conversation? Think about the rules that are often placed on communication: "Don't pass notes in class," or "Don't talk too long on the phone."

Write a description of your personal view of communication, particularly communication between friends. Explain what method is most effective for you and why that is so. Explain the message you would express if you created artwork similar to Rosenquist's.

Prewriting List ways that you communicate with friends, and write friends' names beside the way in which you most often communicate with them. Draw a star next to the category that you use most.

Drafting Focusing on the category with the star by it, write several paragraphs on communication from your perspective. Use the other categories for comparison or contrast. You might mention restrictions that are sometimes or always placed on you, such as phone or computer privileges at home. Your conclusion could sum up the overall message you would want to show in a work of art.

Revising Check your writing for the clear progression of ideas. For example, make sure that you introduce and explain a concept before you describe how that concept should be changed.

Editing Check for correct use of capital letters as well as spelling and grammar.

Publishing Write a final copy and give it to your teacher. Then choose one of the friends you listed in your prewriting. Share your paper with that friend.

Another Look

Capitalizing First Words and the Pronoun *I*
Capitalize the first word of a sentence and of a line of poetry.
(pages L391–L393)
Capitalize the first word in the greeting and the first word in the closing
of a letter. *(page L393)*
Capitalize the first word of each item in an outline and the letters that
begin major subsections of the outline. *(page L394)*
Capitalize the first word in a formal resolution that follows the word
Resolved. (page L394)
Capitalize the first word of a formal statement that follows a colon.
(page L395)
Capitalize the pronoun *I*, both alone and in contractions. *(page L395)*

Capitalizing Proper Nouns
Capitalize proper nouns and their abbreviations. *(pages L399–L409)*
Capitalize names of particular persons and animals. *(pages L399–L400)*
Capitalize geographical names, including the names of particular places,
bodies of water, and celestial bodies. *(pages L400–L401)*
Capitalize names of groups. *(pages L403–L404)*
Capitalize specific time periods, events, and documents. *(page L404)*
Capitalize names of nationalities, races, languages, and religions.
(page L405)

Capitalizing Proper Adjectives
Capitalize most proper adjectives. *(pages L409–L410)*

Capitalizing Titles
Capitalize the titles of persons and works of art. *(pages L412–L414)*
Capitalize a title showing office, rank, or profession when it comes before
a person's name. *(page L412)*
Capitalize a title that is used alone when it is substituted for a person's
name in direct address or when it is used as a name. *(page L412)*
Capitalize the first word, the last word, and all important words that are
used in the following titles: books, stories, poems, newspapers and
newspaper articles, magazines and magazine articles, movies, plays,
television series, and musical songs and compositions. *(page L414)*

Posttest

Directions

Read the passage and decide which word or words should be capitalized in each underlined part. Write the letter of the correct answer. If the underlined part contains no error, write D.

EXAMPLE   Samuel <u>f. b. Morse lived in the nineteenth</u>
                                   (1)
                   <u>century, and he invented the telegraph</u>.

       1 **A**   F. B.
              B   Nineteenth Century
              C   Telegraph
              D   No error

ANSWER   **1** **A**

The term <u>"morse code" refers to the method of communication</u>
                                    (1)
using dots, dashes, and spaces to represent letters and numbers.

<u>in electrical telegraphy, this code</u> consists of short and long pulses;
               (2)
the code can be translated to short and long flashes of light, too.

The <u>telegraph, invented in the u.s. in the 1830s by morse, uses</u>
                            (3)
<u>electrical telegraphy</u>. Similarly, <u>ships can use bright lights to flash</u>
                                           (4)
<u>messages across long distances</u> when radio communications are down.

Many people know the <u>code for the distress call, sos</u>.
                                  (5)

1 **A** Morse Code
   B Morse
   C Method, Communication
   D No error

2 **A** Electrical Telegraphy
   B In, Code
   C In
   D No error

3 **A** U.S., Morse
   B Telegraph, U.S.
   C Electrical Telegraphy
   D No error

4 **A** Ships
   B Long Distances
   C Bright Lights
   D No error

5 **A** SOS
   B Distress Call, SOS
   C Distress Call
   D No error

End Marks and Commas

Directions
Read the passage and choose the mark of punctuation that belongs in each underlined space. Write the letter of the correct answer.

EXAMPLE

The Hercules beetle _(1)_ which is a type of scarab beetle, grows up to eight inches long.

1 **A** period

   B question mark

   C exclamation point

   D comma

ANSWER   1 **D**

   Wow _(1)_ Look over there by the tree at that huge beetle. It must be a Hercules beetle _(2)_ Did you know that a Hercules beetle has a horn that grows up to four inches long _(3)_ My science teacher, Dr _(4)_ Carpenter, told us these facts. Only the male beetle, not the female _(5)_ has this horn. Look at this picture of the beetle on the Internet _(6)_ Scarab beetles, which include the Hercules beetle, are found worldwide _(7)_ Other members of the scarab family are June bugs, Japanese beetles, rhinoceros beetles _(8)_ and dung beetles. Don't these beetles usually have a brilliantly colored body _(9)_ The female Hercules beetle has a layer of red hairs _(10)_ and the Japanese beetle is a shiny green and brown.

1	**A**	period	**6**	**A**	period
	B	question mark		**B**	question mark
	C	exclamation point		**C**	exclamation point
	D	comma		**D**	comma
2	**A**	period	**7**	**A**	period
	B	question mark		**B**	question mark
	C	exclamation point		**C**	exclamation point
	D	comma		**D**	comma
3	**A**	period	**8**	**A**	period
	B	question mark		**B**	question mark
	C	exclamation point		**C**	exclamation point
	D	comma		**D**	comma
4	**A**	period	**9**	**A**	period
	B	question mark		**B**	question mark
	C	exclamation point		**C**	exclamation point
	D	comma		**D**	comma
5	**A**	period	**10**	**A**	period
	B	question mark		**B**	question mark
	C	exclamation point		**C**	exclamation point
	D	comma		**D**	comma

Artist unknown, Egyptian.
Head of Queen Tiy,
ca. 1391–1353 B.C.
Yew wood with silver and glass,
height 3½ inches. Ägyptisches
Museum und Papyrussammlung,
Berlin.

Describe Describe the artistic elements—including line,
color, shape, value, and texture—that the
sculptor used.

Analyze What aspect of this sculpture seems to be its
central focus? Why does this aspect attract
your attention?

Interpret What do you think this sculpture says about
the personality or character of Queen Tiy?

Judge What do you think is the difference in effect
between a sculpture of the head only and a
sculpture of the complete human figure?

At the end of this chapter, you will use the artwork to stimulate
ideas for writing.

Kinds of Sentences and End Marks

A sentence has one of four different functions. It can make a statement, give a command, ask a question, or express strong feeling. Depending on its function, a sentence may be declarative, imperative, interrogative, or exclamatory. The end mark you use with a particular sentence is determined by the function of that sentence.

The first function of a sentence is to make a statement or to express an opinion. Most sentences fall into this category.

A **declarative sentence** makes a statement or expresses an opinion and ends with a period.

The following examples are both declarative sentences, even though the second example contains an indirect question.

Dinosaurs have fascinated people for many years.

I am not sure when dinosaurs lived.
(The direct question would be *When did dinosaurs live?*)

The second function of a sentence is to give directions, make requests, or give commands. Generally *you* is the understood subject of these sentences.

An **imperative sentence** gives a direction, makes a request, or gives a command. It ends with a period or an exclamation point.

If a command is given in a normal tone of voice, it is followed by a period when written. If it expresses strong feeling, it is followed by an exclamation point.

Use this map to get to Dinosaur, Colorado.
(normal tone of voice)

Don't play that silly dinosaur videotape again!
(emotional tone of voice)

Occasionally an imperative sentence is stated as a question, but no reply is expected. Since the purpose of the sentence remains the same—to make a request—the sentence is followed by a period or by an exclamation point.

> Will you please hand me that book on dinosaur extinction.

The third function of a sentence is to ask a question—whether it is completely or incompletely expressed.

> An **interrogative sentence** asks a question and ends with a question mark.

> Have you seen the dinosaur display?

> Where? Did I pass it?

CONNECT TO WRITER'S CRAFT

Watch for interrogative sentences in advertising—both in print and on television. A company will draw you in by asking you a question. Most people feel obligated to answer a question, and so they pay attention to the ad. For example, a magazine page is covered with photos of individual potato chips, and at the top you read, "Can you tell which chip is the fat-free chip?" For a moment, you're tempted to try to answer the question—and the chip company wins your attention!

The fourth function of a sentence is to express strong feeling, such as excitement or anger. Avoid overusing this type of sentence, for it can very quickly lose its impact.

> An **exclamatory sentence** expresses strong feeling or emotion and ends with an exclamation point.

> I think I've found a fossil!

An interjection, such as *wow* or *oh,* may also be followed by an exclamation point.

> Ouch! This cat has teeth like a tiger's.

You can learn more about punctuation with interjections on pages L43–L44.

Fiction writers are especially attentive to their use of end marks when they write dialogue. End marks help give the conversation dynamics—a sense of action—by conveying the speaker's emotions and attitudes quickly through punctuation. Consider the emotions related by the following lines:

> **"Stop,"** he said.
> **"Stop!"** he said.

Simply by looking at end marks, you can tell that the first speaker feels thoughtful and is in no particular hurry, while the second speaker feels a sense of urgent danger or excitement.

PRACTICE YOUR SKILLS

● **Check Your Understanding**
Classifying Sentences

General Interest **Using the following abbreviations, label each sentence.** (Since none of the sentences end with punctuation marks, you will need to label each sentence according to its meaning.)

declarative = *d.*   imperative = *imp.*
interrogative = *int.*   exclamatory = *ex.*

1. Paleontologists study life from the geological past
2. Did you know that fossilized footprints tell us about dinosaurs' habits of movement
3. Will you look at this cast of a footprint
4. Wow, look at the size of it
5. Read the next chapter in your geology textbook
6. What caused the dinosaur extinction at the Cretaceous/Tertiary boundary
7. Everything from asteroids to volcanoes has been blamed
8. I wonder what it was like to watch dinosaurs roam
9. What an exciting time it must have been
10. Dinosaur bones have been discovered in Colorado

11.–20. Rewrite the sentences in the preceding exercise, adding the correct end punctuation.

● Connect to the Writing Process: Editing
Using End Marks

Notice that periods are the only end punctuation used in this E-mail message. Rewrite those sentences that are incorrectly punctuated, replacing periods with question marks and exclamation points where needed.

Alex,

You won't believe what I just found. You know how I'm supposed to be writing that report in science class. I found the perfect place to get all my information. It is this great dinosaur web site that has dozens of links to dinosaur information. Reliable information. A few of the links are broken, but most of them are up to date. You can look at photos of fossils and bones and then print them out. The webmaster calls himself "Virtual Geologist," and he will answer any questions you send him.

Aren't you and your family going camping somewhere this summer. You will want to follow the link to Dinosaur National Monument. This is a park on the border of Colorado and Utah where you can inspect dinosaur bones up close. Maybe your family will take me along. That would be great.

See you later,

Matt

APPLY TO WRITING

Writer's Craft: *Analyzing the Use of End Marks*

As you read the following passage, notice the kinds of sentences and end marks the author uses. Then answer the questions that follow.

> In the store, Thorne held the radio close to his cheek. "Okay," he said. "Sarah? Listen carefully. Get in the car, and do exactly what I tell you."
>
> "Okay fine," she said. "But tell me first. Is Levine there?"
>
> "He's here."
>
> The radio clicked. She said, "Ask him if there's any danger from a green dinosaur that's about four feet tall and has a domed forehead."
>
> Levine nodded. "Tell her yes. They're called pachy-cephalosaurs."
>
> "He says yes," Thorne said. "They're pachycephalo-somethings, and you should be careful. Why?"
>
> "Because there's fifty of them, all around the car."
>
> —*Michael Crichton,* The Lost World

- List the kinds of sentences the author uses in this passage.

- Why do you think the author uses such a variety of sentence types within such a short passage?

- Which sentence do you think would work well with an exclamation point? Why?

- What tone of voice do you think Sarah might be using? Why?

- What kind of sentence do you think should follow this excerpt of dialogue? What would its purpose be?

● Other Uses of Periods

Periods have several uses—in addition to ending a sentence.

With Abbreviations

Using abbreviations is a good way to write faster when you are taking notes, but they should usually be avoided in formal writing, such as in essays and research papers.

Use a period after most abbreviations.

The following list contains some abbreviations that are acceptable in formal writing. Use the dictionary to check the spelling and punctuation of other abbreviations.

ABBREVIATIONS				
TITLES WITH NAMES	Mr. Lt.	Ms. Col.	Mrs. Prof.	Rev. Gov.	Dr. Sr.
INITIALS FOR NAMES	A. E. Housman Samuel T. Coleridge		J. R. R. Tolkien		
TIMES WITH NUMBERS	A.M.	P.M.	B.C.	A.D.	
ADDRESSES	Ave. Rd.	St. Dr.	Blvd. Ct.	Rt. P.O. Box	Dept.
ORGANIZATIONS AND COMPANIES	Co.	Inc.	Corp.	Assoc.	

Some organizations and companies are known by abbreviations that stand for their full names. The majority of these abbreviations do not use periods. A few other common abbreviations also do not include periods.

ABBREVIATIONS WITHOUT PERIODS	
FBI = Federal Bureau of Investigation	km = kilometer
USAF = United States Air Force	mph = miles per hour
ISP = Internet Service Provider	

If a statement ends with an abbreviation, only one period is needed at the end of the sentence. If an interrogative or an exclamatory sentence ends with an abbreviation, both a period and a question mark, or a period and an exclamation point, are needed.

The graduation ceremony begins at 7:00 P.M.
Does the graduation ceremony begin at 7:00 P.M.?

Today, almost everyone uses the post office's two-letter state abbreviations that do not include periods. You usually can find a list of these state abbreviations at the front of most telephone books. The following list includes a few examples.

STATE ABBREVIATIONS		
AK = Alaska	MD = Maryland	OR = Oregon
CA = California	MO = Missouri	TX = Texas
CO = Colorado	NJ = New Jersey	UT = Utah
HI = Hawaii	OK = Oklahoma	VT = Vermont

With Outlines

Periods are used in outlines to help mark each major and minor division.

Use a period after each number or letter that shows a division in an outline.

I. Popular entertainment awards on television
   A. MZTV Music Awards
      1. New Group
      2. Female Solo Artist
   B. Vision Fashion Awards
      1. Fall Collection
      2. Designer
II. Film industry awards
   A. Drama
      1. Original Screenplay
      2. Adapted Screenplay
   B. Comedy

PRACTICE YOUR SKILLS

● Check Your Understanding
Using Abbreviations

Write each item, using proper abbreviations. Include periods where needed. If you are unsure of the spelling or the punctuation of an abbreviation, look it up in the dictionary.

1. George Bush, Senior
2. New Jersey
3. Carlson Lumber Company
4. September
5. Captain Ahab
6. III Conclusion
7. Park Avenue
8. et cetera
9. a liter of milk
10. 1 pound
11. cash on delivery
12. *Anno Domini* 450

● Connect to the Writing Process: Editing
Using Abbreviations and End Marks

Write each sentence, abbreviating the underlined items and using end marks correctly.

13. For the ribbon-cutting ceremony, we bought a 100-<u>foot</u> red ribbon

14. My friends and I were honored by <u>Governor</u> Richmond for cleaning up the old playground at 1300 Elm <u>Avenue</u>

15. At exactly 2:00 *<u>post meridiem,</u>* I will announce the contest winners

16. My sister will receive her <u>Bachelor of Arts</u> degree from the university this May

17. Have you applied for a summer intern position with the <u>Department</u> of Parks and Recreation in Boston, <u>Massachusetts</u>

18. I just passed my driver's test at the <u>Department of Motor Vehicles</u>

19. The City Builders <u>Association</u> gave the Green Builder Award to the Adobe Habitats, <u>Incorporated</u>

20. <u>Lieutenant</u> Raymond <u>Leon</u> Mason, <u>Junior</u>, received the Purple Heart

APPLY TO WRITING

Outline of a Five-Year Plan: *End Marks*

Consider the photograph. What steps do you think these people might have taken to build a foundation for an occupation in the space industry?

What do you want your life to be like five years from now? Write a statement that tells what you want to be doing in five years. Then make an outline of your five-year plan that shows how you intend to get there. In your outline, name the degrees, schools, companies, job titles, and so on that will be necessary to achieve your goal. Use abbreviations and proper end marks and double-check your work for accuracy.

Commas

Although there may seem to be many comma rules, commas have basically only two purposes: to separate and to enclose items.

▶ Commas That Separate

If commas did not separate certain items from each other, all writing would be subject to constant misunderstanding. There is a difference, for example, between *pineapple juice and cheese* and *pineapple, juice, and cheese*. The following specific situations are places in which commas should be used to separate items.

Items in a Series

A **series** is three or more similar items listed in consecutive order. Words, phrases, clauses, or short sentences that are written as a series are separated by commas.

Use commas to separate items in a series.

WORDS	Dinner, movies, and parties are popular date ideas. (nouns)
	We joked, laughed, and talked all evening. (verbs)
PHRASES	I searched for his phone number in my notebook, on my desk, in my book bag, and throughout my house.
DEPENDENT CLAUSES	We aren't sure who should drive, where we should go, or how late we should stay out.
SHORT SENTENCES	The curtain fell, a brief silence followed, and then we applauded loudly.

When a conjunction connects the last two items in a series, a comma is optional. It is always best, however, to include the comma before the conjunction in order to eliminate any possible confusion or misunderstanding.

CONFUSING   My boyfriend makes delicious pea, chicken, tomato and onion soups.
(Does he make tomato soup or tomato and onion soup?)

CLEAR   My boyfriend makes delicious pea, chicken, tomato, and onion soups.
(The last comma makes the meaning clear.)

If conjunctions connect all the items in a series, no commas are needed unless they make the sentence clearer.

This dance is fast **and** difficult **and** fun!

Some expressions, such as *needle and thread,* are thought of as a single item. If one of these pairs of words appears in a series, it should be considered one item.

For our picnic we packed yogurt, fruit and cheese, and oatmeal cookies.

Did you remember the chicken, bread, and ice cream and cake?

Use commas after the words *first, second,* and so on when they introduce items in a series.

Josh's surprise party should include three key things: **first,** a live band; **second,** his favorite food; and **third,** all his close friends.

Notice that when the items in a series have internal commas, commas within the items themselves such as in the preceding example, the items are then separated by semicolons to avoid any confusion.

You can learn more about semicolons on pages L484–L491.

You have probably noticed that newspaper headlines are usually very short—not even a sentence. When headline writers need to write longer headlines, they use commas to join ideas. This usage of commas is similar to using commas to join items in a series. With a headline, however, the "series" may be only two items long.

This headline has a two-item "series" of verbs:

> Expos Shell Shane Reynolds, Withstand Astros' Barrage

This headline has a two item "series" of subjects:

> Braves, Tom Glavine Blow Away Padres

Adjectives Before a Noun

A conjunction sometimes connects two adjectives before a noun. When the conjunction is omitted, a comma is often used instead.

> A busy, enjoyable evening awaits us.

Use a comma sometimes to separate two adjectives that directly precede a noun and that are not joined by a conjunction.

There is a test you can use to decide whether a comma should be placed between two such adjectives. Read the sentence inserting *and* between the adjectives. If the sentence sounds natural, a comma is needed.

COMMA NEEDED	I'll wear my old, comfortable boots to the dance. *(Old and comfortable* sounds natural. When a comma is needed, you can also reverse the adjectives: *comfortable and old.)*
COMMA NOT NEEDED	I'll wear my new black boots to the dance. *(New and black* does not sound natural, nor could you reverse the adjectives to read *black and new.)*

Usually no comma is needed after a number or after an adjective that refers to size, shape, or age. For example, no commas are needed in the following expressions.

ADJECTIVE EXPRESSIONS	
four square boxes	a large Mexican hat

You can learn how to use commas with direct quotations on pages L508–L509.

PRACTICE YOUR SKILLS

● Check Your Understanding
Using Commas to Separate

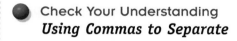

Contemporary Life

Write each series or each pair of adjectives, adding a comma or commas where needed. If commas in a sentence are used correctly, write C.

1. Owen and Daisy ate a dinner of rice beef and cheese enchiladas and salad.

2. I wore a red white and blue shirt to Stan's Fourth of July picnic.

3. Before picking up Marcia, Danny washed and waxed the car and vacuumed the floor mats.

4. For our first date, we didn't know whether to see a movie go to the park or eat dinner.

5. The local dinner theater production of *An Ideal Husband* was a brilliant date idea.

6. Stacey's prom dress was made of red satin and tulle and lace.

7. Stacey and Eric shared a sleek white limousine with Clark and Tabitha.

8. "I have no idea where they went what they are doing or when they'll be back," said Stacey's younger sister Janelle.

9. Shawn and Kelly rode the horses down the hill around the lake and through the trees.

10. The food is planned, the date is set, and the invitations are in the mail.

Use each of the following items in a sentence. Add commas and semicolons where needed.

11. peanut butter and jelly ham and cheese or egg salad

12. June July and August

13. fresh crisp apples and fresh tossed salad

14. large and roomy and bright

15. swam boated and sunbathed

16. first a committee to plan it second a caterer to supply food and third flyers to attract attention

17. in the car in the cafeteria or in the classroom

18. five lavender roses two white carnations and a tall crystal vase

19. chocolate chip peanut butter or cinnamon sugar

20. some cake and ice cream

21. mashed potatoes and gravy and turkey and stuffing

22. cool refreshing lemonade

23. mustard catsup and salt and pepper

24. chairs tablecloths and tables

25. plates napkins and forks

● Connect to the Writing Process: Editing
Using Commas That Separate

Write the following recipe. Insert commas where needed.

Crunchy Nutty Granola Cereal	
14 oz. oats not instant	⅓ cup peanuts chopped fine
½ cup dark brown sugar	1 stick (¼ lb.) butter
½ cup cracked wheat	1 tsp. vanilla
¼ cup bran oat or wheat	½ cup honey
½ cup raisins	1 cup 7-grain cereal
¼ cup wheat germ	

Combine oats brown sugar cracked wheat bran raisins wheat germ and peanuts. Set aside. Melt butter. Stir together the butter vanilla and honey. Pour over cereal mixture stir until well moistened and add the 7-grain cereal. Mix well. Then spread mixture onto two cookie sheets. Bake at 325°, stirring frequently, until lightly browned, about 10–15 minutes.

Communicate Your Ideas

APPLY TO WRITING

Recipes: *Commas That Separate*

Your class is selling a *Senior Favorites Cookbook* as a fundraiser. Write the recipe for a dish you enjoy making— pizza with the works, maybe, or nine-layer dip. Follow the format of the recipe you edited in the preceding exercise. Write a list of ingredients with any necessary adjectives and then write the instructions. Edit your recipe for commas and end marks.

Compound Sentences

The independent clauses in a compound sentence can be combined in several ways. One way is to join them with a comma and one of the coordinating conjunctions—*and, but, or, nor, for, so,* or *yet.*

Use a comma to separate the independent clauses of a compound sentence if the clauses are joined by a coordinating conjunction.

My sister has caught two fish**, but** I haven't caught any.

Friday is Sandy's birthday**, and** I will give her a hermit crab.

She wants a horse**, yet** she's scared to ride one.

No comma is needed in a very short compound sentence—unless the conjunction *yet* or *for* separates the independent clauses.

| No Comma | The car backfired **and** Buster barked. |
| Comma | Tiger hissed, **for** I'd startled her. |

Do not confuse a sentence that has one subject and a compound verb with a compound sentence that has two sets of subjects and verbs. A comma is not placed between the parts of a compound verb when there is only one subject.

| Compound Sentence | I feed the cows each evening, and John milks them each morning. (comma needed) |
| Compound Verb | I worked last night and couldn't feed the cows. (no comma needed) |

A semicolon, or a semicolon and a transitional word, can also be used between independent clauses that are not separated by a conjunction. You can learn more about punctuation with clauses on pages 167–169.

PRACTICE YOUR SKILLS

● Check Your Understanding
Using Commas with Compound Sentences

 **Write *I* if commas are used incorrectly in a sentence. Write *C* if commas are used correctly.**

1. Wild pigs will eat almost anything but they won't overeat.

2. Give the dog some water or he'll dehydrate.

3. The gestation period for an elephant is 21 months and the newborn weighs 90 kilograms.

4. A hippo spends most of its time in water yet grazes for grass on land at night.

5. The cheetah can reach speeds up to 60 miles per hour, and maintain it for nearly half a mile.

6. The silkworm isn't a worm, but is actually a caterpillar.

7. Frogs breathe through their lungs as well as through their skins.

8. At first glance the desert may seem to lack life but it actually is alive with many plants and animals.

9. Cod can lay up to five million eggs at one time, but very few of the eggs hatch and mature.

10. The giant panda is a relative of the raccoon, but can weigh up to 300 pounds.

11. The horseshoe crab is a prehistoric creature, and it has blue blood.

12. Monarch caterpillars eat milkweed so they have a bitter taste that makes birds spit them out.

13. An adult manatee can eat up to 108 pounds of vegetation daily for they are herbivores.

14. The snail has two pairs of tentacles, but it has only one pair of eyes on the longer tentacles.

15. The trilobite cannot be found today for it has been extinct for 245 million years.

Connect to the Writing Process: Editing
Using Commas with Compounds

16.–25. Rewrite the incorrect sentences from the preceding exercise, adding or deleting commas as needed.

Connect to the Writing Process: Drafting
Commas with Compound Sentences

Create compound sentences out of these simple sentences by adding a comma, a coordinating conjunction, and an additional independent clause. (You may add the additional clause either to the beginning or end of the given sentence.)

26. I want a pet.

27. Marshall washed and groomed the poodle.

28. Sparky barked.

29. Black Beauty whinnied and pranced.

30. The catnip spilled onto the floor.

Introductory Elements

A comma is needed to separate certain introductory words, phrases, and clauses from the rest of the sentence.

Use a comma after certain introductory elements.

WORDS	**Yes,** that is my calculator.
	(*No, now, oh, well,* and *why* are other introductory words that are set off by commas—unless they contribute to the meaning of a sentence: Yes *was her answer.*)
PREPOSITIONAL PHRASE	**Throughout the entire math class,** Jessie coughed and sneezed.
	(A comma comes after a prepositional phrase of four or more words.)
PARTICIPIAL PHRASE	**Hunting for my protractor,** I found a long-lost pair of gloves.
INFINITIVE PHRASE USED AS AN ADVERB	**To help Ellen,** I showed her how to find a cube root.
	(A comma does not follow an infinitive phrase that is used as the subject of a sentence: *To pass the math test was my only concern.*)
ADVERB CLAUSE	**Before they left,** they figured out the amount for a 20 percent tip.

Notice in the following examples that the punctuation of shorter phrases varies. Also never place a comma after a phrase or phrases followed by a verb.

OTHER	**In June 1999,** 320 students applied for math scholarships.
	(A comma follows a phrase that ends with a date or number.)

Up above, the compass lay forgotten on the shelf.

(A comma is used to avoid confusion.)

Across the board <u>was</u> the longest equation I've ever seen.

(No comma is used because the verb follows the introductory phrase.)

PRACTICE YOUR SKILLS

● Check Your Understanding
Using Commas with Introductory Elements

Mathematics Topic   **Write the introductory elements that should be followed by a comma. If a sentence is correct, write *C* after the number.**

1. Living in France in the early 1600s René Descartes applied algebraic concepts to geometry.

2. Nowadays we call Descartes's mathematical ideas Cartesian geometry.

3. From Euclid of Alexandria we get Euclidean geometry.

4. Called the leading mathematician of antiquity Euclid explained geometry concepts in *The Elements*.

5. To explain the parallel axiom Euclid said only one line can be drawn through a point parallel to a given line.

6. After leaving Samos around 532 B.C., the Greek Pythagoras lived in Italy.

7. A thousand years earlier the Babylonians had known about the theorem we call Pythagoras's theorem.

8. To prove the theorem was a challenge reserved for Pythagoras.

9. In 1750 Maria Gaëtana Agnesi held the chair of mathematics at the University of Bologna.

10. Noted for her work in differential calculus Agnesi was the first woman to occupy a chair of mathematics.

Using Commas with Introductory Elements

Write sentences using each of these introductory elements. Use commas where needed.

11. the word *no*

12. a prepositional phrase of four or more words

13. the prepositional phrase *within a week*

14. a prepositional phrase followed by a verb

15. a participial phrase

16. an infinitive phrase used as an adverb

17. an adverb clause

18. the phrase *long ago*

19. the phrase *in the year 2000*

20. the word *unfortunately*

● Connect to the Writing Process: Editing
Using Commas with Introductory Elements

Write the following paragraph, inserting commas after introductory elements where needed.

Consisting of a frame with beads on vertical wires the abacus is an ancient arithmetic calculator. Used in China even today the abacus can be found in shops and classrooms. To tally bills quickly a merchant can use an abacus. To teach arithmetic to children a teacher can use an abacus to show, rather than tell, how addition and subtraction work. Oh this handy instrument needs neither batteries nor solar power. For more information you can search for tutorials on the Internet.

Commonly Used Commas

Commas are probably used most often to separate the items in a date or an address, but they are also used in letters.

With Dates and Addresses

Use commas to separate the elements in dates and addresses.

Notice in the following examples that a comma is also used to separate the last item in a date or the last item in an address from the rest of the sentence.

On Monday, October 12, 1999, we founded the Community Music Network.

> Send your résumé to Ms. Faye Buscone, Meals on Wheels, 520 Johnson Street, Madison, Wisconsin 53703, before June 30.
> (No comma is placed between the state and the zip code.)

If items in an address are joined by a preposition, no comma is needed to separate them.

> A homeless shelter has opened at 45 Jackson Boulevard in Tacoma, Washington.

No comma is needed when just the month and the year are given.

> Project Youth Horizons will reach its ten-year anniversary in July 2005.

In Letters

Commas are used in the salutation of many letters and in the closing of all letters.

Use a comma after the salutation of a friendly letter and after the closing of all letters.

SALUTATIONS AND CLOSINGS		
SALUTATIONS	Dear David,	Dear Grandmother,
CLOSINGS	Sincerely yours,	Love,

CONNECT TO WRITER'S CRAFT

E-mail messages are a modern form of letters, and they usually follow the same rules of punctuation as written letters do. However, since some people exchange E-mail messages with friends or co-workers practically all day long, they tend to use very informal salutations and closings. A message might begin "David," or "Hi," instead of "Dear David," but it still uses the comma. Likewise, the closing may be "Later," instead of "Sincerely yours," but the comma is still used to mark the signing off.

Often the use of too many commas is as confusing as not using enough commas. Use commas only where a rule indicates they are needed. In other words, use commas only where they make the meaning of your writing clear.

PRACTICE YOUR SKILLS

● Check Your Understanding
Commonly Used Commas

General Interest **Write *a* or *b* to indicate the sentence that uses commas correctly.**

1. a. You can write to me at the Columbia Children's Refuge, Box 1254, Columbia, Missouri, 65201, after September 1.

b. You can write to me at the Columbia Children's Refuge, Box 1254, Columbia, Missouri 65201, after September 1.

2. a. Dear Professor Tucker,
You are invited to attend the ninth annual International Food Fair on February 9 2001.

b. Dear Professor Tucker,
You are invited to attend the ninth annual International Food Fair on February 9, 2001.

3. a. In 1844 George Williams founded the first YMCA.

b. In 1844, George Williams founded the first YMCA.

4. a. On March 30, 1937, Franklin Roosevelt established the Okefenokee Swamp as a national wildlife refuge.

b. On March 30 1937, Franklin Roosevelt established the Okefenokee Swamp as a national wildlife refuge.

5. a. Write to Student Study Support (SSS), 843 Woodcove Avenue, Pittsburgh, Pennsylvania 15216 for free study guides.

b. Write to Student Study Support (SSS), 843 Woodcove Avenue, Pittsburgh, Pennsylvania 15216, for free study guides.

Writing Sentences with Commas

Write a sentence for each of the following directions. Use commas correctly in each.

6. Include today's date.

7. Tell when you will graduate.

8. Include the complete address of a company for which you would like to work.

9. Tell your school's name and complete address.

10. Tell the name and date of your favorite holiday.

11. Include the address of a local charity.

12. Write the name of an organization to which you belong and its address, including city and state.

13. Include the date on which you were born.

● Connect to the Writing Process: Editing
Using Commas

Rewrite the following friendly letter, inserting commas where needed.

> Dear Friends
>
> Thank you for your hard work on Saturday June 9. The Park Cleanup Day for Triple Oak Park 247 Oak Avenue was a success. I want to invite all of you to the first Park Play Day this Saturday June 16. A picnic and team events will be held in Triple Oak Park from noon to 5:00 P.M. Please let me know if you'll be there. Write me at 203 W. 15th St. Durant OK 74701 by Wednesday.
>
> Best regards
>
> Tiffany

APPLY TO WRITING
Informal Letters: *Commas*

This photograph is on the cover of a brochure from the college you plan to attend. At this college one community-service project per semester is required for your chosen degree program. Write a letter to your friend Erin, who is already at the college. Describe your plans for your first project. Will it be in entertainment? service? education? sports? You might want to ask Erin about some of the community-service projects she has done. As you write your letter, use commas carefully with compound sentences, introductory elements, dates, addresses, and the salutation and closing. After editing your letter, write the final copy.

Write each sentence, adding a comma or commas where needed. If a sentence is correct, write C.

1. Among the inventions of Thomas Edison are the light switch an electric pen and the microphone.

2. The parking meter was invented in Oklahoma City and was the brainstorm of Carlton Magee.

3. To pay off a debt Walter Hunt invented the safety pin.

4. Margaret E. Knight patented an improved paper machine and invented a machine for cutting out shoes.

5. James Watt was not the inventor of the first steam engine but he did improve the steam engine in 1769.

6. After Humphrey O'Sullivan had walked all day on the hot hard pavements of Boston he invented the rubber heel.

7. Joseph Friedman invented the first flexible plastic straw.

8. Amanda Theodosia Jones invented the vacuum process of preserving food and tried to establish a factory that would use her process.

9. To improve methods of farming Englishman Thomas Coke invented a new method of crop rotation during the 1700s.

10. Leonardo da Vinci designed a flying machine and Benjamin Franklin invented bifocals.

11. On June 22 1882 the U.S. Patent Office granted a patent for a propeller-driven rocking chair.

12. Until the envelope was invented in 1839 people folded their letters and sealed them with wax.

13. According to the United States Patent Office records a man named Chester Greenwood held patents on earmuffs and many other items.

14. Fixing a tricycle John Dunlop accidentally invented an inflatable tire.

15. Patented by George B. Hansburg the Pogo stick became an American fad during the 1920s.

16. When Sybilla Masters succeeded in inventing a machine that reduced corn into meal food preparation methods were greatly improved.

17. King Camp Gillette patented the safety razor in the year 1904.

18. Before the twentieth century engine-propelled air travel was not possible.

19. Whitcomb L. Judson patented an early form of the zipper in 1893.

20. Lee De Forest invented a vacuum tube in 1907 and this device helped develop electronic equipment.

Commas That Enclose

Some sentences contain expressions that interrupt the flow of a sentence. These expressions usually supply additional information that is not necessary for understanding the main idea of a sentence.

If one of these interrupting expressions comes in the middle of a sentence, use two commas to enclose the expression—to set it off from the rest of the sentence. If an interrupting expression comes at the beginning or at the end of a sentence, use only one comma.

Direct Address

Any name, title, or other word that is used to address someone directly is set off by commas. These interrupting expressions are called nouns of **direct address.**

Use commas to set off nouns of direct address.

> **Kenneth,** what did you do with my new book?
> Hurry, **Mandy,** or we'll miss Anne Rice's autograph session.
> What is your favorite poem, **Maria?**

Parenthetical Expressions

These expressions add meaning but are only incidental to the main idea of the sentence.

Use commas to set off parenthetical expressions.

The following is a list of common parenthetical expressions.

COMMON PARENTHETICAL EXPRESSIONS		
after all	however	moreover
at any rate	I believe (guess,	nevertheless
by the way	hope, know,	of course
consequently	think)	on the contrary
for example	in fact	on the other hand
for instance	in my opinion	therefore

By the way, did you read Tony's new story?

Your essay**, of course,** was beautifully written.

We will proceed as planned**, nevertheless.**

Commas are used to set off the expressions in the preceding box *only* if the expressions interrupt the flow of a sentence. If the words are an essential part of the sentence, do not use commas.

COMMAS **On the other hand,** we did enjoy the author's book exhibit.

No Commas Wear that glove **on the other hand.**
(*On the other hand* is necessary to the meaning of the sentence.)

COMMAS I noticed, **however,** that the boy never paid for the book.

No Commas Our book club will wait in line for **however** long it takes!
(*However* is part of a phrase that is necessary to the meaning of the sentence.)

Expressions other than those listed in the box can also be parenthetical if they interrupt the flow of the sentence.

> Novels**, like movies,** can change your view of life.

Contrasting expressions, which often begin with *not, but, but not,* or *though not,* are also considered parenthetical expressions.

> Peggy**, not Angela,** will recite a poem at graduation.

> The actor**, though not well known,** will star in the play.

Occasionally an adverb clause will also interrupt a sentence.

> His novel sales**, if they hit nine million today,** will set a national record.

Many of the words listed in the box of common parenthetical expressions can also be used to join two independent clauses. When they do so, they are preceded by a semicolon and followed by a comma.

> I searched the library for hours**; nevertheless,** I could not find the information.

> I had to invite Professor Dinny to my first book signing**; after all,** she had inspired me to write.

To learn more about joining two independent clauses, see pages L167–L169.
Parentheses and dashes are also used to set off parenthetical expressions. To learn more, see pages L528–L530.

Appositives

An appositive with its modifiers renames, identifies, or explains a noun or a pronoun in the sentence.

Use commas to set off most appositives and their modifiers.

> Mr. James**, my English teacher,** attended Ohio State.

> I read Harper Lee's only novel**, *To Kill a Mockingbird.***

An appositive is occasionally preceded by the word *or, particularly, notably,* or *especially.* Some appositives that are introduced by *such as* are also set off by commas.

> Many students**, especially freshmen,** have entered the story contest.
>
> Use visual aids**, such as photos of the author.**

An appositive is not set off by commas if it identifies a person or a thing by telling which one or ones. Often these appositives are names and have no modifiers.

> The verb **write** is an irregular verb. (Which verb?)
>
> My cousin **Lucy** is writing a screenplay. (Which cousin?)

When adjectives, titles, and degrees are in the appositive position, they are also set off by commas.

> ADJECTIVES   The limerick**, short and funny,** is Wanda's.
>
> TITLES   Frank Moore**, Sr.,** is a book editor.
>
> DEGREES   Alicia Ray**, Ph.D.,** teaches Shakespeare.

PRACTICE YOUR SKILLS

● Check Your Understanding
Using Commas with Interrupters

Literature Topic | **Write the word or words in each sentence that should be enclosed in commas. If a sentence does not need any additional commas, write C.**

1. William Carlos Williams M.D. was a noted poet.

2. Uriah Heep the villain in Charles Dickens's *David Copperfield* was the focus of my English composition.

3. The great playwright Lillian Hellman was born in 1905.

4. Lydia have you met Toni Morrison author of *Beloved?*

5. The poet Shel Silverstein died I believe in May 1999.

6. He wrote my favorite story *The Giving Tree*.

7. *Apocalypse Now* Francis Ford Coppola's controversial film on the Vietnam War was based on Conrad's novel *Heart of Darkness*.

8. Epic poetry long and complex usually contains references to mythological gods, battles, and heroes.

9. I recommend poems by authors such as Edna St. Vincent Millay and Robert Frost.

10. Our book club selection for this month by the way is *House of Sand and Fog* by Andre Dubus III.

● Connect to the Writing Process: Drafting
Writing Sentences with Interrupters

Write sentences using interrupters, as directed. Use commas where needed.

11. Use a friend's name in direct address.

12. Use a parenthetical expression.

13. Use an appositive.

14. Use an appositive preceded by *such as* or *particularly*.

15. Use the contrasting expression *but not today*.

16. Use the expression *after all* to interrupt the flow of a sentence.

17. Use the expression *after all* in a way that does not interrupt the flow of a sentence.

18. Use a title or degree following a name.

19. Use an adverb clause to interrupt a sentence.

20. Use *however* to connect two independent clauses.

● Connect to the Writing Process: Editing
Editing Commas with Interrupters

Rewrite each sentence, using the interrupter in parentheses. Use commas where needed.

21. Edmund Spenser wrote *The Faerie Queene*. (not William Shakespeare)

22. Coleridge considered his friend the greatest poet since Milton. (Wordsworth)

23. John Locke is well-known for his essays. (like Jonathan Swift)

24. "A Modest Proposal" is Swift's best known essay. (I believe)

25. Many readers didn't realize Swift was being satirical. (not literal)

26. Modernist writers were very experimental in their writing style. (especially Joyce and Fitzgerald)

27. Many modernist novels do not have "happily ever after" endings. (for example)

28. Stephen Crane is another author who did not believe in happy endings. (if I remember correctly)

29. Oliver Sacks wrote *The Man Who Mistook His Wife for a Hat*. (M.D.)

30. Sack's book was made into a movie of the same name. *(Awakenings)*

Nonessential Elements

Like other interrupters you have just reviewed, some participial phrases and some clauses are not needed to make the meaning of a sentence clear or complete. When a phrase or a clause is not needed to complete the meaning of a sentence, commas are used to enclose it.

Use commas to set off a nonessential participial phrase or a nonessential adjective clause.

A participial phrase or an adjective clause is nonessential (nonrestrictive) if it supplies extra, unnecessary information. To decide whether a phrase or a clause is nonessential, read the sentence without it. If the phrase or the clause could be removed without changing the basic meaning of the sentence, it is nonessential. A phrase or a clause that modifies a proper noun is almost always nonessential.

NONESSENTIAL PARTICIPIAL PHRASE	Birds' nests**, made from grass and twigs,** were visible in the trees. *(Birds' nests were visible in the trees.)*
NONESSENTIAL ADJECTIVE PHRASE	A dog**, which is my favorite kind of pet,** is more loyal than a cat. *(A dog is more loyal than a cat.)*

An essential (restrictive) phrase or clause identifies a person or a thing by answering the question *Which one?* Therefore, no commas are used. If an essential phrase or clause is removed from a sentence, the meaning of the sentence will be unclear or incomplete. (An adjective clause that begins with *that* is usually essential.)

ESSENTIAL PARTICIPIAL PHRASE	The horse **named Prince** should be removed from the show. *(The horse should be removed from the show. The phrase is needed to identify which of many horses should be removed from the show.)*
ESSENTIAL ADJECTIVE CLAUSE	The parakeets **that you wanted** were already sold. *(The parakeets were already sold. The clause is needed to identify which parakeets were already sold.)*

PRACTICE YOUR SKILLS

● Check Your Understanding
Using Commas with Nonessential Elements

Science Topic **Find each interrupter and state whether it is *essential* (E) or *nonessential* (N).** (Note that the commas that should enclose nonessential elements are not present.)

1. The lizard called the gecko can grow a new tail.

2. The carrier pigeon which was once a common message carrier is now extinct.

3. Ralph Winters fishing in Beaver Brook caught a trout.

4. Scientists who classify insects are called entomologists.

5. We watched the geese flying south.

6. A tarantula's bite which is not usually fatal still causes a great deal of pain.

7. The ostrich which is the largest of all birds can outrun a horse.

8. The exoskeleton of an insect is made of chitin which is lighter and far more flexible than bone.

9. The dog that has a black tongue is the chow chow.

10. The underwater enemy threatening the sea otter is the killer whale.

● Connect to the Writing Process: Editing
Using Commas with Nonessential Elements

11.–15. **Write each sentence in the preceding exercise that has a nonessential element, adding a comma or commas where needed.**

● Connect to the Writing Process: Revising
Adding Phrases to Sentences

Rewrite each sentence twice. First, add a nonessential phrase or clause to the sentence. Second, add an essential phrase or clause. Use commas where needed.

16. The dog is next door.

17. The mouse is trapped.

18. Giraffes are majestic.

19. My pet snake got loose.

Communicate Your Ideas

APPLY TO WRITING

Opinion Essay: *Commas That Enclose*

What animal do you think is the most beautiful animal in existence? Prepare an opinion essay for your classmates. Describe the animal and then explain your opinion. Be sure to use essential and nonessential elements correctly.

Science Topic **Write the following paragraphs, adding commas where needed.** (You will add 21 commas in all.)

Elizabeth Blackwell was the first woman to earn a medical degree but she had to travel a long hard road to get that degree. Even though 29 medical schools had refused to admit her she persisted. After three years of private study Blackwell was finally accepted to the Medical Institute of Geneva New York. The director doubtful and concerned passed her application on to the students for their approval. Thinking it was a joke everyone agreed to admit her. When Blackwell arrived however she was greeted with shock and anger. She was ridiculed ignored refused lodging and barred from some classroom activities.

Graduating at the head of her class on January 23 1849 Blackwell continued her studies in London and Paris. She finally returned to New York City and there she opened a hospital in 1853. Called the New York Infirmary for Women and Children it was staffed by women. With the help of Emily her younger sister Blackwell added a medical college for women to the site in 1868.

As a pioneer in medicine Blackwell opened the door for women in the medical field. She required that female students work harder than male students to establish themselves in the medical community. Because of her courage many women comfortably practice medicine today.

Using Commas Correctly

Write each sentence, adding a comma or commas where needed. If a sentence needs no commas, write C.

1. Among the heroes of the American Revolution was a gallant young Frenchman who risked his life and fortune.

2. Lafayette was born in Chavaniac France on September 6 1757.

3. Although at the age of nineteen he was both a French army captain and a popular nobleman he wasn't satisfied with life.

4. When the American colonies declared their independence from England France's ancient foe Lafayette sailed for America.

5. He offered his enthusiastic heartfelt services to Congress which rewarded him with the rank of major general.

6. Lafayette served under Washington who became his friend.

7. Lafayette who proved to be a good officer was slightly wounded in 1777 in his first battle the Battle of Brandywine.

8. His great achievement for the colonies was a treaty of alliance that he persuaded the French government to sign in 1778.

9. When he returned to France after the surrender of Cornwallis at Yorktown he joined the French Revolution.

10. He served as commander-in-chief of the National Guard which was organized to safeguard the revolution.

11. Lafayette however became disenchanted with the revolution.

12. He was proclaimed a traitor and was forced to flee to Belgium where he was imprisoned by the Austrians.

13. After five years in exile Lafayette was freed by Napoleon.

14. His life continued uneventfully until 1830 when he played a leading role in the overthrow of Charles X.

15. Although Lafayette's actions cost him his fortune they won for him the respect of Americans and the French alike.

Kinds of Sentences and End Marks

Write each sentence and its appropriate end mark. Then label each one _D_ for declarative, _IM_ for imperative, _IN_ for interrogative, or _E_ for exclamatory.

1. Scientists estimate that about 100 acres of the remaining tropical rain forests are being cleared every minute

2. How big is an acre

3. In your mind, picture a football field minus the end zones

4. Now picture 100 of these football fields

5. That's how much of the remaining rain forests are being destroyed every single minute

6. Tropical rain forests are found in only seven percent of the world, but they play a vital part in sustaining many life forms

7. Why are rain forests so important

8. The trees provide huge amounts of the earth's oxygen, and the forests are great sources for many needed medicines

9. Of course, the rainforests are also the homes of many endangered species of animals and insects

10. Find out what you can do to stop the destruction of these vital rain forests

Writing Sentences

Write five sentences that follow the directions below. Write about one of the following topics or a topic of your choice: an interesting person from history or an environmental issue such as the rainforests.

Write a sentence that . . .

1. includes a series of nouns.
2. includes two adjectives before a noun.
3. includes an introductory participial phrase.
4. includes an introductory adverbial phrase.
5. includes an appositive.

Language and *Self-Expression*

Do you think a person's character can be seen in his or her face? Consider the sculpture of Queen Tiy's head. Tiy was an Egyptian queen in the 14th century B.C. She participated actively in state affairs and public ceremonies along with her husband, King Amenhotep III. Later she was an adviser to her son, King Amenhotep IV. Looking at her face, can you imagine her performing these royal duties?

In your mind, picture the face of someone in a leadership position that affects you—maybe a school official, a parent, or a coach. Then write a description of how this person's face does or does not reflect his or her true character. For example, do the person's eyes look determined, and does that person show determination in achieving goals?

Prewriting List the facial features and accessories (eyeglasses, jewelry, hats) of your chosen subject. Beside each one, describe the character trait it conveys to you. For example, a baseball cap on a coach makes a different impression than a baseball cap on a mayor.

Drafting Write a character sketch that is three or four paragraphs in length. Describe how your subject's features and accessories imply particular character traits. Your conclusion could state whether these impressions are truly present in the person's character.

Revising Check your writing for organization. For example, you might group the "accessories" ideas in a single paragraph.

Editing Check your writing for correct spelling and grammar as well as for correct use of end punctuation and commas.

Publishing Write a final copy and submit it to your teacher. If you think the subject of your paper would enjoy reading the character sketch, share a copy with that person as well.

Another Look

A **declarative sentence** makes a statement or expresses an opinion and ends with a **period** (.).

An **imperative sentence** gives a direction, makes a request, or gives a command. It ends with a **period** or an **exclamation point** (. or !).

An **interrogative sentence** asks a question and ends with a **question mark** (?).

An **exclamatory sentence** expresses strong feeling or emotion and ends with an **exclamation point** (!).

Using Periods

Use a period after most abbreviations. *(pages L432–L433)*

Use a period after each number or letter that shows a division in an outline. *(page L433)*

Using Commas

Use commas to separate items in a series. *(pages L436–L437)*

Use commas after the words *first, second,* and so on when they introduce items in a series. *(page L437)*

Use a comma sometimes to separate two adjectives that directly precede a noun and that are not joined by a conjunction. *(pages L438–L439)*

Use a comma to separate the independent clauses of a compound sentence if the clauses are joined by a coordinating conjunction. *(pages L441–L442)*

Use a comma after certain introductory elements. *(pages L444–L445)*

Use commas to separate the elements in dates and addresses. *(pages L447–L448)*

Use a comma after the salutation of a friendly letter and after the closing of all letters. *(page L448)*

Use commas to set off nouns of direct address. *(page L453)*

Use commas to set off parenthetical expressions. *(pages L454–L455)*

Use commas to set off most appositives and their modifiers. *(pages L455–L456)*

Use commas to set off a nonessential participial phrase or a nonessential adjective clause. *(pages L458–L459)*

Directions

Read the passage and write the letter of the answer that correctly punctuates each underlined part. If the underlined part contains no error, write *D*.

EXAMPLE   <u>Keller listen</u> to these facts about sugar.
                              (1)

  1 **A** Keller listen,

        B Keller, listen,

        C Keller, listen

        D No error

ANSWER   **1** **C**

Many <u>people including teenagers are</u> unaware of the amount of
                       (1)
sugar they consume. Foods like candy, soda, and maple syrup may

contain more sugar than you think. <u>For example suppose</u> you
                               (2)
drink a twelve-ounce can of <u>soda</u> You have drunk the equivalent of
                          (3)
ten teaspoons of sugar. Are you <u>surprised</u> If you are not surprised
                           (4)
by that <u>fact perhaps</u> this one will surprise you. Foods such as
        (5)
<u>muffins, salad dressings,</u> <u>yogurt and cheese spread</u> may have
     (6)   **(7)**
added sugar. <u>Wow</u> Who would have guessed <u>this</u> Nutritionists
         (8)   **(9)**
suggest a simple response to sugar. If you are in good health, eat

it in <u>moderation</u> If you are overweight, eat sugar sparingly.
     (10)

1
A people, including teenagers, are
B people including teenagers, are
C people, including teenagers are
D No error

2
A For example suppose,
B For example! suppose
C For example, suppose
D No error

3
A soda,
B soda.
C soda?
D No error

4
A surprised!
B surprised?
C surprised.
D No error

5
A fact, perhaps
B fact, perhaps,
C fact. perhaps
D No error

6
A muffins, salad dressings
B muffins, salad, dressings,
C muffins salad dressings
D No error

7
A yogurt and cheese, spread
B yogurt, and cheese spread
C yogurt and cheese spread,
D No error

8
A Wow,
B Wow!
C Wow.
D No error

9
A this?
B this!
C this.
D No error

10
A moderation!
B moderation?
C moderation.
D No error

CHAPTER 11

Other Punctuation

 **Pretest**

Directions

Each underlined part in the passage lacks one type of punctuation. Write the letter of the answer with the punctuation that correctly completes the underlined part.

EXAMPLE   <u>Are you a vegetarian?</u> Abdul asked me.
                              (1)

  1 A   Colon
     B   Italics
     C   Quotation marks
     D   Dashes

ANSWER   **1 C**

Variety and <u>creativity these</u> are the elements that make
                    (1)
a vegetarian diet appealing. Many <u>people and I include</u>
                                        (2)
<u>myself</u> think a dinner of only vegetables would be boring.

Go to a Japanese or Thai restaurant and notice this

<u>restaurants use</u> of flavorings in vegetable dishes. You might
      (3)
taste the <u>following spices garlic, cayenne pepper, and</u>
                              (4)
<u>ginger. Youll get plenty of ideas</u> for your own vegetarian
                    (5)
cuisine.

1   **A**   Dash
    B   Apostrophe
    C   Hyphen
    D   Brackets

2   **A**   Apostrophe
    B   Parentheses
    C   Italics
    D   Semicolon

3   **A**   Colon
    B   Semicolon
    C   Dashes
    D   Apostrophe

4   **A**   Colon
    B   Italics
    C   Parentheses
    D   Quotation marks

5   **A**   Brackets
    B   Italics
    C   Apostrophe
    D   Hyphen

René Magritte. *The Mysteries of the Horizon*, 1955.
Oil on canvas, 19½ by 25⅓ inches. Private collection.

Describe What images has Magritte used in this painting? Describe the elements of color and space.

Analyze Find examples of unity or harmony through repetition of shapes, colors, and images.

Interpret Choose one of the images in the painting. What do you think this image symbolizes? How do you think it contributes to the overall mood or message of the painting?

Judge Which word better describes this painting: *realistic* or *surrealistic*? Why?

At the end of this chapter, you will use the artwork to stimulate ideas for writing.

Apostrophes

Although end marks and commas are the punctuation marks most commonly used, all marks of punctuation are important. This chapter will cover punctuation marks other than end marks and commas. One such punctuation mark is the apostrophe.

You probably use apostrophes with contractions every time you write, but the apostrophe has another important and very common use. It is used with nouns and some pronouns to show possession.

Apostrophes to Show Possession

By using apostrophes, you can indicate that nouns and some pronouns show possession.

Possessive Forms of Nouns

The possessive of a singular noun is formed differently than the possessive of a plural noun.

Add 's to form the possessive of a singular noun.

To form the possessive of a singular noun, write the noun without adding or omitting any letters. Then add 's at the end.

> friend + 's = friend's   This is my friend's cabin.
> cabin + 's = cabin's   The cabin's walls need paint.

Singular compound nouns and the names of most businesses and organizations form their possessives in the way other singular nouns do.

> Her mother-in-law's lakeside barbecue is tomorrow.
> I will order the ribs from Maher's Meat Market.

To form the possessive of a plural noun, write the plural form of the word without making any changes. Then look at the ending of the plural noun. The ending will determine the way you will form the possessive.

Add only an apostrophe to form the possessive of a plural noun that ends in _s_.

If the plural noun ends in _s,_ add only an apostrophe.

girls + ' = girls'   The girls' rowing team has won!

Nelsons + ' = Nelsons'   The Nelsons' raft seats two.

Add _'s_ to form the possessive of a plural noun that does not end in _s_.

If a plural noun does not end in _s,_ add _'s_ to form the possessive—just as you would to a singular noun that does not end in _s._

men + 's = men's   Where are the men's hiking boots?
cacti + 's = cacti's   The cacti's blossoms are pink.

Do not confuse a plural possessive with the simple plural form of a noun.

POSSESSIVE   Marty is the **twins'** rowing coach.
PLURAL   Marty coaches the **twins**.

PRACTICE YOUR SKILLS

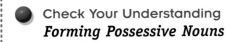

● Check Your Understanding
Forming Possessive Nouns

Write the possessive form of each noun.

1. mother
2. sister-in-law
3. Karen
4. Palmers
5. editor-in-chief

6. oxen
7. women
8. city
9. geese
10. world

11. beaches
12. officers
13. birch
14. children
15. babies

Contemporary Life **Write the correct possessive noun in parentheses.**

16. The two (boys', boy's) canoe was bright orange.

17. (Terrys', Terry's) backpack is waterproof.

18. The primitive campsite is at (Papa Bear's Campground, Papa Bear Campground's).

19. Do you want my life jacket or (Suzys', Suzy's)?

20. This life (jackets', jacket's) strap is broken.

21. Hmm. All the life (jackets', jacket's) straps are broken.

22. Why don't we rent new life jackets from those (women's, womens') supply booth?

23. Look! I see the (McKlintocks', McKlintock's) camper!

24. Later I want to visit the (horse's, horses') stables.

25. Your (brother's-in-law, brother-in-law's) trail map is too old to be useful.

● Connect to the Writing Process: Editing
Using Apostrophes

Correctly write each word that needs an apostrophe or an apostrophe and an *s*.

26. A hunter jacket is usually made of camouflage fabric.

27. Who has November hunting itinerary?

28. All the tent metal poles are in good condition.

29. The poles construction is of aluminum.

30. How long will your father-in-law hunting trip last?

31. We appreciated the other men offer of firewood.

32. Charlies Market on the Highway 52 will buy our venison.

33. Is that bag of corn Paul?

34. He brought it for the deer feeding trough.

35. Mr. Wong four-wheel-drive vehicle saved us from being stuck in that mud hole.

Possessive Forms of Pronouns

Personal pronouns and the pronoun *who* show possession by changing form, not by adding an apostrophe.

The possessive forms of personal pronouns and the pronoun *who* do not use apostrophes.

This is **his** yearbook, but **whose** is that?

None of the following possessive pronouns include apostrophes.

POSSESSIVE PRONOUNS			
my, mine	his	its	their, theirs
your, yours	her, hers	our, ours	

Do not confuse a contraction with a possessive pronoun. A possessive pronoun does not include an apostrophe, but a contraction does. *Its, your, their,* and *theirs* are possessive pronouns. *It's, you're, they're,* and *there's* are contractions.

You can learn more about possessive pronouns on pages L236 and L251–L257.

An indefinite pronoun forms its possessive in the same way a singular noun does—by adding *'s*.

No one**'s** yearbook is signed yet.

Did you ask for anyone**'s** signature?

You can find a list of common indefinite pronouns on page L301.

CONNECT TO WRITER'S CRAFT

Writers often use mnemonic phrases to help them remember the spelling of difficult words. The following sentence, for example, might help someone remember the spelling of the possessive pronoun *theirs*: "The **heirs** in *theirs* did not inherit an apostrophe."

PRACTICE YOUR SKILLS

● Check Your Understanding
Using Possessive Pronouns

Contemporary Life **Write the correct form of each possessive pronoun in parentheses.**

1. (You're, Your) research papers are due on Friday.

2. (Everyone's, Everyones') speeches should be given by Tuesday.

3. I think this ruler is missing (it's, its) markings.

4. (Who's, Whose) is this sketch?

5. (There's, Theirs) is the classroom with the purple walls.

6. This new globe is (hers, her's).

7. (Your's, Yours) arrived first thing this morning.

8. (Someone's, Someones') jacket was left in the bleachers.

9. (Their, They're) report cards should be put over there.

10. (Her, Her's) photograph won a prize.

● Connect to the Writing Process: Editing
Using Possessive Pronouns

Rewrite any incorrectly written possessive pronouns. If all of the pronouns in a sentence are written correctly, write C.

11. The responsibility for sales of the yearbook is our's.

12. Soliciting advertising, however, is you're responsibility.

13. Theirs is a difficult job.

14. They must judge hundreds of amateur photos on each ones' merits.

15. That colorful photo of Mark spiking a volleyball is mine.

16. Who will design the cover is anybodies' guess.

17. The cover design I like best is your's.

18. All of the yearbook members can design there own page of highlights.

19. Somebodys' page design will win a prize of $100.

20. We want this year's book to have its own unique look.

Apostrophes to Show
Joint or Separate Ownership

In written work apostrophes can signal either joint or separate ownership. One apostrophe is used to show joint ownership. Two or more apostrophes are used to show separate ownership.

Add 's to only the last word to show joint ownership.

Add 's to each word to show separate ownership.

In the following example, the audiobook belongs to Paul and Craig. Since both people own the audiobook, an apostrophe is added to the second name only.

> Paul and Craig**'s** audiobook has been returned.

If one of the words in a phrase showing joint ownership is a possessive pronoun, the noun must also show possession.

> Paul**'s** and **his** audiobook has been returned.

In the following example, Paul and Craig own separate audiobooks; therefore, an apostrophe is added to each name.

> Paul**'s** and Craig**'s** audiobooks have been returned.

Apostrophes with Nouns
Expressing Times or Amounts

When you use a noun that expresses time or amount as an adjective, write it in the possessive form.

Use an apostrophe with the possessive form of a noun that expresses time or amount.

> She lost a week**'s** time by reading the wrong book.
> I spent nine dollars**'** worth of quarters on the new book.

Other words that express time include *minute, hour, day, month,* and *year.*

PRACTICE YOUR SKILLS

● Check Your Understanding
Using Apostrophes Correctly

Literature Topic **Write the correct possessive form of the noun or pronoun in parentheses.**

1. My grandparents always read ■ fairy tales to me. (the Grimm brothers and Andersen)

2. *Middlemarch* by George Eliot might be several ■ worth of reading. (month)

3. There is an interesting article about *Treasure Island* in ■ paper. (Sunday)

4. *Jude the Obscure* is one of ■ favorite novels. (LuAnn and her)

5. One of that ■ bestsellers is *A Night Without Armor* by Jewel. (year)

6. ■ novels are often made into movies. (Michael Crichton and Tom Clancy)

7. ■ joint publication is *Lyrical Ballads*. (Coleridge and Wordsworth)

8. ■ poems fill the volume with beautiful imagery. (Coleridge and Wordsworth)

9. ■ poems are always in anthologies of English literature. (Wordsworth and him)

10. You should have seen my hilarious portrayal of Puck in *A ■ Dream!* (*Midsummer Night*)

● Connect to the Writing Process: Editing
Using Possessive Nouns and Pronouns

Rewrite any incorrectly written possessive noun or pronoun. If all possessive forms in a sentence are written correctly, write C.

11. This weeks assignment is to write a poem.

12. Brandy and Kristen's poems will both serve as examples.

13. Kristen's and her works have been published frequently.

14. The first-place winner and the second-place winner's poems will be considered for publication.

15. The newspaper editor and English teacher's decisions are final.

16. She will have several hour's worth of reading to do.

17. Stan's and mine poems are both candidates for prizes.

18. Give me a days time to prepare my acceptance speech.

19. Becca or Nancy's poem will probably win third place.

20. Becca's and Nancy's poems are too somber for my taste.

Communicate Your Ideas

APPLY TO WRITING

Opinion Statement: *Apostrophes*

One of your best friends has asked you to share an apartment after high school graduation. Your friend wants both of you to write a statement of ownership regarding food, furniture, dishes, and so on. What will belong to you jointly, and what will you possess individually? What will be your rights in using one another's personal possessions and food? Write a fair statement of ownership, using apostrophes to show possession. Edit for mistakes in punctuation and then write the final copy.

 **QuickCheck** Mixed Practice

Contemporary Life **Correctly write each word that should be in possessive form.**

1. Alfred applied for the cashier position at the corner gas station.

2. The manager and assistant-manager impressions of him were favorable.

3. He begins his shift by breaking open two dollars worth of nickels, fifty cents worth of pennies, and other rolled coins.

4. His job also includes keeping the women and men restrooms stocked with paper towels and soap.
5. The employees uniform is a lime-green smock.
6. Everyone distaste for the color is apparent.
7. Alfred and Paul decision to ask for new uniforms was applauded by the staff.
8. Paul and his jobs were never in jeopardy.
9. The rest of the employees of Conroys Gas 'N Go supported the young mens request.
10. The new smocks color is black.
11. The Conroy family station hosted an anniversary celebration.
12. Each customer took a minute time to sign up for free prizes such as tune-ups and oil changes.

Other Uses of Apostrophes

In addition to showing possession, apostrophes have several other uses.

Apostrophes with Contractions

An apostrophe is substituted for letters omitted in a contraction.

Use an apostrophe in a contraction to show where one or more letters have been omitted.

CONTRACTIONS		
are n~~ot~~ = aren't	that ~~is~~ = that's	I w~~ill~~ = I'll
we ~~have~~ = we've	let ~~us~~ = let's	~~of the~~ clock = o'clock

The only contraction in which any letters are changed or added is the contraction for *will not,* which is *won't.*

PRACTICE YOUR SKILLS

● Check Your Understanding
Writing Contractions

Write the contraction for each pair of words.

1. do not	**8.** will not	**15.** I would
2. I have	**9.** I am	**16.** there is
3. did not	**10.** is not	**17.** does not
4. let us	**11.** were not	**18.** are not
5. we will	**12.** it is	**19.** we have
6. who is	**13.** you are	**20.** have not
7. they are	**14.** has not	

● Connect to the Writing Process: Editing
Using Contractions

Write the words in each sentence that may be replaced with a contraction. Then write the contraction. Some sentences contain more than one possible contraction.

21. I cannot see the race track from here.

22. They are about to start the race.

23. We will move to better seats.

24. The race will begin at three of the clock sharp.

25. There will be a chance to meet the winners afterward.

26. They will accept their trophies and then mingle with the crowd.

27. I will be sure to get my picture taken next to the champion horse.

28. I have always wanted a horse of my own, but I am not sure I would know how to ride in a race.

29. Let us talk later about how we will buy a horse together and who is going to build the stables in his backyard!

30. I have not had this much fun in weeks, and I will not miss a minute of this race!

Apostrophes with Certain Plurals

To prevent confusion, certain items form their plurals by adding 's.

> **Add 's to form the plural of lowercase letters, some capital letters, and some words used as words.**

> Are these letters *s*'**s** or *e*'**s**?
> Should *O*'**s** be round or oval?

The plurals of most other letters, symbols, numerals, and words used as words can be formed by adding an *s*.

> The Beatles led the British invasion in the 1960**s**.
> Entrepreneurs see $**s** when they recognize a popular fad.

CONNECT TO WRITER'S CRAFT

Some writers prefer to add 's, instead of just *s*, to form the plural of all letters, symbols, numerals, and words used as words. This might lend a look of consistency in poetry, for example. When writing formally, however, follow the preceding rules.

INFORMAL:	I choose my *2*'**s** and my *3*'**s** And add them where I please.
FORMAL:	The children were divided into groups of *2***s** and *3***s**.

Apostrophes with Certain Dates

An apostrophe is also used when numbers are dropped from a date.

> **Use an apostrophe to show that numbers are omitted in a date.**

> We bought this personal computer in '01. (2001)
> Our old PC was manufactured in '92. (1992)

PRACTICE YOUR SKILLS

● Check Your Understanding
Using Apostrophes

Contemporary Life **Write each underlined item in its plural form, and shorten all dates to a two-digit form (such as '85).**

1. The binary numbering system used by computers consists of _0_ and _1_.
2. When I write quick E-mails, I use _&_ for _and_.
3. How many _@_ are in an E-mail address?
4. I've had my E-mail account since the late _1990_.
5. In 1998, I changed my ISP.
6. You can separate parts of your message with a row of _*_.
7. Despite my worries, my computer changed from 1999 to 2000 easily.
8. I remember the concern about whether _PC_ would be Y2K-compliant.
9. I stayed up so late playing a game over the Internet that now I need to get some _z_.
10. How many _w_ are usually found in a typical Website address?

● Connect to the Writing Process: Drafting
Writing Sentences

Write a sentence that follows each direction, using apostrophes and plural forms correctly.

11. Use the two-digit form of the year you were born.
12. Use the two-digit form of the year you will graduate from high school.
13. Use the plural form of the dollar sign.
14. Use the four-digit form of the year that you began school.
15. Use the plural form of the letter _X_.

APPLY TO WRITING

Technical E-mail: *Apostrophes*

You bought a "refurbished" laptop computer, and many of the keyboard keys seem faulty. They type a different letter or symbol than the one printed on the key. Write an E-mail to the technical support division of Global PCs. Describe the keys that aren't working, give the date you purchased the computer, and state how many number 5s are on your proof of purchase seal. Use plurals of all letters, symbols, and words used as words.

QuickCheck   Mixed Practice

Contemporary Life   **Rewrite each incorrectly written letter or word. If a sentence is correct, write C.**

1. A student's life is very busy.
2. Diego's composition was well written, was'nt it?
3. The freshmen and seniors lockers were just painted.
4. The Queen of Englands coronation picture is hanging in my homeroom.
5. Teenager's interests in most areas have changed over the past fifty years.
6. There's their neighbor, waiting at the bus stop.
7. Gorman' advertisement in this mornings' *Herald* offers a discount for graduating seniors.
8. The Raidens' son got two *A*'s on his report card, and their daughter got three on her's.
9. Well need Dad's permission to go on the class trip next week.
10. Aren't there three *ms* in *commencement?*

Semicolons and Colons

By using the semicolon (**;**) and the colon (**:**), you can create sentence variety in your writing.

Semicolons

Use a semicolon between the clauses of a compound sentence when they are not joined by a conjunction.

Two independent clauses not properly joined result in a **run-on sentence**. A run-on sentence can be corrected in several ways. One way to correct a run-on sentence is to join the clauses with a coordinating conjunction and a comma.

RUN-ON	The goldfish is my pet the cat is my mom's.
CORRECTED	The goldfish is my pet, **and** the cat is my mom's.

The clauses in a compound sentence can be joined by a semicolon when there is no conjunction.

A goldfish is a great pet; it demands only food and water from its caretaker.

A cat requires a little time; it needs to be pampered by whoever owns it.

The earthworm has no lungs; it breathes through its skin.

Only closely related clauses should be joined by a semicolon. Ideas not closely related belong in separate sentences.

NOT CLOSELY RELATED	Ferrets make wonderful pets; everyone should have a pet.
CLOSELY RELATED	Ferrets make wonderful pets; they are friendly and use a litter box just as cats do.

You can learn more about correcting run-on sentences on pages L167–L169.

Semicolons with Conjunctive Adverbs and Transitional Words

The clauses in a compound sentence can also be joined by a semicolon and certain conjunctive adverbs or transitional words.

> Use a semicolon between the clauses in a compound sentence when they are joined by certain conjunctive adverbs or transitional words.
>
> He told me the dog was friendly; **however,** it barked ferociously at me.
>
> The kitten's markings could inspire a name; **for example,** you could call her Stripes.

Notice in the previous examples that the conjunctive adverb *however* and the transitional words *for example* are preceded by a semicolon and followed by a comma.

The following are lists of common conjunctive adverbs and transitional words.

COMMON CONJUNCTIVE ADVERBS		
accordingly	furthermore	otherwise
also	hence	similarly
besides	however	still
consequently	instead	therefore
finally	nevertheless	thus

COMMON TRANSITIONAL WORDS		
as a result	in addition	in other words
for example	in fact	on the other hand

Some of the conjunctive adverbs and transitional words listed in the box can also be used as parenthetical expressions within a single clause.

JOINING CLAUSES	A katydid looks much like a harmless green grasshopper**; consequently,** people are surprised when it bites them. (A semicolon comes before the transitional word, and a comma follows it.)
WITHIN CLAUSES	The grasshopper**, however,** doesn't bite. (A comma comes before and after the conjunctive adverb.)

You can learn more about parenthetical expressions on pages L454–L455.

PRACTICE YOUR SKILLS

● Check Your Understanding
Using Semicolons and Commas

Science Topic **Write *I* if the sentence does not use semicolons and commas correctly. Write *C* if the sentence is correct.**

1. Plankton floats at the ocean's surface other sea animals rely on it for food.

2. The bivalve mollusk has two shells hinged together, similarly oysters and mussels have hinged shells.

3. Oysters are prized for the pearls they produce; as a result oyster beds are cultivated as "pearl farms."

4. The sponge is a plantlike animal, and it grows only in an underwater habitat.

5. Jellyfish are stunningly beautiful on the other hand; their sting is stunningly painful.

6. Coral looks like porous rock; however, it is a skeleton secreted by living marine polyps.

7. Polyps such as the sea anemone live individually, others live in colonies and form coral reefs.

8. The octopus has a smooth body with a mouth on the underside furthermore it has eight arms covered with suckers.

9. The ten-armed squid is often used as fish bait; consequently; "squidding" means to fish for squid or to fish with squid as bait.

10. A sea horse's head and neck resemble those of a horse, it swims with its head held upright like a horse's, and its tail curled beneath.

● Connect to the Writing Process: Editing
Using Semicolons and Commas

11.–18. Rewrite the incorrect sentences from the preceding exercise, using semicolons and commas where needed.

Semicolons to Avoid Confusion

To make your meaning clear, you may have to substitute a semicolon for a comma.

Use a semicolon instead of a comma in certain situations to avoid possible confusion.

A semicolon is used instead of a comma between the clauses of a compound sentence if there are commas within a clause.

Military uniforms are often blue, gray, or black; but those are not the only colors used.
(Normally, a comma comes before a conjunction separating the clauses in a compound sentence.)

Semicolons are also used instead of commas between items in a series if the items themselves contain commas.

The President's schedule includes stops in London, England; Paris, France; Florence, Italy; Geneva, Switzerland; and New Delhi, India.
(Normally, commas separate the items in a series.)

You can learn more about using commas on pages L436–L461.

PRACTICE YOUR SKILLS

● Check Your Understanding

Using Semicolons

History Topic **Write each word that should be followed by a semicolon and then add the semicolon.** You may need to replace a comma or commas with semicolons.

1. Armistice Day is November 11 it is the anniversary of the cease-fire of World War I in 1918, which occurred during the eleventh day of the eleventh month at eleven o'clock.

2. The site of the 1898 Klondike gold rush wasn't Alaska in fact, it was the Yukon Territory of Canada.

3. Pocahontas's real name was said to be Matoak *Pocahontas* was a family name.

4. I want to write my research paper on General Douglas MacArthur, General George S. Patton, or General Robert E. Lee but I can't decide which general interests me the most.

5. Robert E. Lee's personal home was made into Arlington National Cemetery during the Civil War therefore, he never went home again.

6. The French and Indian War was 1754–1763 the American Revolutionary War was 1775–1783.

7. Reenactments of battles of the Civil War (1861–1865) will be performed on Saturday, June 8 Sunday, June 9 and Monday, June 10.

8. Alaska was bought from Russia in 1867 for 2.5 cents per acre however, it was not admitted into the union as a state until 1959.

9. Hawaii also was admitted as a state in 1959 it consists of several islands, has its capital in Honolulu, and is 6,424 square miles.

10. The Great Wall of China is more than just stone and mortar in fact, it has over 10,000 watchtowers, hundreds of passes, a rich historical value, and strong cultural influence.

Geography Topic **Write each word that should be followed by a semicolon or comma and then add the semicolon or comma.**

11. The Sahara covers an area of about 3,500,000 square miles Europe covers about 4,100,000 square miles.

12. Florida is not the southernmost state in the United States Hawaii is farther south.

13. I have lived in Detroit Michigan Lincoln Nebraska and Ames Iowa.

14. Some people call Texas the biggest state in the union on the contrary Alaska is the biggest state.

15. Death Valley contains the lowest point in the Western Hemisphere this point is 282 feet below sea level.

16. Death Valley is not confined to one state it stretches across parts of Eastern California and Southern Nevada.

17. Popular European vacation destinations include Paris, France Rome, Italy and London, England however some tourists visit other destinations such as Brussels, Belgium.

18. Unmapped areas of the world include jungles in Papua New Guinea submerged caves in Wakulla Springs, Florida and areas of the Nahanni National Park in Canada.

19. The map of the world in other words is not complete.

20. The United States contains many parks and natural wonders furthermore you don't need a passport to see them.

21. Carlsbad Caverns National Park in New Mexico for example, has one of the world's largest underground chambers and the nation's deepest limestone cave.

22. Mauna Loa in Hawaii is one of the world's largest volcanoes it measures 9,842 yards from the seafloor.

23. Indonesia and Japan rank first and second as nations with active volcanoes the United States ranks third.

24. The giant sequoia is the largest tree on our planet in fact its height often exceeds 300 feet.

Write the following paragraphs, adding semicolons and commas where needed.

The Bermuda Triangle is a mysterious, triangle-shaped area of the North Atlantic Ocean it is located off the coast of Florida. Many ships, planes, and people have disappeared without a trace in this triangle in fact some say there is a powerful vortex beneath the water. Despite numerous accounts of disappearances within the Bermuda Triangle, the U.S. Board of Geographic Names does not record "Bermuda Triangle" as an official name moreover it does not maintain an official file on the area.

The Department of the Navy however acknowledges that there is an area of water where unexplained disappearances occur. The Navy maintains a Website at *http://www.history.navy.mil* called the *Bermuda Triangle Fact Sheet*. Follow the link for the "Frequently Asked Questions" page and then the "Bermuda Triangle" page. The FAQ sheet specifies the triangle's three corners as Miami, Florida San Juan, Puerto Rico and the island of Bermuda furthermore the sheet mentions Coast Guard searches for missing people and ships in that area. A group of five U.S. Navy Avenger Torpedo Bombers for example left Ft. Lauderdale, Florida, on a training mission and never returned. The flight lieutenant's compass failed while over the triangle he is reported to have sent a message before the planes disappeared forever. One of the rescue planes searching for the five planes also disappeared.

 # Colons

Colons are used with lists, independent clauses, long quotations, and in certain conventional situations.

Colons with Lists

A colon is used most often to introduce a list of items that will follow in a sentence.

Use a colon before most lists of items, especially when a list comes after an expression such as *the following*.

When I think of California, I think of the following: beaches, sunshine, and surfing.

My favorite beaches are these: Huntington Beach, Malibu Beach, and Redondo Beach.

A colon, however, does not follow a verb or a preposition.

NO COLON	Ocean water **includes** salt, seaweed, and jellyfish.
COLON	Ocean water includes the following: salt, seaweed, and jellyfish.
NO COLON	Salt is used **for** making glass, building roads, and tanning leather.
COLON	Salt is used in the following processes: making glass, building roads, and tanning leather.

Remember that commas usually separate items in a series. You can learn more about items in a series on pages L436–L441.

Colons with Certain Independent Clauses

Use a colon between independent clauses when the second clause explains or restates the first.

We learned why sodas sell so well: the United States consumes more soft drinks than any country but Mexico.

We now know why she named her new soft drink Key West Cola: she lives in Key West, Florida.

Colons with Long, Formal Quotations and Formal Statements or Propositions

Use a colon to introduce a long, formal quotation or a formal statement or proposition.

Maimonides, the wise Jewish philosopher who lived from 1135 to 1204, wrote this advice: "Do not consider it proof just because it is written in books, for a liar who will deceive with his tongue will not hesitate to do the same with his pen."

The issue before the committee was this: It is necessary that more students be recruited to participate in next month's Trivia Scavenger Trek.

(The formal statement begins with a capital letter.)

You can learn more about long quotations on page L516.

Colons with Conventional Situations

Use a colon in certain conventional situations.

CONVENTIONAL SITUATIONS	
BETWEEN HOURS AND MINUTES	6:30 P.M.
BETWEEN BIBLICAL CHAPTERS AND VERSES	Psalms 46:10

BETWEEN PERIODICAL VOLUMES AND PAGES	*Futura* 16:3–8 Scientific American 9.4:32–44 (In this example, *4* is the issue number; the colon and page numbers follow it.)
AFTER SALUTATIONS IN BUSINESS LETTERS	Dear Sir or Madam:
BETWEEN TITLES AND SUBTITLES	*Star Wars:* The Phantom Menace (movie); "Americans and Weight: Not a Trivial Matter" (article); *The Chieftains:* Tears of Stone (recording)

CONNECT TO WRITER'S CRAFT

More and more employers are giving job applicants the option of submitting cover letters and résumés through E-mail. Most people attach their résumé as a file attachment, but they do write out the cover letter as an E-mail message. These E-mail letters should follow the same rules for punctuating salutations and closings as typed letters; that is, use a colon after your salutation and a comma after your closing.

PRACTICE YOUR SKILLS

● Check Your Understanding

Using Colons

General Interest **Write each word or number that should be followed by a colon and add the colon.**

1. Answer this question How much U.S. trivia do you know?

2. Four women are represented in the U.S. Capitol's Statuary Hall Frances Willard, Maria Sanford, Florence Rena Sabin, and Esther Hobart Morris.

3. The following words are all twentieth-century creations *beautician, highbrow,* and *superhighway.*

4. Theodore Roosevelt stated "The only man who never makes a mistake is the man who never does anything."

5. I had a revelation on my eighteenth birthday I was now old enough to vote.

6. The President's State of the Union address should begin by 7 15 P.M. and be over by 8 30 P.M.

7. Our travel itinerary includes Carlsbad Caverns and the following state capitals Phoenix, Little Rock, and Austin.

8. We learned a valuable lesson Don't travel through the Southwest during the hot summer months.

9. At Bill Clinton's 1997 Presidential Inauguration, his Bible was opened to Isaiah 58 12.

10. John F. Kennedy once said "Ask not what your country can do for you but what you can do for your country."

● **Connect to the Writing Process: Editing**
Using Colons

Write each sentence, adding colons where appropriate. If a sentence is correct, write C.

11. The assignment is this Write a paper about U.S. trivia or culture.

12. I'll expect your finished papers on Friday by 2 00 sharp.

13. You can get help with your research from the librarian, a tutor, or me.

14. Other research paper ideas are these life on an American farm, five American poets, and Native American culture.

15. The principal is making the following announcement Students who submit their research papers for publication in the school newsletter must do so by 2 45 on Wednesday.

Communicate Your Ideas

APPLY TO WRITING

Expository Paragraph: *Semicolons and Colons*

Your history class is creating its own game of American Trivia, and each student must submit one trivia fact and an explanation of the fact. Brainstorm for trivia you know and choose one fact to write about. Write a paragraph explaining the trivia. For example, if your trivia fact is that New York is famous for its pizza, describe why New York pizza is special. Use semicolons and colons to form interesting sentences. Edit your paragraph for correct use of punctuation and then write the final copy. Finally, give your paragraph a title that includes a subtitle.

 **QuickCheck** Mixed Practice

Health Topic

Write the following sentences, adding semicolons, colons, and commas where needed.

1. The average adult uses 1,300 to 1,600 calories a day a child uses an average of 2,400 calories.

2. The Surgeon General has issued the following warning Smoking by pregnant women may result in fetal injury, premature birth, and low birth weight.

3. Bones are vital to the circulatory system they produce blood cells within their marrow.

4. The brain has these three parts the cerebrum, the cerebellum, and the cerebral cortex.

5. I knew that the heart, liver, and kidneys are organs I did not realize that skin is an organ.

6. The skin is in fact the body's largest organ.

7. The blood bank's plea is this Donate blood today.

8. Babies don't develop the cells necessary to see in color until they are six to eight months old therefore everyone is color-blind at birth.

9. A meal eaten at 6 00 P.M. is in some part of the digestive system until 6 00–9 00 A.M. the following day.

10. The guest speaker gave an impassioned plea "While you're still young, develop the healthy habit of exercising for 20–45 minutes several days a week—it could save your life."

Italics (Underlining)

As you know, when words are printed in italics, they slant to the right *like this*. When you are using a computer, highlight what you want italicized and then press *Ctrl-I* for italics or look for the command for italics under *Format*. When you write, you can use underlining as a substitute for italics.

ITALICS	Have you read *Dubliners* by James Joyce?
UNDERLINING	Have you read Dubliners by James Joyce?

Italicize (underline) letters, numbers, and words used as words. Also underline foreign words that are not generally used in English.

LETTERS, NUMBERS	When you write your compositions, your capital *Q*'s look like *2*s. (Only the *Q* and the *2* are italicized— not the 's or s.)
WORDS, PHRASES	In Shakespeare's time the word gentle meant "noble."
	In the same era the phrase for sooth meant "for truth."
FOREIGN WORDS	In Hebrew *shalom* means "peace."

Italicize (underline) the titles of long written works or musical compositions that are published as a single unit. Also underline the titles of paintings and sculptures and the names of vehicles.

Long works include books, periodicals, newspapers, full-length plays, and very long poems. Long musical compositions include operas, symphonies, ballets, and albums. Vehicles include airplanes, ships, trains, and spacecraft. Titles of movies and radio and TV series should also be italicized (underlined).

BOOKS	George Eliot wrote *Silas Marner*. May I use your <u>Dictionary of Symbolism</u>?
MAGAZINES	I subscribe to *Poets & Writers*. I also subscribe to <u>Poetry Horizons</u>.
NEWSPAPERS	I enjoy the movie reviews in the *Philadelphia Bulletin*. Ari reads the comics in the <u>Chicago Tribune</u>. (*The* is generally not considered part of the title of a newspaper or a magazine.)
PLAYS AND MOVIES	Henrik Ibsen's plays *Hedda Gabler* and *A Doll's House* were written in the late 1800s. The movie named <u>A Doll's House</u> after Ibsen's play stars <u>Jane Fonda</u>.
TELEVISION SERIES	The series *Biography* on A&E featured Vincent van Gogh. <u>Star Trek: The Next Generation</u> included quotations of Shakespeare and references to his plays.
LONG MUSICAL COMPOSITIONS	Wolfgang Amadeus Mozart composed the opera *Don Giovanni* in Italian. Mozart composed <u>The Magic Flute</u> in German.
WORKS OF ART	*Story Cloth,* embroidered by Yang Fang Nhu, is fiber art. <u>Listening</u> is an oil on cardboard by Gabriele Münter.
NAMES OF VEHICLES	The *Gudgeon* was the first submarine to circle the earth. Charles Lindbergh flew the <u>Spirit of St. Louis</u>.

You can learn more about the capitalization of titles on pages L412–L417.

As computers become more common in households, many students are using word processing programs to write compositions. These programs allow you to use italics and other special text formatting that typewriting and handwriting do not offer. Remember, though, that italics *replace* underlining— use one or the other. You would not, for example, write <u>*Romeo and Juliet*</u>. Instead, you'd write *Romeo and Juliet*. Also, be sure to use one method—underlining or italics—consistently throughout your paper; that is, do not write <u>Romeo and Juliet</u> in one paragraph and *Romeo and Juliet* in another paragraph.

PRACTICE YOUR SKILLS

● Check Your Understanding
Using Italics (Underlining)

General Interest **Write and underline each letter, word, or group of words that should be italicized.**

1. Often The Learning Channel will air a series called Great Books.

2. Kaddara, an opera produced in 1921, is about Eskimos.

3. Charles Schulz, who created the character Charlie Brown, was once a cartoonist for a well-known magazine, the Saturday Evening Post.

4. The character Snoopy in You're a Good Man Charlie Brown would be a fun part to act.

5. Leonardo da Vinci's painting The Last Supper is considered one of the great art treasures of the world.

6. Why does my English teacher always say I must mind my p's and q's?

7. Biblioteca is Spanish for "library."

8. The name White House was given to the presidential residence by Theodore Roosevelt.

9. The Wall Street Journal offers reports on businesses and the stock market.

10. I read a travelogue on the Queen Elizabeth 2 in Travel Magazine.

11. Children on the Beach is a painting by American Impressionist Mary Cassatt.

12. Do you subscribe to Photomedia Magazine?

13. Of all Dickens's books that I have read, I enjoyed Oliver Twist the most.

14. The Sunday editions of major newspapers (like the Chicago Tribune) have a section on Life and Arts.

15. The term First Lady was not widely used until a comedy about Dolley Madison, called The First Lady in the Land, opened in New York in 1911.

● **Connect to the Writing Process: Editing**
Using Italics (Underlining)

Write the following paragraph, adding italics (underlining) as needed.

My goal is to manage a large bookstore that carries books, music, and periodicals. I would devote funds to a magnificent young adult section with plenty of bestsellers like The Giver by Lois Lowry and The Outsiders by S. E. Hinton. I would feature weekly displays of magazines such as Discover and Writer's Digest and carry major newspapers, including USA Today, the Chicago Tribune, and the Miami Herald. The overhead speaker system would play music from the store's music section. Handel's Messiah would be a good choice during the holidays. Posters of colorful, classical art such as A Sunday on La Grande Jatte by Georges Seurat would adorn the walls of the classical music section. The science and technology section would feature books about

Liberty Bell 7 (the second manned spacecraft) and other overlooked spacecraft. A bookstore with this much variety would require me to dot every i and cross every t, but I could do it.

Communicate Your Ideas

APPLY TO WRITING
Descriptive Web Page: *Italics (Underlining)*

The man in this photograph is an advertising executive who is searching for Websites that will tell him about high school students' interests. Write a descriptive Web page with this man in mind as your audience. Describe your interests in books, magazines, newspapers, plays, movies, television, music, and art. Mention a favorite in each category, using italics (underlining) correctly.

Quotation Marks and Ellipsis Points

Knowing how to use quotation marks correctly when you write fiction is important because conversations cannot be written without them. Authors often use conversation, or **dialogue**, to reveal important information about the characters and to add realism to fiction.

Quotation marks are also essential in research papers. If you omit or incorrectly use quotation marks in a research paper, you may, unwittingly, be plagiarizing someone else's words. Quotation marks show that the words you are writing are not your own—that they belong to someone else.

One of the most important things to remember about quotation marks is that they come in pairs. They are placed at the beginning and at the end of uninterrupted quotations and certain titles.

Quotation Marks with Titles

Use quotation marks to enclose the titles of chapters, articles, stories, one-act plays, short poems, and songs.

The titles of long works of art and publications are italicized (underlined). These long works, however, are usually composed of smaller parts. A newspaper has articles, for example, and a book can include chapters, short stories, short plays, or poems. When the titles of these smaller parts are written, they should be enclosed in quotation marks.

Quotation marks are also placed around the titles of essays, compositions, episodes from TV series, and movements from long musical compositions.

CHAPTERS IN A BOOK	"I Observe" is my favorite chapter in *David Copperfield* by Charles Dickens.

POEMS	Yesterday we read Robert Browning's poem "My Star" in our anthology *English Literature*.
ARTICLES IN MAGAZINES OR NEWSPAPERS	"Facing the Future" was an informative article in *Time*. For homework please read "The Life of a Small-Town Writer" in the local newspaper.
TELEVISION EPISODES	Tonight's episode of *The Simpsons* is "Lisa the Iconoclast."
SONGS	I often listen to "Candle in the Wind" on Elton John's album *Goodbye Yellow Brick Road*.

PRACTICE YOUR SKILLS

● Check Your Understanding
Using Quotation Marks with Titles

General Interest **Find and write each title, adding quotation marks or italics (underlining) where needed.**

1. I'm using Automation on the Line, an illustrated article in the Detroit News, in my research paper.

2. The drama class presented the one-act play The Happy Journey to Trenton and Camden by Thornton Wilder.

3. The band played Yankee Doodle as we marched by.

4. You can find the short story The Bear in the book The Works of William Faulkner.

5. The Elizabethan Stage was the title of my essay.

6. Are we supposed to read Keats's poem To Autumn or Shelley's poem To a Skylark for class tomorrow?

7. In film class I learned that As Time Goes By is the famous song in the movie Casablanca.

8. In music class we're learning Cloudburst, the last movement from Grofé's Grand Canyon Suite.

9. Have you read the chapter The Turning Point in our textbook The History of the World?

10. As soon as I passed my driver's test, I read the article Buying a Used Car.

Connect to the Writing Process: Prewriting

Brainstorming Using Quotation Marks

List the titles of all the printed and recorded materials you have read or listened to in the past week. If you read a poem in an anthology, for example, you would list the anthology's title and the poem's title. Use quotation marks and italics (underlining) correctly.

Communicate Your Ideas

APPLY TO WRITING

Compare and Contrast: *Quotation Marks with Titles*

Use the ideas you developed in the preceding exercise to write a comparison-contrast essay. From your list of titles, choose two items to work with—a song and a story, for example. Write an essay that compares and contrasts the two items. For instance, the song and the story may both tell a love story, but in different ways. Be sure to state complete titles and use quotation marks and underlining correctly. Edit the essay and then write the final copy.

QuickCheck   Mixed Practice

General Interest **Write each title, adding quotation marks or italics (underlining) where needed.**

1. I enjoyed the story The Necklace by Guy de Maupassant.

2. It is in Fiction: A Longman Pocket Anthology, just after The Cask of Amontillado by Poe.

3. Have you read Alfred Noyes's tragic poem The Highwayman?

4. Loreena McKennitt set The Highwayman to music on her album The Book of Secrets.

5. The last episode of this TV show was called Graduation.

6. There is an article called Fairy Tale or Marketing Ploy? in Hollywood Weekly; it's about celebrity weddings.

7. I've read up to the chapter A Wedding Night in The Hunchback of Notre Dame.

8. Wasn't Roy Orbison's performance of Oh, Pretty Woman used in the movie Pretty Woman?

9. I read the chapter entitled Elements of the Novel.

10. I found a great article called How to Write a Poem.

11. The poem When the Frost Is on the Pumpkin by James Whitcomb Riley paints a picture of fall in the Midwest.

12. I'll analyze the chapter News from Lake Wobegon Days by Garrison Keillor.

13. Songs from the Princess by Alfred Lord Tennyson is included in the collection Victorian Poetry and Poetics.

14. Michael Crawford sang The Music of the Night in the London production of The Phantom of the Opera.

Quotation Marks with Direct Quotations

Use quotation marks to enclose a person's exact words.

Quotation marks are placed around a **direct quotation**—the exact words of a person. They are not placed around an **indirect quotation**—a paraphrase of someone's words.

| DIRECT QUOTATION | Bill said, "I'm almost ready." |
| INDIRECT QUOTATION | Bill said that he was almost ready. (The word *that* often signals an indirect quotation.) |

A one-sentence direct quotation can be placed before or after a speaker tag, and it can also be interrupted by a speaker tag. In all three cases, quotation marks enclose only the person's exact words. Notice in the third sentence in the following examples that two sets of quotation marks are needed because quotation marks enclose only a person's exact words, not the speaker tag.

BEFORE	"The game was very suspenseful," he said.
AFTER	He said, "The game was very suspenseful."
INTERRUPTED	"The game," he said, "was very suspenseful."

Only one set of quotation marks is needed to enclose any number of quoted sentences—unless they are interrupted by a speaker tag.

He said, "The game was very suspenseful. We were tied in the last inning. Then Will hit a home run."

PRACTICE YOUR SKILLS

● Check Your Understanding
Using Quotation Marks with Direct Quotations

Contemporary Life **Write *I* if quotation marks are used incorrectly. Write *C* if quotation marks are used correctly.**

 1. "The volleyballs are low on air, Coach Mabry said."
 2. "I'm not sure," I said, "where the air pump is."
 3. Someone said "that the pump is in the supply closet."
 4. The crowd chanted, "Two, four, six, eight! "Whom do we appreciate? The Rockets!
 5. Did you say that you're going to resign as team captain?
 6. I certainly did not say that, "Mark protested."
 7. I replied, "Go ask Tyler. He heard it too."
 8. "The new gym, our principal promised, will be everything we've hoped for."
 9. "The builders said that the gym is nearly finished."
 10. "Do fifty push-ups and no cheating, the coach commanded." "Then run ten laps around the track."

11. I can hardly breathe, puffed Taylor.

12. Chris added, "I prefer running laps over doing push-ups."

13. Raquel asked, "What's next?"

14. "I'd like," Suzanne suggested, "to practice my relay.

15. "Finish warming up! Coach shouted. You haven't even begun to work!"

● Connect to the Writing Process: Editing
Using Quotation Marks with Direct Quotations

16.–25. Rewrite the incorrect sentences from the preceding exercise, using quotation marks correctly. In this exercise place a comma or an end mark that follows a quotation *inside* the closing quotation marks.

Capital Letters with Direct Quotations

A capital letter begins a quoted sentence—just as it begins a regular sentence.

Begin each sentence of a direct quotation with a capital letter.

"**H**appiness is a long Saturday with nothing to do," Priscilla said.

Priscilla said, "**H**appiness is a long Saturday with nothing to do."
(Two capital letters are needed: one for the first word of the sentence and one for the first word of the quotation.)

"**H**appiness," Priscilla said, "is a long Saturday with nothing to do."
(*Is* does not begin with a capital letter because it is in the middle of the quotation.)

"**H**appiness is a long Saturday with nothing to do," Priscilla said. "**T**hat is the best antidote to stress I can give you."
(*That* is capitalized because it starts a new sentence.)

PRACTICE YOUR SKILLS

● Check Your Understanding
Using Capital Letters with Direct Quotations

General Interest **Write *I* if the sentence does not use capital letters and quotation marks correctly. Write *C* if it is correct.**

1. "the happy do not believe in miracles," Goethe stated.

2. "Happiness is not a state to arrive at, but a manner of traveling," Commented Margaret Runbeck.

3. "Those who won our independence . . . believed liberty to be the secret of happiness and courage to be the secret of liberty," declared Justice Louis D. Brandeis.

4. "When one is happy, there is no time to be fatigued. being happy engrosses the whole attention, E. F. Benson said."

5. Don Marquis mused, "Happiness is the interval between periods of unhappiness."

6. "When a happy moment, complete and rounded as a pearl, falls into the tossing ocean of life," Agnes Repplier said, "it is never wholly lost."

7. Happiness is not being pained in body or troubled in mind, commented Thomas Jefferson.

8. C. P. Snow said, "the pursuit of happiness is a most ridiculous phrase. If you pursue it, you'll never find it."

9. William Lyon Phelps mused, "If happiness truly consisted in physical ease and freedom from care, then the happiest individual, I think, Would be an American cow."

10. "happiness is not a matter of events. it depends upon the tides of the mind," Alice Meynell once said.

● Connect to the Writing Process: Editing
Using Capital Letters with Direct Quotations

11.–17. Write each incorrect sentence from the preceding exercise, adding capital letters and quotation marks where needed. In this exercise place a comma or an end mark that follows a quotation *inside* the closing quotation marks.

Commas with Direct Quotations

A comma is used to separate a direct quotation from a speaker tag.

Use a comma to separate a direct quotation from a speaker tag. Place the comma inside the closing quotation marks.

Notice in the following examples that when the speaker tag follows the quotation, the comma goes *inside* the closing quotation marks.

"You should enter the story contest," she said.
(The comma goes *inside* the closing quotation marks.)

She said, "You should enter the story contest."
(The comma follows the speaker tag.)

"You should," she said, "enter the story contest."
(Two commas are needed to separate the speaker tag from the parts of an interrupted quotation. The first comma goes *inside* the closing quotation marks.)

PRACTICE YOUR SKILLS

● Check Your Understanding
Using Commas with Direct Quotations

Literature Topic — **Write *I* if the sentence uses commas, capital letters, or quotation marks incorrectly. Write *C* if the sentence is correct.**

1. Agatha Christie said, "The best time for planning a book is while you're doing the dishes."

2. "I see but one rule: to be clear", wrote Stendhal. "If I am not clear, all my world crumbles to nothing."

3. Aristotle once said "The greatest thing in style is to have a command of metaphor."

4. "A book ought to be an ice pick" wrote Kafka, "to break up the frozen sea within us."

5. "Regarding writing," Guy de Maupassant advises "get black on white."

6. Isaac Bashevis Singer commented, "A story to me means a plot where there is some surprise . . . because that is how life is—full of surprises."

7. "One writes to make a home for oneself," Says Alfred Kazin, on paper, in time and in others' minds."

8. Fitzgerald wrote, "You don't write because you want to say something; you write because you've got something to say."

9. "When you're writing, you're trying to find out something which you don't know", James Baldwin commented.

10. Baldwin went on to explain "The whole language of writing for me is finding out what you don't want to know, what you don't want to find out. But something forces you to anyway."

● **Connect to the Writing Process:** Editing
Punctuating Direct Quotations

> **11.–17.** **Rewrite the incorrect sentences from the preceding exercise, adding commas, capital letters, and quotation marks where needed.**

End Marks with Direct Quotations

A period marks the end of a statement or an opinion, and it also marks the end of a quoted statement or opinion.

> **Place a period inside the closing quotation marks when the end of the quotation comes at the end of the sentence.**

He said, "I think I'll order lasagna."
(The period goes *inside* the closing quotation marks.)

"I think I'll order lasagna," he said.
(The period follows the speaker tag, and a comma separates the quotation from the speaker tag.)

"I think," he said, "I'll order lasagna."
(The period goes *inside* the closing quotation marks.)

If a quotation asks a question or shows strong feeling, the question mark or the exclamation point goes *inside* the closing quotation marks. Notice that the question mark goes *inside* the closing quotation marks in the three examples that follow.

> She asked, "Where did you pick the apples**?**"
> "Where did you pick the apples**?**" she asked.
> "Where," she asked, "did you pick the apples**?**"

The exclamation point also goes *inside* the closing quotation marks in the following three examples.

> He exclaimed, "It is time for dessert**!**"
> "It is time for dessert**!**" he exclaimed.
> "It is," he exclaimed, "time for dessert**!**"

A quotation of two or more sentences can include various end marks.

> "Did you see the cooking exhibit**?**" Laura asked.
> "I accidentally knocked over the wok**!**"

Question marks and exclamation points are placed inside the closing quotation marks when they are part of the quotation. Occasionally a question or an exclamatory statement will include a direct quotation. In such cases the end mark goes *outside* the closing quotation marks. Notice in the following examples that the end marks for the quotations themselves are omitted. Only one end mark is used at the end of a quotation.

> Did Nancy say, "The Chinese food has arrived"**?**
> (The whole sentence—not the quotation—is the question.)
>
> I couldn't believe it when Ben said, "They forgot our eggrolls"**!**
> (The whole sentence—not the quotation—is exclamatory.)

Semicolons and colons go *outside* closing quotation marks.

> My dad specifically said, "No parties while I'm gone"**;** therefore, I'll plan the pizza party for this weekend.
>
> The following are today's "savory selections"**:** baked beans, creamed corn, and mini-sausages.

● Check Your Understanding
Using End Marks and Commas with Direct Quotations

Contemporary Life **Write _I_ if end marks and commas are used incorrectly. Write _C_ if the sentence is correct.**

1. "Where is the saltshaker," Cindy asked.

2. I shouted "Don't touch that—it's hot"

3. "Those fresh tomatoes were delicious," Megan said. "Did you grow them yourself?"

4. Who said "Taste this unusual fruit."

5. "Wow" exclaimed Andie "Are these luscious brownies made from scratch"

6. "First you blend the dry ingredients," explained my mom. "Then you add the milk."

7. I asked "Should we use buttermilk or whole milk"

8. Did I actually hear you say, "I promise to wash all the dishes after dinner"?

9. "Yeast" she said "is what makes the dough rise".

10. He walked through the kitchen shouting "Brownies! Brownies! Who wants a brownie"

11. Do you think we use chocolate chips? asked Megan, I think we use cocoa.

12. I'm sure Mom said, "Use baking powder for your rising agent," so we don't need the yeast.

13. Max called out, "Make some ham and cheese sandwiches, too!"

14. Did Bart say, The Pattersons have arrived?"

15. "Is the food ready? Emily asked, I'm starving?"

● Connect to the Writing Process: Editing
Using End Marks and Commas with Direct Quotations

16.–25. Rewrite the incorrect sentences from the preceding exercise, using end marks and commas as needed.

Communicate Your Ideas

APPLY TO WRITING

Interviews: *Direct Quotations*

You are writing an article for the school newspaper, and you need several direct quotations to make the article come alive. Working with a classmate, interview him or her about a topic of your choice. (Possible topics include a student's right to privacy, what to do if your best friend deserts you, and key ingredients to a successful date.) Write down your interviewee's statements exactly, using quotation marks and end marks correctly. Your classmate can then interview you for his or her article.

Working alone now, write a short article that incorporates some of the direct quotations from your interview. Edit for correct use of all punctuation and then write the final copy.

QuickCheck Mixed Practice

Literature Topic
Rewrite each sentence, adding capital letters, quotation marks, and other punctuation marks where needed.

1. the applause of a single human being is of great consequence Samuel Johnson said

2. the most beautiful adventures explained Robert Louis Stevenson are not those we go to seek

3. we need to restore the full meaning of the old word *duty* Pearl Buck remarked it is the other side of *rights*

4. Joseph Conrad stated an ideal is often but a flaming vision of reality

5. make up your mind to act decisively and take the consequences no good is ever done in this world by hesitation Thomas Huxley warned

6. Janet Erskine Stuart said to aim at the best and to remain essentially ourselves are one and the same thing

7. welcome everything that comes to you André Gide advised but do not long for anything else

8. can anything be sadder than work left unfinished Christina Rossetti asked yes, work never begun

9. did the poet W. B. Yeats say good conversation unrolls itself like the dawn

10. when people talk, listen completely stated Ernest Hemingway most people never listen

 ## Other Uses of Quotation Marks

In long quotations in reports and in conversations in stories, quotation marks require special applications.

Unusual Uses of Words

Quotation marks can draw attention to a word that is used in an unusual way.

Use quotation marks to enclose slang words, technical terms, and other unusual uses of words.

SLANG	"Surfing channels" and "surfing the Net" are slang expressions for watching TV and browsing the Internet.
TECHNICAL TERMS	A computer "crash" is a system failure. You will probably need to "reboot" your computer.
OTHERS	He plays so many computer games that I call him a "game-oholic." (invented word)
	Please don't "help" me anymore. You crashed my system! (irony/sarcasm)

Dictionary Definitions

When you write a dictionary definition within a piece of writing, you must include both italics (underlining) and quotation marks.

When writing a word and its definition in a sentence, italicize (underline) the word but use quotation marks to enclose the definition.

DEFINITIONS OF WORDS	The word *mouse* can mean either "a computer input device" or "a small, furry rodent."

CONNECT TO WRITER'S CRAFT

Writers often include definitions in their materials to clarify the meaning of words or phrases that might not be familiar to the reader. Technical terms, such as those related to the computer, are evolving at a phenomenal rate, and their definitions might be difficult to find in a standard dictionary.

Dialogue

When you write **dialogue**—conversation between two or more people—begin a new paragraph each time the speaker changes. A new paragraph clearly indicates who is speaking.

"Class," said Ms. Spoffard, turning from the board with a smile. "Who would like to help design the official Website for our school?"

"I'll help," said Stephen, who had already designed his own site.

"Excellent!" said Ms. Spoffard. "Who else?"

"I volunteer David," said Alma, smiling brightly. She added, "He already works part time as a Webmaster."

In the preceding example, notice that actions or descriptions of the speakers are sometimes included within the same paragraph in which each one speaks.

If the speaker's sentences form more than one paragraph, begin each paragraph with a quotation mark, but place a closing quotation mark at the end of the last paragraph only.

> Ms. Spoffard said, "Let me begin by telling you what the major sections of the Website will be.
>
> "First, we need an attractive home page, where people can find basic information and links to other pages.
>
> "Next, we need pages on each major aspect of our school, including sports, clubs, social activities, and even the week's cafeteria menu.
>
> "Finally, we need a map of the school."
>
> The students sat silently, taking notes.
>
> "May I design the map?" Jordan asked. "I have a few ideas to share."
>
> "We need a floor plan of the actual structure," continued Ms. Spoffard, "that the viewer could surf through.
>
> "In addition, we need realistic details which will require an observant team."

CONNECT TO WRITER'S CRAFT

Some experimental writers deliberately omit quotation marks from dialogue or place more than one speaker's words in the same paragraph. James Joyce, for example, uses dashes to indicate the beginning of a speaker's words.

> Then he asked:
> —Are you good at riddles?
> Stephen answered:
> —Not very good.
> Then he said:
> —Can you answer me this one? Why is the county of Kildare like the leg of a fellow's breeches?
>
> —*James Joyce*, A Portrait of the Artist as a Young Man

Remember, though, that your writing will be understood more easily when you follow standard rules of punctuation. Always use correct punctuation with formal writing for school and business.

Long Passages

When you quote five or more typed lines in a research paper, quotation marks are not necessary. Instead, begin on a new line and indent the quoted passage ten spaces along the left margin; the right margin remains even with the rest of the paper. This format is called a "blocked quote." After the blocked quote, begin your next sentence in the paper on a new line. Add text at the original margin width and continue in this format until you wish to add another quote.

> In his book *Editing Your Newsletter,* Mark Beach explains that with illustrations, you can have too much of a good thing:
>
> > Clip art was developed for display ads, not editorial matter. When using clip art in a newsletter, keep your objectives clear. Novice editors tend to use too many illustrations and to place them poorly. Even some experienced designers think readers like lots of drawings scattered at random.
>
> Beach urges newsletter editors to use clip art sparingly.

Another way to quote a long passage is to set it off from the rest of the text by indenting both left and right margins. If you are using a computer, you also could set the passage in a smaller type size. When you use this method of quoting a long passage, no quotation marks are needed.

CONNECT TO SPEAKING AND WRITING

As you have learned, there is more than one way to format a long quoted passage. When you write a research paper, therefore, be sure to consult your teacher's guidelines or the style handbook that your class uses to learn what format you should use. Then follow that format consistently.

You can learn more about using colons with formal quotations and with formal statements and propositions on page L492. You can learn about citing sources on pages L540–L543.

Quotations Within Quotations

If a title or a quotation is included within another quotation, a distinction must be made between the two sets of quotation marks. To avoid any confusion, use single quotation marks to enclose a quotation or certain titles within a quotation.

"Is the chapter 'Graphics and E-mail' a long one?" Li asked.
Lou said, "I heard him say, 'The answers are on page 101.'"
Lou asked, "Did he say, 'The answers are on page 101'?"

Notice in the second example above that the closing single quotation mark and the closing double quotation marks come together. The period is inside both of them.

PRACTICE YOUR SKILLS

 Check Your Understanding
Using Quotation Marks

Technology Topic — **Write *I* if quotation marks are used incorrectly. Write *C* if the sentence is correct.**

1. A "mouse potato' is someone who sits at the computer all day.
2. "Faith asked, Did someone say, Reboot all the computers now?"
3. You say you're working, but your work looks like personal E-mails.
4. A "computer virus" or "computer bug" causes a program to malfunction.
5. You probably remember hearing the news hype about the 'millenium bug.'
6. The word *click* "means to press a button on the mouse."
7. Does netiquette mean etiquette for the Internet?
8. The computer lab monitor said, "Print the warning that begins, 'Software piracy will be prosecuted.'"
9. A chatroom is a location on the Internet where you exchange written dialogue with other computer users.

10. When your computer is connected to the Internet, you are "on line."

11. "I heard Garrett say, 'The Internet is a technical highway of computerized information.'"

12. The word *E-mail* means 'electronic mail.'

13. The links on a Web page might include pictures or underlined text on which you would click to jump to another Web page.

14. Jason likes to "surf the net."

15. Have you contacted your "server" about better access to the Internet?

● Connect to the Writing Process: Editing
Using Quotation Marks

16.–25. **Rewrite each incorrect sentence from the preceding exercise, using quotation marks correctly.**

● Connect to the Writing Process: Drafting
Writing Quotations Using Quotation Marks

26.–35. **Write ten quotations of statements people have made to you in the past two days. Include at least two quotations within quotations. Use quotation marks where needed.**

Communicate Your Ideas

APPLY TO WRITING

Dialogue: *Quotation Marks*

You are writing "A Typical Day in My Senior Year" for your Senior Scrapbook. Write a conversation in which you speak to a friend, teacher, or other acquaintance. (To begin, you may want to use one of the statements from the preceding exercise.) Punctuate and indent the dialogue following the rules you have learned.

QuickCheck Mixed Practice

Correctly rewrite the following dialogue between Ebenezer Scrooge and Bob Cratchit. Add punctuation and indentation as needed.

Hallo growled Scrooge in his accustomed voice as near as he could feign it. What do you mean by coming here at this time of day? I am very sorry, sir said Bob. I am behind my time . . . . Yes. I think you are. Step this way, sir, if you please It's only once a year, sir pleaded Bob, appearing from the tank. It shall not be repeated. I was making rather merry yesterday, sir. Now, I'll tell you what, my friend said Scrooge. I am not going to tolerate this sort of thing any longer. Therefore . . . I am about to raise your salary!

—*Charles Dickens*, A Christmas Carol

Ellipsis Points

Most often ellipsis points (**. . .**) are used with quotations to show that part of a complete quotation has been dropped.

Use ellipsis points to indicate any omission in a quoted passage or a pause in a written passage.

QUOTED PASSAGE	"With malice toward none **. . .** let us strive on to finish the work we are in **. . . .**" Abraham Lincoln (Notice that part of the quotation is omitted at the end of the statement; the three ellipsis points are followed by a period.)
WRITTEN PASSAGE	"Well **. . .** I don't know who won the election," said the ballot-counter.

● Check Your Understanding
Using Ellipsis Points

Government
Topic

Write the following paragraphs, omitting the underlined portions and inserting ellipsis points as needed.

Four score and seven years ago our fathers brought forth on this continent, a new nation, conceived in Liberty, and dedicated to the proposition that all men are created equal.

Now we are engaged in a great civil war, testing whether that nation, or any nation so conceived and so dedicated, can long endure. We are met on a great battle-field of that war. We have come to dedicate a portion of that field, as a final resting place for those who here gave their lives that that nation might live. It is altogether fitting and proper that we should do this.

—*Abraham Lincoln*, "The Gettysburg Address"

● Connect to the Writing Process: Revising
Using Ellipsis Points

Write a shortened version of this paragraph, using ellipsis points to indicate where you omit words.

The other day, one of the gentlemen from Georgia, an eloquent man, and a man of learning, so far as I can judge, not being learned myself, came down upon us astonishingly. He spoke in what the Baltimore American calls the "scathing and withering style." At the end of his second severe flash I was struck blind, and found myself feeling with my fingers for an assurance of my continued physical existence. A little of the bone was left, and I gradually revived. He eulogized Mr. Clay in high and beautiful terms, and then declared that we had deserted all our principles, and had turned Henry Clay out, like an old horse, to root. This is terribly severe. It cannot be answered by argument; at least, I cannot so answer it. I merely wish to ask the gentleman if the Whigs are the only party he can think of, who sometimes turn old horses out to root. Is not a certain Martin Van Buren an old horse, which your own party have turned out to root? and is he not rooting a little to your discomfort about now?

—*Abraham Lincoln*
(from a speech in the House of Representatives)

Communicate Your Ideas

APPLY TO WRITING
Pauses in Written Dialogue: *Ellipsis Points*

You have a serious issue to discuss with a friend, and you're not sure what to say. For example, the issue might be her unkindness toward you or your deep appreciation of his friendship. Write a "practice dialogue" to this friend; express your thoughts in writing as though you were actually speaking. Use ellipsis points to show where you would pause, either to think or to wait for a response to an idea or question. Check your work carefully for correct usage of ellipsis points, and then write the final copy.

Other Marks of Punctuation

Hyphens, dashes, parentheses, and brackets are the other marks of punctuation covered in this section.

 **Hyphens**

A hyphen (**-**) has several uses besides its most common use, dividing a word at the end of a line.

Hyphens with Divided Words   When you write a research paper or a composition, you should—wherever possible—avoid dividing a word at the end of a line.

Use a hyphen to divide a word at the end of a line.

If you must divide a word, use the following guidelines.

GUIDELINES FOR DIVIDING WORDS

---

1. **Divide words only between syllables.**
   hu-morous or humor-ous

2. **Never divide a one-syllable word.**
   laugh   brought   save   lead

3. **Never separate a one-letter syllable from the rest of the word.**
   Do Not Break   a-dore   e-mit   i-ris

4. **Hyphenate after two letters at the end of a line, but do not carry a two-letter word ending to the next line.**
   Break   be-lieve   re-call   in-vite
   Do Not Break   tight-en   shov-el   over-ly

5. **Usually divide words containing double consonants between the double consonants.**
   shim-mer   oc-cur   ship-ping   stag-ger

---

6. Divide hyphenated words only after the hyphens.

spur-of-the-moment   father-in-law   self-confident

7. Do not divide a proper noun or a proper adjective.

Olivero   Yonkers   Himalayan   Polish

If you do not know how to hyphenate certain words, you can always look in a dictionary to find out where they can be divided between syllables.

PRACTICE YOUR SKILLS

● Check Your Understanding
Using Hyphens to Divide Words

Write each word, using a hyphen or hyphens to show where the word can be divided at the end of a line. If a word should not be divided, write *no*.

1. educate	**6.** governor	**11.** puzzle	**16.** decent
2. squeeze	**7.** octave	**12.** immune	**17.** Reggie
3. follow	**8.** permit	**13.** dress	**18.** method
4. event	**9.** planet	**14.** Nigerian	**19.** carefully
5. holiday	**10.** traitor	**15.** tuition	**20.** respect

● Connect to the Writing Process: Editing
Editing for Hyphens that Divide Words

Some of the following words have been divided incorrectly. Rewrite each word, using a hyphen or hyphens to show where the word can be divided. If a word is correct, write *C*.

21. pepp-er	**26.** yes-terday	**31.** tele-vision
22. tab-le	**27.** Lin-coln	**32.** John-son
23. thre-ad	**28.** a-void	**33.** ampli-fier
24. bask-etball	**29.** envelo-pe	**34.** tab-let
25. sweat-er	**30.** mer-ry-go-round	**35.** ba-tter

Hyphens with Certain Numbers
Hyphens are needed when you write out certain numbers.

Use a hyphen when writing out the numbers *twenty-one* through *ninety-nine*.

> Seventy-four new math textbooks were shipped to us today.
> Since we ordered eighty-nine, we are missing fifteen.

Hyphens with Some Compound Nouns and Adjectives
Some compound nouns and adjectives need one or more hyphens.

Use one or more hyphens to separate the parts of some compound nouns and adjectives. Also use one or more hyphens between words that make up a compound adjective located before a noun.

HYPHENATED COMPOUND WORDS	
COMPOUND NOUNS	sister-in-law, flare-up, secretary-general
COMPOUND ADJECTIVES	skin-deep, long-term, run-of-the-mill

A hyphen is used only when a compound adjective comes before a noun—not when it follows a linking verb and comes after the noun it describes.

> ADJECTIVE BEFORE A NOUN — This is a well-written paper on Pythagoras.
>
> ADJECTIVE AFTER A NOUN — This paper on Pythagoras is well written.

A hyphen is used only when a fraction is used as an adjective—not when it is used as a noun.

> FRACTION USED AS AN ADJECTIVE — A **one-fourth** minority of the students knows Pythagoras's theorem.
>
> FRACTION USED AS A NOUN — **Three fourths** of the students had never heard of Pythagoras.

Never use a hyphen between an adjective and an adverb ending in –ly.

> That **fairly difficult** geometry test yielded no low scores. (no hyphen)

Hyphens with Certain Prefixes   Several prefixes and one suffix are always separated from their root words by a hyphen.

Use a hyphen after the prefixes *ex-, self-,* and *all-* and before the suffix *-elect.*

A hyphen is used with all prefixes before most proper nouns or proper adjectives.

HYPHENS WITH PREFIXES AND SUFFIXES			
ex-champion	self-control	all-around	mayor-elect
mid-Atlantic	pre-Columbian	pro-American	

PRACTICE YOUR SKILLS

● Check Your Understanding
   Using Hyphens

General Interest   **Correctly write each word that should be hyphenated. If no word in the sentence needs a hyphen, write C.**

1. Is Maya Nenno the write in candidate for class president?

2. The ex mayor of Morrisville teaches trigonometry at the University of Nebraska.

3. I still must work twenty five more equations.

4. Fifty six bushels of corn were picked today.

5. Have you heard of this mathematician from the mid Victorian era?

6. The metal used in the sculpture is one fourth copper.

7. This report includes up to date statistics.

8. Jamie is self confident about lecturing in math class.

9. These terrifyingly written word problems are difficult to answer!

10. I request your all out effort in helping me find biographies of famous mathematicians.

● Connect to the Writing Process: Editing

Using Hyphens

Some of the hyphens in these sentences are used incorrectly; others are missing. Correctly write each word that should be hyphenated. If a sentence is correct, write C.

11. Thirty nine seniors are enrolled in honors math.

12. A three-fourths majority voted to host a free math clinic for the nearby junior high.

13. We expect only one-half of those who signed up actually to attend the clinic.

14. The student assistants at the math clinic must be self motivated-workers.

15. The day's program is all encompassing, including beginning and advanced skills.

16. This all encompassing format should meet the needs of every student.

17. We expect the entire day's worth of sessions to be an all around success.

18. In addition, we know that approximately two thirds of these students who participate will enter our high school next year.

19. These freshmen to be will already have a head start in math skills covered in our clinic.

20. We want our schools—all of them—to be seen as math-friendly environments.

Hyphens to Avoid Confusion   Without a hyphen, some words would be difficult to read.

Use a hyphen to prevent confusion or awkwardness.

re-edit, anti-irritant, re-elect
(prevents awkwardness of two identical vowels)

co-operator
(prevents confusion with the word *cooperator*)

re-sign the contract
(prevents confusion with the word *resign*)

PRACTICE YOUR SKILLS

● **Check Your Understanding**
Using Hyphens

 Correctly write each word that should be hyphenated. If a sentence is correct, write C.

Contemporary Life

1. I would like to reexamine those photographs.

2. At least one half of these photographs are of historical buildings in town.

3. Many of the buildings are of pre World War II construction.

4. We should repetition the town hall to hang these photos in the lobby.

5. A three fourths portion of the wall space is now covered in tattered travel posters.

6. These quality photographs would create a much improved look.

7. If the photo display is long term, perhaps it will attract customers to your gallery.

8. After all, the run of the mill citizen goes inside the town hall only occasionally.

9. The photos should be displayed long enough to be seen by at least one half of the townspeople.

10. Twenty to twenty five photographs should be sufficient for the display.

Dashes, Parentheses, and Brackets

A dash (—) or (--), parentheses ( ), and brackets [ ] are used to separate certain words or phrases from the rest of a sentence. Do not overuse these marks of punctuation and do not substitute them for other marks of punctuation such as commas or colons.

Dashes

Like a comma, a dash is used to separate words or expressions. A **dash**, however, indicates a greater separation than a comma does. Dashes should be used in the following situations.

Use dashes to set off an abrupt change in thought.

> Several students—there were five—applied for the job.
> I've misplaced the book—oh, I see you have it.

Use dashes to set off an appositive that is introduced by words such as *that is, for example,* or *for instance.*

> If an item is lost—for example, a book or a tape—pay the fee.
>
> Sam's job—that is, assistant librarian—is interesting.

Use dashes to set off a parenthetical expression or an appositive that includes commas. Also use dashes to call special attention to a phrase.

> Let's find a novel—mystery or historical—for you.
> You can return the novel to me Monday or Wednesday—or Friday, for that matter—right after school.

Use dashes to set off a phrase or a clause that summarizes or emphasizes what has preceded it.

> June 6, 7, and 8—these are the dates of the book auction.
> A book and a T-shirt—I received these gifts for my birthday.

When you write a dash, remember that it is twice as long as a hyphen. If you are using a typewriter, use two hyphens to make a dash. If you are using a computer, you can use the special symbols menu to insert a dash (—), or you can type two hyphens to make a dash (--). Some word processing programs will automatically convert two hyphens into one dash.

Parentheses

Parentheses separate from the rest of the sentence additional information that is not necessary to the meaning of the sentence. Definitions and dates, for example, are sometimes enclosed by parentheses. When using parentheses, remember to use pairs.

Use parentheses to enclose information that is not related closely to the meaning in a sentence.

To decide whether you should use parentheses, read the sentence without the parenthetical material. If the meaning and structure of the sentence are not changed, then add parentheses. Keep in mind that parenthetical additions to sentences slow readers down and interrupt their train of thought. As a result, you should always limit the amount of parenthetical material that you add to any one piece of writing.

Dylan Thomas **(**1914–1953**)** read his own poetry brilliantly.

Samuel Clemens did not invent the name Mark Twain **(**which means "a depth of 2 fathoms, or 12 feet"**)**.

Use parentheses to identify a source of information such as a reference to an author or a page number.

"Arthur Conan Doyle realized he could make more money writing mystery stories than practicing ophthalmology" **(**Garrett 22**)**.

When the closing parentheses come at the end of a sentence, the end mark usually goes outside of the parentheses. However, occasionally the end mark goes inside the parentheses if the end mark actually belongs with the parenthetical material.

> Many people enjoy Doyle's mystery stories. **(I'm not one of them, though.)**

Brackets

When you write a research paper that includes quoted passages, you may need to use brackets.

Use brackets to enclose an explanation within quoted material that is not part of the quotation.

> Richard Ellman wrote, "He **[W. B. Yeats]** displayed and interpreted the direction in which poetry was to go."

The following summary may help you decide when to use certain kinds of punctuation.

PUNCTUATING PARENTHETICAL INFORMATION

Parenthetical (nonessential) information is always set off from the rest of the sentence by special punctuation. Depending on how important the parenthetical material is, use one of the following marks of punctuation.

- Use commas to enclose information that is loosely related to the rest of the sentence yet is nonessential. This method is the most common.
- Use parentheses to enclose information that is not essential to the meaning of the sentence but that adds an interesting point.
- Use dashes to signal a break in the train of thought.
- Use brackets to enclose your own words inserted into a quotation.

PRACTICE YOUR SKILLS

● Check Your Understanding
Using Dashes, Parentheses, and Brackets

Literature Topic **Write *I* if the sentence is punctuated incorrectly.
Write *C* if it is punctuated correctly.**

1. The Victorian poet, Alfred Lord Tennyson, 1809–1892 wrote *In Memoriam* over a period of seventeen years.

2. "Mariana," "Ulysses," and "Maud" all these are poems by Tennyson.

3. A number of Victorian authors—for example, Charles Dickens, Wilkie Collins, and Arthur Conan Doyle—wrote mystery stories.

4. At Dickens's death he died in 1870 his novel *The Mystery of Edwin Drood* was unfinished.

5. One of the most interesting characters was what was her name? Her Royal Highness the Princess Puffer.

6. Conan Doyle had interesting friends—for instance, the magician Harry Houdini.

7. Houdini [then known as "Ehrich, The Prince of the Air"] began his career in show business as a trapeze artist and contortionist.

8. "A Scandal in Bohemia" begins, "To Sherlock Holmes, she (Irene Adler) is always *the* woman."

9. I cannot—I repeat, cannot—find my copy of *The Moonstone* by Wilkie Collins.

10. Collins's *The Woman in White* was an instant sensation —published in 1860—that inspired a perfume and a dance.

● Connect to the Writing Process: Editing
Using Dashes, Parentheses, and Brackets

11.–18. Rewrite the incorrect sentences from the preceding exercise, using commas, dashes, parentheses, and brackets correctly.

Communicate Your Ideas

APPLY TO WRITING

Narratives: *All Punctuation*

To help you make plans for the future, your school counselor has asked you to write a scene showing what you would like to be doing twenty years from now. Write freely, exploring ideas for action and dialogue. Then create a scene that places you twenty years in the future. Limit your narrative to a single location and add only one or two other characters. Include realistic dialogue to help the characterization come alive and use appropriate marks to set off parenthetical information. As you edit your narrative, check for the correct use of all punctuation.

QuickCheck Mixed Practice

General Interest **Write the following sentences, inserting hyphens, parentheses, dashes, and brackets as needed.**

1. Running, swimming, and riding these are good forms of exercise.

2. Because Mr. Pearson values sports, I think we should reelect him to the school board.

3. I think you are how shall I say it too short to be good at basketball.

4. The dates for some of this year's competitions football, tennis, and track have already been set.

5. Who was it that said, "He Tom Landry was the greatest football coach of all time"?

6. Let me tell you something and this is just between you and me.

7. I already know who the head coach to be is.

8. We need to add forty eight chairs that's four dozen.

9. Sasha she's our head cheerleader broke her leg.

10. A number of cheerleaders for instance, Terry, Holly, and Keisha have already asked to take Sasha's place.

Language Topic **Write the following paragraphs, adding any punctuation marks and capital letters that are needed.**

There arent any hard and fast statistics nevertheless the expression OK is probably the most widely used American expression in the world. For example, during World War II, there was a special international soccer match. One team was composed of members from the following four countries Poland, Czechoslovakia, Denmark, and Norway. The team had serious difficulties because of the language differences. Finally one of Polands players shouted, OK! Feeling confident that everyone finally understood the same thing, the team members went on to win the game.

Despite its international acceptance, the expression OK is really an all American expression. It first appeared in print in 1839 in a Boston newspaper, the Morning Post. A year later President Martin Van Buren he was born in Kinderhook, New York ran for a second term of office. He was called Old Kinderhook by his backers. The initials of his nickname were then used during the campaign. Later OK came into wide use as a catchword meaning all is right.

Using Correct Punctuation

Write each sentence, adding punctuation where needed.

1. The conservation department puts rainbow trout into the streams the lakes are stocked with salmon, herring, pickerel, and perch.

2. The prop committee still hasnt found the following items a straw hat, a wicker chair, and a large desk.

3. Everyones enthusiasm at the pep rally encouraged the players on Newtons all star team.

4. In the code the 2s stood for es.

5. The Eighteenth Amendment the prohibition amendment was not ratified by Connecticut and Rhode Island.

6. Most insects have no eyelids thus, their eyes are always open.

7. Six, forty, and ten these are the three correct answers.

8. Its time to apply for the dogs new license.

9. We have our choice of pink, aqua, or lavender unfortunately, we dont know which color would be best for the room.

10. A tree snake appears to fly through the air however it merely glides on air currents.

11. We couldnt possibly be at your house by 7 30.

12. Shiny metals for example, tin and copper turn into black powders when finely ground aluminum is an exception.

13. Gregor Mendel 1822–1884 was the Austrian botanist who developed the basic laws of heredity.

14. Bobs and Teds scores in their last bowling game were the best theyve ever had.

15. Only two copies of the works of the Greek sculptor Myron have survived one of those is the sculpture Discus Thrower.

Punctuating Direct Quotations

Write each sentence correctly, adding end marks, commas, and quotations marks where needed.

1. Ogden Nash mused, I marvel that such small ribs as these can cage such vast desire to please

2. A dog's ideal is a life of active uselessness stated William Phelps

3. If dogs could talk Karel Capek said perhaps we would find it as hard to get along with them as we do with people.

4. A dog is a lion on his own street states a Hindu proverb

5. When did a dog ever turn up his nose at a smell asked C. E. Montague

6. I have always thought of a dog lover quipped James Thurber as a dog that was in love with another dog

7. Bertrand Wilberforce said Dogs are evidently intended to be our companions, protectors, and in many ways, our examples

8. Alexander Pope once said Histories are more full of examples of the fidelity of dogs than of friends

9. Money will buy a pretty dog, but it won't buy the wag of its tail commented Josh Billings

10. Outside of a dog, a man's best friend is a book inside of a dog, it is very dark cracked Groucho Marx

Writing Sentences

Write five sentences that follow the directions below.

Write a sentence that . . .

1. includes the possessive form of the nouns *cousins* and *six months*.

2. includes the joint ownership of something.

3. includes a series of dates, including month, day, and year.

4. includes a colon at the beginning of a list.

5. includes a dash or pair of dashes.

Language and *Self-Expression*

René Magritte once said, "The mind loves the unknown. It loves images whose meaning is unknown, since the meaning of the mind itself is unknown." How does Magritte use this idea in *The Mysteries of the Horizon*?

Does the painting remind you of mysterious mental images of your own? Can you imagine images like these coming to you in your sleep? If you painted the images from one of your dreams, would you use artistic elements in the way Magritte has? Why or why not? Write an essay answering these questions.

Prewriting Freewrite for ten minutes, answering the above questions. Don't worry about grammar, punctuation, or spelling at this point; rather, focus on getting as many ideas as you can onto paper.

Drafting Use your freewriting to create a first draft, perhaps devoting a separate paragraph to each question. The topic sentence for each paragraph could be a one-sentence answer to the question, and the body of the paragraph could explain in more detail.

Revising Make sure your paragraphs include specific references to artistic elements such as line, color, shape, and value. These descriptions will help your reader envision your ideas.

Editing Check your paper for errors in spelling and capitalization. Be sure you have used punctuation such as italics, apostrophes, and semicolons correctly.

Publishing Write a final copy for your English teacher. You could also use a copy of your paper to begin your own "dream journal," complete with descriptions and sketches.

 **Another Look**

Using Apostrophes
Add 's to form the possessive of a singular noun. *(page L471)*
Add only an apostrophe to form the possessive of a plural noun that ends in *s*. *(page L472)*
Add 's to form the possessive of a plural noun that does not end in *s*. *(page L472)*
Add 's to only the last word to show joint ownership. *(page L476)*
Add 's to each word to show separate ownership. *(page L476)*

Using Semicolons and Colons
Use a semicolon between the clauses of a compound sentence when they are not joined by a conjunction. *(page L484)*
Use a semicolon between the clauses in a compound sentence when they are joined by certain transitional words. *(pages L485–L486)*
Use a colon before most lists of items. *(page L491)*
Use a colon between independent clauses when the second clause explains or restates the first. *(page L492)*

Italics (Underlining), Quotation Marks and Ellipsis Points
Italicize letters, numbers, and words used as words. *(page L496)*
Italicize certain titles. *(pages L496–L497)*
Use quotation marks to enclose certain titles. *(pages L501–L502)*
Use quotation marks to enclose a person's exact words. *(pages L504–L505)*
Use ellipsis points to indicate any omission in a quoted passage or a pause in a written passage. *(page L519)*

Using Other Marks of Punctuation
Use a hyphen to divide a word at the end of a line. *(pages L522–L523)*
Use a hyphen when writing out certain numbers. *(page L524)*
Use dashes to set off an abrupt change in thought. *(page L528)*
Use parentheses to enclose information that is not related closely to the meaning in a sentence. *(page L529)*

Directions
Each underlined part in the passage may lack one type of punctuation. Write the letter of the answer with the punctuation that correctly completes the underlined part. If the underlined part contains no error, write D.

EXAMPLE

René <u>Magritte the artist we studied in class</u>
                    (1)
<u>yesterday was</u> a master of Surrealist painting.

   1 **A**   Italics
       B   Quotation marks
       C   Dashes
       D   No error

ANSWER   **1** **C**

<u>René Magritte 1898–1967 was</u> a Belgian artist who established
          (1)
a reputation as a talented artist in the Surrealist style. Horror,

comedy, and <u>mystery these are some</u> of the moods he created in
        (2)
his paintings. If you study a number of his paintings, you'll notice

certain symbols are repeated <u>throughout many of them the female</u>
               (3)
torso, the bowler hat, the castle, and others. <u>Although Magrittes</u>
                (4)
<u>work is famous today</u>, he had to work earnestly for his success. His

humble beginnings included <u>nonglamorous jobs such as designing</u>
               (5)
<u>wallpaper</u> and sketching advertisements.

1   **A**   Parentheses

   B   Quotation marks

   C   Italics

   D   No error

2   **A**   Italics

   B   Parentheses

   C   Dash

   D   No error

3   **A**   Hyphen

   B   Semicolon

   C   Colon

   D   No error

4   **A**   Semicolon

   B   Dash

   C   Apostrophe

   D   No error

5   **A**   Semicolon

   B   Colon

   C   Dash

   D   No error

A Writer's Guide to Citing Sources

Whenever you write a research paper, you need to know how to use citations. **Citations** in a research paper direct readers to the original sources of borrowed words or ideas. The following guidelines will help you determine when to cite a source of information.

CITING SOURCES

- Cite the source of a direct quotation. Use direct quotations only when the author's wording makes the point better than you could in your own words.

- Cite the source of any paraphrased fact or idea that your readers might otherwise assume is your own.

- Do not cite facts or ideas that are considered to be common knowledge.

You can document your sources using parenthetical citations, footnotes, or endnotes. **Parenthetical citations** briefly identify the source in parentheses. **Footnotes** are numbered notes at the bottom, or foot, of a page. The numbers correspond to numbers that appear in the text immediately after borrowed material. **Endnotes** are also notes that correspond to numbers in the text; however, endnotes appear on a separate page at the end of the paper.

The style of citation is often determined by your subject matter. Standards are set by professional organizations, such as the Modern Language Association (MLA) in the language arts or the American Psychological Association (APA) in the social sciences. Scholars of history and the humanities often refer to *The Chicago Manual of Style* (CMS) for guidelines. These styles of citation vary slightly.

For most literary research papers, you will use the MLA style of parenthetical citations. The examples on the following page should help you use parenthetical citations.

BOOKS WITH A SINGLE AUTHOR	Give author's last name and a page reference: (Nostbakken 66).
BOOKS WITH TWO OR MORE AUTHORS	Give all authors' last names and a page reference: (Fujita and Pronko 220).
ARTICLE WITH AUTHOR NAMED	Give author's last name and a page reference: (Alleva 17). Omit the page reference if the article is a single page: (Greenlaw).
ARTICLE WITH AUTHOR UNNAMED	Give a shortened form of the title (unless full title is already short) and a page reference: ("Seminarian" 36–37). Omit the page reference if the article is a single page: ("Playful").
ARTICLE IN A REFERENCE WORK; AUTHOR UNNAMED	Give title (full or shortened). No page reference is necessary if the article is a single page from an encyclopedia arranged alphabetically: ("Sonnet").
AUTHOR NAMED IN TEXT	Give only the page reference from the text being cited: (56).

If you are citing a different page from the work you have most recently cited in the paragraph, you do not need to include the author's name (or the title) again. List only a page reference.

You should keep parenthetical citations close to the words or ideas being credited without interrupting the flow of the sentence. Place them at the end of a phrase, clause, or sentence. Refer to the following guidelines for help in placing a citation.

PLACEMENT OF PARENTHETICAL CITATIONS

- If the citation falls next to a comma or end punctuation, place the citation before the punctuation mark.

- If the citation accompanies a long quotation (three or more lines) that is indented and single-spaced, place the citation after the end punctuation.

- If the citation falls next to a closing quotation mark, place it after the quotation mark but before the end punctuation.

The CMS cites sources with footnotes or endnotes. For either type of note, you mark any borrowed material with a number raised halfway above the line of a text—a **superscript**. The number refers the reader to citation information with the same number located either at the foot of the page, a footnote, or at the end of the paper but before the works cited page, an endnote. The following examples will help you write footnotes or endnotes.

BOOKS WITH A SINGLE AUTHOR	[1] Faith Nostbakken, <u>Understanding Macbeth: A Student Casebook to Issues, Sources, and Historical Documents</u> (Westport: Greenwood Press, 1997) 99.
BOOKS WITH MORE THAN ONE AUTHOR	[2] Minoru Fujita and Leonard Pronko, eds., <u>Shakespeare East and West</u> (New York: St. Martin's Press, 1996) 220.
GENERAL REFERENCE WORKS	[3] Paul A. Jorgensen, "Macbeth," <u>Encyclopedia Americana</u>, 1999 ed. [4] "Sonnet," <u>World Book Encyclopedia</u>, 1998 ed.
ARTICLES IN MAGAZINES	[5] Lavinia Greenlaw, "Shakespeare in Love: The Love Poetry of William Shakespeare," <u>New Statesman</u> 7 June 1999: 56.
ARTICLES IN NEWSPAPERS	[6] Eileen Blumenthal, "That Power-Mad Couple Seems So Familiar," <u>New York Times</u>, 1 Mar. 1998, sec. 2: 5.
INTERVIEWS	[7] Stephanie Smith, telephone interview, 25 Sept. 1999.

Use an abbreviated footnote for a work you have already cited by including the author's last name (or the title if there is no author) and the page reference. If you have cited more than one work by the same author, also include the title (full or shortened).

REPEATED REFERENCES	[1] Nostbakken 3. [2] Blumenthal, "That Power-Mad Couple," 5.

A **works-cited page** is a complete listing of all the sources you have cited in a research paper. You should compile a works-cited page in addition to whatever parenthetical citations, footnotes, or endnotes appear in your paper. The works-cited page is alphabetized by the author's last name or by title (if no author is given). It should appear on a separate page at the end of the paper.

Refer to the following examples for help formatting a works-cited page, but note the differences in formatting between a works-cited page and footnotes and endnotes.

GENERAL REFERENCE WORKS	Jorgensen, Paul A. "Macbeth." <u>Encyclopedia Americana</u>. 1999 ed. "Sonnet." <u>World Book Encyclopedia</u>. 1998 ed.
BOOKS WITH A SINGLE AUTHOR	Nostbakken, Faith. <u>Understanding Macbeth: A Student Casebook to Issues, Sources, and Historical Documents</u>. Westport: Greenwood Press, 1997.
BOOKS WITH MORE THAN ONE AUTHOR	Fujita, Minoru, and Leonard Pronko. <u>Shakespeare East and West</u>. New York: St. Martin's Press, 1996.
ARTICLES IN MAGAZINES	Greenlaw, Lavinia. "Shakespeare in Love: The Love Poetry of William Shakespeare." <u>New Statesman</u> 7 June 1999: 56.
ARTICLES IN NEWSPAPERS	Blumenthal, Eileen. "That Power-Mad Couple Seems So Familiar." <u>New York Times</u>. 1 Mar. 1998, sec. 2: 5.
INTERVIEWS	Smith, Stephanie. Telephone interview. 25 Sept. 1999.
CD-ROM	<u>Discovering Shakespeare</u>. CD-ROM. Dedham: Bride Media International, Inc., 1998.
ARTICLE FROM AN ONLINE DATABASE WITH A PRINT VERSION	Siemens, R.G. "Disparate Structures, Electronic and Otherwise: Conceptions of Textual Organisation [sic] in the Electronic Medium, with Reference to Electronic Editions of Shakespeare and the Internet." <u>Early Modern Literary Studies</u> Jan. 1998: 29 pars. 20 Sept. 1999 <http://www.shu.ac.uk/emls/03-3/siemshak.html>.
ONLINE MATERIAL WITH NO PRINT VERSION	<u>The Complete Works of William Shakespeare</u>. Ed. Jeremy Hilton. 20 Sept. 1999 <http://www-tech.mit.edu/Shakespeare/works.html>.

Spelling Correctly

• •

 **Pretest**

Directions

Read the passage. Write the letter of the answer that correctly respells each underlined word. If the word is correct, write *D*.

    EXAMPLE   British poetry is part of our <u>curiculum</u>.
                                                (1)

           1 **A**   curicculum
               B   corriculum
               C   curriculum
               D   No error

    ANSWER   **1** **C**

    We <u>recentally</u> read a poem by John Keats called "Ode to
          (1)
a Nightingale." This <u>melencholy</u> poem expresses the poet's
                   (2)
<u>emoteons</u> as he listens to the bird's song. He remarks that
    (3)
the bird is <u>imortal</u> and that the same song he hears was heard
            (4)
by ancient <u>emporers</u>. The poet speaks of the <u>numbness</u> he
              (5)   **(6)**
feels at the <u>tyrany</u> of time. His heartache contrasts with the
              (7)
<u>happyness</u> of the bird's melody. He speaks of flying to the
    (8)
bird on the <u>invisable</u> wings of poetry. In <u>dispair</u>, he wonders
                (9)   **(10)**
whether he is awake or dreaming.

1	**A**	recently	6	**A**	numness
	B	recenttly		**B**	nummness
	C	reccently		**C**	numbeness
	D	No error		**D**	No error

2	**A**	melancoly	7	**A**	tirrany
	B	melancholy		**B**	tiranny
	C	melancholly		**C**	tyranny
	D	No error		**D**	No error

3	**A**	emoteions	8	**A**	happiness
	B	emotions		**B**	hapiness
	C	emottions		**C**	happynes
	D	No error		**D**	No error

4	**A**	imortle	9	**A**	invizable
	B	inmortal		**B**	invissable
	C	immortal		**C**	invisible
	D	No error		**D**	No error

5	**A**	emperors	10	**A**	despair
	B	empirers		**B**	dispare
	C	emporrers		**C**	despare
	D	No error		**D**	No error

Strategies for Learning to Spell

Learning to spell involves a variety of senses. You use your senses of hearing, sight, and touch to spell a word correctly. Here is a five-step strategy that many people have used successfully as they learned to spell unfamiliar words.

1 Auditory

Say the word aloud. Answer these questions.
- Where have I heard or read this word before?
- What was the context in which I heard or read the word?

2 Visual

Look at the word. Answer these questions.
- Does this word divide into parts? Is it a compound word? Does it have a prefix or a suffix?
- Does this word look like any other word I know? Could it be part of a word family I would recognize?

3 Auditory

Spell the word to yourself. Answer these questions.
- How is each sound spelled?
- Are there any surprises? Does the word follow spelling rules I know, or does it break the rules?

4 Visual/Kinesthetic

Write the word as you look at it. Answer these questions.
- Have I written the word clearly?
- Are my letters formed correctly?

5 Visual/Kinesthetic

Cover up the word. Visualize it. Write it. Answer this question.
- Did I write the word correctly?

If the answer is no, return to step 1.

Spelling Strategies

Being a good speller is an ongoing process. As you read and build your vocabulary, you also increase the number of words whose spellings you will want to master. The strategies in this chapter will help you spell new words as well as familiar words.

STRATEGY **Use a dictionary.** If you're not sure how to spell a word, or if a word you've written doesn't "look right," check the word in a dictionary. If you don't want to stop and check a word while you are writing, that is okay. Instead, circle the word and look it up when you finish.

STRATEGY **Proofread your writing carefully.** Read your paper one word at a time, looking only for spelling errors. Also, watch for words you're not sure you spelled correctly. If you are working on a computer, you can use the spell checker.

PRACTICE YOUR SKILLS

● Check Your Understanding
Recognizing Misspelled Words

Identify the misspelled word in each set. Then write the word correctly.

1. (a) occurrence	(b) neice	(c) stretch
2. (a) fiery	(b) drought	(c) arial
3. (a) condemn	(b) weight	(c) interupt
4. (a) courtesy	(b) milage	(c) regrettable
5. (a) assistence	(b) biscuit	(c) carriage
6. (a) immigrant	(b) fasinate	(c) pitiful
7. (a) business	(b) bargain	(c) campain
8. (a) ilustrate	(b) seize	(c) reference
9. (a) chord	(b) luxury	(c) napsack
10. (a) analyze	(b) ordinery	(c) cooperate

Be sure you are pronouncing words correctly.
"Swallowing" syllables or adding extra syllables can cause
you to misspell a word.

PRACTICE YOUR SKILLS

● Check Your Understanding
Pronouncing Words

> Oral Expression **Practice saying each syllable in the following words to help you spell the words correctly.**

1. am•big•u•ous
2. si•mul•ta•ne•ous
3. phe•nom•e•non
4. ca•tas•tro•phe
5. bank•rupt•cy

6. li•ai•son
7. a•non•y•mous
8. fo•li•age
9. pop•u•lar•i•ty
10. sim•i•le

STRATEGY **Make up mnemonic devices.** A sentence like "**Ants** have
many descend**ants**" can help you remember that *descendant*
ends with *ant*. "There are a pair 'a' **ll**'s in **parallel**" can help
you remember where the double *l*'s belong in *parallel*.

STRATEGY **Keep a spelling journal.** Use it to record the words that
you've had trouble spelling. Here are some suggestions for
organizing your spelling journal.

- Write the word correctly.
- Write the word again, underlining or circling the part of
  the word that gave you trouble.
- Write a tip that will help you remember how to spell the
  word in the future.

colossal	*colossal*	*Colossal has two a's, two l's, and two s's, but only the s's are side by side.*

Spelling Generalizations

Spelling generalizations are rules that apply to many different words. Knowing a few spelling generalizations can help you spell many different words correctly. The information that follows can help you decide when to use certain letter patterns, how to form plurals, and how to add prefixes and suffixes.

Spelling Patterns

Probably the most well-known spelling generalization is the "*i* before *e,* except after *c*" pattern. Another familiar generalization covers spelling the "seed" sound at the end of words.

Words with *ie* and *ei*

When the vowel sound is long *e,* write *ei* after *c* and *ie* after other consonant letters.

	IE AND *EI*			
EXAMPLES	ceiling field	receive chief	deceive believe	deceit achieve
EXCEPTIONS	seize weird	either protein	neither	leisure

When the sound is long *a* or any vowel sound other than long *e,* write *ei.*

	VOWEL SOUNDS OTHER THAN LONG *E*			
EXAMPLES	weigh height	neighbor heir	freight forfeit	reign heifer
EXCEPTIONS	view sieve	friend fierce	mischief tie	ancient pier

The generalizations do not apply if the *i* and *e* are in different syllables.

IE AND *EI* IN DIFFERENT SYLLABLES			
be•ing	de•ice	re•imburse	re•iterate
pi•ety	fi•esta	di•et	sci•ence

Words with *–sede*, *–ceed*, and *–cede*

The syllable that sounds like "seed" can be spelled *–sede, –ceed,* or *–cede.*

–SEDE, –CEED, AND *–CEDE*			
–SEDE (ONLY ONE WORD)	super**sede**		
–CEED (ONLY THREE WORDS)	ex**ceed**	pro**ceed**	suc**ceed**
–CEDE (ALL OTHERS)	ac**cede**	con**cede**	pre**cede**

There is no –seed ending except in words derived from the noun seed, *such as* reseed, *which means "to sow again."*

PRACTICE YOUR SKILLS

● Check Your Understanding
Using Spelling Patterns

Write each word, adding *ie* or *ei*. If you are unsure about a spelling, check the dictionary.

1. br ■ f
2. for ■ gn
3. th ■ r
4. n ■ ce
5. rec ■ pt
6. p ■ ce
7. l ■ sure
8. perc ■ ve
9. w ■ gh
10. y ■ ld
11. s ■ ge
12. hyg ■ ne
13. s ■ zure
14. rec ■ ve
15. conc ■ t
16. dec ■ ve
17. n ■ ther
18. med ■ val
19. rel ■ ve
20. counterf ■ t

Write each word, adding –sede, –ceed, or –cede.

21. re ■

22. con ■

23. ex ■

24. inter ■

25. super ■

26. pro ■

27. se ■

28. ac ■

29. suc ■

30. pre ■

Connect to the Writing Process: Editing
Using Spelling Patterns

History Topic **Read this article, paying particular attention to the underlined words. Decide whether they are spelled correctly. Then rewrite those that are misspelled.**

Today much is known about the culture of <u>ancent</u> Egypt. Two centuries of study have <u>yeilded</u> a wealth of information about the religious <u>beliefs</u> and practices of <u>anceint</u> Egypt. At the beginning of the nineteenth century, Egyptian civilization was <u>veiled</u> in mystery. Jean-François Champollion was the first scholar to work in this <u>field</u>. He is <u>veiwed</u> as the founder of Egyptology.

Champollion worked with the Rosetta Stone to <u>piece</u> together the principles of <u>heiroglyphics</u>. The Rosetta Stone, which was discovered by Napoleon's troops near Alexandria, had been inscribed by <u>priests</u> of Ptolemy V. On it, the same text appears in <u>hieroglyphic</u>, demotic, and Greek. Using the stone, Champollion <u>proceded</u> to compare the Egyptian text to the Greek text and <u>succeded</u> in figuring out the key to <u>hieroglyphics</u>. For the study of <u>ancient</u> Egypt, this was an <u>excedingly</u> important <u>acheivement</u>.

Plurals

There are a number of useful generalizations that will help you spell the plural of most nouns.

Regular Nouns

To form the plural of most nouns, add *s*.

To form the plural of nouns ending in *s, ch, sh, x,* or *z,* add *es*.

MOST NOUNS				
SINGULAR	geologist	frog	bicycle	rose
PLURAL	geologist**s**	frog**s**	bicycle**s**	rose**s**

S, CH, SH, X, AND *Z*				
SINGULAR	moss	bea**ch**	wi**sh**	ta**x**	walt**z**
PLURAL	moss**es**	beach**es**	wish**es**	tax**es**	waltz**es**

The following related plurals are alike, except one ends in *s* and the other in *es*. Form the plurals carefully, because their meanings differ.

cloths—[plural noun] pieces of fabric with specific uses; often part of a compound word: *tablecloths, dustcloths, washcloths*

> There are cleaning **cloths** in the broom closet.

clothes—[plural noun] garments or apparel, usually made of cloth

> Everyone wore formal **clothes** to the prom.

Nouns Ending with *y*

Add *s* to form the plural of a noun ending with a vowel and *y.*

VOWELS AND *Y*			
SINGULAR	essa**y**	journe**y**	allo**y**	monke**y**
PLURAL	essay**s**	journey**s**	alloy**s**	monkey**s**

Change the *y* to *i* and add *es* to a noun ending in a consonant and *y*.

CONSONANTS AND Y				
SINGULAR	ene**my**	falla**cy**	catego**ry**	sup**ply**
PLURAL	ene**mies**	falla**cies**	catego**ries**	sup**plies**
EXCEPTIONS	For proper nouns ending with *y*, just add *s*.			
	Jeremy	Avery	Nancy	
	Jeremys	Averys	Nancys	

PRACTICE YOUR SKILLS

● Check Your Understanding
Forming Plurals

Write the plural form of each noun.

1. fantasy
2. editor
3. latch
4. thistle
5. tragedy

6. fox
7. alley
8. phrase
9. hoax
10. reply

11. casualty
12. holiday
13. ally
14. railway
15. class

16. bench
17. six
18. sketch
19. melee
20. blueberry

● Connect to the Writing Process: Editing
Spelling Plural Nouns

General Interest **Edit this paragraph, changing the underlined nouns from singular to plural.**

The names people give their baby go in and out of fashion. This is true of names given to both sex, but switch in popularity are particularly common for very old names given to boy. Consider Henry. The name Henry has been around for century. It means "one who rules the home and estate (amassed property)." History is full of famous Henry. There were eight monarch of England named Henry and six

Holy Roman underline{emperor}. Other recent historical underline{personality} include Henry Ford and Henry Kissinger. But for a while, during the middle underline{decade} of the twentieth century, the name Henry was not very popular. There were many underline{Gary} and underline{Barry}, but not very many underline{Henry}. Today underline{family} are once again naming their underline{baby} Henry. How many underline{Henry} do you know?

Nouns Ending with *o*

Add *s* to form the plural of a noun ending with a vowel and *o*.

VOWELS AND *O*				
Singular	stud**io**	rat**io**	ster**eo**	kangar**oo**
Plural	stud**ios**	rat**ios**	ster**eos**	kangar**oos**

Add *es* to form the plural of many nouns that end with a consonant and *o*.

CONSONANTS AND *O*				
Singular	toma**to**	torpe**do**	he**ro**	ec**ho**
Plural	toma**toes**	torpe**does**	he**roes**	ec**hoes**

Add *s* to form the plural of musical terms, proper nouns, and some other nouns that end in *o*.

MUSICAL TERMS, FOODS, ETC.				
Singular	piccol**o**	tangel**o**	tac**o**	Pocon**o**
Plural	piccol**os**	tangel**os**	tac**os**	Pocon**os**

When dictionaries give two forms for the plurals of some nouns ending in a consonant and *o*, the first form is the preferred one.

PREFERRED FORMS			
SINGULAR	tornad**o**	zer**o**	mosquit**o**
PLURAL	tornad**oes** or tornad**os**	zer**os** or zer**oes**	mosquit**oes** or mosquit**os**

Nouns Ending in *f* or *fe*

To form the plural of some nouns ending in *f* or *fe*, just add *s*.

F OR FE					
SINGULAR	che**f**	staf**f**	roo**f**	wai**f**	giraf**fe**
PLURAL	che**fs**	staf**fs**	roo**fs**	wai**fs**	giraf**fes**

For some nouns ending in *f* or *fe*, change the *f* to *v* and add *es* or *s*.

F OR FE TO V					
SINGULAR	shel**f**	lea**f**	hoo**f**	wi**fe**	kni**fe**
PLURAL	shel**ves**	lea**ves**	hoo**ves**	wi**ves**	kni**ves**

When unsure which rule applies, consult a dictionary to find out the correct plural form of a word that ends with *f* or *fe*.

PRACTICE YOUR SKILLS

 Check Your Understanding
Forming Plurals

Write the plural form of each of these nouns. Check a dictionary to be sure you've formed the plural correctly.

1. half   **6.** placebo   **11.** belief   **16.** gulf

2. cello   **7.** scenario   **12.** banjo   **17.** proof

3. tomato   **8.** soprano   **13.** silo   **18.** self

4. burrito   **9.** pimento   **14.** wharf   **19.** folio

5. sheriff   **10.** ratio   **15.** stereo   **20.** radio

Spelling Plural Nouns

Music Topic **Rewrite this paragraph, correcting any spelling errors.**

Of all the stringed instruments, the violin is the most versatile. It is unusual to see violas and celloes in a country music group, and you will rarely see banjoes and guitars in the symphony orchestra. Violins, however, have dual lifes. Going by the name of "fiddles," they do themselfs proud, playing with folk or bluegrass comboes. As violins, they are the principal voices in symphonies, sonatas, and concertoes. Alone, they can play soloes. With a cello and a viola, they can play trios. They are almost as versatile and popular as pianoes, and they are much more portable!

Plurals of Numbers, Letters, Symbols, and Words Used as Words

To form the plurals of most numerals, letters, symbols, and words used as words, add an *s.* However, to prevent confusion, it is best to use an apostrophe and *s* with lowercase letters, some capital letters, and some words used as words.

EXAMPLES
The 7**s** in this column should be 4**s.**
Interest rates were high in the 1980**s.**
Ampersands (&**s**) replace the *ands* in some company names.

EXCEPTIONS
If *e***'s** are closed at the top, they look like *i***'s.**
(Without the apostrophe, *i*'s become *is.*)
*A***'s** are easy letters to write. (*A*'s become *As.*)

Some writers prefer to add 's to form the plural of all numerals, letters, symbols, and words used as words.

Other Plural Forms

Irregular plurals are not formed by adding *s* or *es.*

IRREGULAR PLURALS				
SINGULAR	child	woman	tooth	mouse
PLURAL	child**ren**	wom**en**	t**ee**th	m**ice**

For some nouns, the singular and the plural forms are the same.

SAME SINGULAR AND PLURAL				
sheep	moose	corps	scissors	Chinese
salmon	trout	species	series	Swiss

Compound Nouns

The plurals of most compound nouns are formed in the same way other plural nouns are formed.

MOST COMPOUND NOUNS			
SINGULAR	stepchild	eyetooth	bookshelf
PLURAL	step**children**	eye**teeth**	book**shelves**

In compound words in which one part of the compound word modifies the other, make the word that is modified the plural.

SELF-MODIFYING COMPOUNDS			
SINGULAR	musk-ox	son-in-law	runner-up
PLURAL	musk-**oxen**	**sons**-in-law	**runners**-up

Foreign Plurals

The plurals of some foreign words are formed as they are in their original language. For some foreign words, there are two ways to form the plural.

FOREIGN WORDS				
SINGULAR	alga	alumnus	bacterium	ellipsis
PLURAL	algae	alumni	bacteria	ellipses
SINGULAR	formula	index	hippopotamus	
PLURAL	formulas or formulae	indexes or indices	hippopotamuses or hippopotami	

Check a dictionary when writing the plural of foreign words. When two forms are given, the first one is preferred.

 Listen and watch for foreign words that are becoming more commonly used. If you use them in your writing, be sure to form the plurals correctly.

chapeau—[noun, plural *chapeaux*, French] a hat
> Brett put his **chapeaux** on the shelf.

cravat—[noun, plural *cravats*, French] a scarf or a tie
> He bought two **cravats** in the shirt department.

PRACTICE YOUR SKILLS

● Check Your Understanding
Forming Plurals

Write the plural form for each item. If you are not sure about the correct form, check a dictionary.

1. memorandum
2. genus
3. stylus
4. thesis
5. nucleus
6. *but*
7. 8
8. 1890
9. dormouse
10. grandchild
11. die
12. ?
13. goose
14. goldfinch
15. tempo

Forming Plurals

Decide if the underlined plurals in these paragraphs are formed correctly. Check a dictionary if you're not certain. If any of the underlined plurals are incorrectly formed, write the correct forms.

Everyone knows something about dude ranches, where tenderfoots go to pretend they are cowpokes. Probably fewer people have heard of tourist farms because there hasn't been much publicity in the mediums yet. Tourist farms are one of the vacation phenomenons of the late 1990s. These farms offer city-dwellers who spend their workdays in offices the opportunity to experience life as their forefathers (and foremothers) might have in the 1890's. Parents and their childs spend their vacations on working farms, not as bystanders or looker-ons, but as farmhands. They plow fields and plant crops. They feed the poultries and collect the eggs. They milk the dairy cattles. They pick fruits from orchards. They learn the importance of windmills and other farm apparatus to traditional farms. If the windmills do not turn, the guests will help figure out how to pump water for the sheeps and other farm animals. Familys might spend mornings picking buckets of blackberrys, which later become pies, jellys, and jams. Farms may not be ideal vacation spots for couch potatoes or sticks-in-the-mud, but for people looking for relief from stress, farms can be ideal.

APPLY TO WRITING

Travel Brochure: *Plurals*

Imagine that this picture is an illustration for an advertising brochure for a vacation farm. You are an ad writer, and it is your job to write the copy for the brochure. Write one or two paragraphs that tell about the fun folks can have if they spend their vacations on farms. Use at least ten plural nouns in your brochure copy.

Spelling Numbers

When you are writing, you may be unsure whether you should write a number as a numeral or in words. The following generalizations can help you decide.

Numerals or Number Words

Spell out numbers that can be written in one or two words. Use numerals for other numbers. Always spell out a number that begins a sentence.

> Our journey lasted **fifteen** days.
>
> We traveled **3220** miles, from Portland, Maine, to Portland, Oregon.
>
> **Three hundred eighty-seven miles** was the farthest we traveled in one day.

Be consistent. When you have many numbers in a passage, use numerals for them all.

> We traveled an average of **230** miles a day, but one day we went **387** miles and another day we traveled only **95** miles.

Ordinal Numbers

Always spell out numbers used to tell the order.

> On the **first** day, we got a very late start.
> By the **tenth** day, we were getting tired of traveling.

 Word Alert Use ordinal words to represent the names of streets numbered first through tenth. For street names greater than tenth, use ordinal figures: numbers ending in *st, nd, rd,* and *th.*

Fifth Avenue   44th Street   33rd Street

Other Uses of Numerals

Use numerals in dates, addresses, times of day, and statistics and for numbers that identify.

USES OF NUMERALS			
DATES	September **9, 2001**	A.D. **1066**	**500** B.C.
ADDRESSES	**220** West End Avenue Hudson, OH **43210-2104**		
TIME	**9:45** A.M. **7:15** P.M. (If you use *o'clock,* then write the hour: **six** o'clock)		
STATISTICS	**90** degrees **16** ounces **51** percent **47** points		
NUMBERS THAT IDENTIFY	Route **66** Channel **11** Room **213** Box **549** pages **11–17**		

PRACTICE YOUR SKILLS

● Check Your Understanding
Spelling Numbers

 If the underlined number is written correctly, write C. If it is written incorrectly, rewrite it correctly.

1. Grandma received <u>80</u> birthday cards on her <u>eightieth</u> birthday.

2. On the <u>17th</u> of July, the hottest day of the summer, the temperature soared to a humid <u>ninety-nine</u> degrees.

3. Our <u>1st</u> dog weighed <u>47</u> pounds, but the new puppy will weigh about <u>80</u> pounds when it is grown.

4. It's almost <u>5</u> o'clock, and in <u>60</u> minutes, <u>12</u> people will walk through that door, expecting dinner.

5. The drawing on page <u>thirty-nine</u> shows the Great Pyramid of Khufu, which was built in <u>twenty-six eighty</u> B.C. and is one of the <u>Seven</u> Wonders of the Ancient World.

6. A sonnet is <u>14</u> lines of iambic pentameter; each line has <u>10</u> beats and every <u>2nd</u> beat is emphasized.

7. The final score was <u>ninety-five</u> to <u>ninety-three</u>, and Channel <u>Three</u> is showing game highlights at <u>11</u> o'clock.

8. Phillis Wheatley, the <u>1st</u> published African American poet, was kidnapped from Africa when she was <u>7</u>; she published her first book of poems when she was <u>17</u>.

9. In <u>1803</u>, the United States purchased <u>eight hundred twenty-eight thousand</u> square miles of land from France at a cost of about <u>four</u> cents an acre.

10. For <u>36</u> seasons, the Major League record for home runs was <u>61</u>, but Negro League player Josh Gibson, who died in 1947, had a season record of <u>89</u> homers.

● Connect to the Writing Process: Editing
Writing Numbers

Geography Topic **Rewrite this paragraph, correcting any mistakes in writing numbers.**

Of the 48 contiguous United States, Minnesota is the state located farthest north. Minnesota covers a total of eighty-four thousand four hundred two square miles, and 4,567,267 people lived there in 1990, making Minnesota the 12th largest in size and 20th in population.

8 percent of all Minnesotans live in Minneapolis, the state's largest city. With a population of three hundred sixty-eight thousand three hundred eighty-three, Minneapolis ranks 42nd among the country's 50 largest cities. Minneapolis ranks much higher when it comes to quality of life. 6,000 acres of the city are devoted to parks, and a total of 5.5 square miles are covered by water. There are one hundred fifty-three parks in the city's park system, and there are 12 lakes within the city limits.

Prefixes and Suffixes

A **prefix** is one or more syllables placed in front of a base word to form a new word. The base word's spelling does not change.

PREFIXES	
anti + toxin = **anti**toxin	**re** + enact = **re**enact
re + introduce = **re**introduce	**over** + rule = **over**rule
pre + suppose = **pre**suppose	**in** + animate = **in**animate

When the prefix re– *is followed by a word that begins with* e, *some writers prefer to hyphenate the word:* re + enact = re-enact.

Word Alert

The prefix *anti–* and the prefix *ante–* sound alike, but don't confuse them. Their meanings are quite different.

anti—[prefix] adds the meaning "against" or "opposite"

> Many college students were part of the **anti-war** movement of the 1960s.
> Raising interest rates is an **anti-inflation** strategy.
> Vitamin K is a common **antitoxin**.

ante—[prefix] adds the meaning "before" or "prior"

> In architecture, **antebellum** means before the Civil War and *prewar* means before World War II.
> Many buildings in Boston **antedate** the Revolutionary War.

A **suffix** is one or more syllables added at the end of a base word to change its part of speech and possibly also its meaning.

Suffixes –*ness* and –*ly*

The suffixes –*ness* and –*ly* are added to most base words without any spelling changes.

–NESS AND –LY	
even + **ness** = even**ness**	usual + **ly** = usual**ly**
great + **ness** = great**ness**	friend + **ly** = friend**ly**

Words Ending in *e*

Drop the final *e* in the base word when adding a suffix that begins with a vowel.

SUFFIXES WITH VOWELS	
imagine + **ary** = imagin**ary**	note + **able** = not**able**
refuse + **al** = refus**al**	destine + **y** = destin**y**

Keep the final *e* when the suffix begins with a consonant.

	SUFFIXES WITH CONSONANTS	
EXAMPLES	excite + **ment** = excite**ment**	
	grace + **ful** = grace**ful**	
EXCEPTIONS	judge + **ment** = judg**ment**	awe + **ful** = aw**ful**
	true + **ly** = tru**ly**	mile + **age** = mile**age**

When the base word ends with *ce* or *ge*, the final *e* must stay to retain the soft sound of the consonant. In some base words ending with *ce*, *e* is changed to *i* before adding a suffix that begins with a vowel.

CE OR *GE*	
change + **able** = change**able**	courage + **ous** = courage**ous**
notice + **able** = notice**able**	grace + **ous** = grac**ious**

Word Alert

Pronounce the difference between *re'fuse* and *refuse'* by stressing the correct syllable. If you add a suffix to *refuse'* and mispronounce it, the word will not make sense.

refuse'—[verb] to express unwillingness to believe or to participate

> I **refuse'** to watch the news coverage.

re'fuse—[noun] trash or garbage

> The disaster left **re'fuse** throughout the city.

refuse' + **al** = **refus'al**

> I accept your **refus'al** to watch.

PRACTICE YOUR SKILLS

● Check Your Understanding
Adding Prefixes and Suffixes

Combine these base words and prefixes or suffixes. Remember to make any necessary spelling changes.

1. dis + appear

2. re + elect

3. nerve + ous

4. imitate + ion

5. ir + regular

6. use + able

7. im + mobile + ity

8. under + rate

9. space + ous

10. store + age

11. argue + ment

12. manage + able

13. outrage + ous

14. grieve + ous

15. final + ly

16. true + ly

17. co + operate

18. race + al

19. style + ish

20. arrange + ment

● Connect to the Writing Process: Editing
Spelling Words with Prefixes and Suffixes

General Interest **Locate the words in this paragraph that have prefixes or suffixes, and rewrite correctly those that are misspelled.**

   The nineteenth century saw the establishment of many utopian communities. Often founded in lovly locations, these communities were based on a combineation of socialism and religious commitment. "From each according to his gifts to each according to his needs" is a statment of the harmony and fairness these communities truely struggled to attain. Each member worked for the benefit and betterment of all members. Unfortuneately, self-interest is more natureal to humankind than concern for communal good. Too often selfishness and self-involvment stood in opposetion to the achievment of true community. As a result, many utopian communities ultimatly failed.

Words Ending with *y*

Keep the *y* when adding a suffix to words that end in a vowel and *y*. Change *y* to *i* when adding a suffix to words that end in a consonant and *y*.

SUFFIXES WITH *Y*		
EXAMPLES	employ + **able** = employ**able** pay + **ment** = pay**ment** ally + **ance** = all**iance** merry + **ly** = merr**ily**	
EXCEPTIONS	rely + **ing** = rely**ing** hobby + **ist** = hobby**ist**	day + **ly** = da**ily** shy + **ness** = shy**ness**

Doubling the Final Consonant

Double the final consonant when adding a suffix that begins with a vowel if the base word satisfies both these conditions: (1) It has only one syllable or is stressed on the final syllable and (2) It ends in one consonant preceded by one vowel.

DOUBLE CONSONANTS	
ONE-SYLLABLE WORDS	hop + ing = ho**pp**ing wet + est = we**tt**est fog + y = fo**gg**y
FINAL SYLLABLE STRESSED	upset + ing = upse**tt**ing permit + ed = permi**tt**ed rebel + ion = rebe**ll**ion

Word Alert

Don't confuse *personal* and *personnel*. *Personnel* is the French word for *personal,* but in English it has a special meaning.

personal—[adjective] specific to a certain person; done in person; involving human beings

> This store is my **personal** favorite.
> Customers receive **personal** attention.
> The management values **personal** relationships.

personnel—[noun] people employed by a business establishment

> The store's **personnel** are well trained and courteous.

Words Ending with *c*

When adding a suffix that begins with *e, i,* or *y* to a word that ends with a vowel and *c,* do not double the final *c.* Instead add the letter *k* after the *c* to retain the hard *c* sound.

FINAL *C*	
picnic + **ing** = picni**ck**ing	colic + **y** = coli**ck**y

PRACTICE YOUR SKILLS

● **Check Your Understanding**
Adding Suffixes

Combine these base words and suffixes. Remember to make any necessary spelling changes.

1. lobby + ist
2. deny + al
3. vary + ance
4. study + ing
5. permit + ed
6. transmit + al
7. compel + ed
8. regret + able
9. politic + ing
10. worry + some
11. deter + ent
12. occur + ence
13. rely + able
14. shellac + ed
15. thirty + ish
16. person + al
17. panic + y
18. apply + ance
19. mimic + ed
20. profit + able

Adding Suffixes

General Interest **Read these paragraphs, looking for words with suffixes that are spelled incorrectly. Write each word correctly.**

Many people experience recuring dreams. These dreams sometimes reveal things about the dreamer's personallity. Some people's recurring dreams are undenyably their very own. They are unique and unlike any other. Other people have dreams that are shared, with some personnal varyation, by many people.

A common recurring dream is the one in which the dreamer must take the final exam in a course she either didn't know or forgot she was registerred for. This can be a very upseting dream, and the dreamer is often panicing when he or she wakes up. Experts say that this dream is typickally experienced by people who are worried—sometimes excessively—about doing well.

Another dream that is reported frequentely to experts includes the action of jumping or flying. The dreamer often is comforted by the upward movement. Experts say that this dream usualy reveals a subconscious acknowledegment of the ability to overcome obstacles or to move beyond challenging situations. Those who have recuring dreams of this kind are sincerly appreciatetive of the positive explanation.

APPLY TO WRITING

Narrative: *Suffixes*

Write a story about a recurring dream similar to either one described on page L569. Create a character who might have such a dream. Describe what happens in the dream and what the character does—in the dream and upon waking. Use five of the following words with suffixes in your writing.

- *panic + y*
- *regret + able*
- *scary + est*
- *early + est*
- *enjoy + able*

- *compel + ed*
- *excel + ence*
- *deny + ing*
- *refuse + al*
- *prepare + ation*

✔ QuickCheck Mixed Practice

Add the prefix or suffix to each of these base words, and write the new word.

1. admit + ance
2. lazy + ness
3. day + ly
4. argue + ment
5. un + notice + able
6. repel + ing
7. hobby + ist
8. acknowledge + ment
9. buoy + ancy
10. re + place + able

11. courage + ous
12. lonely + ness
13. face + al
14. frolic + ing
15. picnic + er
16. mis + spell
17. infer + ed
18. il + logical
19. even + ness
20. study + ous

Make it your goal to learn to spell these fifty words this year. Use them in your writing, and practice writing them until spelling them correctly comes automatically.

accommodate	espionage	perceive
adolescence	fission	physician
allegiance	fulfill	plagiarism
anonymous	guarantee	psychology
atmosphere	harassment	reminiscent
bibliography	hypocrisy	rendezvous
bizarre	initiative	specimen
boulevard	interference	strategic
camouflage	larynx	symbolic
caricature	maintenance	symmetrical
complexion	maneuver	theoretical
conscientious	melancholy	thesaurus
curriculum	mischievous	tyranny
despair	naive	unscrupulous
dilemma	obsolete	vehicle
dilettante	orchestra	villain
environment	parallelism	

Spelling Words Correctly

Write the letter preceding the misspelled word in each group. Then write the word, spelling it correctly.

1. (A) proceed   (B) sharing   (C) stereos
   (D) acurracy   (E) rendezvous

2. (A) deceive   (B) occurred   (C) managable
   (D) eyeglasses   (E) forgettable

3. (A) piece   (B) excede   (C) feign
   (D) fifes   (E) echoes

4. (A) thesaurus   (B) usualy   (C) descendant
   (D) gauge   (E) notaries public

5. (A) rarity   (B) chefs   (C) alloys
   (D) rein   (E) rehersal

6. (A) apparant   (B) concede   (C) referral
   (D) patios   (E) outrageous

7. (A) releive   (B) seize   (C) veil
   (D) wives   (E) thesis

8. (A) leisure   (B) overrule   (C) alumnuses
   (D) obedient   (E) bizarre

9. (A) changeable   (B) disimilar   (C) loneliness
   (D) mosquito   (E) bushes

10. (A) recurence   (B) license   (C) overture
    (D) sieve   (E) neither

Another Look

Spelling Patterns *(pages 549–551)*

When the vowel sound is long *e*, write *ei* after *c* and *ie* after other
consonant letters. When the sound is long *a* or any vowel sound other
than long *e*, write *ei*. The generalizations do not apply if the *i* and *e*
are in different syllables.

The syllable that sounds like "seed" can be spelled *sede*, *ceed*, or *cede*.

Plurals *(pages 552–560)*

To form the plural of nouns ending in *s, ch, sh, x,* or *z,* add *es*.

Change the *y* to *i* and add *es* to a noun ending in a consonant and *y*.

Add *es* to form the plural of many nouns that end with a consonant and
o. For some nouns ending in *f* or *fe*, change the *f* to *v* and add *es* or *s*.

In compound words in which one part of the compound modifies the
other, make the word that is modified the plural.

Spelling Numbers *(pages 561–563)*

Spell out numbers that can be written in one or two words. Always spell
out a number that is used to tell the order or that begins a sentence.

Use numerals in dates, addresses, times of day, and statistics and for
numbers that identify.

Prefixes and Suffixes *(pages 564–570)*

Drop the final *e* in the base word when adding a suffix that begins with
a vowel. Keep the final *e* when the suffix begins with a consonant.

When the base word ends in *ce* or *ge*, the final *e* must stay in order to
retain the soft sound of the consonant. In some base words ending in
ce, *e* is changed to *i* before adding a suffix that begins with a vowel.
Change *y* to *i* when adding a suffix to words that end in a consonant
and *y*.

Double the final consonant when you add a suffix that begins with a
vowel if the base word satisfies both these conditions: (1) It has only
one syllable or is stressed on the final syllable and (2) It ends in one
consonant preceded by one vowel.

When you add a suffix that begins with *e* or *i* to a word that ends with a
vowel and *c*, do not double the final *c*. Instead add the letter *k* after
the *c* to retain the hard *c* sound.

Posttest

Directions

Read the passage. Write the letter of the answer that correctly respells each underlined word. If the word is correct, write **D**.

EXAMPLE   This is a <u>remarkable</u> book about a young boy.
                              (1)

      1 A   remarkeable
          B   remarkible
          C   remmarkable
          D   No error

ANSWER   **1 D**

The *Catcher in the Rye* is an <u>extreamly</u> popular book about
                                   (1)
<u>adolesence</u> and coming of age. The hero, Holden Caulfield, runs
(2)
away from his prep school as Christmas <u>vacation</u> begins. On the
                                              (3)
<u>bulavards</u> of New York, he finds himself involved in a <u>serie</u> of
(4)   **(5)**
adventures.

Holden is a <u>fascinateing</u> character, at once both worldly and
                    (6)
<u>niave</u>. His <u>disatisfaction</u> with the adult world around him is
(7)   **(8)**
evident as he rails against <u>hypocracy</u> and dishonesty. Holden's
                                (9)
feelings are <u>remaniscent</u> of the teenage rebellions that took place
                    (10)
in the 1960s.

1	**A**	extremally	**6**	**A**	fastenating
	B	extremely		**B**	fascinating
	C	exstreamly		**C**	fascanating
	D	No error		**D**	No error
2	**A**	adolescence	**7**	**A**	nyive
	B	adolecense		**B**	naiv
	C	adolesense		**C**	naive
	D	No error		**D**	No error
3	**A**	vacasion	**8**	**A**	disatissfaction
	B	vaccasion		**B**	dissatisfaction
	C	vacateon		**C**	dissatisfashion
	D	No error		**D**	No error
4	**A**	boulevards	**9**	**A**	hippocracy
	B	bullavards		**B**	hypocrasy
	C	boulavards		**C**	hypocrisy
	D	No error		**D**	No error
5	**A**	series	**10**	**A**	reminiscent
	B	serieses		**B**	remeniscent
	C	seria		**C**	reminicent
	D	No error		**D**	No error

A Study Guide
for Academic Success

Success in school is often measured by how well you perform on tests, both in your daily classes and in standardized testing situations. Developing good study skills and test-taking strategies, therefore, may be your key to success as a student.

There are a number of effective methods you can use when studying for tests. Many of these may seem simple—just using common sense—as they are outlined in this chapter. However, if you employ the strategies suggested in the following pages, you will develop the skills you need to tackle specific types of problems that occur regularly on tests.

The end result, however, is not simply a higher grade for a class or better scores on exams. Your ability to decipher the main idea of a reading passage or correct errors within a text enhances your ability to discriminate between accurate, well-written texts and those that are incorrect, biased or ambiguously written. You will rely on these skills throughout your life.

Learning Study Skills

Tests are designed to evaluate how much you know about certain subjects. How well you do on these tests, however, often reflects how effectively you study and prepare assignments on a daily basis. How effective are your study habits?

Strategies for Effective Studying

- Choose an area that is well lighted and free from distractions.
- Equip your study area with everything you need for reading and writing, including, if possible, a dictionary, a thesaurus, and other print and non-print reference tools.
- Keep a notebook for recording assignments and due dates.
- Allow plenty of time. Begin your assignments early.

 Adjusting Reading Rate to Purpose

Whenever you read, it is important to understand your purpose for reading the material. Reading a story for entertainment requires different kinds of reading strategies than reading a textbook to learn important information. Reading textbooks requires an organized approach that enables you to focus your attention and achieve your purpose. The following strategies can help you read textbook material more effectively.

Scanning

Scanning is reading to get a general impression and to prepare for learning about a subject. Scan a chapter or section by reading the title, headings, subheadings, picture captions, words and phrases in boldface and italics, parenthetical and appositive phrases, information set off by dashes, and any focus questions to determine quickly what the reading is about and what questions to keep in mind as you read.

Skimming

After scanning a chapter, section, or article, skim the introduction, the topic sentence and summary sentence of each paragraph, and the conclusion. **Skimming** is reading to identify quickly the purpose, thesis, main ideas, and supporting ideas.

Close Reading

After skimming a selection to learn the main ideas, read it more slowly to learn the details. **Close reading** is for locating specific information, following the logic of an argument, or comprehending the meaning or significance of information.

● Taking Notes

Note-taking is an important skill for helping you remember what you have read in a textbook or heard in class. Three methods for taking notes are the informal outline, the graphic organizer, and the summary.

In an **informal outline**, words and phrases are used to record main ideas and important details. When you study for an objective test, such as a multiple-choice test, an informal outline will help you easily see and review the important facts and details.

In a **graphic organizer,** words and phrases are arranged in a visual pattern to indicate main ideas and supporting details, among many other possibilities. A graphic organizer, or a cognitive map, is an excellent tool to use for studying information for an objective test, for an open-ended assessment, or for writing an essay. The visual organizer allows you, instantly, to see important information and its relationship to other ideas.

In a **summary**, sentences are used to express important ideas in your own words. Writing summaries is useful in preparing for an essay test because you must think about the information, see relationships among ideas, and draw conclusions.

In the following passage from a textbook, the essential information is underlined.

Thomas Hardy had two distinct literary careers, the first as a novelist and the second as a poet. His deepening pessimism in *Jude the Obscure,* coupled with the public burning of the book by an Anglican bishop, turned him away from novel writing and toward poetry.

Until the age of fifty-eight, Hardy was known only as a novelist. Among his best-known novels are *The Return of the Native* and *The Mayor of Casterbridge.* These novels show Hardy's pervasive gloominess, yet his rustic characters also reveal an underlying sense of humor. Hardy considered himself a meliorist, one who believes that things tend to improve.

For the last 30 years of his life, Hardy wrote nothing but poetry. His great epic drama, *The Dynasts,* is less well known than his shorter poems, such as "The Man He Killed," "Channel Firing," and "In Time of 'The Breaking of Nations.'" These poems tend to be sad and pessimistic, like his novels, but they also suggest the heroic dignity of humanity's struggle.

Thomas Hardy

Informal Outline:

1. Until age fifty-eight—known only as a novelist
   a. Novels show gloominess but also humor
   b. Meliorism—belief things tend to improve
2. Last 30 years of life—wrote only poetry
   a. Short poems most familiar
   b. Display sadness and pessimism
   c. Reveal heroic dignity of human beings

Graphic Organizer:

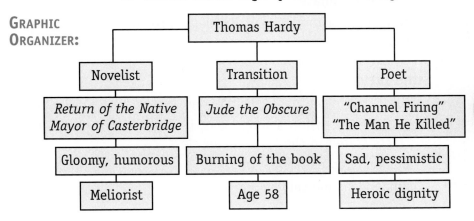

Thomas Hardy

Novelist — Transition — Poet

Return of the Native / *Mayor of Casterbridge* — *Jude the Obscure* — "Channel Firing" / "The Man He Killed"

Gloomy, humorous — Burning of the book — Sad, pessimistic

Meliorist — Age 58 — Heroic dignity

SUMMARY:
Thomas Hardy
Hardy had two different writing careers. He was a novelist until age fifty-eight and a poet thereafter. His most well-known novels are gloomy but show an underlying humor. Hardy believed that things tend to improve. His short poems, for which he is best known, display sadness and pessimism but also reveal humans' heroic dignity.

Strategies for Taking Notes

- Label your notes with the title and page numbers of the chapter or section, or the topic and date of the class.
- Record only the main ideas and important details.
- Use the titles, subtitles, and words in special type or color to help you select the most important information.
- Use your own words; do not copy word for word.
- Use as few words as possible.

Modified Outline

- Use words and phrases.
- Use main ideas for headings.
- List any supporting details under each heading.

Graphic Organizer

- Use a logical visual representation.
- Use words or phrases.
- Place main ideas and supporting details to show relationships.

Summary

- Write complete sentences, using your own words.
- Show the relationship among ideas, being careful to use only the facts stated in the textbook or class.
- Include only essential information.
- Organize ideas logically.

Preparing Subject-Area Assignments

Using the strategies you have learned for reading textbooks, taking notes, and preparing for tests can be valuable when doing assignments in any subject area; using those study aids specific to various subject areas can be of special help. Mathematics and science texts often list important rules, formulas, charts, graphs, equations, or models. Consequently, you may spend much of your study time in these areas applying rules and practicing your analytical and computational skills along with problem-solving strategies. History materials, on the other hand, often emphasize such skills as analyzing and interpreting maps, charts, graphs, chronologies, time lines, documents, and statistical data, which you will use in preparing assignments. Use the following study tips to help you prepare assignments for whatever subject area you are studying.

 Tips for Preparing Subject-Area Assignments

- Carefully read all directions.
- Adjust your reading rate to suit your purpose.
- Take notes from both readings and classes. Use the technique of highlighting to help you remember important information, such as names, dates, terms, or facts.
- Be organized. For example, you will find it helpful to keep your reading notes and class notes on the same topic together in your notebook or journal.
- Keep a separate list of vocabulary words, key terms and concepts, or rules and equations for review.
- Keep a running list of questions that arise as you read, listen, or review. Seek answers promptly. If there is anything you do not understand, get help.
- Participate in study groups, following the principles of cooperative learning.
- In preparing for tests, leave ample time for study. Focus on anticipating and answering the questions you will be asked by your teacher. Ask for clarification of concepts.
- Practice applying what you have learned using the specialized learning aids and skills for the particular subject area in which you are working.

Taking Standardized Tests

A standardized test assesses your abilities, skill, progress, and achievement. One section of the test assesses your understanding of the meaning of words and the way they are used in sentences. Questions within this section are often analogy questions, which assess your ability to understand word relationships; and sentence-completion questions, which require you to use the context to complete a sentence.

Standardized tests also include reading comprehension sections and writing assignments. Your skills are often checked with objective questions about grammar, usage, and mechanics as well as with open-ended questions and time-limited essays.

The best way to prepare for taking a standardized test, as for any other kind of test, is to work conscientiously on class work all along. Reading widely and becoming familiar with the standard testing formats is also good preparation.

Strategies for Taking Standardized Tests

- Read the test directions carefully. Answer sample questions to be sure you understand what the test requires.

- Relax. Concentrate on doing the best you can.

- Preview the whole test by quickly skimming. This will give you an overview of the kinds of questions on the test.

- Plan your time carefully, allotting a certain amount of time to each part of the test.

- Answer first the questions you find easiest. Skip those you find too hard, coming back to them if you have enough time.

- Read all choices before you answer. If you are not sure of an answer, eliminate choices that are obviously wrong. Making an educated guess is usually wise, but check the test directions to find out if you will be penalized for guessing.

- If you have time, check your answers. Look for omissions and careless errors on your answer sheet.

Analogies

Analogy questions assess your skill at seeing word relation-ships. Your first step is to decide how the words in capital letters are related. In the analogy HAND : FINGER, for example, the relationship is whole-to-part. The hand (whole) includes the finger (part). Your next step is to find the pair of words among the choices that shows the same relationship. The word order must be exactly the same in the answer as it is in the question. Determine the correct answer in the following analogy.

HAND : FINGER ::
(A) author : story   (B) top : bottom   (C) state : city
(D) handle : mug   (E) joke : laughter

(The answer is *(C) state : city* because it contains the only whole-to-part relationship among the choices.)

Sometimes analogies are written in sentence form.

Decipher is to *decode* as *proclaim* is to ■.
(A) influence   (B) acknowledge   (C) announce
(D) annoy   (E) encode

(The first two italicized words are synonyms. Therefore, the correct answer is *announce,* a synonym for *proclaim.*)

Knowing some common types of analogies, such as those in the following chart, will help you figure out word relationships.

COMMON TYPES OF ANALOGIES	
Analogy	**Example**
word : synonym	evade : escape
word : antonym	feasible : impossible
part : whole	caboose : train
cause : effect	exercise : fitness
worker : tool	mason : trowel
worker : product	publisher : magazine
item : category	lobster : crustacean
item : purpose	bus : transport

● Check Your Understanding
Recognizing Analogies

Write the relationship using the preceding list of analogy types. Then write the letter of the word pair that has the same relationship as the word pair in capital letters.

1. VERTEBRATE : MAMMAL ::

(A) crustacean : snake   (B) money : bank

(C) fog : precipitation   (D) element : copper

(E) silver : ore

2. INSPECT : EXAMINE ::

(A) condemn : encourage   (B) cease : begin

(C) attempt : try   (D) lead : inspire

(E) inform : confuse

3. TRIVIAL : IMPORTANT ::

(A) windy : wet   (B) patron : client

(C) lazy : tired   (D) complete : finished

(E) stale : fresh

4. EAVES : ROOF ::

(A) road : driver   (B) forest : tree

(C) steps : staircase   (D) germ : bacteria

(E) pen : ink

5. BRUSH : PAINTER ::

(A) sports : competitor   (B) jeweler : gem

(C) stonecutter : chisel   (D) shirt : price

(E) bowl : chef

● Check Your Understanding
Completing Analogies

Use the chart on page L583 to determine the relationship of each analogy; then complete the analogy by writing the letter of the word that best completes the analogy.

6. *Purpose* is to *intention* as *surplus* is to ▩.

    (A) excess   (B) equipment   (C) storage

    (D) discussion   (E) determination

7. *Heat* is to *expansion* as *wind* is to ▩.

    (A) erosion   (B) donation   (C) dismissal

    (D) breeze   (E) temperature

8. *Talent* is to *achievement* as *genius* is to ▩.

    (A) innovation   (B) prodigy   (C) failure

    (D) shrewdness   (E) underachievement

9. *House* is to *frame* as *body* is to ▩.

    (A) skin   (B) torso   (C) joint

    (D) skeleton   (E) brain

10. *Merge* is to *separate* as *flippant* is to ▩.

    (A) swimming   (B) unbalanced   (C) talkative

    (D) thrown   (E) respectful

● Sentence-Completion Tests

Sentence-completion questions assess your ability to use the context to complete a sentence. These questions ask you to figure out what word or words make the most sense in the blanks of a sentence. Although the sentences cover a wide variety of subjects, they do not require that you have a prior knowledge of those subjects. By using key words, you should be able to determine the answers from the context alone.

First read the following sentence from beginning to end. Then choose the most appropriate word to complete the sentence.

> Because you failed to meet the April 30 deadline and have since refused to say when or whether you will complete the work, we are forced to ▩ our contract with you.
> (A) honor   (B) discuss   (C) terminate
> (D) negotiate   (E) extend

(The answer is *(C) terminate.* The rest of the sentence clearly suggests that the contract has not been honored and that the time for negotiating has passed. The other choices do not make sense in the context of the sentence.)

Sentence-completion questions sometimes have two blanks in the same sentence. Find the correct answer in this example.

Despite ■ to the contrary, the detective was ■ that Mrs. Arnold had mislaid her jewels.
(A) suspicions . . . pleased   (B) evidence . . . convinced
(C) feelings . . . certain   (D) confessions . . . depressed
(E) furor . . . surprised

(The answer is *(B) evidence . . . convinced.* The key words that help you determine this are *contrary* and *mislaid.* *Feelings . . . certain* contains a contradiction, while the other choices do not make sense in the context of the sentence.)

When you answer an item like this, read the sentence to yourself with the words in place to be sure it makes sense.

PRACTICE YOUR SKILLS

● Check Your Understanding
Completing Sentences

Write the letter of the word or words that best complete each of the following sentences.

1. Since we had to meet at the station at exactly 2:35 P.M., we decided to ■ our watches.

(A) synchronize   (B) ignore   (C) wind

(D) consider   (E) hide

2. An economist stated that the ■ of foreign currency could stimulate the small country's economy.

(A) influx   (B) suppression   (C) study

(D) suitability   (E) lack

3. The giraffe is ■, feeding only on plants.

(A) quadruped   (B) hoofed   (C) herbivorous

(D) huge   (E) endangered

4. Her acceptance speech was so long that we can print only an ■ of it in the newspaper.

(A) extension   (B) array   (C) excerpt

(D) overture   (E) understatement

5. As a young man, the actor was slim and lithe; but as the years passed, he became a ■ character actor.

(A) loose-limbed   (B) portly   (C) well-paid

(D) forgotten   (E) lackluster

● Check Your Understanding
Completing Sentences with Two Blanks

Write the letter of the pair of words that best completes each of the following sentences.

6. The detective claimed that the suspect, in his ■ to leave the scene, ■ left a laundry ticket behind.

(A) aversion . . . randomly   (B) haste . . . inadvertently

(C) anger . . . purposely   (D) decision . . . foolishly

(E) plot . . . absentmindedly

7. Great Britain, with its long coastline and ■ ports, is one of the leading ■ nations in the world.

(A) many . . . agricultural   (B) outstanding . . . industrial

(C) excellent . . . nautical   (D) crowded . . . financial

(E) overabundant . . . debtor

8. When the ■ was cut to 18 players, Phil was retained despite his ■ playing.

(A) team . . . superb   (B) choice . . . exuberant

(C) staff . . . improved   (D) roster . . . inconsistent

(E) management . . . unsatisfactory

9. After a lengthy discussion, the ▣ of the group was that our ▣ affairs should be handled by an accountant.

(A) disagreement . . . legal   (B) intent . . . basic

(C) equality . . . fund-raising   (D) vote . . . important

(E) consensus . . . budgetary

10. We agreed that any ▣ who could play both Juliet and Lady Macbeth had to be very ▣.

(A) woman . . . elderly   (B) performer . . . tricky

(C) actress . . . versatile   (D) stagehand . . . flexible

(E) amateur . . . professional

Reading Comprehension Tests

Reading comprehension tests assess your ability to understand and analyze written passages. The information you need to answer the questions may be either directly stated or implied in the passage. You must study, analyze, and interpret a passage in order to answer the questions. The following strategies can help you answer such questions.

> **Strategies for Answering Comprehension Questions**
> - Begin by skimming the questions that follow the passage.
> - Read the passage carefully and closely. Notice the main ideas, organization, style, and key words.
> - Study all possible answers. Avoid choosing one answer the moment you think it is a reasonable choice.
> - Use only the information in the passage when you answer the questions. Do not rely on your own knowledge or ideas on this kind of test.

Most reading comprehension questions will ask you to interpret or evaluate one or more of the following characteristics of a written passage.

- **Main idea** At least one question will usually focus on the central idea of the passage. Remember that the main idea of a passage covers all sections of that passage, not just one section or paragraph.

- **Supporting details** Questions about supporting details test your ability to identify the statements in the passage that back up the main idea.

- **Implied meanings** In some passages not all information is directly stated. Some questions ask you to interpret information that the author has merely implied.

- **Tone** Questions on tone require that you interpret or analyze the author's attitude toward his or her subjects.

PRACTICE YOUR SKILLS

Check Your Understanding
Reading Comprehension Passage

Read the passage and answer the questions that follow.

A pebble begins as part of a large rock and often ends up as part of a larger rock. As rocks erode, break away, become fragments, and are transported by water, they become pebbles. Pebbles are generally rounded and smooth, some more so than others. If the rounding and smoothing proceed far enough, the pebbles become gravel or sand. Although pebbles, gravel, and sand all exist independently, they can also form the basis of new rocks.

Pebbles of any size can be bonded together to form either a breccia or a conglomerate. Some rock fragments travel only a short distance by stream or river, and thus retain the sharp, angular features of the fragments produced by the original fracturing. If consolidation occurs at this point, the result is a breccia. A *breccia* is a rock formed by the natural cementing together of sharp, unrounded fragments into a fine-grained matrix.

As the traveling distance of the original eroded rock increases, rounding continues. The bonded rock that is made is called a *conglomerate*. Many of the pebbles in a conglomerate, unlike those in a breccia, will not have derived from rocks in the immediate vicinity. Some will have been transported long distances, perhaps moved along a seacoast by the action of tides. One famous deposit is in Devon, England. The pebbles in this conglomerate are thought to have come from the rock of the mountains in Brittany, France, and to have been washed to England by the tides.

1. The best title for the passage is

    (A) Rocks, Wind, and Waves.

    (B) What Is a Conglomerate?

    (C) A Brief Look at Geology.

    (D) The Life Cycle of Pebbles.

    (E) Pebbles at Budleigh Salterton.

2. Breccia contains sharp, angular pebbles because

    (A) there was no water to transport the pebbles.

    (B) the water molded the pebbles into that shape.

    (C) the pebbles did not go far in a stream or river.

    (D) some pebbles are too hard to round off.

    (E) cementing made the pebbles sharp.

3. The writer's attitude toward the subject of pebbles is

    (A) impassioned.

    (B) skeptical.

    (C) friendly.

    (D) pessimistic.

    (E) objective.

The Double Passage

Some tests may also ask you to read two passages together and then answer questions about each passage individually and about similarities and differences between the two. The questions about the individual passages are typically just like single-passage questions. The questions about both passages ask you to compare and contrast such issues as viewpoints, tones, and implied meanings. A short introduction that precedes the passages may help you anticipate the ways in which the passages are similar and different.

On these tests, both reading passages are presented first, followed by questions about Passage 1 and then questions about Passage 2. Then come the comparison questions. You may find it helpful to read Passage 1 first and immediately answer the questions related to that passage before you read Passage 2. When you have finished the Passage 1 questions, you can return to read the second passage and answer the remaining questions.

PRACTICE YOUR SKILLS

● Check Your Understanding
Reading for Comprehension with Double Passages

The following passages present two views of heroes and heroism. The first passage is from the introduction of a popular book about heroes and heroines in our time. The second is from a book on mythology by Edith Hamilton. Read each passage and answer the questions that follow.

Passage 1

In a simple society such as the Greeks' of three thousand years ago, the heroes' world was straightforward and uncomplicated. It was, in the words of Joseph Campbell, a world of "monomyths": it had single goals, definite and clear purposes. The heroes and heroines of that society spoke for and perpetuated humankind's goals and purposes. In more complicated societies, such as our own, heroes and heroines wear many faces because of their numerous responses to the varied needs of individuals, groups of people, and national purposes.

As a society's needs become more complicated, so too do the heroes and heroines; as people become more sophisticated, the heroes and heroines become less modeled on the conventional demigods of the past, less clear-cut and obvious. In a swiftly moving society like America today, heroes and heroines undergo rapid transformation. They frequently develop in ways and for purposes that are not immediately apparent. Twentieth-century American heroes and heroines, existing in a highly technological society and driven by the electronics of mass communication, change quickly. They are often hailed as heroic today and forgotten tomorrow. But though they may disappear rapidly, they serve useful and needed purposes while they endure. So we continue to create heroes and heroines because they can concentrate the power of the people—of a nation—and serve as the driving force for the movement and develop-ment of individuals and society.

Passage 2

The world of Norse mythology is a strange world. Asgard, the home of the gods, is unlike any other heaven men have dreamed of. No radiancy of joy is in it, no assurance of bliss. It is a grave and solemn place, over which hangs the threat of an inevitable doom. The gods know that a day will come when they will be destroyed. Sometime they will meet their enemies and go down beneath them to defeat and death. Asgard will fall in ruins. The cause the forces of good are fighting to defend against the forces of evil is hopeless. Nevertheless, the gods will fight for it to the end.

Necessarily the same is true of humanity. If the gods are finally helpless before evil, men and women must be more so. This is the conception of life which underlies the Norse religion, as somber a conception as the mind of man has ever given birth to. The only sustaining support possible for the human spirit, the one pure unsullied good man can hope to attain, is heroism; and heroism depends on lost causes. The hero can prove what he is only by dying. The power of good is shown not by triumphantly conquering evil, but by continuing to resist evil while facing certain defeat.

1. According to the author of Passage 1, which of the following factors best explains why heroes in Greek society differ from heroes of today?

(A) lack of monomyths

(B) mass communication

(C) technological advancements

(D) simple versus complicated societies

(E) development of nations

2. In relation to paragraph 1 in Passage 1, the purpose of paragraph 2 is mainly to

(A) define heroes.

(B) trace the development of heroes through the centuries.

(C) contrast contemporary heroes with ancient heroes.

(D) elaborate the point made in sentence 1.

(E) illustrate the concept of monomyth.

3. According to the author of Passage 2, heroism in Norse mythology is achieved by

(A) overcoming the forces of evil.

(B) triumphing over death.

(C) fighting to the death against forces of evil.

(D) accomplishing great deeds.

(E) mastering godlike powers.

4. According to the author of Passage 2, which describes mythology's sphere of influence in Norse culture?

(A) spiritual   (B) social   (C) political

(D) intellectual   (E) artistic

5. Which of the following ideas from Passage 1 holds true for the idea of heroism as described in Passage 2?

(A) Heroes undergo rapid transformation.

(B) Heroes may disappear rapidly.

(C) Heroes are not clear-cut and obvious.

(D) Heroes can concentrate the power of a people.

(E) Heroes are varied to reflect cultural diversity.

Tests of Standard Written English

An objective test of standard written English assesses your knowledge of writing skills. The test contains passages or sentences with underlined words, phrases, or punctuation. The underlined parts may contain errors in grammar, usage, mechanics, vocabulary, and spelling. You must find each error or, on some tests, identify the best way to revise a faulty sentence or passage.

Error Recognition

This kind of question tests grammar, usage, capitalization, punctuation, word choice, and spelling. As a rule, each item consists of a sentence with five underlined parts. Four of these underlined parts suggest possible errors in the sentence. The fifth indicates that there is no error. No sentence has more than one error. Read the following sentence carefully and identify the error, if there is one.

> The Pacific <u>Ocean</u> is 36,198 feet deep in the Mariana's
>   **A**
>
> Trench, even <u>deeper</u> <u>then</u> Mount Everest or the
>   **B**   **C**
>
> mountain K2 <u>is</u> high.
>   **D**
>
> (The answer is *C*. Standard usage requires *than* rather than *then* in this sentence.)

Sometimes you will find a sentence that contains no error. Be careful, however, before you choose *E* as the answer. The errors included in this kind of test are often common errors that are hard to notice.

Remember, however, that everything not underlined is presumed to be correct. You can often use the correct parts to help identify the error in the sentence.

● Check Your Understanding
Recognizing Errors in Writing

Write the letter of the underlined word or punctuation mark that is incorrect. If the sentence contains no error write *E*.

(1) The Reverend William Spooner, who's last name
    A   B
became a common noun, had an unusual quirk of speech.
                      C   D
(2) Spooners' quirk was to transpose the initial sounds of
    A   B
two or more words. (3) There are a great many examples of
C   D   A   B
his odd, humorous mistakes. (4) When Spooner spoke, "a
C   D   A
well-oiled bicycle," for example, would come out as "a well-
        B   C
boiled icicle". (5) Spooner was an experienced, knowledgeable
        D   A
teacher who his students liked and respected. (6) If you
        B   C   D
was to ask most of his students, they would say he was
A   B   C   D
unforgettable. (7) After all, how could anyone forget a man
                        A   B
who said, "Let me sew you to your sheet," when he intends
                                                        C
to show you to your seat? (8) Everyone who knew Reverend
                    D   A
Spooner had their own story to tell about him. (9) Still, as
        B   C   D
time went by, the old man's long service at New College,
                        A   B
Oxford, was all but forgotten. (10) Spoonerisms, however,
        C   D
are remembered to this day, and are the classic examples
                        A   B
used in all dictionary definitions of the word based on his
C   D
name.

Sentence Correction

These questions assess your ability to recognize appropriate phrasing. Instead of locating an error, you must select the best way to write a sentence. In this kind of question, part of the sentence is underlined. Following the sentence are five different ways of writing the underlined part. The first way shown, (A), is the same as the underlined part. The other four ways present alternatives. The choices may involve questions of grammar, usage, capitalization, punctuation, or diction. Your answer must not change the meaning of the sentence.

> We all agreed that the guest lecturer was well informed, articulate, and he had a nice personality.
>
> (A) he had a nice personality.
> (B) he had a pleasant personality.
> (C) a nice personality.
> (D) likeable.
> (E) nice personality wise.
>
> (The answer is (D). The problem with the original sentence, as well as with choices (B) and (C), is lack of parallelism. Choice (E) is parallel but contains an awkward construction. Notice that (D) includes a new adjective, *likeable*, although *personable* would have been satisfactory.)

PRACTICE YOUR SKILLS

● Check Your Understanding
Correcting Sentences

Write the letter of the correct or best way of phrasing the underlined part of each sentence.

1. "Fair is foul, wrote Shakespeare, and foul is fair."

    (A) foul, wrote Shakespeare, and

    (B) foul, "wrote Shakespeare, "and

    (C) foul", wrote Shakespeare, "and

    (D) foul," wrote Shakespeare, "and

    (E) foul," wrote Shakespeare, and

2. Each <u>of us in the audience hopes</u> to learn your views on the bond issue.

(A) of us in the audience hopes

(B) of we in the audience hopes

(C) of us in the audience hope

(D) of we in the audience hope

(E) member of the audience hope

3. The prince, along with all <u>his supporters, were observed coming toward</u> the village.

(A) his supporters, were observed coming toward

(B) his supporters were observed, coming toward

(C) his supporters, was observed coming toward

(D) his supporters, was observed, coming toward

(E) his' supporters, was observed coming toward

4. Was it Jacqueline who said, <u>Its not too late to get a collar for your puppy?</u>

(A) Its not too late to get a collar for your puppy?

(B) "Its not to late to get a collar for your puppy"?

(C) "It's not too late to get a collar for you're puppy?"

(D) It's not to late to get a collar for your puppy.

(E) "It's not too late to get a collar for your puppy"?

5. The <u>alarm should of begun</u> ringing by now.

(A) alarm should of begun

(B) alarm, it should of begun

(C) alarm should have begun

(D) alarm should have began

(E) alarm should of began

Revision-in-Context

Another type of question you may encounter on a standardized test is revision-in-context. You will be asked to read a brief essay, one that represents an early draft of a student's work. In the questions that follow the essay, you will be asked to choose the best revision of a sentence, group of sentences, or the essay as a whole and to demonstrate your understanding of the writer's intention.

PRACTICE YOUR SKILLS

● Check Your Understanding
Correcting Sentences

Carefully read the passage and answer the questions that follow.

(1) Recently, a questionnaire was developed that asked people to give their opinions. (2) What they were to give their opinions about was the value of leisure time. (3) Most people said that their favorite pastime was watching television. (4) Commenting on the quality of the shows, however, the programs were not very satisfying. (5) Most people felt that their time would be better spent if they pursued physical activities such as sports and athletics. (6) They felt such activities would make a noticeable change in the way they felt. (7) Unfortunately, they also felt there was little likelihood that they would take up exercise on a regular basis. (8) Many people, it seems, are willing to settle for so-so pastimes despite the fact that they know other pastimes might enhance the quality of their lives.

1. In relation to the rest of the passage, which of the following best describes the writer's intention in sentence (8)?
   (A) to restate the opening sentence
   (B) to draw a conclusion
   (C) to provide examples
   (D) to contrast active versus passive pastimes
   (E) to offer contradictory evidence

2. Which of the following is the best revision of the underlined portion of sentence (4) below?

Commenting on the quality of the shows, <u>however, the programs were not very satisfying.</u>

(A) , however; the programs were not very satisfying.
(B) however the viewers reported that the programs were not very satisfying.
(C) , however, the viewers reported that the programs were not very satisfying.
(D) ; however, the programs were not very satisfying.
(E) , however, the viewers reported that, the shows were not very satisfying.

3. Which of the following is the best way to combine sentences (1) and (2)?
(A) Recently, a questionnaire was developed that asked people to give their opinions, and what they were asked to give their opinions about was the value of leisure time.
(B) Recently, a questionnaire was developed that asked people to give their opinions on the value of leisure time.
(C) Recently, people were asked to give their opinions of leisure time.
(D) Recently, a questionnaire was developed, it asked people to give their opinions on the value of leisure time.
(E) A recent questionnaire developed to ask people to give their opinions on the value of leisure time.

Taking Essay Tests

The main difference between a classroom writing assignment and an essay test is time. Since you have a limited amount of time on a test, you must organize and express your ideas quickly, clearly, and logically.

● Kinds of Essay Questions

Before you begin to write your answers on an essay test, plan the amount of time you should spend on each part of the test. (The time you spend should be in proportion to the number of points allotted to each part.) Then when it comes time to begin your first question, look for key words, such as those listed in the following box. Such key words will tell you precisely what kind of question you are being asked to answer.

KINDS OF ESSAY QUESTIONS	
ANALYZE	Separate into parts and examine each part.
COMPARE	Point out similarities.
CONTRAST	Point out differences.
DEFINE	Clarify meaning.
DISCUSS	Examine in detail.
EVALUATE	Give your opinion.
EXPLAIN	Tell how, what, or why.
ILLUSTRATE	Give examples.
SUMMARIZE	Briefly review main points.
TRACE	Show development or progress.

As you read the instructions, jot down everything that is required in your answer, or underline key words and circle instructions. For instance, the key words are underlined and the instructions are circled in the following example.

> When Francisco Pizarro first landed in 1531 on the coast of what is now Ecuador, the Inca Empire was larger than any European city of the time. Nevertheless, within only several years, the Spanish were able to destroy this mighty empire. Analyze three possible reasons for the rapid collapse of the Inca Empire. Include specific details to support each point.

PRACTICE YOUR SKILLS

● Check Your Understanding
Interpreting Essay Test Questions

Write the key word in each question. Then write one sentence that explains what the question is asking you to do.

1. Explain how carbon-14 is used to date objects.

2. Contrast an ode and an elegy.

3. Briefly summarize the plot of *Silas Marner,* a novel by George Eliot.

4. Trace the development of a tornado.

5. In your own words, define *market economy.*

6. How does the working of a gasoline engine compare with that of an electric engine?

7. In his *Dictionary of the English Language,* Samuel Johnson defines youth as "The part of life succeeding to childhood and adolescence; the time from fourteen to twenty-eight." Do you agree? Discuss Johnson's definition.

8. Briefly evaluate the scientific contributions of lasers.

▶ Writing an Effective Essay Answer

Since the procedures for writing an essay test are basically the same as those for a typical writing assignment, you should recall and apply all that you have learned about the process of writing an essay. However, because your time will be restricted in a test situation, you must do some extra preplanning.

You should first decide how much time you will work on each question and how much time you will spend on each step in the writing of each answer. A general guideline is to allow two minutes of planning and one minute of revising and editing for every five minutes of writing. As you calculate according to this timetable, plan to give more time to the essay answers worth the most points.

Knowing what you are going to write—and in what order you are going to write it—is essential before you begin to write your essay answer. Your first step, therefore, should be to organize your answer by writing a plan in the form of a simple informal outline or a graphic organizer. Study the following example.

Reasons for the Collapse of the Inca Empire

INFORMAL OUTLINE:
(thesis statement)
1. Reason 1: weapons
2. Reason 2: transportation
3. Reason 3: internal war
(conclusion)

GRAPHIC ORGANIZER:

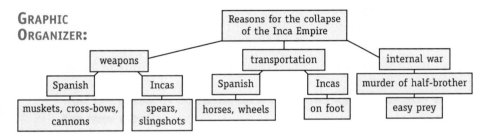

Your next step is to write a thesis statement that states the main idea of your essay and covers all of your major supporting ideas. A helpful hint when writing an essay answer is to reword the test question itself—if possible—into a thesis statement.

ESSAY QUESTION:
When Francisco Pizarro first landed in 1531 on the coast of what is now Ecuador, the Inca Empire was larger than any European city at the time. Nevertheless, within only several years, the Spanish were able to destroy this mighty empire. Analyze three reasons for the rapid collapse of the Inca Empire.

THESIS STATEMENT:
Although the Inca Empire was larger than any European city in 1531, the Spanish were able to destroy this mighty empire for three reasons.

As you write your essay answer, keep the following strategies in mind.

> ## Strategies for Writing an Essay Answer
>
> - Begin with a thesis statement that states the main idea of your essay and covers all of your major supporting ideas.
> - Follow the order of your plan, writing at least one paragraph for each main point.
> - Provide adequate support for each main point—using specific facts, examples, and/or other supporting details.
> - Make certain the essay contains a logical progression of ideas.
> - End with a strong concluding statement that summarizes, or brings closure, to the main idea of the essay.
> - Be certain the essay has an overall sense of unity.
> - Communicate your ideas clearly and effectively.
> - Write legibly, using standard English.

Model: Essay Test Answer

THESIS STATEMENT

Although the Inca Empire was larger than any European city in 1531, the Spanish were able to destroy this mighty empire for three reasons. Perhaps the most obvious reason was the discrepancy in the weapons that the Spanish and the Incas used. Having no knowledge of iron, the Incas fought mainly with bronze-edged spears and slingshots. The Spanish returned such attacks with muskets, crossbows, and full-sized cannons.

The Spanish were able to transport themselves, their cannons, and their supplies into the interior of the Inca Empire because they not only had horses, but they also had the use of the wheel.

Even though they had built a sophisticated system of roads, the Incas traveled only on foot. They did not have horses, and they could only carry, not pull, things since the wheel was unknown to them.

When Pizarro entered the empire, Atahuallpa had successfully captured the throne from his half-brother. Realizing the threat from the Spanish, Atahuallpa had his half-brother killed. However, shortly afterward the Spanish killed Atahuallpa himself. As a result the Incas, greatly divided and lacking a strong leader, became easy prey for the Spanish. At the time the combination of these

CONCLUSION: three factors was too much for the Incas. Could the course of history have a taken a different turn, however, if someone like Pizarro had come only 20 or 30 years later?

Revising   Writing Process

Always leave yourself a few minutes to revise your essay answer. As you revise your work, ask yourself these questions.

- Did you thoroughly follow the instructions?
- Did you begin with a thesis statement?
- Did you include supporting details and examples?
- Did you use transitions to connect ideas and examples?
- Did you have a logical progression of ideas?
- Did you end with a strong concluding statement that summarized your essay?
- Did you create a sense of unity?
- Did you communicate your ideas clearly and effectively?

Once you have made any necessary revisions, quickly read your essay for any mistakes in spelling, usage, or punctuation. To keep your paper as neat as possible, use proofreading symbols to make any corrections. If time permits, look for the following problems:

- lack of agreement between subjects and verbs *(pages L289–L317)*
- lack of agreement of pronouns and antecedents, especially indefinite pronouns *(pages L267–L273)*
- tense shift problems *(page C373)*
- incorrect verb inflections *(pages L181–L192)*
- incorrect form of adjectives and adverbs in the comparative and superlative forms *(pages L327–L333)*
- incorrect capitalization of proper nouns and proper adjectives *(pages L399–L411)*
- incorrect use of commas *(pages L436–L460)*
- incorrect use of apostrophes *(pages L471–L483)*
- incorrect divisions of words at the end of a line *(pages L522–L523)*

Communicate Your Ideas

APPLY TO WRITING
Drafting: *Essay Test Question*

Select any subject area, including English, and write an essay question that is likely to be included on an upcoming test. Answer the question by following the strategies on pages L601–L602. First prepare a brief outline or graphic organizer and a thesis statement. Then draft your answer. Finally, revise and edit your essay answer.

Timed Writing

The more you practice writing within a limited time period, the more confident you will feel as you enter a test situation in which you must complete a timed writing assignment.

Time limits can vary from 20 to 60 to 90 minutes depending upon the purpose and complexity of the task. Following the steps in the writing process, you might organize your time for a 20-minute essay in this way:

5 minutes: Brainstorm and organize ideas.

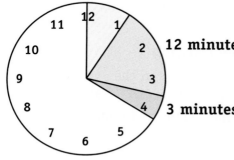

12 minutes: Write a draft.

3 minutes: Revise your work and edit it for mistakes.

Communicate Your Ideas

APPLY TO WRITING

Prewriting, Drafting, Revising, Editing: *Timed Writing*

Give yourself 20 minutes to answer the following:

- Keeping yourself informed of national and world news is an important task. Compare and contrast the strengths and weaknesses of television news programs and newspapers. Give specific examples from your own experiences.

Plan time for every step of the writing process, set a timer, and begin your answer.

A **Abstract** summary of points of writing, presented in skeletal form.

Abstract noun word that names a quality, a condition, or an idea.

Action verb word that tells what action a subject is performing.

Active voice the voice a verb is in when it expresses that the subject is performing the action.

Adjective word that modifies a noun or a pronoun.

Adjective clause subordinate clause that is used like an adjective to modify a noun or a pronoun.

Adjective phrase prepositional phrase that is used to modify a noun or a pronoun.

Adverb word that modifies a verb, an adjective, or another adverb.

Adverb clause subordinate clause that is used like an adverb to modify a verb, an adjective, or an adverb.

Adverb phrase prepositional phrase that is used like an adverb to modify a verb, an adjective, or an adverb.

Alliteration repetition of a consonant sound at the beginning of a series of words.

Allusion reference to persons or events in the past or in literature.

Analogies logical relationships between pairs of words.

Antecedent word or group of words that a pronoun replaces or refers to.

Antonym word that means the opposite of another word.

Appositive noun or a pronoun that identifies or explains another noun or pronoun in a sentence.

Assonance repetition of a vowel sound within words.

B **Body** one or more paragraphs comprised of details, facts, and examples that support the main idea.

Brainstorming prewriting technique of writing down everything that comes to mind about a subject.

C **Case** form of a noun or a pronoun that indicates its use in a sentence. In English there are three cases: the nominative case, the objective case, and the possessive case.

Cause and effect method of development in which details are grouped according to what happens and why it happens.

Characterization variety of techniques used by writers to show the personality of a character.

Chronological order the order in which events occur.

Citation note that directs reader to the original source.

Classification method of development in which details are grouped into categories.

Clause group of words that has a subject and a predicate and is used as part of a sentence.

Cliché overused expression that is no longer fresh or interesting to the reader.

Clustering a visual form of brainstorming that is a technique used for developing supporting details.

Coherence logical and smooth flow of ideas connected with clear transitions.

Common noun names any person, place, or thing.

Comparative degree modification of an adjective or adverb used when two people, things, or actions are compared.

Comparison and contrast method of development in which the writer examines similarities and differences between two subjects.

Complement word that completes the meaning of an action verb.

Complete predicate all the words that tell what the subject is doing or that tell something about the subject.

Complete subject all the words used to identify the person, place, thing, or idea that the sentence is about.

Complex sentence one independent clause and one or more subordinate clauses.

Compound adjective adjective made up of more than one word.

Compound-complex sentence two or more independent clauses and one or more subordinate clauses.

Compound noun word made up of two smaller words that can be separated, hyphenated, or combined.

Compound sentence two or more independent clauses in one sentence.

Compound subject two or more subjects in one sentence that have the same verb and are joined by a conjunction.

Compound verb two or more verbs that have the same subject and are joined by a conjunction.

Concluding sentence a strong ending to a paragraph that summarizes the major points, refers to the main idea, or adds an insight.

Conclusion paragraph that completes an essay and reinforces its main idea.

Conflict struggle between opposing forces around which the action of a work of literature revolves.

Conjunction word that joins together sentences, clauses, phrases, or other words.

Connotation the meaning that comes from attitudes attached to a word.

Consonance repetition of a consonant sound, usually in the middle or at the end of words.

Context clue clue to a word's meaning provided by the sentence or passage in which the word is used.

Coordinating conjunction single connecting word used to join words or groups of words.

Correlative conjunction pairs of conjunctions used to connect compound subjects, compound verbs, and compound sentences.

D **Dangling modifier** phrase that has nothing to describe in a sentence.

Declarative sentence statement or expression of an opinion that ends with a period.

Demonstrative pronoun word that substitutes for a noun and points out a person or a thing.

Denotation the literal meaning of a word.

Descriptive writing writing that creates a vivid picture of a person, an object, or a scene by stimulating the reader's senses.

Developmental order information that is organized so that one idea grows out of the preceding idea.

Dewey decimal system system by which nonfiction books are arranged on shelves in numerical order according to ten general subject categories.

Dialect regional variation of a language distinguished by distinctive pronunciation and some differences in word meanings.

Dialogue conversation between two or more persons.

Direct object noun or a pronoun that receives the action of a verb.

Direct quotation passage, sentence or words written or spoken exactly as a person wrote or said them.

Drafting stage of the writing process in which the writer draws together ideas on paper.

E | **Editing** stage of the writing process in which the writer polishes his or her work by correcting errors in grammar, usage, mechanics, and spelling.

Elaboration addition of explanatory or descriptive information to an essay, such as supporting facts, details, and examples.

Electronic publishing various ways to present information through the use of technology. It includes desktop publishing (creating printed documents on a computer), audio and video recordings, and online publishing (creating a Website).

Elliptical clause subordinate clause in which words are omitted but understood to be there.

E-mail electronic mail that can be sent all over the world from one computer to another.

Essential phrase or clause group of words essential to the meaning of a sentence and is therefore not set off with commas.

Etymology a word's history from its earliest recorded use to its present use.

Exclamatory sentence expression of strong feeling that ends with an exclamation point.

Expository writing writing that explains or informs with facts and examples or gives directions.

F | **Fact** statement that can be proved.

Fiction prose works of literature, such as short stories and novels, that are partly or totally imaginary.

Figurative language imaginative, nonliteral use of language.

Formal English conventional rules of grammar, usage, and mechanics.

Free verse verse without meter or a regular, patterned beat.

Freewriting prewriting technique of writing freely about ideas as they come to mind.

G | **Gerund** verb form ending in –ing that is used as a noun.

Gerund phrase a gerund with its modifiers and complements working together as a noun.

Glittering generality words and phrases most people associate with virtue and goodness.

H | **Helping verb** auxiliary verb that helps to make up a verb phrase.

Hyperbole use of exaggeration or overstatement.

I | **Imagery** use of concrete details to create a picture or appeal to senses other than sight.

Imperative mood verb form used to give a command or to make a request.

Imperative sentence a direction, a request, or a command that ends with either a period or an exclamation point.

Indefinite pronoun word that substitutes for a noun and refers to an unnamed person or thing.

Independent clause group of words that can stand alone as a sentence because it expresses a complete thought.

Indicative mood verb form used to state a fact or to ask a question.

Indirect object noun or a pronoun that answers the question *to or from whom?* or *to or for what?* after an action verb.

Infinitive verb form that usually begins with *to* and is used as a noun, an adjective, or an adverb.

Inquiring prewriting technique in which the writer asks questions such as *Who? What? Where? Why?* and *When?*

Intensive pronoun word that adds emphasis to a noun or another pronoun in the sentence

Interjection word that expresses strong feeling.

Internet a worldwide network of computers (see also *Basic Internet Terminology in a Writer's Guide to Using the Internet*).

Interrogative pronoun word used to ask a question.

Interrogative sentence a question; a sentence that ends with a question mark.

Intransitive verb an action verb that does not have an object.

Introduction paragraph that introduces a subject, states or implies a purpose, and presents a main idea.

Inverted order condition when the subject follows the verb or part of the verb phrase.

Irregular verb does not form its past and past participle by adding *–ed* or *–d* to the present.

L **Linking verb** links the subject with another word in the sentence. This other word either renames or describes the subject.

Literary analysis interpretation of a work of literature supported by appropriate responses, details, quotations, and commentaries.

M **Metaphor** figure of speech that compares by saying that one thing *is* another.

Meter the rhythm of a specific beat of stressed and unstressed syllables found in many poems.

Misplaced modifier phrase or a clause that is placed too far away from the word it modifies, thus creating an unclear sentence.

Mood overall atmosphere or feeling created by a work of literature.

N **Narrative writing** writing that tells a real or an imaginary story.

Nonessential phrase or clause group of words that is not essential to the meaning of a sentence and is therefore set off with commas.

Nonfiction prose writing that contains facts about real people and real events.

Noun a word that names a person, a place, a thing, or an idea. A common noun gives a general name. A proper noun names a specific person, place, or thing and always begins with a capital letter. A collective noun names a group of people or things.

Noun clause subordinate clause that is used like a noun.

O **Objective complement** noun or an adjective that renames or describes the direct object.

Occasion motivation for composing; the factor that prompts the writer to decide on process for communication.

Onomatopoeia use of words whose sounds suggest their meaning.

Opinion belief or judgment that cannot be proved.

Oral interpretation performance or expressive reading of a literary work.

Order of importance order in which supporting evidence is arranged from least to most or (most to least) important.

Outline information about a subject into main topics and subtopics.

P | **Paraphrase** restatement of an original work in one's own words.

Parenthetical citation source and page number (in parentheses) within a sentence in which the source of information must be credited.

Participial phrase participle with its modifiers and complements—all working together as an adjective.

Participle verb form that is used as an adjective.

Passive voice the voice a verb is in when it expresses that the action is being performed upon its subject.

Peer conference a meeting with one's peers, such as other students, to share ideas and offer suggestions for revision.

Personal pronoun type of pronoun that can be categorized into one of three groups, dependent on the speaker's position: first person, second person, and third person.

Personal writing writing that expresses the writer's personal point of view on a subject drawn from the writer's own experience.

Personification comparison in which human qualities are given to an animal, an object, or an idea.

Persuasive writing writing that states an opinion and uses facts, examples, and reasons to convince readers.

Phrase group of related words that functions as a single part of speech and does not have a subject and a verb.

Phrase fragment phrase written as if it were a complete sentence.

Play a composition written for dramatic performance on the stage.

Plot sequence of events leading to the outcome or point of the story.

Point of view vantage point from which a writer tells a story or describes a subject.

Portfolio collection of work representing various types of writing and the progress made on them.

Positive degree adjective or adverb used when no comparison is being made.

Possessive pronoun pronoun used to show ownership or possession.

Predicate adjective adjective that follows a linking verb and modifies the subject.

Predicate nominative noun or a pronoun that follows a linking verb and identifies, renames, or explains the subject.

Prefix one or more syllables placed in front of a root or base word to modify the meaning of the root or base word or to form a new word.

Preposition word that shows the relationship between a noun or a pronoun and another word in the sentence.

Prepositional phrase group of words that begins with a preposition, ends with a noun or a pronoun, and is used as an adjective or an adverb.

Prewriting invention stage in the writing process in which the writer plans for drafting based on the subject, occasion, audience, and purpose for writing.

Principal parts of a verb the *present*, the *past*, and the *past participle*. The principal parts help form the tenses of verbs.

Pronoun word that takes the place of one or more nouns.

Proofreading carefully rereading and making corrections in grammar, usage, spelling, and mechanics in a piece of writing.

Propaganda effort to persuade by distorting and misrepresenting information or by disguising opinions as facts.

Protagonist principal character in a story.

Publishing stage of a writer's process in which the writer may choose to share the work with an audience or make the work "public."

Purpose reason for writing or for speaking.

R

Reflexive pronoun pronoun formed by adding –*self* or –*selves* to a personal pronoun and is used to reflect back to another noun or pronoun.

Regular verb verb that forms its past and past participle by adding -*ed* to the present.

Relative pronoun pronoun that relates an adjective clause to the modified noun or pronoun.

Repetition repeat of a word or phrase for poetic effect.

Research paper a composition of three or more paragraphs that uses information from books, magazines, and other sources.

Résumé summary of a person's work experience, education, and interests.

Revising stage of a writer's process in which the writer rethinks what is written and reworks it to increase its clarity, smoothness, and power.

Rhyme scheme regular pattern of rhyming in a poem.

Root part of a word that carries the basic meaning.

Run-on sentence two or more sentences that are written together and are separated by a comma or have no mark of punctuation at all.

S

Sensory details details that appeal to one of the five senses: seeing, hearing, touching, tasting, and smelling.

Sentence fragment a group of words that does not express a complete thought.

Sequential order the order in which details are arranged according to when they take place or where they are done.

Setting environment (location and time) of a story.

Short story short work of narrative fiction.

Simile figure of speech comparing two unlike objects using the words *like* and *as*.

Simple predicate main word or phrase in the complete predicate.

Simple sentence one independent clause.

Simple subject main word in a complete subject.

Sound devices ways to use sounds in poetry to achieve certain effects.

Spatial order order in which details are arranged, according to their location.

Speech oral composition presented by a speaker to an audience.

Standard English conventions of usage accepted most widely by English-speaking people throughout the world.

Style visual or verbal expression that is distinctive to an artist or writer.

Subject word or group of words that names the person, place, thing, or idea the sentence is about.

Subjunctive mood words such as *if*, *as if*, or *as though* or that are used to express a condition contrary to fact or to express a wish.

Subordinate clause group of words that cannot stand alone because it does not express a complete thought.

Subordinating conjunction single connecting word used in a complex sentence to introduce an adverb clause.

Suffix one or more syllables placed after a root or base word to change the word's part of speech and possibly its meaning.

Summary information written in a condensed, concise form, touching only on the main ideas.

Superlative degree modification of an adjective or adverb used when more than two people, things, or actions are compared.

Supporting sentences specific details, facts, examples, or reasons that explain or prove a topic sentence.

Symbol object, an event, or a character that stands for a universal idea or quality.

Synonym word that has nearly the same meaning as another word.

T **Tense** form a verb takes to show time. The six tenses are the present, past, future, present perfect, past perfect, and future perfect.

Theme underlying idea, message, or meaning of a work of literature.

Thesis statement statement of the main idea that makes the writing purpose clear.

Tone writer's attitude toward the subject and audience of a composition (may also be referred to as the writer's *voice*).

Topic sentence statement of the main idea of the paragraph.

Transitions words and phrases that show how ideas are related.

Transitive verb action verb that passes the action from a doer to a receiver.

U **Understood subject** unstated subject that is understood.

Unity combination or ordering of parts in a composition so that all the sentences or paragraphs work together as a whole to support one main idea.

V **Verb** word that expresses action or state of being

Verbal verb form used as some other part of speech.

Verb phrase main verb plus one or more helping verbs.

Voice particular sound and rhythm of language that the writer uses; writer's attitude toward the subject of a composition (may also be referred to as *tone*).

W **World Wide Web** a network of computers within the Internet, capable of delivering multimedia content and text over communication lines into personal computers all over the globe.

Working thesis statement that expresses the possible main idea of a composition or research report.

Works cited page alphabetical listing of sources cited in a research paper.

Writing process recursive series of stages a writer proceeds through when developing ideas and discovering the best way to express them.

Note: Italic page numbers indicate skill sets.

Note: Italic page numbers indicate skill sets.

Note: Italic page numbers indicate skill sets.

INDEX

Direct object
clauses and phrases, used
as, L112, L155
compound, L72, L85, L243
defined, L72-L73, L91, L611
objective case, L242
placement of, L73, L74,
L243
pronoun as, L243, L247
sentence diagram, L85, L86
of a verbal, L246
Direct quotation
blocked quote, L516
capitalization, L392
punctuation, L517
Discover, invent, L364
Double passage and reading
comprehension tests,
L591, *L591-L593*
Drafts and drafting
defined, L611

E *Each, every* L299
Ei, ie, spelling rule for,
L549-L550, L573
Either, or, L267, L283, L298,
L374
Elaboration, L611
Ellipsis points (ellipses)
defined, L146
omissions from quotations,
L146, L519, L520-L521,
L537
pauses in written passage,
L519, L537
Else, other, L335-L336, L349
E-mail. See Internet.
Emigrate, immigrate, L365
End marks
abbreviations, L433, L465
ellipsis points (ellipses),
L519
exclamation point, L427-
L428, L465
parenthetical citations, L541
period, L427-L428, L465
question mark, L428, L465
sentences, kinds of, L427-
L429, L429-L431, L465
Endnotes, L540, L542
English, standardized testing
error recognition, L594,
L595
revision-in-context, L597-
L598, L598-L599
sentence correction, L595-
L596, L596-L597
Error recognition,
standardized test, L594-
L595
Essay tests
drafting, L603
editing, L605, L607
evaluating and revising,
L604

kinds of questions, L600-
L601
prewriting/organization,
L602
time limitation, L599-L601,
L606
Writer's model, L603-L604
Essential clause or phrase
adjective clause and phrase,
L150-L151, L458-L459
appositive and appositive
phrase, L104-L105
participial phrase, L109,
L458-L459
Etc., L365

F Fact, L611
Farther, futher, L366
Fewer, less, L366
Figurative language
cliché, L609
defined, L611
hyperbole, L611
imagery, L611
onomatopoeia, L612
personification, L613
Footnotes, L540, L542
Formal English, L353, L611
Formal writing
abbreviations, L432
contractions, L18
fragments, L70, L164
hyphens and dividing words,
L522-L523
plurals of letters, symbols,
and numerals, L481
pronouns as predicate
nominatives, L237
punctuation, L515
Standard English, L198,
L353
Former, latter, L366
Fraction used as adjective,
L524
Free verse, L611
Freewriting, L611

G Gender, L267-L268,
L269-L270, L271, L272-
L273
Gerund, L112, L113, L114-
L115, L133, L252-L253,
L611
Gerund phrase
defined, L112-L113, L113-
L115, L133, L611
fragment, L123
objective case, L246
possessive form of noun or
pronoun, L113, L252-L253
sentence diagram, L128
Good, well, L329-L330, L341-
L342, L349, L368
Graphic organizer, L578, L579,
L580, L602

H *Had of*, L368
Have, L18, L290-L291
Have, of, L368-L369
Hear, here, L369
Helping verb/auxiliary verb,
L18, L108, L184, L197,
L290-L291, L611
Here, there, L62, L303-L304
Hisself, theirselves, L264, L378
Historical present tense, L198
Hole, whole, L369, *L373*
Hyperbole, L611
Hyphen, L6, L26, L412, L537
L522-L527, L537

I *I*, L391, L395, *L396-L397*
Imply, infer, L369
In, into, L369
Indirect object
compound, L73, L243
defined, L73-L74, *L74-L75*,
L91, L612
object of preposition, not,
L74
gerund phrase, used as, L112
noun clause, used as, L155
objective case and
pronouns, L242-L243
sentence diagram, L86
Infinitive (verb), L208-L209
Infinitive (verbal), L115,
L128-L129, L133, L612
Infinitive clause, L116-L117
Infinitive phrase defined,
L116-L117, *L117-L119*,
L133
fragments and combining
sentences, L124-L125
introductory element, L444
objective case, L246
prepositional phrase,
distinguished between,
L115
sentence diagram, L128-
L129
Informal English, L353-L354
-ing word
gerund, L112
present participle (verb),
L182
present participle (verbal),
L107
Inside of, L374
Interdisciplinary writing. *See*
Writing across the
curriculum.
Interjection, L43, *L43-L44*,
L51, L428, L612
Internet.
defined, L612
E-mail, L611
Interrogative pronoun, L14,
L28, L51, L258-L260,
L260-L261, L612

INDEX

Note: Italic page numbers indicate skill sets.

Note: Italic page numbers indicate skill sets.

INDEX

Note: Italic page numbers indicate skill sets.

Note: Italic page numbers indicate skill sets.

Note: Italic page numbers indicate skill sets.

Note: Italic page numbers indicate skill sets.

Note: Italic page numbers indicate skill sets.

INDEX

Barrett Kendall Publishing has made every effort to trace the ownership of all copyrighted selections in this book and to make full acknowledgment of their use. Grateful acknowledgment is made to the following authors, publishers, agents, and individuals for their permission to reprint copyrighted material.

Language

L153: Reprinted by permission of the publishers and the Trustees of Amherst College from *The Poems of Emily Dickinson*, Ralph W. Franklin ed., Cambridge, Mass. The Belknap Press of Harvard University Press, copyright © 1998 by the President and Fellows of Harvard College. Copyright 1951, 1955, 1979 by the President and Fellows of Harvard College. **L214:** From *Green Eggs and Ham* by Dr. Seuss. TM and copyright © 1960 and renewed 1988 by Dr. Seuss Enterprises, L.P. Reprinted by permission of Random House, Inc. **L256:** By permission of J.P. Seaton. **L386:** © 1999, The Washington Post Writers Group. Reprinted with permission. **L392:** Reprinted by permission of the publishers and the Trustees of Amherst College from *The Poems of Emily Dickinson*, Ralph W. Franklin ed., Cambridge, Mass. The Belknap Press of Harvard University Press, copyright © 1998 by the President and Fellows of Harvard College. Copyright 1951, 1955, 1979 by the President and Fellows of Harvard College. **L392:** From *I Wouldn't Have Missed It: Selected Poems by Ogden Nash.* Copyright 1940 by Ogden Nash. First appeared in *Saturday Evening Post.* By permission of Little, Brown and Company, Inc. **L393:** By William Carlos Williams, from *Collected Poems 1909-1939*, Volume I. Copyright © 1938 by New Directions Publishing Corp. Reprinted by permission of New Directions Publishing Corp. **L397:** From *The Poems of John Keats*, edited by Jack Stillinger. Copyright © 1978, 1982 by the President and Fellows of Harvard College. Reprinted by permission of The Belknap Press of Harvard University Press. **L397:** From *The Love Song of J. Alfred Prufrock*, by T.S. Eliot. From *Collected Poems 1909-1962*, by T.S. Eliot. © 1936, 1963, 1964 by Harcourt. **L398:** Reprinted by permission of the publishers and the Trustees of Amherst College from *The Poems of Emily Dickinson*, Ralph W. Franklin ed., Cambridge, Mass. The Belknap Press of Harvard University Press, copyright © 1998 by the President and Fellows of Harvard College. Copyright 1951, 1955, 1979 by the President and Fellows of Harvard College. **L398:** From *Byron's Letters and Journals*, Volume V, edited by Leslie A. Marchand. Editorial matter copyright © 1976 by Leslie A. Marchand. Byron copyright material © 1976 by John Murray. Reprinted by permission of The Belknap Press of Harvard University Press. **L591:** "Introduction" from *Contemporary Heroes and Heroines* by Ray Brown. © 1990 Gale Research, Inc.

PHOTO CREDITS

Key: (t) top, (c) center, (b) bottom, (l) left, (r) right.

Language

L4, L50: Courtesy of Ronald Feldman Fine Arts, New York. © 2001 Andy Warhol Foundation for the Visual Arts/ARS, New York. Photograph by D. James Dee. **L15:** Spencer Collection, The New York Public Library. Astor, Lenox and Tilden Foundations. **L20:** Noriyuki Yoshida/SuperStock. **L30:** © 1997 Artists Rights Society (ARS), New York/ADAGP, Paris. **L56, L90:** Courtesy of Linda Jones Enterprises. **L560:** Richard Hutchings/PhotoEdit. **L61:** Print Collection Miriam and Ira D. Wallach Division of Art, Prints and Photographs, New York Public Library, Astor, Lenox and Tilden Foundations. **L96, L132:** © Andy Goldsworthy. Photograph courtesy of the artist. **L122:** Billy R. Allen Folk Art Collection. African American Museum, Dallas, Texas. Gift of Mr. and Mrs. Robert Decherd. **L138, L174:** From *Why Mosquitoes Buzz in People's Ears* by Verna Aardema, pictures by Leo and Diane Dillon, pictures copyright © 1975 by Leo and Diane Dillon. Used by permission of Dial Books for Young Readers, a division of Penguin Putnam Inc. **L180, L228:** Musée d'Orsay, Paris/SuperStock. **L211:** Art Guys Worldwide Photos. **L234, L282:** © 1993 Vietnam Women's Memorial Project, Inc. Photo by Gregory Staley, courtesy of Goodacre Studio, Santa Fe. **L241:** Jeffrey Sylvester/FPG International. **L250:** AP/Wide World Photos. **L 278:** Vladimir Pcholkin/FPG International. **L288, L320:** Scala/Art Resource, NY. **L296:** © Sam Ogden. **L320:** Erich Lessing/Art Resource, NY. **L326, L348:** Private collection/SuperStock. **L332:** Bob Daemmrich/Stock Boston. **L332:** Bob Daemmrich/Stock Boston. **L338:** Artwork © Wang Shiqiang. Courtesy of Byron Preiss Visual Publications/New China Pictures. **L338:** Trustees, National Gallery, London. Photograph © SuperStock. **L373:** Steve Vidler/SuperStock. **L386:** Mitch Kezar/Tony Stone Images. **L416:** Courtesy of Barbara Baldwin's Antiques. **L426, L464:** Ägyptisches Museum und Papyrussammlung, © BPK, Berlin, 1998. Photo by M. Büsing. **L435:** Chris Salvo/FPG International. **L446:** G & V Chapman/The Image Bank. **L451:** © Bob Daemmrich. **L470, L536:** Christie's Images/SuperStock. © 2001 C. Herscovici, Brussels/Artists Rights Society (ARS), New York. **L500:** Barrett Kendall photo by Andrew Yates. **L521:** George Glod/SuperStock.